Success Habits

by Dirk Zeller

A Wiley Brand

Success Habits For Dummies®

Published by: **John Wiley & Sons, Inc.,** 111 River Street, Hoboken, NJ 07030-5774, www.wiley.com

Copyright © 2019 by Dirk Zeller and John Wiley & Sons, Inc., Hoboken, New Jersey

Published simultaneously in Canada

For general information on our other products and services, please contact our Customer Care Department within the U.S. at 877-762-2974, outside the U.S. at 317-572-3993, or fax 317-572-4002. For technical support, please visit https://hub.wiley.com/community/support/dummies.

Wiley publishes in a variety of print and electronic formats and by print-on-demand. Some material included with standard print versions of this book may not be included in e-books or in print-on-demand. If this book refers to media such as a CD or DVD that is not included in the version you purchased, you may download this material at http://booksupport.wiley.com. For more information about Wiley products, visit www.wiley.com.

Library of Congress Control Number: 2019936523

ISBN 978-1-119-50884-7 (pbk); ISBN 978-1-119-50883-0 (ebk); ISBN 978-1-119-50885-4 (ebk)

Manufactured in the United States of America

C10009166_04/02/19

Contents at a Glance

Table of Contents

PART 6: THE TIME AND SUCCESS CONNECTION..........283

CHAPTER 17: **Setting Your Habits for Time Management Success** 285

Introduction

Congratulations on making the investment in yourself and your success. The decision to take action to study and learn more about success and how to achieve it is one of the most important you can make in life. Most people want to be more successful, but they don't do anything to make it happen. You, my friend, are a doer!

I had a "line in the sand" moment with my lack of success. At 27 years of age, I was embarking on a new career hoping the next 5 years would not be like the previous 5 years. I was broke and in debt, wanting to earn a six-figure-plus income, but very behind on my goals. I decided I needed to study and read about success. I wanted to be successful but lacked a plan, strategies, and a system. I was a hard worker, but being a hard worker wasn't enough. I knew there was something more, so I set about to find it. That decision has changed my life, my income, my relationships, and my bank account. If you are having the type of moment that caused you to pick up this book, I applaud you.

Success leaves clues; it leaves a trail. Success has a recipe, just as making a Caesar salad has a simple recipe that anyone can follow. My objective is to share with you the recipe to success, to teach you the combination of ingredients and how to mix them in the right order. Once you learn and master the recipe, then you can make your own adjustments and change the recipe to your taste.

This book comes out of my passion to help people live the life they dream about. I want to help you define what you desire in life and then help you craft a plan to achieve it. I will coach you on the mindset, habits, skills, strategies, systems, and tools that will guarantee your success and speed up the timeframe to acquisition of it.

I am personally excited about our journey to success together. I frequently conclude correspondence with "To Your Success" before my signature. What I am stating is that I celebrate and cheer for you as you progress to greater success. So let's clink our glasses and celebrate success!

To Your Success!

About This Book

This book is about becoming more successful by building strong habits. It's also about clearly defining what success is to you so it's more easily achieved. The only definition of success that really matters is *yours*. This book is a guide that helps you achieve the goals and dreams that you have for yourself and your family.

I'm delighted to share with you the keys I've found for success and to help you avoid the mistakes I've made along the way. (I'm a firm believer in the idea that we often benefit more from failures than from successes — but that doesn't mean you have to repeat my failures.) My hope is that you learn from both my warnings and positive examples.

The habits, techniques, skills, and strategies I present throughout this book are the same ones I've used and tested to perfection personally and with thousands of coaching clients and hundreds of thousands of training program participants. We certainly live in a technology empowered world today. The influence of social media is prevalent. But the foundational principles of success, personal habits, wealth, relationships, productivity, proper usage of time, and being healthy have not changed as much. This is not a book of theory but of "real stuff" that works and is laid out in a hands-on, step-by-step format. You'll also find time-tested tools, strategies, and systems, not fluff, contained in this book.

If you apply the information contained in this book with the right attitude, and if you're consistent in your approaches and in your success expectations, your success is guaranteed.

Foolish Assumptions

When I wrote the book, I assumed a few things about you, my dear reader. I assumed you picked up the book because you wanted to achieve a higher level of success. You want to earn more income, create wealth, enhance your family relationships, be more valuable at work, run your business better, and optimize your health. Any or all of the above may apply to you, or you might be on a quest to define success more completely and personally for you. As they say, you have come to the right place.

Icons Used in This Book

To help you navigate this book a bit better, you can rely on icons in the book's margins. The icons are little signposts that point out the important info.

TIP

This icon points out little-advertised nuggets of knowledge that are certain to give you an edge in increasing your success in life.

REMEMBER

This icon denotes critical information that you really need to take away with you. Remember these points if nothing else. They address the issues that you will come across repeatedly in climbing higher on the mountain of success.

WARNING

Consider this the flashing red light on the road to success. When you see the this icon, you know to steer clear of whatever practice, behavior, or response I indicate.

ANECDOTE

When you see this icon, I'm giving examples from my personal life or from the lives of close family and friends.

Beyond the Book

In addition to the material and content in the print or e-book version you are reading now, there are also additional resources that I created that you can access on the web. There is a valuable Cheat Sheet, a Dummies staple. You can access it by going to www.dummies.com and typing for "*Success Habits For Dummies* cheat sheet" in the search box. The Cheat Sheet is a wonderful reference to keep handy and refer to frequently. It is comprised of key reminders, quick strategies, and focus points for achievement. It's a great tool to have on your phone, computer, tablet, or even printed out and taped to the mirror.

Where to Go from Here

To tackle a book so packed with tools, techniques, and strategies, Part 1 is a good place to start. It deals with the formulas and principles of achieving success, and reading this section first will create a solid foundation upon which to build your success.

After that, you might use the table of contents or index to pick out topics that you have the greatest interest or need in. Select the chapters that are most important to your definition of what success is to you. Feel free to move around the book in any way that suits you. Even this approach will lead you to a vast array of new knowledge and strategies for success. If you feel well-versed in, say, your relationships, then you might want to dive into Part 5, "Success with Wealth and Money," or Part 6, "The Time and Success Connection." These two parts of the book cover the most common roadblocks to achieving success.

The truth is, no matter where you take your first plunge, the water is fine. You will find a vast array of valuable information that you can use to increase your performance, income, relationships, and quality of life.

1

Principles and Formulas for Success

IN THIS PART . . .

Get familiar with the formula for success.

Learn success from the successful people around you.

Discover discipline's role in the achievement of success in life.

Chapter **1**

Success Is a Habit

The pursuit of success is not new. People for all ages have been trying to unlock the mysteries of human behavior, peak performance, and success. Why is it that some people seem to, at first observation, achieve success easily while others try but repeatedly fall short? Just about everyone has the desire to improve their lives, but only a few of us actually achieve it.

Aristotle said, "We are what we repeatedly do. Excellence therefore is not an act, but a habit." He was using success interchangeably with excellence. While you might define them differently, they must be thought of as close cousins. Aristotle studied and wrote about success until his death in 322 BC. The big picture in this quote is the connection between repeatedly doing something and the establishment of a habit. The conclusion is that you can create the habit of success or you can create the habit of failure.

Success, or excellence, will always be created through establishing positive, repetitive habits. Unfortunately, almost anything we do repeatedly can lose its luster, passion, and energy. Without doing something repeatedly, you won't establish it as a habit. When you focus on repeating the actions that lead to success, you create habits. So repeating and success are like peas and carrots: They go together. There is always a yin and a yang in the pursuit of success. Right actions repeatedly done create habits and guarantees success. That would be the yin. The yang would be not engaging in the right actions repeatedly over time, creating bad habits that guarantee failure.

REMEMBER

We all will create habits in either direction in life. The establishment of our habits is inevitable. We are the ultimate arbiters of what those habits will be. First, we will create our habits, and then our habits will create us.

In this chapter, I will describe success from a number of different angles. My desire is to start you off with the broad brush strokes and give you a little background scenery. In subsequent chapters, we'll approach the painting with finer brushes and explore more specific aspects of the beautiful landscape of success habits.

What Is Success?

Success is many things to different people. We all have our own personal and unique definition of what success is to us. The dictionary defines success as the fact of getting or achieving wealth, respect, or fame. It also defines success as the correct or desired result of an attempt. I feel those two definitions capture the essence and objectives of success. Earl Nightingale, who is called "The Dean" of the personal motivation industry, describes with a twist: Success as the *progressive* realization of a worthy goal or worthy ideal.

Too many of us attach the moniker of success to the end result of achieving success: the achievement of the purchase of a new Mercedes, the finish line of becoming a millionaire, our kids graduating high school or college, or the corner office in the company. Mr. Nightingale brings a new perspective to success through the word "progressive." As long as you are progressing toward a predetermined goal, you are in fact a success. What is most important is not how I define success. I can certainly add ideas, insight, and guidance in your journey to achieving of success. What is more important and personal is how you define success for your life.

>> Success is you as a business owner providing valuable service to your clients, and that you enjoy helping your clients and customers. You go home content in the fact that you did a good job for each person you served, delivered value to, and treated with honesty.

>> Success is that you went home to meaningful relationships with people you love. You have community, communication, and fun with those loved ones. You have people you love and who love you.

>> Success is having interests that bring you joy, whether that is a serving opportunity at church, the community center, or a homeless shelter. A recreational interest creates success, whether that's golf, pickle ball, hunting, fishing, mountain biking, or more sedentary interests like painting or knitting.

» Success is the feeling of security you have when you sit down to pay bills each month and there are funds left over. What you are doing in that moment is increasing your assets and reducing your liabilities. You are taking a few steps more toward financial security.

» Success, at the end of the day, is being grateful as you turn out the lights. You are grateful to people who have helped you today or whom you have been able to help and serve.

What Isn't Success?

The biggest *isn't* of success is failing to define it for yourself, as a couple, or as a family. It's easy to get sidetracked or pursue someone else's definition of success. Our brains are bombarded with images of success in social media, the news, the television, or even in the parent drop-off lane at school. We can't avoid seeing Sally's new Porsche or her daughter's new designer clothes. Or we notice that Amy looks so tan and rested after her family's trip to Barbados.

TIP

Observe others to encourage and remind yourself of what is possible. Don't observe to compare or keep score. The truth is, the only score card that matters is yours.

ANECDOTE

Being successful is granting grace to yourself and others when the achievement you desire takes a little while longer than you expected. I had a coaching call recently with a wonderful client, Sandy. Her goal was to sell enough homes to make $250,000. She had a challenging year because she and her business partner decided to end the partnership. There was a lot of drama to say the least. We were reviewing what she had earned and what was still to be collected in income, and we came to the realization she would not make her $250,000 goal. When that fact was confirmed, she didn't feel very successful. Frequently, our timeline for success can be slightly off. In reviewing her sales numbers, I ventured that her sales in escrow that were set to close by the middle of January would put her at that $250,000 mark. So she missed her goal, but she only missed it by two weeks. In the overall scheme of things, that's nothing.

The Only Thing That's Important: What Success Is to You

Success is personal. It's a personal experience of well-being, confidence, and accomplishment. That is why you must decide what success is for you. We all have wishes to lose weight, save more money, and improve our relationships. But success is not in the wish business. It's in the desire, habit, and commitment business. The do it or else business. A wish has not morphed into desire, where you are willing to lay everything on the line to achieve it. It doesn't come with the resolve that causes you to say to yourself, "I will do it or else." In order for you or I to achieve success, we must have desire for something and a big enough reason why we desire it.

REMEMBER

You are in control of what you desire or wish. We all have the authority and power to decide what we want and then determine our motivation level to achieve it. You need to have clarity about what's important to you and who's important to you. What legacy you want to leave is the process of refining your definition of success.

Too many people get caught up in the *how* of reaching success or even a specific benchmark or goal of success. They spend little time focusing on the clarity of the *why*. Why we want something is the power source. If the why is large enough, the how becomes easy. We often focus on the wrong end of the equation. Why do you want to be financially independent? Why do you want to build a business to a large scale? Why do you want to be married and have children? Why do you want to lose weight? Why do you want the luxury house or second home? Why do you want to retire early?

I don't think there are hundreds of whys in our life. I think we have a handful of whys that can interconnect to our goals and dreams. This small handful of whys create the power source in our life to become a good spouse, parent, child to older parents, business owner or employee. It helps us establish a legacy of service and love even after our journey on Earth is over.

A why can come from a past positive or a negative experience. There are thousands of stories of successful people who grew up in abject poverty, and that fueled their why. There are stories, like my own, where I grew up more privileged, and that also fueled the why. There is really no difference between the two pathways to the result. Each person taps into their unique why to power themselves to achievement to their desired life. The why can come from a desire to achieve the highest level of personal performance. Some people are motivated to excel, but the question is always, "Why?" Why do some have a passion for improvement and others don't?

No one else can give you your why; you must discover it for yourself. As a coach, I can ask questions and guide clients to their unique set of whys. I can't give them their why, though. That is one big value to having a coach in all the stages of your career, as they have the ability to help you draw out the whys buried inside of you. Your why can come from your envisioned future of your life and business. Your why can come from your love of another and the devotion and commitment you have for them in areas of your life.

I learned from my late friend, Jim Rohn, that life is not about what you acquire but what you become. We set goals to become the person we need to become to accomplish the goal. I had to become a different person to attract the success that I had in real estate sales. I've had to become a more skilled and more knowledgeable person to become a coach, speaker, and author. A specific example is that I had to become more disciplined to become the author of ten books and counting. As an author, you must be free to remove distractions, sit in the seat, and write, type, or speak your thoughts into words.

The important whys are like a magnet that pulls you to success. The more compelling the whys of your life, the more bumps in the road and adversity you will face. You might be asking, why more adversity? Because of the clarity, you recognize and are bothered by the distractions, and you are aware that they are taking you further way from your goals. A powerful why doesn't remove the challenges; it just renders them to being less important. The clarity of why fires up your resolve to overcome any obstacle to achievement. You recognize the obstacles and your sense of urgency dispatches them.

The Different Categories of Success

Success can be evaluated through different lenses. I find that most people want to achieve their definition of success in these categories:

Health

Success in the health area of life means to be reasonably healthy and free of ailments, to be physically active, free of pain, and able to enjoy activities that require movement. One could determine success in the health category with numbers if you are more analytically inclined: your cholesterol number, waist size, minutes of cardio exercise per week, your weight, your body mass index, and so on.

Your definition of health might be affected by a chronic disease that you merely need to manage well rather than cure. My definition of successful health has evolved since being diagnosed with Meniere's disease more than eight years ago. There is no cure for Meniere's disease, so my expectations of successful health is focused on reducing the vertigo episodes and lowering their intensity so that I can enjoy work, family, and life's other pleasures more completely. Along with the weight, cholesterol, and exercise levels, the controlling of the Meniere's is a big marker in being successful in my health.

Financial

We all need to achieve some level of financial success. What constitutes success financially can vary widely from person to person. Some attach success to a large lifestyle of luxury homes, automobiles, and exotic trips. For others, financial success is humbler: having their home paid off and being reasonably prosperous. If you don't take the time to evaluate your desires in the financial category, it's easy to wander in the wilderness, pursue stuff, and develop envy of others that have achieved more financial wealth.

There are two realizations that I have come to in achieving financial wealth. The first is that there will always be people who have acquired more wealth than I will. The second is that I won't be taking any of it with me when I die.

Relationships

Being successful in your key relationships in life can bring the greatest joy. We are made for relationships with others. Our significant others, children, parents, siblings, friends, and coworkers are all key relationships that need to be developed and maintained to create meaning in our lives.

Career

The average person invests more than 90,000 hours of their lifetime at work. For many, a third of your life is invested in work. Some of us work more than 40 or 50 years of our life until retirement. Advancing your career, becoming more valuable, and embracing new challenges at your job, career, or business can bring definition and clarity to how you define success.

And more . . .

Health, wealth, relationships, and career are just a few examples of success categories. You may have different measuring sticks for success: happiness, peace of mind, security, length of life, a nice home, personal growth, and freedom.

These categories all could be developed into primary aims for your pursuit of success.

SOME SUCCESS CATEGORIES ARE HARDER THAN OTHERS

We were all created to crave. The desire to pursue improvement, success, and personal self-worth is hardwired into us as humans. In the Declaration of Independence, Thomas Jefferson expressed to King George that we are "endowed" by our Creator with certain unalienable rights that include "life, liberty, and the pursuit of happiness." That craving was placed there by our Creator, and each of us has the right, an obligation, to pursue life as we desire to define it. We have the right to pursue happiness based on our unique and personal definition of it. Success is the pursuit of living out your goals in each category of life that is important to you.

There are certainly some categories that offer up a greater challenge in the pursuit of success. The categories of health, wealth, and relationships, in my observation of self and others, are the most challenging of all to achieve success. When it comes to health, more than 69 percent of the people in the United States are obese or overweight. It's obvious that achieving and maintaining good health is a huge struggle for most people.

In relationships, our most important is probably the one we have with our spouse or significant other. Relationships require work, introspection, forgiveness, and grace. I applaud you if you have mastered the relationships in your life, because frequently I feel less than accomplished in this category.

The final of the triad of challenges is our finances. The United States one of the richest countries, and we currently live in one of the most prosperous times in human history. According to the United States Census Bureau, the average net worth of people less than 35 years old is $6,936. The average net worth of people 65 to 69 years old is $193,833. While that might seem like a lot, it includes the net worth in their home. Many who are 65 to 69 years old have worked for more than 40 years. If you take $193,833 and divide it by 40 years, that is $4,845.83. That $4,845.83 is the average annual net worth growth over 40 years, which encompasses savings, investment returns, and appreciation growth in their home and mortgage payments of principle only, not interest, over 40 years. The average person doesn't have a high success score when it comes to finances. If I were handing out report cards for the $193,833 after 40 years, it's truly D grade work at best.

We all fall short in a category or two

One or two of the success categories will be more challenging for you, so you will need to study, plan, and work more on those categories. Some will come easily for you and may simply require more maintenance in your attention to detail. The best investment in your success right now is brutal honesty with yourself:

>> What categories of success are easy for you?

>> Which one is most challenging for you?

>> Which one is most important to change?

>> What is the most important thing you could do right now to change it?

If I am being fully authentic and transparent, the wealth or money category has been the easiest for me to master. Whether that's due to my parents' instructions, my clear focus on it from a young age, or the learning, reading, and planning I have done, I have been successful in generating wealth. The health category has been the most challenging for me, but not because I lack knowledge about health. I know that I need to move my body more and take in fewer calories. My problem comes from not being consistent and balanced in my workout routine, and this comes from a guy who played racquetball at the professional level in my 20s.

Creating the Habit of Success

Whether your pursuit of success is in the business world or in your personal life, being successful or winning seems to carry forward and create more victories. Making the right decisions also frequently aligns with getting good breaks and positive circumstances. Understanding that success begets more success, people can get on a roll. A business can build momentum and reach a tipping point. A salesperson can get on a hot streak where all meetings with prospects result in sales for a period of time. As you lose weight and see that scale number start to drop, it fires you up to stick with your new eating and exercise habits. The feelings of self-worth and self-confidence grow, and as a result, success habits are solidified.

Deciding to be successful

The most powerful driver of success is a decision, and by that I mean the decision itself and the commitment to the decision. Here are some examples:

>> The decision to shed weight and never allow it back

>> The decision that you will never utter the "divorce" word to your spouse even in the most heated verbal exchanges

>> The decision through words and demonstrated actions to show love and acceptance to your children

Success is a decision, just as wealth is a decision. Gary Smalley, author and relationship expert, had a seminar series he called *Love Is A Decision*. I know because Joan, my wife, and I attended it early on before we were married. (I tell more of that story later in the book.) We recently celebrated our 29th anniversary. We decided early on to be committed to each other.

REMEMBER

The decision and commitment to success come before the achievement of it.

We are all faced with choices. You will make millions of large and small choices in your lifetime. We labor over the small ones, like whether to have soup or salad at dinner, but we miss the big ones entirely that come each day, like deciding to be happy rather than miserable, or choosing a positive attitude each morning when we wake up. These choices can establish your success each day.

If you choose to be happy, then you must understand what makes you happy. You have to uncover what makes you fulfilled, energized, valued, and loved. You also have to link in small accomplishment benchmarks each day, so you feel good about your day and the results you have achieved, no matter how small. Abraham Lincoln stated it so well: "Most folks are happy as they make up their minds to be."

Knowing where you want to go

Steven Wright, the famous comedian, said, "You can't have everything. Where would you put it?" In achieving success, there are a lot of things we have to personally say "no" to. The act of saying no crosses off the things in life that we must give up to accomplish what we really desire. We have to say no to eating unhealthy and high-calorie foods to lose the weight we desire. We have to say no to a sedentary lifestyle in order tone our muscles and stay fit. As you are deciding what you want, what your success targets are for life, and what you are saying "yes" to, you must also decide what you don't want and what you have to say no too.

Deciding on your yeses and nos gives you a more complete definition of success and what you must do to achieve it. It takes the decision to a whole other level. You are defining what you want to attract yourself to and also what you want to repel yourself from.

Setting your expectations for success

When you make the effort to plan your success, when you prepare for success to happen through deciding, prioritizing, and planning, your mind then will expect to be successful in your endeavors. The internal winner within us all emerges. That expectation doesn't mean success happens automatically and without effort. That is certainly not the case. You expect to extend effort, but you expect that effort to be rewarded. Of course, your path isn't always going to be smooth and straight. You will hit roadblocks, detours, and traffic jams. No one really becomes an overnight success. The famous actor Adrien Brody said, "My dad told me, 'It takes 15 years to be an overnight success,' and it took me 17 and a half years."

We will all encounter twists and turns on the road to success. One of the key reasons is that few people are as interested in your achievement of success as *you* are in life. If you have a small handful of people who are rooting, praying, encouraging, and helping you achieve success, you are blessed with more people than most. Some people will be working to sabotage your success because they are small thinkers, or your competitors, or the type of people who pull everyone down. You must hold on and expect that you will succeed in all endeavors that you are passionate about.

Building success momentum

Every thought, action, or discipline is drawing you closer to your goals and objections or pushing you further away. The stacking of positive thoughts and actions together builds momentum. Sir Isaac Newton stated that a body in motion tends to stay in motion. Our motion toward success tends to stay in that positive motion. When we apply new force consistent with our direction toward our primary objectives, this action creates growing momentum.

The opposite is true as well. If you are moving away from success through poor habits or no habits, you will eventually be much farther away from the success you desire.

The habit of working each day, to take small steps and actions toward your goals, is the key to success and momentum.

Establishing a Consistent Process of Success

If you have ever watched the show *The Profit* on CNBC, Marcus Lemonis goes into partnership with the failing business owner. He evaluates the business and invests his capital to upgrade the business and fix the problems. His mantra is "people, product, process." You have to fix the people in the business, get the product right, and create a process of manufacturing, fulfillment, sales, administration, and so on.

It's a simple but effective formula for business and life success. In this section, I want to focus on process, which is really aligned with habits. What is your process in the morning? When do you wake up? What is your morning routine? There is a direct correlation between waking up early and success. Ninety percent of executives wake up before 6:00 a.m. on weekdays. Fifty percent of self-made millionaires wake up at least three hours before the start of their work day.

As I write these words, it's 3:02 a.m. I always get up at 5:00 a.m. There are times when I have book or project deadlines on my plate that I get up even earlier because I know I can squeeze in a few more highly productive hours in the day by rising earlier. There are countless benefits to having an early morning routine to start your day earlier than most people:

>> Your competitors are doing it, so you don't want to fall behind.

>> The distractions and interruptions increase and intensify as the day goes on (which is why I am writing at 3:05 a.m. right now).

>> Your mental strength and willpower are higher in the morning.

>> Starting early sets the tone for a productive day, which will likely continue.

>> You create an enhanced feeling of control, that you are the captain of your ship.

The morning process or routine is the foundation for a successful day. I perform so much better when I follow my morning routine compared to when I don't. Success is contained in the daily pursuit and the daily routine.

Win the day

I am a fan of Oregon Ducks football. One of the team slogans is "Win the day." The slogan is simple, clean, and concise. But more important than that, it's true. The objective in the pursuit of success is to win the day.

What you control is today. I don't presently control anything other than today. Tomorrow has not yet become today, so I have limited influence on tomorrow. That last statement doesn't mean I'm being laissez-faire about tomorrow. I have a plan I am working toward. I have a business plan, life plan, and objectives for the week to complete as well as deadlines that might be significant for tomorrow. But in order to accomplish all that I need to, I must win today first. I have to prioritize that as number one.

Emphasizing today over tomorrow is not a new way of thinking. Ancient scripture says, "Therefore, do not worry about tomorrow, for tomorrow will worry about itself. Each day has enough trouble of its own." To paraphrase, win today. That's all that matters right now.

Create your success routine

As I said earlier, a success routine starts in the morning, likely early in the morning. A routine is just a process you follow to create consistently high results. It creates a pattern of behavior and actions that link to positive outcomes based on the law of cause and effect. The word "routine," to some people, causes them to feel confined, regimented, non-flexible, or lacking freedom. I'd ask you to look at it from another angle: A routine creates peak performance, efficiency, productivity, and proven and repeatable outcomes. It allows you to do more in less time, creating more freedom. The end result of routine is freedom, options, and choices because you are rewarded those by being more productive and efficient.

ANECDOTE

When I started my real estate sales career in 1990, my routine was to be at my office by 7:15 a.m. It was about a 25-minute drive from my home. I was up by 5:15 a.m. to be at my athletic club by 5:30 a.m. when it opened. I worked out for 60 minutes, showered, shaved, and dressed. My target time to walk out the door of the club was 6:55 a.m. I was the only one in my real estate office at 7:15 a.m. Most of the time, the first other people coming in were administrative staff at 9:00 a.m. I was on the phone by no later than 8:00 a.m. making calls to newly expired listings, which were sellers who recently were unsuccessful in selling their homes.

Today, my day still starts early at 5:00 a.m. I make my tea, and by 5:15 a.m., I am in my morning devotion time reading the Bible and praying (especially for my teenagers and for patience and endurance for Joan and myself). I make my second cup of tea at 6:00 a.m. and start reading my newspapers at 6:15 a.m.: *The Wall Street Journal, Washington Post, USA Today,* and our local *Bend Bulletin*. There are many days when I don't get through all the newspapers, so I read at lunch or at end of my work day. I hit the shower by 7:45 a.m. to be working by 8:00 a.m. I work from my home office a majority of the time. I personally enjoy the quietness, solitude, and lack of distractions.

A home office has a yin and yang to your routine and success. For highly disciplined people, it can provide what it does for me, which is a more productive environment with fewer distractions. For people who are easily distracted by unfinished chores, television, neighbors, or the multitude of other things going on around the home, a home office may not be the best option over the routine of getting ready, driving to the office, and starting your day. And on the flip side, working at home also means you have the temptation of working longer hours by sneaking in a few more things to get done.

In designing the right morning routine for you, my advice is to incorporate the following actions:

>> **Gratitude:** Start your day with gratitude. What are you grateful for? What is really a blessing in your life? What are you thankful for that recently happened? What is going to happen in the near future that will be a blessing to you? When we start our day with gratitude, we empty some of our cup of life so that the universe, the world, our higher power, or God can fill it up again with new and better blessings.

>> **Quiet time/prayer/meditation:** Take some amount of time to turn inward to connect with yourself, God, or your higher power and to center yourself and calm yourself each day. Your ability to pause, listen, breathe, and relax is worthwhile.

>> **Read:** Your mind is receptive after being fully rested. Whether you are reading a book, newspapers, the Bible, or other spiritual texts, reading is essential in a morning routine. You want to be learning and increasing your knowledge.

>> **Journal:** I always journal a few entries on what I am learning, what hit me as profound, and what God is saying to me. I also note what questions I am still trying to find solutions for.

>> **Exercise:** Doing some form of exercise is a wonderful way to establish health habits and routines. It also raises your energy level for the day. In raising your heart rate in the morning, you burn calories at a higher efficiency throughout the day.

REMEMBER

You don't need to do all of these activities, but if you do most of them, you have the foundation to win the day. And when you win enough days, you will win the week, month, quarter, year, and lifetime.

I would select the activities that apply to you and fit your style and timeline. Create a schedule based on time blocks to do two, three, or all five of these activities in your morning routine. Be exact and then try it out, understanding you will likely need to make an adjustment or refinement in roughly a week. Focus on forcing yourself to hit the appointed time with the next activity in your schedule.

Turn consistency into repetition

Creating your win-the-day process, or system, is a significant tool that will enable you to reach consistency. Success is created through consistency turned into repetition. A singular morning routine is not habit, nor is it repetition. A morning routine executed a single time is an act. An act by itself will not determine success or failure. It must be linked together in succession and consistency to create success. You can create new habits, have them take hold, and apply commitment to continue in a day or even a week. It takes weeks of repeating that act to establish and cement it as a habit in your routine of success. If you miss a day, even one day, that breaks the cycle of routine and consistency. If the new routine or behavior hasn't been engrained as a habit, my counsel is that you should start tomorrow as if it's day one in your journey to establishing your routine or new habit.

Staying on Track to Your Success

We all get off track. We all have moments or even days where we have a lack of focus. It feels like we aren't accomplishing much. It's as if we are swimming in a bowl of porridge.

Lose the notion that successful people are on track all the time. The unknown truth is that they likely have more distractions, problems, and issues that can and do derail them. The secret is, from the moment they go off track to the time they get refocused or back on track, the span of time between off track and back on is dramatically less. Most people, when they get off track, stay that way for a day or two. Successful people are off track for an hour or less. They have programmed their mind to recognize that they are off track, distracted, non-focused, dealing in unproductive pursuits, or handling issues with no solution. They get through those moments quickly and refocus on the key objectives and agenda.

Measuring where you are

Evaluate your time throughout the day. A key measure is your time usage and how it aligns with your objectives to success. Ask yourself, "Is what I am doing right now drawing me closer to my goals? Am I doing something whose value is at or above what I am worth per hour?"

A good attorney has the focus to be able to bill a certain number of hours per day to a client or multiple clients. Are you billing out enough hours of your expertise each day? A doctor needs to see a certain number of patients per day. Whether you are an entrepreneur or employee, you must measure based on that standard of billable hours. As an employee, you might be thinking, why does that matter? All employees want to increase what their companies pay them. As an employee, you become more valuable to your company through increased productivity, handling more problems well, increasing company sales and revenue, and providing wonderful customer service experiences.

Evaluate how well you maintain your morning routine. Are you able to stay on it five out of five days, four out of five, or lower? Are you saving money out every paycheck for retirement, emergency fund savings, your next car, next family trip, or college for your kids? Are you measuring or monitoring your food intake and amount of exercise? How about the amount of time you are spending with the people you love? Is your spouse or significant other getting enough of your attention? Is it a habit for just the two of you to be together at least once per week?

Here's a key tenant of success: When actions are measured, actions improve.

Speeding up the process of success

Charles Coonradt, who wrote the book *The Game of Work*, stated, "When performance is measured, performance improves." If you measure something, it will get better. The whole premise of Weight Watchers is the weekly weigh in. When you have to weigh yourself in front of God and everyone in your Weight Watchers group, it helps you follow the plan better because you know you have the day of reckoning on Tuesday at the meeting and weigh in.

Mr. Coonradt further states, "When performance is measured and reported, performance improves faster." If you want to speed the process of success, find someone to report to. That person could be a friend, colleague, your spouse or significant other, your kids, a coach, or personal trainer. The measuring, with the addition of reporting to someone who can hold you accountable to your stated goals and objectives, is key. You might even have a few people you report to, which is fine. The magic comes from both the measurement and the reporting.

Chapter **2**

Success Leaves Clues

People have been searching for success since the dawn of time. Ten thousand years ago, success might have been more rudimentary and basic, like not getting eaten by a saber-toothed tiger meant that you had a successful day. You can observe any era of human history and learn from the small numbers of people who are successful rather than the larger group who are not.

In 1906, Vilfredo Pareto, an economist in Italy, observed that about 20 percent of the population had acquired all the wealth and influence in society. He further surmised that the vast majority of the people, 80 percent, had no influence, power, or wealth. He called the 80 percent with little the "trivial many." He stated the 20 percent were the vital few. At that moment the *80/20 rule*, or the *Pareto principle*, was born. (I discuss this rule in more detail in Chapter 19.)

Even at that time, you could observe much of what those top 20 percent did, read, attended, and engaged in. A person who desired success back then, as today, needed only observe and learn because success is never created in a vacuum or hidden from view. The truth is, success leaves clues to follow. You don't need the intellect of Sherlock Holmes to find clues to achieve success.

Even in Biblical times, success principles, habits, and clues were revealed. Take the advice in Matthew 7:7: "Keep on asking, and you will receive what you ask for. Keep on seeking, and you will find." This statement from Jesus, which appears in each of the four gospels, states clearly that asking is part of receiving. In fact, it's the most important part of receiving. You won't receive without asking, or worse, you might receive what you don't want.

Joan and I were a few years into our marriage and Christmas was approaching. My parents asked us both what we wanted for Christmas. Joan was launching her new home-building company, so she said that she needed some tools to be more hands-on in the construction process. My father's eyes lit up because he loves tools and working with his hands.

I thought about what I would want but couldn't really come up with anything and forgot to tell my parents in the ensuing weeks. So Christmas morning came and my father presented Joan a few wrapped gifts. She received a toolbox with all kinds of quality hand tools: hammers, wrenches, pliers, screwdrivers, tape measures, and so on. She was fully outfitted with high quality tools.

When it came time for me, my parents handed me a couple small boxes. I opened the first one and found silverware in it: spoons with extremely long handles. I asked, "What are these?" My mom exclaimed they were iced tea spoons. It was a struggle for me to be gracious, but I faked it. All the while I'm thinking, "Wow, I just got iced tea spoons. How exciting. My wife gets all these cool tools from my parents and I receive iced tea spoons." So I learned the lesson: Ask and you shall receive, or if you don't ask, you won't receive, or you might receive iced tea spoons instead.

The second part of the verse is seek and you will find. If you are a seeker in life, you will also be a finder. I know you are a seeker because you've picked up this book to read, which means you will also be a finder.

What we can't do is seek for everything all at one time. We must organize our seeking based on what's most important to us. The quickest way to frustration and failure is to say yes to everything or try to do everything. In success, saying yes to one thing requires saying no to another. There are some things in success that are choice-driven with a corresponding "no." For example, if you want to achieve physical health, you likely have to say no to eating burgers and fries most of the time.

Success leaves clues you can follow. You also need mentors to follow, people who have been successful before you and are relatable examples of how to live life to the fullest, build relationships, and attract wealth into their lives. In this chapter, we will explore what makes a good mentor an example to follow. True, I want you to look at the maps that others have followed to create their success, but ultimately, I want you to create our own treasure map.

Ask a Successful Person to Be Your Mentor

We learn through the observation of others. The power of observational learning is ingrained from a young age. That's how all babies, toddlers, and young children learn best. We observe how people walk and listen to how people talk, and we mimic what we hear and see. We process the stimuli and repeat, correct ourselves when we fail, and try again.

Do you know someone that has a grand lifestyle and wonderful relationships along with physical health and wealth? Is that person someone you could approach and talk to or have lunch with? Would that person be willing to become a mentor to you? Usually, someone who is willing to mentor someone realizes that success is not achieved in a vacuum. Their success in whole or part is from well timed advice, supportive people, and even fortunate circumstances in their life. That's not to say that success is random or happenstance. It's not.

I do believe that, as I stated earlier, when you ask, you will receive. For someone seeking help or seeking a mentor, that person or help will be manifested in their life. And mentors, because of their success and awareness of others' influence of their success, have the "pay it forward" attitude. One of the reasons I write, speak, and coach is paying it forward to help others. My success was not achieved without mentors, both those I met personally and those I encountered through books, audio programs, seminars, and coaching.

The heavyweights of the personal coaching industry, like Napoleon Hill, W. Clement Stone, and Earl Nightingale, through books and audio programs, mentored my thinking, actions, and disciplines. These men were the founding fathers of the personal development industry. Other heavyweights, like Jim Rohn and Brian Tracy, I got to know through live programs and later as colleagues in the personal development and success industry we all work in. If you haven't read the books these titans have published, you are denying yourself the privilege.

ANECDOTE

My most personal and formative mentor was Zig Ziglar, who wrote the original *Success For Dummies*. I was a young entrepreneur who had done very well in the last six years of the late 90s. I was asked to speak on a national tour of success programs in the real estate industry. Zig was the headliner, the keynote the draw for the program. Through those programs in different cities over a number of weeks, I was able to meet with, eat with, and talk with Zig about success, business, speaking, and impacting people's lives. I have letters and notes from Zig dating back almost 30 years that I cherish. He delighted in my success probably even more than I did. That's the type of person that you want as a mentor.

Evaluating good mentors

Plenty of people have achieved success in a few areas of life at the expense of other aspects of their lives. You are looking for a mentor who seems to have achieved a healthy balance. As you are evaluating and looking for role models and mentors, ask the following questions:

- » Do they have the relationships that I would desire?
- » How is their closeness with their kids?
- » How is their marriage?
- » Do they speak with honor and respect toward their spouse?
- » Do they have friends — true friends?
- » Are they happy in life?
- » Are the people around them happy?
- » How is their health?
- » Is their weight in control?
- » If they have health issues, were they caused by unavoidable circumstances or neglect?
- » Do they have a regular exercise routine?
- » How is their mental and emotional health?
- » How is their spiritual wellbeing?
- » Are they clear in their beliefs?
- » Does their spirituality bring them joy?
- » Do they equate success to their spiritual pursuits?
- » How are their finances?
- » Do they have the lifestyle you aspire to?
- » Are they stressed out by money and bills?
- » Are they saving for retirement and their kids' college education?

Believe it or not, there are people who have it all together in just about every aspect of life. These are the people you need to be watching and learning from. They have balanced all the distractions and temptations to achieve success, and they aren't robbing Peter to pay Paul. They aren't, for example, sacrificing the health of their personal relationships in the pursuit of wealth.

No one is perfect

Early in my business career, I found a mentor to model my life after. I was in my mid-twenties, so I was not well rounded as a person. My goal was to achieve wealth because I didn't have it. I figured if I learned how to become wealthy, my other challenges in life would be solved as well. Don't get me wrong, wealth is important. You are more likely to feel satisfied with life and feel lower levels of stress when you have enough money.

This mentor I chose to model had money. He had a high income and a grand lifestyle that included beautiful homes, luxury cars, fine dining, and resort vacations. He had achieved stature in his field and was considered an expert. So I was captivated and drawn in. I decided to follow his example because I wanted what he had in life: wealth and status.

So he took me under his wing, and I started implementing in my life what he told me. But I started to notice a few areas of his life that I didn't want to model. He went through a divorce. Now I realize that divorce is part of life and society, so I'm not making any judgments. But this divorce happened to be his fourth, and he has since had number five. I began to realize that while my mentor knew how to generate income, he certainly didn't have marriage figured out.

He later became estranged from most of his kids, which also caused me to raise an eyebrow. In terms of wealth, on a scale of 1 to 10, he was an obvious 10. But in the father and husband department, his score was much lower. I share this with you because, especially if you are young in your 20s or 30s like I was, you mostly define success in financial terms.

You may need multiple mentors and models

In determining a model or mentor for your life, a category or compartmentalization approach might work better. So if you accept that everyone has flaws, rather than looking for just one model or mentor, look for several:

>> Someone to mentor you on wealth

>> Someone else who has outstanding relationships

>> Someone who has vibrant health and vitality

So the best course could be to accurately observe the pluses and the minuses of multiple mentors.

Every person in your life can teach you something on your journey to greater success. In fact, I would contend that everyone occupies a place in one of two categories:

>> **Examples:** These people are clearly successful, so do what they do. If you follow their formula or recipe, you will likely achieve the level of success they have achieved.

>> **Warnings:** These people have made obvious mistakes. Don't do what they've done. If you take the actions they've taken, you will encounter the same problems and challenges that they have to deal with.

The categories are clear. So ask yourself this: In which category will my life be placed when others evaluate me? I personally want to avoid the warning column in my life. You create a legacy created in either column you occupy. Your children, friends, and acquaintances are watching to see where you end up.

If you follow, you get it all

Success leaves clues. Success follows the law of cause and effect. The law of cause and effect states that certain causes create certain effects. If I make time for my kids, Annabelle and Wesley, focus on being interested and engaged in what's important to them, if I spend time with them and am 100-percent present in that time, the effect will be a successful relationship and being a successful parent. It doesn't guarantee that we won't encounter challenges or rough patches or even that I will be able to navigate them away from trouble, difficulty, and hurt. My efforts won't erase all errors they might make. The best parents still have kids who make poor choices. What it will mean to Wesley and Annabelle is that our relationship is healthy, and they will know confidently that they are valuable and loved.

REMEMBER

Being able to objectively review success is a benefit. Evaluate a mentor's whole life, not just the one that attracted you in the first place. Realize if you follow the pattern, pathway, or model, you most likely reap all of what they have sown.

Approaching Success Like Preparing a Recipe

A recipe is in simple terms a series of ingredients put together in the right order to cook something specific. What are you trying to cook up in your life? You can have anything you want as long as you understand what it is and find or create a recipe to get it. For those of us who live in the United States, we have boundless opportunity for success. People from other countries, especially those with less affluence and opportunity, are desperate to come to the United States because they understand it's a land of opportunity unlike any other. If you live in the United States, you have many of the ingredients for your success recipe already.

Are you passionate about what you do? Do you love going to your job, business, or career? Being in love with your work is a key ingredient of success. You will spend more than one-third of your hours during your working years . . . working. I would suggest you love what you do or find something else to do that you love. If you want to be a business owner, you need to love what you do, especially because you'll work long hours doing it.

REMEMBER

Passion is also a key ingredient to success. You either have passion or you don't for what you do. I passionately love watching people grow, expand, and achieve their goals and provide a better life for their families. When someone comes up to me after I speak and tells me how I inspired them, no amount of money is equal to that in life for me. My writing flows from that passion to reach more people, serve more people, and help more people where it's cost effective for them. There is a small audience that can afford my services in coaching them personally. The books allow me to translate my philosophy of success to more people.

Finding the right recipe for you

What is it that you want? What skills do you need to acquire to achieve your goals? What changes in your attitude must you take on? What new habits and disciplines must you add? What type of income and lifestyle do you desire? Can you accomplish your goals in your present field? Can you achieve success with your present grades? Are you playing at your all-out effort level?

These are some of the questions you need to ask yourself to arrive at your recipe. In addition to my book, I would point you to other resources that will help you find your recipe:

>> *Think and Grow Rich* by Napoleon Hill. This book is the foundation, besides the Bible, of the motivational success industry. It's rare for a highly accomplished, successful person to have not read this book.

>> *The Richest Man in Babylon* by George S. Clason. This small but powerful book packs a large amount of financial wisdom in an evening of reading. If your desire is financial independence some time in life, you can't miss this book in refining your financial success recipe.

REMEMBER

Success is attracted by the person you become. It's not the million dollars that makes the millionaire. The money is actually the least valuable part of the equation. That might seem crazy to some, but hear me out. The million dollars in merely the *result* of newly acquired, habits, skills, abilities, or strategies. The real value, or success, is what you had to *become* to attract the million dollars. If you lost the money, you can remain confident that you can create it again. You did it the first time, right? You will be a changed person from the work and experience you gained when earning your first million.

TIP

Here is my bold guarantee: If you will change, then everything will change for you. Don't be looking for circumstances to change, and by circumstances, I mean things like the economy, or taxes, or the government, or your relationships. Those will all likely be the same more or less your whole life. Yes, there will be times of economic growth and economic contraction, but you don't control that. What you control is you and your growth in your skills, thinking, attitude, and value in the marketplace. You control what you learn and how fast you learn. You control the books you read, new skills you develop, and disciplines you implement.

What new skills do you need to acquire? What change in attitude must you embrace? What new actions must you implement in your daily life? Your answers to these questions will change who you become so that you better attract what you desire. It's who you want and need to become that will be the right recipe of success.

Determining the ingredients you are missing

We all lack skills, habits, and tools that are required to increase our success. I believe that most of us, if we are willing to look honestly at ourselves in the mirror, can see our own flaws; we know what we are lacking. Most of us just choose not to go to that level of self-analysis or introspection. I realize it takes being uncomfortable.

Let's take a dive into our health area of life. We know that we eat too much, consume the wrong combination of foods, and exercise too little. We only have to look in that full-length mirror and see the excuses placed around our midsection or hips. And if you honestly have no clue of what you are lacking in life, then ask a trusted friend. Ask, "Why do you think I am not as successful as I would like? What changes would you suggest that I make in my attitude, character, or actions and activities?" If you can find a mentor, ask him or her. For the vast majority of us, we know the ingredients we are missing from our success recipe if we simply look in the mirror of our life.

Another key factor of success is to narrow down what are most important of all the actions and activities you must do. My belief and experience is that success is not contained in doing a few things with excellence, or even at a world-class level. Early in the chapter, I introduced the Pareto principle, or the 80/20 rule. Allow me to use it as an illustration again:

REMEMBER

Eighty percent of the success you achieve in a given pursuit will be due to executing well a half-dozen things.

If you want to increase your value and earnings in your chosen career, for example, there will be about a half-dozen things you must do with passion, intensity, and consistency to increase your value and earnings. You have to determine those half-dozen things yourself, but I will share what a half-dozen might look like:

1. Arrive 30 minutes early and stay an additional 15–30 minutes each day to increase output.

2. Read at least 30 minutes per day something related to your career to increase your skill.

3. Ask your boss once per week, "Is there anything that I can help with or take off your plate?" And then get it done for him or her.

4. Talk with your boss once per month about any training you could take or skills you need to help you advance or be more valuable.

5. Partake in regular physical activity (you know, exercise) for 60 minutes per day, 4 days per week.

If you did those five with consistency, passion, and energy, I guarantee that you would increase your income and value at your work.

You will notice that I stopped at five, and that's because half-dozen is a flexible term. It could be only five, a full six, or maybe seven, but it shouldn't be more than seven because then you have too many pans in the fire. What you are trying to create is a priority system so that you focus on the most important tasks to create the biggest impact. You could use this method effectively in your career, your relationships, your business, or your finances. Any improvement toward your success can be used in creating your key half dozen. You will notice that my examples are specific and measurable: Each week I ask my boss; every day I read for 30 minutes. You want to craft your recipe in a manner that allows you to say for certain you did that action today, or this week, or whenever the frequency needs to be. Don't give yourself an out by being vague.

Use a reminders app on your smartphone to create a checklist for your regular activities. You can attach an alarm to some activities if needed, and you can set up the reminders to repeat on a daily, weekly, or monthly basis. As you complete the tasks in your reminders list, check them off.

Expecting the recipe to be delicious

Most successful cooks and chefs start with a recipe. As they perfect their dish or meal, they make adjustments to enhance the flavor or make the meal healthier. Even as they experiment with the ratios of ingredients, one thing is certain: They expect what they are making to be tasty and delicious.

The same is true as you experiment with your formula or recipe for success. You have to expect, as you make changes and adjustments, that what you are striving for will be accomplished and you will become more successful in whatever your objective is at the time. Part of being successful is having a positive attitude of expecting success. Once you begin to achieve a goal, don't let the negative creep into your mind. Focus on remaining positive through observing other challenges you have previously overcome. You might try writing or saying affirmations like, "I will shed 25 pounds of weight in less than six months from today." Or, "I will have a net worth of a million dollars in less than ten years from today."

People who remain positive in challenging times and circumstances weather the trials better. In fact, they seize those times to create a grand future and the achievement of their goals.

In 2008, when the economy was challenging, to say the least, when the banks were failing, and the overall economy was grinding to a halt, my businesses and income were trending much lower than normal. I was not a Pollyanna in believing that only positive thinking was going to turn around my companies' lower sales numbers. But I was certain that we would weather the current economic malaise. I expected to be one of the many businesses that actually thrived.

In fact, as 2008 closed out and the negative trends continued into 2009, I was more confident than ever that there would be actual opportunity in this adversity. First, I stayed positive. I found a number of new opportunities created by the economic crisis, and the vast foreclosure crisis had created a rare opportunity to create wealth. So I needed to change my recipe. I cut the overhead in my companies, and that meant trimming budgets, overhead, and even staff. Anything that was not creating revenue or not increasing our customers' experience was gone. I even cut out what we thought had been sacred cows in the business. I learned that sacred cows make the best hamburgers.

We looked for new problems that the economic change had created in our core market niches in sales, real estate sales training, and education. We embraced new delivery systems for our training and coaching, like live virtual classrooms. We brought our brand of success to the marketplace at lower costs so that we could appeal to a broader customer base.

I recognized key investment opportunities in bank-owned and short-sale real estate investments. That was the biggest game changer of all. In Chapter 14, I cover in depth how I approached that windfall. That change led to multiple millions of dollars in wealth because I was willing to stay positive, expected success, and seized new opportunities that presented themselves.

Chapter **3**

Discipline: The Magic Habit

I f you lined up all the habits to develop to create success — planning, saving, being present with loved ones, love, faith, integrity, trustworthiness, passion for learning, and personal improvement — there is one element that is required to make all the others go. Think about it this way: You can have a marvelous luxury car like a Bentley, Mercedes, or McLaren, one that just says to everyone, "I am successful." You keep it in tip-top shape by having the best mechanics work on it, but if you don't fill it with the right gasoline, it won't go anywhere.

That's basically how *discipline* relates to all the other skills, attributes, and characteristics of success. You could be highly educated and have a vast amount of stored knowledge, but if you lack discipline to turn that knowledge into action, you will fall extremely short of your goals and objectives. It doesn't matter if you go to all the seminars or read all the books. If you have knowledge but lack the discipline to implement and take action on what you know, it's as if you don't posses the knowledge in the first place.

I should add the word *self* in front of discipline, because that's what I am really talking about. Self-discipline is the magic habit of successful people. It takes discipline to break free from some of the bad habits we have in our lives — the ones that we have cultivated over time and have grown from smalls weed to large trees with deep roots. And keep in mind that everyone has a few trees that started as weeds.

It takes discipline to craft your success plan and evaluate all the factors and determine your goals. You then need to be disciplined to execute the plan, dealing with the setbacks, adjusting the plan, and learning from your errors. Discipline is required to be fully objective in why you aren't where you want to be and why your plan results have been less than expected. It's been my experience that the most successful people are the most honest with themselves.

ANECDOTE

When Wesley, my oldest child, was born, I started to create a list of skills, characteristics, and attributes I wanted to teach him. This list I called "The Tools of Success." I kept thinking about it and adding to the list over a few months. Then one day I had this thought: What if I wasn't around long enough to teach and instill everything on the list? Yes, I will admit, it was kind of a morbid thought, but it then got me thinking about priorities. When I asked myself which of these skills is the most important of all on this list? It honestly came to me right away: discipline.

I knew that if Wesley was able to develop and master discipline, he would have the foundational skill required to acquire the others when he needed them most.

REMEMBER

All other life skills are subservient to discipline.

Discipline Is a Reward, Not a Punishment

Too frequently, we equate discipline to punishment or something negative. For example, we discipline our children by putting them in timeouts. We are correcting behavior and demonstrating the law of cause and effect. So acting disrespectfully to others will create the effect of being in timeout for a period of time. But discipline is not a negative tool, as some believe, but a positive tool that creates leverage in life. And just as you use leverage to lift heavy objects, discipline allows you to overcome the problems and challenges you face.

Also misunderstood is the placement of reward for discipline. In today's world, we want everything immediately, even our accomplishments and rewards.

We also live in a society where everyone gets a participation trophy. It doesn't take much discipline to be awarded a trophy for participation. Our kids get participation trophies for being on the soccer team, whether or not they play, and I find this practice to be detrimental to discipline growth. After all, if you are going to step into "the arena," there will be winners and losers. Losing is merely an opportunity to improve and learn from your errors, where you can apply great discipline in preparation so that you win the next time.

The rewards we reap for a disciplined approach to life are frequently delayed to some time in the future. The penalties for a lack of discipline are immediate but sometimes imperceptible. They can be so small that we don't notice them. And a lack of discipline in your life repeated over time leads to regret.

Here's an example: The failure to save 10 to 15 percent of your income over the span of 30 to 40 years will lead to regret. When we realize at age 50, 60, or 70 that we have not saved enough over our working lifetime, that we have little in savings and few earning years left to correct the problem, then we certainly encounter regret and wish we could go back 20 years to make more disciplined choices. The weight of regret is a burdensome weight to carry. On the other hand, the weight of small disciplines repeated over time is like carrying around a 5-pound weight. You know it's there, but you also know it's making you better and stronger.

Emphasize the positive rather than the negative

We all have some areas where we struggle to be disciplined. For you, it might be your eating or exercise, or finances even. We tend to focus on what we are not doing and what we could be doing better. While there is importance in accurate self-evaluation, I would suggest a different approach as you are working on your discipline: Focus on the positive of implementing a new discipline instead of trying to remove a negative habit or activity.

I want you to focus on addition. Focus on that new, positive action or habit you can start today.

Don't worry so much about removing undisciplined behavior and actions. Rather than focusing on stopping smoking, as an example, focus on adding exercise regularly to your routine. By adding a new discipline or action, you create a positive new habit. Every new discipline you add has a positive effect on all your other disciplines. Every new activity you add increases your performance and success. As you exercise regularly, you feel better about yourself; your self-confidence increases. This self-confidence increase will make it easier for you to stop smoking in the near future.

Even adding a small discipline creates positive momentum and positive motivation. Select the smallest new discipline you can think of. When you start it and keep consistent with it for a few weeks, this new discipline will start feeding your self-confidence.

One of the biggest barriers to success is the lack of self-confidence, which chokes out the willingness to try new disciplines.

So what new disciplines do you need to add to your day?

Think of discipline as a gift

We all like to receive gifts, and the anticipation of a gift is a powerful motivator. Think about the excitement kids feel on their birthday or Christmas morning. That's the attitude we need to have as we develop discipline in our lives.

Discipline is a gift that can be given through demonstration, and it can be received through observation. I received discipline as a gift from my father. He demonstrated the power of discipline throughout my formative years. Even at 87 years of age, he still demonstrates it daily through routine of early rising, working diligently on his goals and objectives, controlled spending, and passionate service and philanthropy. When I visited him recently, he was building an addition to his barn, framing the roof, and standing 12 feet up in the bucket of his tractor. He is amazing. Discipline is a gift my father wanted to give to everyone he encountered, especially the people that he loves. All you had to do was observe him and you would receive it.

Most of us look at success as a very complex combination of skills, abilities, attitudes, and actions joined together in a magical or secret formula to achieve grand results. Discipline is the fundamental building block that most successful people utilize to achieve greater success in life. Once you have acquired the skill of discipline, it doesn't matter what the economy is doing or what business you are in, your success is within reach at all times. You possess the most important tool to help you through the storms and changes of life.

Discipline is a crucial missing piece for many people. Most people don't have someone to demonstrate discipline to them, as I have had. That's why I truly believe it's a gift. I would encourage you to make a goal to demonstrate and give discipline to your loved ones.

I believe that, because our country has become so prosperous, we take the need for discipline for granted. Older people in our society remember the sacrifices they had to make to achieve a greater measure of success. People like myself, who were born in the 1960s and beyond, have grown up in a vacuum compared to older generations. We are far too removed from the struggles of the World War I generation, Depression generation, World War II generation, and even the Korean War generation. Those generations needed discipline just to survive. In modern-day America, you don't need discipline to survive. We have slowed the train down so that undisciplined people can stay on the train. Discipline is the secret weapon of successful people. It is the one big tool that separates them from all others.

Deciding Where to Focus Your Discipline

If we can control and discipline three key areas of our life, we can control and discipline anything. These three areas are the toughest for most people to discipline themselves to take control of:

>> **Our finances:** I meet too many high producers and high achievers who can't control their money. Their hands are like a colander with lots of holes: The money just runs right through, and it all runs out. In the end, it's not what you gross; it's what you net. It's not what you make; it's what you keep.

I always tell salespeople that I can easily teach them how to make another $100,000 in less than a year, but if they don't discipline themselves to save a good portion of it, I haven't really helped them that much. We have to learn the skill of increase, coupled with the skill of discipline and control, to dramatically change our financial picture.

>> **The cleanliness of our home:** It takes discipline and hard work to maintain your home. For my wife Joan and me, the battle has increased exponentially with our children, Wesley and Annabelle. Those of you with children know what a challenge this is daily. It's easy to let the laundry pile up, to not make the beds, to not control the kitchen. It's easy to let the garage get filled with everyone's stuff to the point you can't park the cars in it anymore. Keeping the house in order is hard.

>> **Our weight:** For many of us, controlling what we eat and how much we move daily is a tremendous battle. I have to admit this is the one that gets me. I like to say that I'm too short for my weight presently. Given the low probability of an increase in height, I need to be more disciplined about my weight. What I eat, when I eat, and how much I move are disciplines that are a high priority. The discipline part really kicks in when it comes keeping the weight off for the long haul. Anyone can have success with a fad diet to lose some or all of the weight. It takes real discipline to change your eating and exercise habits for the long haul.

As I've said before, anyone who desires success must have discipline. Success is attracted to you because of the person you become. It comes to you due to the plan you are working and the specific actions you take to implement the plan. Success aligns with the law of attraction. You attract success to you. Have you ever known anyone that basically is successful at almost anything they try? That person is adept at the law of attraction.

It takes discipline to plan, to set the necessary time aside to evaluate the conditions, and to construct the plan that takes advantage of the current conditions and skills that you possess. You also need to evaluate the weaknesses that must be addressed to increase the probability of your success. So it takes discipline to plan, and it also takes discipline to implement the plan.

Most people quit before the plan can take full root and work. We live in a society where we all want instant success without significant effort. If we really knew the grand future that awaits us, if we could really see it, touch it, and feel it, we would be ready to implement disciplined activity to achieve it. In short, we would be willing to pay the price to get there.

An effective strategic plan should inject emotion and passion into you. You should be able to feel that emotion and passion. And that feeling, coupled with discipline, will move you to take action.

REMEMBER

Taking action is really the goal for a successful person. Discipline is not magical; it's merely movement — regular, consistent, purposeful. Discipline is the link between your thoughts and your accomplishments.

The Keys to Success

Discipline truly is the key that universally unlocks the doors of success. By universal key, I mean it unlocks the doors to health, happiness, wealth, self-esteem, recognition, respect, accomplishment, and self-worth. Any door you encounter can be unlocked if you are prepared and willing to apply discipline. Even if the lock is stuck due to past misuse and neglect, you'll have the resolve to work it free.

In order to effectively use discipline as your tool or key, you must *start.* It's the starting of the new discipline that stops most people. A journey to success begins with a single step. The first step is what stops most people. Without that first step of faith and discipline, you are guaranteed to not accomplish your objectives. For some, that means reaching out for a new customer. For others, a first step is just a walk around the block for exercise. And then there are those who need to open a savings account. What is the first step you have been delaying because you aren't ready? What step do you need to take before today becomes yesterday?

Mastering your circumstances

We all are faced with circumstances we would prefer not to face. It's how we approach these circumstances in our daily life that determines the level of success we achieve. The bad things that happen to us happen to all of us. While you might be dealing with a horrible health diagnosis, you must recognize you aren't the only one who has received this bad news.

Frequently, opportunity and success come to us with an exterior wrapper, like market problems or misfortune. We focus so much on the outside wrapper that we fail to open what's really in store for us inside.

ANECDOTE

In late 2008, when the economy was in free fall, the real estate market was tanking. The stock market was correcting to new lows. My personal finances and my businesses were taking a large hit in revenue. I had lost 50 percent of the value in my retirement accounts. It was hard to see beyond the wrapper of my latest set of problems. My circumstances, while not dire, caused me to be concerned about my devastated retirement assets. What was required was more discipline on my part to research and understand my options to correct my now significant retirement shortfall. I had been passive in my thinking that a financial planner was more skilled to invest my retirement money than I was. They are trained and educated to make wealth and money decisions. It was undisciplined thinking that caused me to passively let someone else captain my retirement ship. I threw that undisciplined thinking out the window.

I dove into learning and exploring the options I had with retirement assets. What I discovered through study was that I could self-direct my retirement assets into real estate. Real estate is an asset class I know a lot about, so I decided to go all-in on real estate investments from 2009 to 2011 when the real estate market was well below historic values. The banks had foreclosed homes and were giving them away below replacement costs. I knew this circumstance was a rare opportunity. Now almost a decade later, the disciplined action at that time has exploded my retirement account's asset value.

TIP

Being able to master your circumstances, remain positive, and discipline yourself to continue searching for a solution will always lead to success.

Balancing discipline with procrastination

Being more disciplined creates a greater awareness of the need to take action. Change is a constant in life, especially in the pursuit of success. We have to be willing to take action on small changes that are needed and avoid any delays. If I am more disciplined, I am naturally more aware of the power of my actions and how important implementation is in success.

The voice of discipline inside both you and me says, "Get it done." It says, "Always do the best you can with what you have." It shouts, "Do it now!" The voice of procrastination says, "We can do it later." And you think that doing it tomorrow, or when you get around to it, will be good enough. We are regularly cornered with the decision to do it now or do it later. If you develop the habit of taking action now, or very soon, your success will be guaranteed.

REMEMBER

Be aware of the age-old concept called the law of diminishing intent. This law creates countless casualties on the road to success. It states that the greater the span of time from when you know a certain action must be taken, to when you actually start to take that action, the lower the odds you will ever take action or do it.

Let's say you have been spurred through reading this chapter to add a new discipline of an exercise routine to your daily life. You feel quite good and resolved in that decision. But the longer you wait until you actually put on your athletic shoes and start your walk around your neighborhood, the less likely you will ever take that first step. So you can't wait until tomorrow or next week. You're just killing your chances of getting anything done.

TIP

My best advice: Avoid the procrastination pattern employed by so many. If you're resolved to do something, then do it now!

Balancing the price versus the promise

We all know in life the concept of delayed gratification: We delay receiving something today for something better, more meaningful, or valuable in the future. We have to understand, balance, and connect paying the price today with the promise of the reward in the future. The challenge is that if we can't see the promise clearly, we are unlikely to pay the price, or any price for that matter.

If we can see the future — next week, next month, or next year — if we have comfort or assurances that the promise will be delivered to us, then the price becomes inconsequential. The society of today is less aware of the connection. Farmers understand the price and the promise. They prepare the ground for the seed with expectation of the promise this fall of a crop. They then plant the seeds and tend to them by watering and weeding. The promise is fulfilled with a bountiful harvest (with very few exceptions involving drought and other forms of bad weather).

What would you do in a disciplined manner for a spectacular promise? Would you get up an hour earlier and devote it to reading the books? Would you stay up late to craft your goals and success plan? Would you save 15 percent of what you make for the promise of wealth? What discipline do you need to connect the price and the promise to?

Mastering the Law of Sowing and Reaping

One of the most powerful paths to success is derived from the law of sowing and reaping, which was first written down in the Bible as the Parable of the Sower, told by Jesus in Matthew 13:3–9:

> A farmer went out to sow his seed. As he was scattering the seed, some fell along the path, and the birds came and ate it up. Some fell on rocky places, where it did not have much soil. It sprang up quickly, because the soil was shallow. But when the sun came up, the plants were scorched, and they withered because they had no root. Other seed fell among thorns, which grew up and choked the plants. Still other seed fell on good soil, where it produced a crop — a hundred, sixty or thirty times what was sown. Whoever has ears, let them hear.

There's a lot to take from this story. We know the farmer in the story had discipline. He was at work probably early to be able to sow seeds. He had a small window of time to plant the seeds where the frost had ceased in covering the ground, but it was early enough in the growing season where he had plenty of days to grow his crop before harvest. He had to hit that window just right so that he could produce the largest crop. I am sure he observed and maybe even recorded each year the day and month he planted annually.

In those ancient days, he didn't have tractors or other heavy equipment to aid him. He did the back-breaking work of preparing the ground by hand or using animals to pull a plow. He then scattered or planted the seeds, which are actually two different strategies to success:

>> **In scattering the seed,** you have to factor in that a portion of your seed will be eaten, blown away, dried up, and not return a crop. You must scatter more seed than you expect will germinate and take root. Less still will be harvested in the fall. It's the awareness that Murphy's Law (anything that can go wrong will go wrong) will take a portion of your seed. This is true of the pursuit of success in the modern day. Some of your hard work and seed will dry up, get eaten, or be blown away. When using discipline as our focus in the scatter-seed system, we need to go beyond what seems necessary, becoming hyper disciplined, knowing that some of our efforts will be for naught.

>> **When using the planting approach,** as the farmer does to success, we know we will have less breakage, but we won't be able to plant as many acres of land because we take more time tending to those acres in the planting stage.

REMEMBER

Whatever method you choose, the key is to keep sowing and expanding. Both of these strategies are valid approaches to success for different times and different areas of life.

Let me share an example: For many years, I used the planting approach with my children, almost exclusively. We would spend time together on the rug crawling around, going to the park, having tea parties, baking cookies. In those periods of time, I was planting seeds of love, self-confidence, discipline, learning to finish what you start. In those activities, I was able to plant the seeds of future success in their soil (or minds). Because when kids are young, they're more impressionable and more likely to listen to their parents.

Today as teenagers, my kids have to deal with so many other sowers of influence who are trying to plant and scatter seeds into their soil. And my strategy has shifted to focus more on scattering the seeds. I have moments where I try to plant seeds, but being teenagers, they want greater control over who plants seeds in their soil. They want a little independence, so my strategy needed to change.

In creating financial success, there are times to scatter seed, to be more broadly invested in a wider pool of balanced investments. Then there are other times when you encounter a rare opportunity. This is the time to plant a larger portion of your asset base in the one right field. I did that from 2009 to 2012 in the real estate crash. It has proven to be an extremely effective strategy to create wealth.

The changes we go through in life are similar to the weather changes we experience during the seasons of the year: spring, summer, fall, and winter. We have to recognize the season and pick up the right tool and summon the discipline to create the successful outcome we desire. These changing seasons happens in business, relationships, finances, and even spirituality.

We are all farmers in life. We are growing crops in our place of work. We are growing crops in our relationships, with our health, with our finances. You might not live on an actual farm, but you are still a farmer. It takes productivity and discipline to bring forth a crop of success. You must think like a farmer and ask, "What season am I presently in?" Then anticipate when the next season may come.

Multiplying your rewards from your sowing efforts

As Jesus explained in Matthew 13:3–9, when the seed landed in good soil, a crop was produced. But that crop wasn't one to one. You don't plant one seed and get one of anything back. You receive a multiple. In the scripture it says, "a hundred, sixty or even thirty times what was sown." Think about it: By the disciplined act of first sowing, I can get a thirty-times return, and that's on the low end.

To put this in perspective, I will use money as my example. Why? Because money is easy to count and is relatable to everyday life. If you gave your financial planner $10,000 and he gave you $30,000 in return in 6 months to a year, you would likely be delighted with his services. That is what the scripture is expressing on the low end of the scale. The truth is, you get nothing if you don't sow. The only way to receive a return is to sow. What the law of sowing and reaping says is that we actually reap more than we sow. In focusing on discipline, when you take disciplined actions and perform activities with discipline, you will reap more than you sow in seeds of discipline.

Here is the bad news as well. When you don't take disciplined actions toward your success, you will reap more negative outcomes than you expect. This is called the *compound effect:* Everything in life compounds in its return. We often think of the compound effect for just money and wealth, but *everything* in life compounds. Healthy eating or unhealthy eating both compound in different directions in our bodies. You can give your kids attention, love, and time, or you can show them neglect and negativity. Both options compound in their lives.

And in your business, if you provide a unique and better customer service experience, if you give your customers good value, your business will multiply in gross revenue and net profit. Your reward will be compounded.

Dealing with the four types of soil you will encounter in life

We will encounter different types of people and different types of circumstances in life. Most of what we encounter can be broken down into the four different types of soil described in the Parable of the Sower. The key to success is to never stop your disciplined act of sowing. The second key is to observe the type of soil that you're sowing efforts are being invested in.

Along the path

Sometimes we sow seeds in minds that are pathlike. The seeds bounce off the path or just sit there to be snatched away. This is true not only of people but situations. You might be working on a sale at work that just seems like no matter what you do, you can't break through the wall to make the sale. We have to look at ourselves and assess the odds. Is this ground fertile enough? Does what I am proposing solve a big enough problem for them? Am I talking with the right person? Am I better to continue on with them or find someone else who might be better soil in which to make a sale?

We have the option to change soil in many areas of our lives. In parenting, as well, the soil can be different from child to child. There are also times when the soil between Wesley's or Annabelle's ears is not receptive to my ideas. Their top layer of soil is hard as a path, so I'm wasting my effort trying to get through to them. Human beings, and especially in family dynamics, have the right to have different soil in their heads at different times. Discovering what soil might be present is important if you want to achieve success together.

Rocky places

The seeds you plant in rocky soil might get off to a fast start of germination and growth, but because roots cannot form due to thin soil, the growth stops, and the plant is scorched out by the sun.

We all encounter people, even ourselves, who are good starters but lack the staying power to hit the finish line. We get excited about new ideas or opportunities but have not done a soil examination before we start. When our idea attempts to take root in ourselves or others, it runs into the rocky soil.

This type of soil is more discouraging than the path. At least with the path you know your seeds are bird food quickly. The rocky soil encouraged you by quick germination and growth of your seed, but it then dealt the blow of adversity and failure to create a crop. The discouragement can stop you from further sowing seeds. When sowing stops, whether it's business or personal relationships, it creates a chokepoint to success.

Thorny soil

The Biblical text says the least about this type of soil. Thorny soil has a lot going on. It has invasive thorns and weeds that will overtake your efforts to sow success. We ourselves could be the thorny soil when we are trying to juggle too many things at once, not focusing intently enough on a few things that will make the biggest difference in our discipline and success.

Our lives can be so consumed by trivial pursuits and responsibilities that the weeds take over the garden. We all need to go through a regular process of pruning and removing the unimportant and marginally important from our lives.

TIP

To gain clarity on what are truly important objectives and goals in our lives, take a look at the complete process of goal setting in Chapter 5.

Good soil

The good soil is where meaningful things happen. It's where the compound effect takes hold. The key is to just keep scattering and planting seeds, and you will eventually find good soil. The real problem for most of us is that when we don't hit good soil on the first attempt or two, we quit.

Based on the law of averages, I will only hit good soil about one out of four times. What if I stop at three attempts? Then I have little chance of hitting good soil. This ratio or law of averages is true in all areas of my life. If I expect to tell my children something one time and have them grasp it, the odds are I will quit, become discouraged, and maybe even throw my hands up in frustration. The same is true for a staff member as well. What are the law of averages for your business? What is the law of averages for your health and relationships?

If you are in sales and you expect to only make a call or two to prospects to open up the relationship to a sales opportunity, you are falling far short of what success requires. You haven't even exhausted the possible types of soil you encounter once you actually can engage in a conversation with them. Then you need to discover needs, wants, desires, and problems they are experiencing. All of this must be done before you can even begin to talk about solutions you offer.

The Parable of the Sower is one of the best examples and illustrations of how to use discipline in life to achieve success. It incorporates the law of averages, the Pareto principle, and the compound effect all inside the sowing and reaping principles of a successful life. Our objective is to farm our way to success in our relationships, spiritual life, career, health, and wealth.

2

Putting Together Your Success Plan

IN THIS PART . . .

Craft your blueprint for success.

Develop your goals and objectives for life.

Master the skills to deal with inevitable adversity and setbacks.

Chapter 4

Tapping into Personal Motivation

Motivation is a key tool of success. It is the fuel that powers our engine speeding down the track of success. The importance of motivation is right up there with persistence, self-worth, and a positive mental attitude.

To understand motivation's power, we have to define what motivation is. The dictionary defines motivation as the condition of being eager to act or to work. I feel that's a splendid definition. Motivation is not the planning process. It's not about preparing endlessly. You can spot a motivated person based on their *actions*.

We see a person who has unlimited energy and excitement, and we think that's motivation, and those characteristics can be outward signs of motivation. But there are many people who talk a good game of success. They say all the right words and phrases to identify them as successful. But when you see them in real life, problems are readily apparent. What you're hearing and what you're seeing don't match. In a motivated person, the audio and video are in alignment. You can observe their actions and know that they are successful.

We all are motivated in different ways and by different things. The journey to become motivated is knowing thy self and being true to thy self. Don't wish you were different. Instead, we can wish and then choose to have different habits.

We can also create new habits due to our motivation to change. Be the best you that you can be by discovering what you are skilled at and then developing those skills.

The Benefits of Being Motivated

The benefits of motivation are significant but not always clear. Let me share with you how important and beneficial motivation can be:

>> **Productivity:** People who are more motivated get more done. They accomplish more in shorter periods of time, whether that amount of time is an hour, a few hours, a day, a week, or a month. They accomplish more in a year and their lifetime. Motivated people have a sense of urgency. They attack what needs to be done with energy, intensity, and focus. They move quickly to action. They stay engaged in actions longer without losing steam.

>> **Energy:** This characteristic is what we usually see in others and equate it to motivation. The natural excitement when you are motivated creates an adrenaline rush. Your body, from that excitement, requires less sleep. As you sleep, your subconscious mind is turning over your problems and challenges like a rotisserie turning a chicken until it is roasted to perfection. Then when you wake, your energy level is high because the solution you have been searching for came to you in the middle of the night!

>> **Charisma:** When you have motivation, your highly energetic, positive personality draws people to you. Those people are attracted to you and want to be part of helping you. If we can link mutual benefits, you both will be increasing your motivation. This is especially true for a cause that is larger than you. Motivated people are attractors of people and success.

>> **Compounding:** When you create the state of being motivated, your efforts are exponential. These benefits cross over and compound in all areas of your life. You are just layering success upon itself to create explosive, almost unbelievable outcomes.

What Motivates Most People

I have been in the sales field for more than 30 years. I have sold both tangible and intangible products and services. I've done both business-to-business and business-to-consumer selling. The reason I give you this background on myself is because sales is a field that requires large amounts of motivation. In fact, I believe it's the career that requires the greatest amount of motivation, especially if you are in 100-percent commission sales, which has been my compensation model for more than 30 years. As a 100-percent salesperson, you have to get up every day and must be motivated to find leads, prospects, and clients to earn your income. You are starting every day at zero. You are starting every day unemployed, working to find people to serve. Being highly motivated is a big deal!

I have studied motivation and have seen it executed well and poorly for decades, and here is what I have found out. When you strip all the factors away, there are three motivators that get people into action:

>> Desire for gain

>> Fear of loss

>> Pain or pleasure

We all have these three motivators lurking inside us. And we all are using these three to spur us to action. We can all view circumstances that occur to us through the lens of these motivators. The same circumstance could happen to you and me, and you might look at it as a gain while I might view it as a loss. In my research, the fear of loss is most used and most powerful to move people to action. Now you might be thinking, not me. And I wouldn't argue because I don't know you. But for most people, the potentially negative situation creates more action.

Desire for gain

The desire to gain wealth, recognition, acceptance, power, freedom, choices, wisdom, health, or honor are all huge motivators. Outward signs of prosperity are all around us. Being motivated to acquire wealth is not wrong. Wealth can provide security, comfort, self-confidence, freedom, and even generosity.

The danger comes in when it's *the* motivation, not *a* motivation. I can say that there have been periods in my life that wealth was *the* motivation. Wealth had too much control over my reasons to take action. I think it's easy to fall into this trap. It's also easy to go overboard in the motivation to acquire the trappings of wealth, to focus on the new car, new house, and overall consumerism in pursuit of a wealth lifestyle.

If you are out of balance in your motivation, or if your motivation for wealth is not tempered with other key motivations, then when you achieve the wealth goals of life, you will go through a period of being out of focus and unmotivated. As you draw closer to wealth goals, it will become more difficult to motivate yourself because money or wealth will have less pull for you. You will need to reset, adjust, or increase your goals. You might shift your focus to giving the surplus wealth away.

NASA discovered in the 1970s that the astronauts who had reached the pinnacle in space travel, landing on the moon, were having motivation and assimilation issues back on earth. As they conducted interviews over a series of months and years, they discovered that because these astronauts had invested years, and some lifetimes, toward the goal of landing on the moon, they were having significant challenges establishing lofty new goals to push for. It actually makes sense, when you consider it. When you've gone to the moon and back, what could be a loftier goal than that? You have accomplished something that only a dozen human beings in history have accomplished, and none since 1972.

There are many people whose most significant motivation is power. Many of these people go on to create and run large companies. Many in our political system are in this camp as well. An elected official can also have the motivation to serve our community and nation, but there are a large number for whom power is their primary motivator.

Fear of loss

Fear is a real part of life. Fear has been a teacher and motivator since we were small. I have loved my father from an early age, but I also feared him. The proverbial "Wait until your father gets home" threat kept me on the straight and narrow — most of the time. I knew if I strayed off that path, the odds were, upon him getting home, a belt would be used on my bare backside. I am not advocating corporal punishment but merely relating an illustration that was a reality for many families not all that long ago.

Having realistic fears for realistic reasons can place boundaries and shape motivation. The fear of getting a poor grade drives a student to study more. The fear that we might have a second heart attack changes our eating and exercise habits. And there are healthy fears that are ingrained in us for survival purposes, like the fear you experience as you walk across a small ledge high in the air, or the fear you feel driving too fast on a slippery road.

Fear-based motivation is frequently shorter in duration because once the fear passes, the feared outcome is less of a threat. We can put our guard down. Fear is a temporary way to make us perform in a more motivated state.

Pain or pleasure

We are all wired to seek pleasure and also avoid pain. We have both of these motivation impulses inside of us. I have used both with clients whom I coach in getting people unstuck and into action. Let me share a few of my favorites.

Most of us have causes that we are for or against with significant passion. Think of the various political causes that cause people to march or protest. Find whatever elicits a passionate response in yourself, based on your values and beliefs, and can connect that with pain. Doing something that might benefit a cause you are against would be pain.

ANECDOTE

Let's say I'm working with a client to establish motivation and new habits, and that guy is an avid Democrat. We agree to a commitment level and activity level, and we decide what actions should be taken. He agrees that if he falls short, there is a pain action he is required to take. For example, he sends me a check for $100 or $500 made out to a Republican candidate or the Republican National Committee. If he falls short on his commitment, then I send the check. I actually have checks like this in my desk frequently. I can count on one hand the number of times, in 20 years of coaching, when I have had to mail them. The clients, because of the pain of contributing to something inconsistent with their values and believes, motivate themselves to action.

Using pleasure also works well for some of us. Creating pleasurable rewards, small or large, can motivate us to action. Give yourself an extra day off for hitting your sales goals for the month. Dangle the mani-pedi afternoon of pampering if you get the garage fully cleaned and organized by midday on Friday. Either pain or pleasure speaks to your motivation more deeply. There isn't an absolute right or wrong, but figure out what works for you.

Personalizing Your Drivers

What we can personally feel and personally be rewarded for does increase motivation. The motivation for recognition status, honor, acceptance, and security can link in with desire to create a powerful draw. Remember, it's all about thrusting thought, emotion, and ideas into action. The more I can personally attach my emotions of wellbeing into the actions of that I must take today, the higher the odds of my success.

Increasing the power of your drivers

The power of motivation increases when you limit the options and choices. When you don't have the option of doing nothing, and when all other courses of action are untenable, then your motivation to take action increases.

Think of the heart attack patients who smoke, for example. They knew for years that smoking was bad for them before the heart attack. Now faced with no choice but to quit, backed up by the specter of death, it's amazing how their willpower exceeds their won't power.

The problem for most of us is that we rely on external influences to motivate us to operate or change. It's not due to discipline actions or internal resolve. The frequently negative external consequences limit our choices. We get painted into a corner with no other option. That is when our *will*power surges ahead of our *won't* power.

Tying drivers to those you love

The most powerful driver in the world is love. It is the big why and the big motivator. The emotion of love will cause you to be more motivated in your behavior and actions because you're doing things for someone else. Most of us will never love ourselves as much as we love someone else. The love we feel for our kids and significant other can be a dominant driver in our motivation.

ANECDOTE

Joan and I tried for years to conceive a baby. We went through rounds of infertility shots, insemination, and invitro treatments to no avail. When the miracle of adopting Wesley just appeared out of nowhere, our years of prayers became a reality. I was emotionally at an all-time high. This story is pertinent because I connect those years of infertility struggle with subsequent positive action. Within a month of Wesley being born, I had opened a 529 college savings account for him. We have fully funded that account for 17 years straight. We did it through two recessions because of our love for Wesley and the desire for him to graduate college without the massive debt that most people start their work lives with. Removing that debt from his plate will give him an advantage in life that few enjoy. It will also allow us to not have to raid our retirement funds to pay for his or our daughter Annabelle's college education.

TIP

Who do you love so much that you will get up early for them and stay late to help them? What actions can you take? Connect your love for them with your motivation to take action and you have a powerful combination.

The Three Categories of Motivation

Our ability to increase motivation can be linked to a process that can be created, revised, and refined over time. It can also be triggered by an emotion or feeling. Some of us can access higher motivation like flipping on a light switch. The wonderful journey of motivation is to figure out what turns you on.

The inducement

A carrot placed in front of a horse builds his anticipation of a treat. His eyes see the carrot but it's just a few steps out in front. It's the enticement of a reward that is just out of reach that can trigger the motivation to go take action. Most people need both long-term goals as well as short-term goals to create motivation. The promise of the payoff in the near future causes most people to begin.

Creating inducement rewards and even celebrations can increase motivation. If I have made any mistake in motivation, it has been too many long-term rewards and not enough short-term rewards. One of my big goals in life has been financial independence. It has been a large driver and motivator. The challenge with financial independence is it's honestly a long way off. For even the most successful people, it's a 20-year journey. Being motivated every day for 20 years is a high bar. You must also reward progress and the journey along the way.

The benchmark

Having benchmarks means placing markers in your pathway to success. It's setting small rewards along the road when partial completion has been accomplished. You can use benchmarks for a project, relationship, earnings, or health. My counsel would be to set specific targets and timelines.

As I'm writing this chapter, I've decided that I'm going to reward myself with a walk outside after finishing this section on the three categories of motivation. When I finish the whole chapter later this evening, Joan and I will drop the kids off to go ice skating while we have a quiet dinner out. I am setting specific benchmarks and rewards.

The more we can reward ourselves with small but important rewards as we reach benchmarks, the more motivation we stir up in ourselves. Because we haven't fully completed the task but merely a benchmark, we must select a reward that has a small investment of time as well as small cost. I'll limit my walk to 15 minutes so that I can get right back at it. If I go for an hour, it'll be too much time away from writing, and I run the risk of not completing the chapter today, which is the bigger objective.

TIP

This strategy works extremely well with children, even teenagers. Because kids look at the totality of a task or project, they are easily overwhelmed, which leads to demotivation. Most kids lack the skill to break a task down to benchmarks or smaller pieces. As the adult, we need to help them and create small rewards at benchmarks. Then mix in a little encouragement.

The reward

The reward is what we are really shooting for. We have crossed the finish line and completed a task or accomplished a goal. It helps to add drama, significance, celebration, or ceremony to achievement. We need to claim our rewards when they happen. We also need to slow down to enjoy and savor them. The process of savoring solidifies the accomplishment in your subconscious mind and builds your self-confidence. You'll want to have that feeling again and again.

The danger of motivation being kicked into hyper drive is that we never pause and savor. Once we accomplish whatever achievement we desire, we tend to cross that one off our list and cue the next one up to go after. Pausing to reflect and enjoy locks it in. It helps us avoid burnout, which leads to demotivation. Since I accomplished the benchmark of completing this section, it's time for my walk, where I get to feel the sun on my face and observe nature's beauty. It's my reward of 15 minutes.

Diving Deeper into Your Behavioral Style

Motivation drives us to achieve more. It provides the energy, passion, and power when we encounter obstacles. Being clear on what drives you or motivates you can have both short-term and long-term benefits, and it all starts with three key things. The first is knowing what you want. Then you need to know why you want it. (I cover both of those topics in the next chapter.) Finally, you need to know what motivates you. What is your behavioral style?

Behavioral style is a critical piece of the puzzle in personal motivation and success. I'm going to discuss several in the following sections, but there is no one behavioral style that is more successful than others. Research has proven that there are different patterns of success based on the different behavioral style you might have.

REMEMBER

The key is to know who you are behaviorally. Then know what gets you going, keeps you going, and what turns the key off.

Behavioral style and motivation

Everyone reacts differently to any given situation. Say you're in a meeting to hear the bad news that your company earnings are down. If I were there, I might demand facts, numbers, and possibly hurt some people's feelings by my direct approach to finding the source of the problem. You might launch into a pep talk, pat the others on the back, and assure everyone that this is just a hiccup. Another attendee might latch onto a finance report, poring over every detail and attempting varying analyses. And someone else may simply sit calmly, taking in the responses of the others before speaking up.

These are examples of varying responses defined within a behavioral model known as the *DISC model.* According to the DISC theory, a widely followed behavioral model — adopted and modified by numerous behavioral-modeling programs — each person exhibits one or more of the following behaviors in varying degrees:

>> A **Dominant** is motivated through competition, contests, and goal achievement.

>> An **Influencer** is motivated through recognition and relationships.

>> A **Steady** is motivated through harmony, peace, and persistence.

>> A **Compliant** is motivated to plan and follow a process.

What motivates and drives people with these four behavioral styles is very different. Whichever style you have, you have to create systems and opportunities to drive you and reward you as you progress to success.

Identifying your DISC behavioral style

To be most effective in your efforts toward success, you must first understand yourself. Then you can figure out how to adapt your strategy and objectives in order to effectively reach success, both personally and professionally. To advance your career by using the DISC model, you must take one action step right now: Take the test!

To identify your primary behavioral style, go to the Sales Champions website, `www.SalesChampions.com/FreeDISC`, and take the free behavior-style assessment. It takes less than 10 minutes to answer the 12 questions, and you get the results, which pinpoint your behavioral style, via e-mail within minutes. This report points you in the right direction so that you can begin to use your behavioral style in your day-to-day life.

So how did it turn out? Did you say, "Yes, that's me!" after reading the information? That's the typical reaction of most people. Before diving deeper into DISC, you must rid yourself of two ideas before you make any wrong assumptions about people:

>> **No behavioral style is better than another.** In truth, each style carries with it strengths and weaknesses, opportunities, and challenges.

>> **Most people exhibit a combination of behavioral styles, with one or even two commanding the mix (called primary behavioral styles).** Very few people — less than 4 percent — score high in only one style.

A person's primary behavioral style is the style with the highest score when using an assessment instrument. It's the style that is most notable especially in pressure situations. The secondary DISC style influences behavior to a lesser degree.

I dissect each behavioral style in the following sections in this chapter. DISC was based on William Marston's research on human behavior dating back to the early 1900s. DISC does not factor in education or experience. Having said that, I find it to be extremely accurate in the prediction of behavior and acts.

ANECDOTE

DISC has been well validated. One of my most vivid life experiences with DISC involves my oldest son, Wesley. At 9 months old, he started to talk, and he was soon using complete sentences. It didn't take long for us to realize that he was wired in the womb to be a High I (influencer). He has the classic yin and yang of a High I. On one hand, he can strike up a conversation with anyone and has a rare gift of verbal communication. A friend is merely someone he hasn't met yet. On the other hand, he has the attention span of a flashbulb. We have long discussions about tools, systems, and strategies he must use to keep himself focused. Most people in the High I category are great starters but lousy finishers.

Understanding and Motivating Yourself as a Dominant

The Dominant person — in some DISC systems referred to as a driver panther, organizer, guardian, or economist — exhibits the characteristics that many perceive to be those of a leader. The High D is often described with these characteristics:

- » Aggressive
- » Bold
- » Competitive
- » Confident
- » Controlling
- » Decisive
- » Demanding
- » Direct
- » Results focused
- » Risk oriented

I bet you're thinking that most of these characteristics describe a successful salesperson, executive, or entrepreneur. And indeed, they often do. These folks are invigorated by challenges and the feelings of accomplishment.

What makes the Dominant tick?

Dominants are bottom-line oriented. They thrive when they have a clear, tangible goal, and they're in it — whether we're talking sports, stardom, or sales — to win it. You find a lot of Ds in the sports world. Vince Lombardi's famous quote of "Winning isn't everything; it's the only thing" sums up life's philosophy for a High Dominant person. Dominants also love a challenge and are enthusiastic when the challenge results in an "est" reward: the highest salary, the biggest corner office, and so on.

I remember watching a *60 Minutes* interview a number of years ago. Cohost Ed Bradley asked golf mega-star Tiger Woods, "If we played ping pong, would you want to beat me?" Woods responded, "No, I would want to kick your butt!" Then Mr. Bradley said, "What if I won?" Tiger's response was classic High D: "We would play again until I won."

How does a D operate?

Dominants thrive on results, but how does that play out in their lives? Dominants are . . .

- » **Self-motivated,** with a need to direct and control all situations that have an impact on them. They can prefer to work alone rather than serve as part of a team. And if they're part of the team, they prefer to be the leader.

- » **Focused on the destination,** working hard to achieve their goals and eliminating steps they consider unimportant. If you've ever said, "Don't ask how I achieved it; only notice that I did it," your core behavioral style is most likely that of a Dominant.

- » **Direct.** Some would call them forthright, straightforward, or to the point; others would describe them as curt or brusque.

> **»** **Willing to work long and hard to make their plans happen.** People with a D behavioral style get to the office early, stay late, and pay almost any price necessary to achieve the success that they desire.

> **»** **Quick in thinking and action and expect others they work with to be as quick.** Your D boss wants to know your numbers; she's impatient when you attempt to explain the hows and whys.

What's the downside to Ds?

Fast thinking, fast talking, and fast acting, Dominants can easily overpower or intimidate others. Dominants are by nature direct, aggressive, and to the point. When aggravated by stress, the High D can come across as egotistical, arrogant, too fast, not caring, inattentive, and pressuring.

Dominants also tend to get bored easily and need the constant stimulation of a worthy challenge. In their efforts to control all factors that affect their success, Dominants often attempt to control other people as well, which can cause discord. The good news is that when the battle's over, it's over. No grudges, no rehashing. For a Dominant, it's water under the bridge.

The High D has a primary fear of being taken advantage of. A High D must be convinced that he's getting a fair shake or a good deal before he's comfortable moving ahead. A High D also needs the straight story upfront. He's the type who walks into a car dealership and says, "Give me your best price." If he discovers that they didn't give it to him at the get-go, he walks out. What's the High Ds' blind spot? His short fuse often has him exploding in anger. The fireworks go off, with little consideration for the aftermath, and sometimes he's surprised when others seem cold after one of his outbursts.

Understanding and Motivating Yourself as an Influencer

As the name implies, Influencers or expressives are recognized for their contagious energy and enthusiasm, which can inspire others to action. An Influencer may exhibit some of these qualities:

>> Communicative	>> Gregarious	
>> Emotional	>> Optimistic	
>> Entertaining	>> Personable	
>> Enthusiastic	>> Persuasive	
>> Expressive	>> Popular	

When you channel the gift of gab, high energy, and powers of persuasion into human interaction at home or on the job, you're reckoning with a powerful force. The Influencer makes things happen!

What drives the I?

Influencers are people people. They enjoy working with groups as well as having one-on-one interactions. Influencers like a lot of attention, so in group dynamics, they tend to wind up angling for the spotlight. Being liked, being popular, and being recognized rank high with the I.

Optimism and can-do certainty make Influencers comfortable with the often high-pressure demands at work or home. Their unbounded enthusiasm and desire for personal glory helps them reach sales achievements — especially if it earns them a gold plaque on the wall for all to see.

High Is are also drawn to the newest, cutting-edge, trendiest, most-exclusive products, services, and experiences available. They feel it is part of their image and that it affects the way others see them. A High I wants to be recognized by other people for her purchase or sound decision.

An Influencer in action

An I is the easiest of the four behavioral types to identify. Even in the midst of a crowd, look for the most colorful, most vocal, most expressive of the flock, and you've found your I. Influencer's command of language and strong verbal skills turn to his advantage in situations in which he must be persuasive. High Is are extremely social and personable.

One on one, Influencers exude the same amount of energy and optimism. They connect and build a high level of trust in others quickly and easily. For example, in your mind, replay some of the times you saw President Clinton on television. He's certainly the classic High Influencer. I don't think there has been as effective, friendly, persuasive, optimistic, and verbally persuasive of a politician in my lifetime.

Too much of a good thing?

High Influencers can be bigger than life and sometimes overwhelming. Under fire, a High I can appear scattered, showy, lacking substance, out of touch, verbose, too familiar, self-promoting, and unrealistic.

High Influencers are also often highly emotional. Feelings and emotions can influence their actions heavily — often to the detriment of objective clarity. Focusing on the details — filling in the paperwork and adding up the numbers — just doesn't add up to a priority for an I. In fact, a High I may neglect most activities that don't involve social interaction or "fun."

Influencers tend to be trusting to a fault. They give their trust to people easily without checking all the facts.

Understanding and Motivating Yourself as a Steady

The Steady behavioral style is also known as a relater or amiable in some models. A Steady is rarely described as a high-pressure salesperson but instead sells on these other qualities:

- ❯❯ Good listener
- ❯❯ Harmonious
- ❯❯ Loyal
- ❯❯ Patient
- ❯❯ Persistent
- ❯❯ Predictable
- ❯❯ Reliable
- ❯❯ Service oriented
- ❯❯ Sincere
- ❯❯ Team oriented

What gets a Steady going?

Steadies live to serve. They're driven to please and meet the needs of their family, friends, community, and job. They're extremely loyal to the people around them and are always willing to give help and support. An environment of collaboration and cooperation is the most comfortable place for the S.

The High S develops deep, long-term relationships, and in business, they retain clients for years or even decades. They want to finish what they start and go through each step or stage of a project for their own fulfillment, as well as for their family, friends, or job.

Distinguishing a Steady

If you want to see a Steady, look for the Energizer Bunny. This type adheres to the established routing or cycle and keeps going and going and going. The predictable Steady sticks to the program, especially under fire.

Spotting High Steadies can sometimes be hard. They're behind-the-scenes operators, steering clear of center stage and opportunities for attention. That doesn't mean Steadies don't like working with people. In fact, they're very sociable, but in more of a what-can-I-do-for-you way, rather than a look-at-me way. Steadies treasure long-standing relationships and work hard to maintain them.

A High Steady is the type who sticks with her hairdresser of ten years — even though she's less than dazzled with her recent haircuts. The High S possesses unlimited amounts of patience for people's needs, wants, concerns, and hesitations. Although not dramatically emotive like the High Influencer, the Steady is empathetic and exudes a caring attitude.

Steady challenges

Although patience is a virtue, sometimes Steadies are steadfast to a fault, sometimes taking too long to make decisions or allowing their processes to hinder their productivity. Their lack of self-focus often translates to lack of self-confidence, and their discomfort with sudden change can paralyze them in times of upheaval.

The nature of the Steady is to proceed with caution when pressure increases. Steady people are likely to contain their emotions and react slowly to a threat. They're uncomfortable with confrontation, especially if they sense a change in emotion on the person they are interacting with. A High Steady in extreme can be viewed as uncaring, uncreative, slow to act, unable to change, afraid, inflexible, hesitant, and unconcerned.

The High Steady craves harmony in all interactions. She wants everyone to get along, work together, and talk it out. If a High S senses friction, her inclination is to flee. But to those she's connected with, a High S is a loyalist. Despite their strong commitments, High Steadies can come across as disengaged or uncaring because they tend not to express their emotions, and people may have a hard time reading them.

Understanding and Motivating Yourself as a Compliant

The Compliant, also referred to as rational or analytical in other behavioral models, yearns more than any other type for quality and perfection. C qualities include these characteristics:

- Detailed
- Harmonious
- Exacting
- Intrinsically motivated
- Logic driven

- Precise
- Process oriented
- Reserved
- Structured
- Thorough

Compliants are into facts and figures. They are measured in their responses. Nothing gets them really high or really low.

What puts a High C into gear?

High Compliants aren't motivated by recognition, rewards, and other incentives. They are more internally motivated by quality. They're there to compete with themselves based on the standard they've committed to meet. For High Cs, the focus is on the process and on achieving accurate and high-quality results.

In any endeavor, having a clear grasp of all the details is important to a High C. For example, a High C wouldn't buy a new TV until he's researched all the features and comparison-shopped with every store in town and on the Internet — even if it takes months.

High Cs thrive when they clearly understand the expectations and are given the time and resources to achieve accuracy and quality in their outcomes. They don't demand the sort of control that a Dominant does, but they crave control over the factors that affect their results. They research thoroughly, wanting to take all risk out of the equation. They fear making a mistake.

How does a High C act?

Compliants, like Steadies, often fly under the radar. They can be quiet, reserved, and — although they're agreeable to team situations — often found working alone. Compliants are meticulous planners. They're polite and courteous in their approach. For a manager, Compliants provide the fewest problems in regard to following the rules, procedures, and paperwork.

High Cs need to follow the process and be clear on their objectives. Naturally reserved and painstakingly thorough, they become more so under pressure, especially if they're being pressured to make a sudden change or break with the plan in any way. Under these circumstances, they turn to the procedures and carefully review the facts, the data, and the situation. High Compliants seek absolute accuracy. They often fear making the wrong decision and assess every situation thoroughly. High Cs often let their exacting nature lead to fear — a fear that they'll make a bad decision.

When Compliants turn uncompliant

Considering their moniker, Compliants can be the most difficult, contrary, and uncompliant of the four types. In fact, High Cs are actually in compliance to a higher standard — one of thoroughness and accuracy at all costs. If they're pressed to compromise in a way that betrays these standards, they can become just plain belligerent.

Compliants, like Steadies, can be resistant to change and slow to adapt, especially from what they believe to be the right process or system. At their worst, High Compliants are viewed as perfectionists, unyielding to change, overly questioning, too sensitive, slow moving, nitpicky, pessimistic, and not focused enough on the results.

Choosing Other Types of Motivation

There are almost countless types of motivation categories and targets. Motivation is unique to each of us. It's truly the ultimate journey of self-discovery. What motivates one person can demotivate another. As I describe different strategies to motivate yourself, consider the strategy based on your thoughts, ideas, and drivers. Ask yourself, would this potentially work for me? How long would this strategy work? Can I see myself using this method? How would I change or adjust it to work more effectively for me?

Focusing on the power of personal development

Pursuing personal improvement or personal growth can be a big motivator. Being a better boss, spouse, or parent can fire up our desire and consequences. The striving to be the best version of ourselves possible and seeing the progress makes us feel better about ourselves. When we feel good about ourselves, our confidence and self-worth increases.

When we pursue improving our knowledge and skills, we increase our value to our company as well as the marketplace. We then gain the reward of more earnings and income because our value is enhanced. The new knowledge and skills are really new assets and tools that you can use for the length of your life. They even enable you to leave a broader, more valuable legacy to your children, friends, and associates.

When you engage in a focus of learning and growth, you start to formulate positive habits. The simple habit of reading each day for 30 minutes to grow and learn can lead to spectacular results of success. That 30 minutes each evening, repeated over a year, is 183 hours of reading time. The typical book can be read in 6 hours, so that's better than 30 books read in a year.

TIP

Using your car as an auto-university, rather than listening to the radio, is life changing. When I started my personal development journey in earnest at the age of 29, I was never in my car listening to the radio. Instead, I had a cassette tape teaching me success, motivation, sales, wealth, finance, investing, time management, marketing, and many other success topics. That leads me to the next topic. . . .

Using activities to increase motivation

Drawing a line in the sand and taking physical action is a wonderful habit and great motivator. Doing something feeds your body and mind. Physically taking a walk around your neighborhood, biking along the river, or lifting weights can fire up your motivation to other actions. When you take physical action, it triggers your realization that you are responsible. If you are waiting around hoping to feel more motivated, there will be many times when that feeling does not show up. Even in the most motivated people, that feeling can't be counted on to come. What they have done is connect in the habit of taking action. The first step in any action is a decision.

It can help to engage in actions and activities with others. As an example, let's consider working out or exercising. If you engage a spouse, coworker, or friend, you will be likely to show up to avoid letting them down. I find for me, because I am a High D behavioral style, an exercise routine that enables me to compete is easier for me to maintain. Getting on the treadmill is less exciting than playing a match of squash against a worthy competitor. I love to win and get fit at the same time.

Getting motivated through loss and failure

We frequently will learn more from our failures than our successes. We learn how not to do something, which is usually vastly more valuable than how to do something. For all humans, making mistakes and errors is a normal occurrence of life.

Some of the greatest accomplishments have come out of the great losses. Candace Lightner established one of the most influential nonprofit organizations in the world, Mothers Against Drunk Driving. Candace lost her 13-year-old daughter, Cari, who was killed by a drunk driver. MADD has increased public awareness of the dangers of drunk and drugged driving, and its influence has been felt in the halls of Congress and state legislatures throughout the United States.

ANECDOTE

I was personally not the most successful, popular, or engaging kid in middle school. In fact, I was picked on, ridiculed, and made fun of relentlessly. It created in me toughness and resolve to ignore people who occupy the cheap seats in my life. It made me determined to be a success. What could be more validating personally in achieving success than being asked to write *Success Habits For Dummies!*

Increasing motivation through gratitude

We all have much to be grateful for in our lives. Just getting to the place of being born is a 1 in 400 trillion shot. The fact that you are actually alive to read this means you have overcome the longest odds that you will ever face. There will be nothing harder than actually being born. Be grateful at the opportunity of life. You are more than matter. You matter!

We can always find something to be grateful for. You might be going through a particular tough stretch financially or physically with your health. You might have an estranged relationship with a parent or a child. I would encourage you to look around and try to find a small thing to start a gratitude moment. Flip through a photo album and recall some fun moments you had with your family. Or at work, take a look around your office and remember those days when you had to work out of a cubicle next to someone who never stopped blowing her nose. It could be as simple as realizing you have good food on the table for today or this week. It could be how close you live to family and friends. Go outside and feel the warm sun on your face or walk outside and feel the crunch of the new snow or the warm sand on a beach.

If you are really struggling, go volunteer in a place where you're guaranteed to run into people who are less fortunate than yourself. Serve a meal at a homeless shelter, help in a food pantry, or at your church. Volunteer to read at a school in an economically challenged area. There are countless people who have less than you do.

The ability to pause, meditate, and pray can also trigger gratitude. It can recalibrate our place and size in the world. For me, I know that God is in my corner and that He is much bigger than me or any of my problems. That triggers for me a mental awareness of gratitude. I recall this ancient text: "What then shall we say to these things? If God is for us, who can be against us?" That gives me comfort in knowing I have help.

Using progress and completion for motivation

There is power in seeing movement toward completion of a task or goal. As we draw closer to completion, our motivation increases. If you have ever ridden a horse late in the afternoon, as you head back to the barn, when the horse realizes where you are going, he picks up his cadence. He knows his meal is not far off. The motivation for dinner grows with each step toward the barn. While we are not horses, the same is true for us humans as we approach completion.

Our brains need to see tasks completed. The completion triggers our feelings of self-worth, well-being, and accomplishment. Why not purposefully create those feeling first thing in the morning? One way to do that is to make your bed when you get up in the morning. That made bed signifies a completed task. As you walk by that bed, with its clean lines, crisp pillows, and lack of wrinkles on the comforter, you know you did that!

The Swiss-cheese approach: Poking little holes in the task

When approaching a major or complicated task seems overwhelming, start with the easier pieces — the aspects that you know you can complete quickly and with little effort. In this way, you poke holes in the project, making lighter work of the steps that remain after you polish off the manageable aspects. This approach increases your motivation and momentum to complete the project.

For example, suppose you're facing your kitchen after a dinner party: dishes piled to the tops of the cupboards, leftovers cooling in their serving dishes, the sink clogged with kitchen scraps, and the roaster pan caked with burned food and tenacious grease. The job is more than you can fathom at midnight. You're tempted to turn around, go to bed, and hope the kitchen fairies come in the night to transform your kitchen into its former spotless self.

Or you can tell yourself you'll do one simple thing before you turn out the lights. So maybe you put away all the food and scrape the scraps into the compost bin or garbage disposal. And then when you make short work of that, you tell yourself that filling up the dishwasher with at least one load won't take that long. When that's done, you decide you can at least rinse and stack the other dishes. By the time you poke these holes into the project, not too much is left. Even if you give up at this point, the task that awaits you in the morning isn't nearly so formidable.

The salami approach: Finishing it one slice at a time

The salami approach is a great tactic for those long-term projects in which the deadline seems so far away that you convince yourself you don't need to start yet. So that you don't resort to cramming at the 11th hour, take the time immediately to cut up the project into bite-sized pieces. These slices should be small enough that you can schedule them day-by-day or at least week-by- week.

The number of ways you can slice and dice a large task are many. The slicing creates benchmarks that increase your feelings of accomplishment and your motivation as well. Here's one option for breaking things down:

1. Set time aside to plan the project completely so that you can begin working on it and cut it down to size.

2. Create an action order of what needs to be done and when.

   This timeline helps you segment the task into pieces.

3. Figure out what materials you need for the task.

4. Collect all the materials and make them ready and available.

By taking these steps, while you haven't "officially" started working on the project, you're organizing the project in your mind. You see the task more clearly and also see the *completed* task more clearly. As you complete the steps, your desire and motivation peak.

ANECDOTE

When I begin my book projects, the publisher gives me a certain amount of time, usually several months, to complete the manuscript. I know from experience that I can't look at the project as a single huge step; it's too daunting. So I break it up. For example, if I have six months to write the book and it's 24 chapters long, I break down the project into chapter slices. So instead of "write book in six months," it's "write chapter this week." Or it may be "write ten pages per day this week" or some other breakdown that's meaningful to me.

» Getting your Fabulous 50 goals down on paper

» Prioritizing your Fabulous 50

» Finding the motivation to speed up achievement

» Gathering additional resources

Chapter **5**

Goals: The Power Source of Achievement

Today, more than at any time in history, you have limitless opportunities, especially if you're living in the United States. However, having so many choices can lead to confusion, distraction, and wasted time. Achievement in anything in life takes focus, diligence, and patience. So the question arises: Can getting a handle on your most precious lifelong dreams and desires help you get more done on a day-to-day basis? Absolutely! Say, for example, you and your spouse have always dreamed of taking six months to travel the world while you're still young enough to hoist a backpack. Such a focus may motivate you to put in extra hours or accelerate your sales quotas at work to build up the necessary funds and time for that adventure.

Even long-range goals can shape the way you use your time, invest your resources, energy, and savings. Suppose your goal is to retire early so that you can enjoy a simpler lifestyle in the sun of Hawaii, where you can walk along the beach and feel the wind and waves, relax, and center yourself each day. Even if that goal is 30 years away, your priority *now* is more likely to be on investing your income, saving, and advancing your earning power.

REMEMBER

Everyone has dreams and goals for the future. But in order to accomplish more of them, to enable yourself to accomplish them in less time, and to create a sense of urgency in yourself, your goals need to be clear, compelling, and measurable. Having a clear sense of goals, in numerous areas of your life, is paramount.

In this chapter, I guide you in the process of committing your goals to paper; categorizing, balancing, and breaking them down into manageable chunks; and allowing that powerful action to spur your achievement and productivity.

Understanding the Power of Goals: We Become What We Think About

We were born and created for achievement and success. I truly believe that we *all* have natural gifts placed in us by God to become successful. We have to define what success is to us, and a large part of that is through the setting of goals.

Think of goals specifically as just creating a target. If you were into archery, the chief objective or aim is not to just pull the bow back slowly and steady to release the bow string so the arrow flies through the air. The objective to archery is to hit the target. Think of goal setting in the same manner. The purpose and power of goals is to create a specific target like a bullseye. You focus on that bullseye so that all your effort, focus, and concentration is harnessed to a primary aim.

Earl Nightingale, the dean of the personal success industry, creator of the recording *The Strangest Secret*, coined the statement, "We become what we think about." The great truth in life throughout history is this: People with goals succeed and people without goals then fail. Why? Because a well-constructed goal causes you to think about its accomplishment. We think about that goal, how to accomplish it, what it will feel like when we do, and how it will affect our lives. Those thoughts are automatic when you create goals, so even the outcome of reaching your goals is assured.

Consider what Ralph Waldo Emerson said: "A man is what he thinks about all day long."

Without a clear target of what you want, the most advanced computer ever created — the human mind — isn't switched on. The ability of the human mind to solve problems, innovate new products, and create new services will be in the constant reboot mode with the wheel of death on screen. We must plant goals in to our mind so that it can create the opportunities and solutions and fire up our imagination and motivation to achievement and success.

Overcoming the Barriers to Goal Setting

The biggest barrier to setting goals is complacency or lack of urgency. It's the "I have plenty of time" mentality. That mindset is really just an excuse to be lazy.

TIP

My advice is to embrace the Nike slogan: "Just do it."

Why not set as many goals as you can for what those goals will create in you? After all, you will have to develop skills and discipline in order to accomplish them. How's that a bad thing?

The greatest barrier to goal setting is a span of about six inches. That is the average span between your left ear to your right ear. It's the space between those ears that causes the barriers to goal setting and achievement. As my friend, Zig Ziglar, who authored the first *Success For Dummies,* says, "It's *stinkin' thinkin'.*"

Lack of knowledge

Lack of knowledge shouldn't stop you from setting a few goals to help pull you on your way to success. The "I'm not smart enough" personal mantra most people play in their head over and over should be turned off. You don't need to be the smartest person in the room. In fact, knowledge is overrated as a critical component of success.

Your formal education will help you make a living. Your personal education will help you make a future. I heard Jim Rohn say that almost 30 years ago when I was broke, hadn't finished college, and was unemployed. And given the fact that I had graduated in the part of the high school class that made the top half possible, my prospects at that time were dim.

TIP

By continuing to read this chapter, the barrier of knowledge about goal setting and goal achievement will be removed. You will no longer be able to use that as an excuse to block your success. I give you the knowledge plan and a system of goal setting.

Fear of rejection

Some people fail to set goals and advance themselves because they fear being rejected by others. This is especially true in the case of family. For some families, they want everyone to stay together at the same socioeconomic class. They want everyone to be in one big happy poor family. When one of us climbs out, like a crab in a bucket, the other crabs grab him and pulls him back in.

As you set big goals for your life and then achieve those goals, there will be people in your life presently that you will leave behind. You will outgrow them as people. The small challenges that you have conquered will cause them to continue to struggle. The errors of judgement that you have put aside are the ones that they will keep making. You are likely to also outgrow their influence of you. That is honestly a natural happening in life. As you set higher goals and climb upward in life, it's like climbing a mountain. A mountain is smaller at the top than it is at the base. There is less surface area, so there is less room for people. The fear of being rejected, an outcast, or ridiculed is a real emotion, and it's a barrier to goal setting and achievement.

Fear of success

The fear of success is real, and it's sometimes linked to the fear of rejection. There are people who come close to achieving their goals only to sabotage themselves just before accomplishment. Think of people you know who work hard to lose weight through a good balanced diet and exercise program. When they get close to their objective weight, they yo-yo back up beyond their previous weight. Are there experiences in your past where you felt you weren't good enough? Has anyone told you that personally? Without putting those feelings behind us, we can be trapped in fear.

To set more effective goals, dig deeper into how you might feel when you accomplish your goals. Why do you want to achieve a certain goal? What will these goals do for you? Why do you desire to have this? What is the motivator to achieve this goal? Is it recognition, freedom, security, accomplishment, or respect? These are all valid powerful emotions and feelings, so embrace them to conquer your fears.

Fear of failure

Playing it safe with your goals and goal setting doesn't serve anyone well. You can't allow yourself to ask the "what if I don't succeed" question. Ask yourself this instead: "What would my goals be if I was all but guaranteed to accomplish them?" If there was no fear and failure was not an option, what would you go after in life? Most adults have learned over time to play it safe. We don't look for or even embrace failure for what it is: learning.

I had a mild obsession with the fear of failure until my late 20s. I thought that making a mistake or failing at something was a catastrophe. It was a root cause of my lack of success in my income and wealth to that point. That fear caused me to be cautious when I should have been trying new opportunities and using failure as a teacher.

Failure is a good teacher in life if you don't repeat your mistakes. To play it safe without goals or big goals doesn't protect you from the downside of failure. I almost guarantee that it will occur. Failure is an opportunity to start anew. It's the confirmation that the way you tried doesn't work and you are close to finding the solution.

Harnessing the Power of Paper

Some studies calculate that only about 3 percent of goal-setters document their aspirations. And I can assure you that these folks are the ones who have the most money, influence, power, prestige, freedom, and time to work toward their dreams. Why? Because as numerous studies suggest, people who clearly define and write down their goals are more likely to accomplish them — and in a shorter timeframe. People who don't clarify and write out their goals invest more time and accomplish less.

When you take the time to write down your goals, you clarify them and sharpen your vision for attaining them. You are telling your brain that this isn't a dream to be ignored as a hope-to, wish-to, or would-like-to. It's really something for which you're willing to invest time, effort, energy, and emotion.

When I speak at conferences and events, I frequently have people who approach me at the conclusion to ask questions and talk. They want to share their goals in achieving success. I love to learn about the plans of others, and as I listen, I think, "How can I help and support them to succeed?" The vast majority of people start expressing their goals with "I would like. . .." The second "I would like" comes out, I stop them from even sharing their goal. I say, "Wait a minute. Did you hear yourself?" I wait, and most of the time, they don't catch the issue. The statement, "I would like," is a dead giveaway that their goals are not written down. They have not committed to them 100 percent.

There are just some things you have to commit your heart and soul to, and those are your goals.

What people really mean when they say, "I would like" is "If it happens, I would be happy, grateful, pleased." That "it would be nice" or "fine" if they achieved it. Those two words, "nice" and "fine," should evoke a warning. When I ask my wife Joan how her day was and she says, "Fine," I know with certainty after 29 years of marriage, things are most certainly not fine!

The phrase "I would like" comes from people who haven't really committed. They would gladly accept a million-dollar lottery payout if they ever got that lucky, but this book isn't about luck. What they haven't done is connected the goal to "I will do it no matter what." So they have a wish, not a goal.

Create commitment to your goals

The act of writing goals down on paper fires up a connection in your mind. I realize that most people today work on tablets, phones, and laptops. We type our thoughts into the software as it cascades across the screen. I believe that to increase commitment to your goals, you need to handwrite them on paper. There is a connection between the brain and our hands in writing something down on paper. Our minds retain, refine, and lock in thoughts, ideas, and goals so that they become more clear, compelling, and achievable.

TIP

Create a written journal of your goals. Carry this notebook with you and check off every goal once it's accomplished.

Map out the most direct route to achievement

When you put your goals in writing, you're setting your sights on the destination before you begin. Your life goals become the framework for how you prioritize and manage your time. We all need more focused use of our time so that we can achieve greater success. You begin the process of planning and strategizing about the steps you can take to achieve that goal. Your brain starts to look for the best, most direct route and the route with the lowest time investment. You engage your subconscious mind to work on figuring out solutions and strategies while you sleep. The subconscious mind will contemplate the goal, problem, or challenge, helping you figure out the most direct path to success. Thinking about the most direct route will help you order the steps into a system or strategy to create success.

Limit detours

Consider this saying: "If you don't know where you're going, any road will take you there." If you head off on just any road, you're likely to end up in a place you don't want to be. By documenting your goals, you can more easily gauge whether an effort is likely to bring you closer to or further away from them. With your goals in front of you, you make fewer wrong turns, invest less time in trial-and-error, and encounter fewer dead ends.

If you know that "be an outstanding father" is at the top of your written goal list, then overtime, extra work assignments, business travel, and other actions that take you away from your kids won't distract you as easily. You know you're more likely to achieve this goal by spending time with your kids, going to their games, taking walks, throwing a ball, playing dress-up, going to the park, having a tea party, or writing a note. These are all actions that bring you closer to being an outstanding father.

Establishing Your Fabulous 50

As you put together your list of goals, you need to consider the five core aspects of wants that I cover in this section. My mentor Jim Rohn taught them to me when I was in my 20s. These five questions will focus you in crafting better and clearer goals that you can break down more easily into manageable steps, so you'll dramatically reduce the amount of time you need to achieve your goals. These same questions can help you expand your thinking that so you can have more, be more, and achieve more.

As soon as you finish reading this section, read no further until you get your goals on paper. Your task after reading this section is to come up with at least 50 goals that you want to accomplish within the next 10 years. As you brainstorm your list of goals, keep a few points in mind to make your goal-setting effective:

>> **Make sure your goals line up with your wants.** Don't evaluate goals based on what you think you need, deserve, or can realistically achieve. Focus on what you want. With your goal set, don't allow your mind out of the want and desire zone. Frequently, we can slip into the "how" zone. How am I going to achieve it? "Wow, that seems too far out. How can I do that?" At this stage, it's only the what you want that's important, so don't allow your mind to wander. Your success is determined by what you want and the passion of why you want it.

>> **Think big.** "Go big or go home" is a philosophy I encourage my clients and workshop participants to embrace. Many shy away from setting big goals for a range of reasons, from fear of disappointment to concern that they may not have the drive to pursue them. While in the future you might cross the goal off as unimportant, in this early stage of goal setting, focus on *what* and the *big whats*. There really are no unrealistic goals — ever. The timeline to achievement might be longer than you expected, but if your desire, passion, persistence, and determination are high, there is never an unrealistic goal.

REMEMBER

If you approach your dreams conservatively — going after what you think is reasonable or realistic — your odds of getting beyond that are slim to none. But if you let your imagination go and pursue the big dream, the odds of reaching that level of joy and fulfillment are in your favor. Big goals and big dreams cause you to stretch, strain, and go for what you really want in life.

They connect with the best use of your time and energy. They draw you to remove the things in your life that don't serve you well.

>> **Pick a time somewhere in the future and work backward from there.** For any goal that stretches further than ten years, break it down into smaller goals with shorter timeframes to increase your focus, intensity, and commitment. See the later section "Assigning a timeframe to each goal" for details.

>> **Set measurable goals.** When you establish a measurable, quantifiable goal, you know you can't fudge on whether you achieved it or not. You either hit the target or you don't. You also know where you stand at any given time. Goal measurement naturally falls into two categories:

- **Number-based goals:** Measuring your progress toward a goal is pretty easy when the goal is number based. You know when you've acquired a million dollars or lost 30 pounds, for example. The bank statement or scale are pretty simple to read. As you craft financial and other goals that are associated with numbers, be specific. Do you want to earn a certain annual salary? To put away a certain amount of money each year? To run a certain number of miles by September?

- **Non-number-based goals:** To measure a non-number-based goal, focus on how you'll know when you've accomplished it. For example, will some organization's seal of approval establish you as a world-renowned archeologist? Will being elected president of the chamber of commerce constitute being a business leader in the community? Will having your children expressing greater thanks for your efforts as a parent equate to being a better dad or mom?

As you identify and record 50 goals that you'd like to achieve in the next 10 years, contemplate the following five core questions to guide your goal setting.

What do you want to have?

The question of what you want to have focuses on material acquisitions. What possessions do you yearn for? A swimming pool? A sailboat? Do you fantasize about owning a sports car? Do you dream of a formal rose garden landscaped into your backyard? Someone to cook and clean for you? Your own private jet? Winter vacations in the Caribbean? If your home environment is a priority, imagine the place you want to live. An expansive ranch overlooking the Pacific Ocean? A Fifth Avenue penthouse? An off-the-grid abode that runs on solar and wind power? A villa in Tuscany?

REMEMBER

Although possessions are important to consider, they're typically a means to an end: They enable you to create the lifestyle that you want to have. We all work to fund a specific lifestyle that we aspire to or currently have now.

ANECDOTE

One of the best goals I set and achieved was to own two houses, one as my primary residence and one to which I could retreat. The goal flowed from my childhood because my parents owned a second home that we enjoyed as a family. Some of my fondest memories of my childhood are attached to that second home at the Oregon coast. Once I achieved that goal, I wanted to spend more time there. That created in me a high motivation to work hard and advance my career further. It focused me to invest time during work hours so that I could enjoy spending long weekends at my second home.

What do you want to see?

When you ask yourself what you want to see, think experiential acquisition. Travel is likely to be a key focus. I'm certain you can easily come up with at least ten places you want to see. Have some world wonders fascinated you? The Pyramids of Egypt? The Great Wall of China? I travel internationally a few times a year on business, and it only fuels my desire to see more parts of the world and expand my awareness of how other people live.

I've found that exposure to different cultures and places in the world has a secondary benefit. Through world exposure, we can develop our gratitude and patriotism. It allows us to recognize how fortunate we are to live where we live. How blessed we are to have the lifestyle we have today. In the United States, even if you are on one of the lower rungs of wealth and earnings, you are rich compared to others in the world.

What do you want to do?

Most likely, many of your goals are connected with the question of what you want to do at some point in your life. Whereas the possessions that you want to acquire help create your lifestyle, the action-oriented question you consider here focuses more on bigger events and feats outside the daily realm. Because this category is vast, I have my clients consider three main aspects of this question:

>> **Activities:** You may want to include some once-in-a-lifetime experiences, such as snorkeling with sea turtles or hiking Mt. Kilimanjaro. What about a goal of regular exercise four times per week? Or maybe you want to see Lady Gaga in concert.

>> **Skills:** For example, have you always wanted to speak Spanish or Mandarin Chinese? Do you wish you could play the piano or electric guitar? Have you put off a new experience — snow-skiing, surfing, fly fishing — because you thought it was too late to learn? Whether these skills can enhance your career or financial state or are simply actions that bring personal pleasure, cast a wide net and list the ones that intrigue you most.

>> **Career:** How do you want to seek fulfillment through your career? Be honest with yourself and sort out how you'd like to measure that success. Do you yearn to be recognized as the top authority in your field? To win an international award? To write an influential book?

What do you want to give?

Andrew Carnegie, the great steel entrepreneur, met his goal to amass a fortune in the first half of his life. His goal for the second half was to give it all away. Many of the public libraries in the United States, Canada, and the United Kingdom exist today because of his philanthropy.

An important way to balance all the want, see, and do items on your Fabulous 50 list is to include give goals as well. What are you willing or interested in giving back? How do you want to share your good fortune with others? Which causes are near and dear to you?

I personally have developed more philanthropy goals as I have aged. Perhaps that's due to a higher awareness of the many blessings in my life. Or maybe it's being more aware of the needs others have around me, or it could be due to having achieved more. My belief is this greater awareness is normal for a successful person. If you aren't feeling very philanthropic, that doesn't make you a bad person. It just means there are other goal categories that are more important to you in achieving first. A giving focus, as well as giving goals, can broaden your perspective and well-being.

Who do you want to become?

To a degree, what you want to have, see, do, and give determine the person you want to become. But you should still envision and write down how you see yourself developing while you achieve these goals. The real value of goals isn't what you achieve; it's in the accumulation of knowledge, skills, discipline, and experience you gain through learning, changing, improving, and investing yourself as you work toward your goals. Often, those newly discovered or carefully developed traits are the only lasting acquisitions that stand the test of time.

Don't get me wrong. I'm not suggesting that you become someone other than who you are; rather, I'm encouraging you to earnestly and honestly evaluate the characteristics and disciplines best suited for your ambitions. To identify the areas you should focus on, take a look at all the goals you've written down so far. (If you haven't yet read the preceding sections, complete them before moving on here.) Then ask yourself the following questions when considering your goals as a whole:

>> What personal characteristics do you need to change or improve? Do you need assertiveness training to deal more effectively with your boss or coworkers? Do you need to work on interpersonal skills? Does your anger get in the way of your success because you get frustrated so easily?

>> What disciplines do you need to work harder at practicing consistently? Are you able to delay gratification and do what you need to when it needs to be done? Are you able to save regular amounts from your current paycheck, or are you waiting to make more money before you start the savings process? What if that extra money never shows up?

TIP

If you're struggling to identify areas where you need to work on personal development, take a look at people who have achieved what you want; then evaluate your characteristics and disciplines as compared to theirs.

APPRECIATING PERSONAL GROWTH

Consider this true-life story: I made my first million by the time I was in my early 30s, but I can wholeheartedly say the value I gained from attaining that goal wasn't the money (which, unfortunately, I lost a pretty good chunk of through some poor investments). Of deeper and lasting value are the personal characteristics and skills that I gained through the process of strategizing, acting, and investing my time on my way toward the goal. I'd changed as a person as a result of the process, and the characteristics I developed through the process enabled me to meet other goals as well. Because I learned to create the money, when the money evaporated, I was confident I had the skills to earn it again.

I grew with each new goal I worked toward. To reach my goals in real estate sales, I had to increase my focus and discipline. When I decided to go into coaching and speaking, I had to develop better behavioral analysis and leadership to get others to follow my coaching and teaching. And to reach my goal of writing books that would help readers achieve success, I had to gather new skills in organization, critical thinking, and patience due to the demands all the pesky editors in the publishing business.

Labeling and Balancing Your Fabulous 50

After you draft a list of the 50 goals you want to achieve in the next ten years, your next task is to assign a category and timeframe to each of them.

Creating categories for your goals and establishing timeframes to achieve them sharpens your focus and increases your intensity, which can reduce the time required to achieve your goals. It also allows you to quickly and easily see whether your time investment to the various areas of your life as well as the size and difficulty of your goals are appropriately balanced.

REMEMBER

The objective isn't to spread an equal number and depth of goals among the six categories; the aim is to identify whether one or two of the categories is light compared to the others and to determine whether you need to pay more attention to those areas of your life to develop them. In the end, the purpose is to create a well-rounded system of goals that addresses your whole person and that you'll have the motivation to actually work toward.

Categorizing your goals

After you assign a timeframe to each of your 50 goals, your next step is to assign a category to each one. Typically, your goals fall into one of six categories:

> C = Career
>
> H = Health
>
> F = Family
>
> M = Money/financial
>
> S = Spiritual
>
> P = Personal

When determining which category each goal falls under, you'll find that some goals fall naturally in one specific category. A goal to get be promoted to supervisor at work, for example, is an easy C. Other goals, however, aren't so easy to peg. Going back to school to earn an MBA may be a C for career, but it also may be a P for personal. Place the goal in whichever category you most closely associate with it, or feel free to place some goals in multiple categories.

Now go back through your list of 50 goals and write the appropriate category letter next to each one. After you label each goal with a category, count the total number of goals you have for each category and record those numbers in Figure 5-1. Then assess the spread of your goals across those categories to see whether they're well balanced. Are you light on health goals? Should you pay more attention to your spiritual life?

FIGURE 5-1:
Balance your
goals across
categories with
this chart.

Category	Number of Goals in This Category
Career (C)	
Health (H)	
Family (F)	
Money/Financial (M)	
Spiritual (S)	
Personal (P)	

Assigning a timeframe to each goal

I firmly believe you can have anything you want; you just can't have it all at once and all right now. Just because you establish a goal to lose 20 pounds doesn't mean you'll wake up tomorrow with 20 pounds missing from your body. Realizing your goal involves a process that requires specific activity and time.

Remember that your Fabulous 50 list names goals that you want to accomplish within the next 10 years. That said, you may want to see some of them come to fruition much earlier. Some may be immediate — just a year away. Others may require you to first achieve some intermediate goals. For instance, say your goal is to double your income within 3 years. You know you're unlikely to receive any-where close to a 100-percent raise at your current job, so you start exploring other options: a new job that pays more and has a fast-track career path, a second job, freelance or contract projects that you can do on your off-hours, or a real-estate investment that brings in rental income.

Before you head to the next section, go back through your list of 50 goals (which you created earlier in "Establishing Your Fabulous 50") and write a 1, 3, 5, or 10 next to each goal to indicate whether you want to achieve that goal within 1, 3, 5, or 10 years.

When you start thinking about the time you need to attain your goals, make sure you're being reasonable. Whether or not the timeframe for your goals is reasonable depends entirely on your situation. To help you stay on track, follow these steps:

1. Consider the timeframe you'd ideally like to accomplish this goal.

   Would you be happy if you accomplished it one year or even three years later than your ideal, or are you intent on accomplishing it by a certain time?

2. Assess the complexity of the goal.

3. Determine what new knowledge or other resources you may need to accomplish the goal.

   See the "Pinpointing Your Resource Needs" section, later in this chapter, for guidance.

4. Consider what timeframe someone else needed to accomplish a similar goal.

After you label each goal with a timeframe, tally up the number of goals you have for each time slot and record those totals in Figure 5-2. Then assess the spread of your goals across those timeframes to see whether they're well balanced.

FIGURE 5-2:
Use this table
to tally your
goals for each
timeframe.

Timeframe	Number of Goals in This Timeframe
1 year	
3 years	
5 years	
10 years	

REMEMBER

Especially when finances are involved, keep in mind that you should enjoy the process of working toward your goals. Although planning for the future is important, you're guaranteed only the present. You don't want to rob yourself of all enjoyment now. Better to live a balanced life while you implement your plan and adjust it as needed when circumstances throw you for a loop.

Creating Your Success Tournament

At this point, you should have a list of 50 goals you want to accomplish over the next 10 years, all labeled according to the timeframe you want to achieve them in and the aspect of your life that they fall under (as discussed in the preceding section). A large list ensures that you have new goals to move to when you accomplish your first goals. However, concentrating on *all* your goals at once leads to frustration, distraction, and ultimately, failure.

The next step is to break down your list of 50 into some manageable chunks, which helps you focus your energy where you need it most. You won't allow others to interrupt you as frequently, and you'll work with a greater sense of urgency because you have things to do, places to go, people to meet, things to see, time-frames in which to accomplish them, and goals to cross off.

Sometimes actually prioritizing your goals is the most difficult part of goal set-ting. Many of us can create our Fabulous 50 or even 75 or 100 things we want to accomplish and experience. The hardest part is breaking them down to a few that are the most important, highest priority. If we do that in our head, we often have less certainty of our goals and objectives. Again, paper is really our best friend in this process of clarity.

TIP

Focus always comes before success. Very little is accomplished without removing what we don't want so that we focus on what we truly do.

To clarify your goals into specific priorities, we are going to have a tournament. The concept is the same for sports playoffs or at a tennis or racquetball tourna-ment. In the bracket of competitors, winners advance and losers stay put and are considered a lower priority. Then an ultimate or outright winner is declared.

If you have ever played competitive athletics where the competition is head to head, you'll understand. My experience in athletics is mostly in the arena. As a former professional racquetball player in my later teens and 20s, in each match, I was playing against a specific person. To win the overall competition, you have to follow the tournament bracket. To accurately compare specific goals, a tourna-ment bracket is an efficient way to evaluate their importance.

Setting up your tournament brackets

You can create your tournament brackets in two ways: timeframe or category. In either case, the bracket should look like Figure 5-3.

Timeframe tournament

You can organize your list of goals based on timeframe for a bracket. You would place all your one-year goals on the outside lines of the tournament bracket. They would be placed in head-to-head competition, and you would play off those two goals to see which is the winner. The winner is the one that is the most important and meaningful to you.

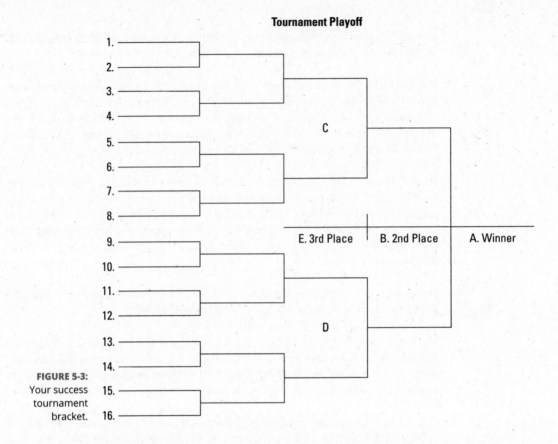

Tournament Playoff

1.
2.
3.
4.

C

5.
6.
7.
8.

E. 3rd Place | B. 2nd Place | A. Winner

9.
10.
11.
12.

D

13.
14.
15.
16.

FIGURE 5-3:
Your success
tournament
bracket.

When you have determined the more important, you advance it forward to go against another goal that has advanced out of the first round as well. You repeat that process until you have the ultimate winner. This one goal has won out and is your most desirable goal for that timeframe. All your efforts should be focused on achieving this primary goal or objective.

Be sure to play off your goals for third and fourth place. The two semi-final goals need to be prioritized because it's likely you will have the time and passion to work on them to accomplishment. They might also aid or help you in the achievement of your number-one goal. Your first-round goals that lose are less likely to be achieved in the timeframe prescribed because they lack the level of importance to advance further. This process creates the awareness of how what you want most influences decisions and effort.

Category tournament

The other option is to arrange a tournament bracket based on the categories of goals. So arrange all your financial goals, regardless of timeframe, and play them off in a tournament. You might find that the long-term goal of financial independence and being worth $5 million is more important than saving money to pay cash for a new Mercedes Benz. The freedom, choice, and security speaks to you more deeply in achieving the $5 million in net worth than does the luxury car.

TIP

You might even consider doing both a category tournament and timeframe tournament. It's possible you will organize your goals to a highly defined level. This organization and focus will make it easier for you to create and enact execution plans and strategies to increase the odds of them being accomplished.

When you compare the two ways to create a tournament, the results could be different than you expect. The exciting part about using a tournament strategy is that there is no general right and wrong. You're trying to discover with clarity what is right and wrong for you.

Here are some examples goal matchups for a one-year timeframe:

>> 5 days a week quiet time vs. Increase reading by 2 hours per week = Increase reading

>> Save $50 more each week vs. Increase tithe = Increase tithe

>> Run 3 miles daily vs. 5 days weekly workouts = 5 days weekly workouts

>> Eat 3 servings of vegetables each day vs. Reduce cholesterol to 150 = Reduce cholesterol

Realizing who the winner is: You

In all this tournament playoff action, the true winner will be you. In fact, you have no way to lose unless you don't do this. Most goal setting exercises stop at categorizing the goals. To create goals that pull you toward their achievement, you must prioritize. Focusing on what you want intently really moves you closer to success.

Increasing the Speed to Achievement

To achieve more and become successful, we need to accomplish more in less time. Speed matters. We want to be able to cross more goals off our goal list so that we can attack the next group of goals with the same passion and focus we accomplished the last.

Time is the great equalizer of life. We all have the same amount in a given day. We are given 86,400 seconds each day when we wake up. But we don't know how many days of 86,400 seconds our life on Earth will consist of, so speed to achievement does matter. The skill to force efficiency of action and efficiency of implementation of your goals can determine your well-being and sense of success.

Forced efficiency is the ability to look for and find time savings in accomplishing your pursuits. If you can prepare an outstanding meal in 30 minutes, where for most it takes an hour or more, that savings of time in 30 days adds up to more than 15 hours in a month. You can apply this kind of time saving to other goals, objectives, or pursuits.

Determining the why

The why you want a particular goal is the power source to success. Once you determine the what you want and organize the categories, you have to dig deep inside yourself to understand why you want that goal or achievement. Some of the most powerful goals come out of childhood experiences that are ingrained over many years.

Think of the people who had challenging childhoods that involved constant poverty and struggle no matter how hard their parents worked. Their parents maybe lacked the education to be able to land a high-paying job, so they were forced to work multiple jobs to provide barely enough. That experience is such a powerful why to some that the goal of achieving an advanced degree consumes them. They have connected their education through a "big why" to filling the belly and providing a more stable lifestyle for the family.

It's been nearly 28 years since my success and personal development journey began. I was in my late 20s when I first read Napoleon Hill's landmark book, *Think and Grow Rich*. The book guided me to probe deep into myself to explore the why's of my goals, aspirations, and motivations to achieve success. That book led me to other amazing books, speakers, and authors over the last few decades.

Since that time, I have become well known worldwide in the real estate sales arena as the guy who was able to sell 150 homes a year with a four-day workweek schedule. The truth is, that schedule was no accident. It was a goal of mine to work only four days a week since I was a child. And I accomplished that goal due to the power of why.

ANECDOTE

Here's my story: My dad worked a four-day week when I was growing up. He was able to do that because of his successful dental practice. He was always around on Friday when I came home from school. But the biggest benefit came in the summer, when we left Portland every Thursday afternoon to spend three days at a second home on a lake near the Oregon coast. Some of my fondest childhood memories are of swimming, sailing, waterskiing, walking the beach, and playing at our lake house. I wanted to replicate that life exactly. As I built my real estate sales business, that desire drove my success. It led me to build a vacation home in Bend, Oregon, where Joan and I spent three days a week for more than five years until which time we moved into our vacation home in Bend full time.

Although my why happened to come from a positive childhood experience, keep in mind that reasons can just as easily come from a negative place. Either way, they're motivating factors to keep you pressing on. Thousands of success stories have germinated from the seeds of abject poverty or personal tragedy.

REMEMBER

When the why is large enough, the how becomes easy. The bigger and more powerful the "why" of your goals, the "how" or path to achievement becomes easier and easier as you progress. So why are the goals you selected important to you?

Using emotion to fuel the fire

Emotions are powerful drivers of success and goal achievement. If you can tie powerful emotional to your goals, you increase the odds of accomplishment. The emotions of excitement, recognition, status, exclusivity, disgust, and fear are just a few that can be used as a fulcrum to success. You can use either positive or negative emotions to drive you. The avoidance of pain and the pursuit of pleasure can be used equally as well.

In my experience, the biggest, most powerful emotional driver is love. If you can connect love, especially love of others, to your goals as your key why, there is nothing that will block your path to success.

ANECDOTE

My father's why, for example, was born out of his love for my mother, who was diagnosed with multiple sclerosis. My father's goal was to earn enough income as a dentist to provide my mother with the most extraordinary life possible: to travel in a wheelchair to Mexico, Asia, Hawaii (annually), and many other locations — always with three sons in tow. But mostly, he wanted to be able to care for her in the home where she raised her children and provide her the best quality of life imaginable for someone in her physically challenged condition. He accomplished that goal for her whole lifetime. She never had to live outside of her home that contained the memories of more than 40 years of comfort, security, and family.

Pinpointing Your Resource Needs

Achieving your goals requires resources, be they money, contacts, knowledge, skills, time, or all of the above. Some fortunate folks may have an abundant supply of all resources, but most are short on at least a couple. I may have the income to allow me to train to become a world-class figure skater, but because I lack the skill, I'm unlikely to have enough time to become good enough to achieve the goal of qualifying for the Winter Olympics in 2022.

Even if you approach your goals with an imbalance of resources, by carefully leveraging those that you have at your disposal, you can overcome many short-falls. If you're lacking in one or more resources, you may have to invest more of the resources you have. Take my Olympics example: I'm short on time and skill, so I may need to invest more money to devote myself to full-time training, or I may have to borrow time and aim for the 2026 Olympics instead.

Increasing your capital

Most goals, if they aren't about money, seem to require money: building your dream home, taking a cruise, sending your kids to an Ivy League school, opening your own coffee shop. Even a goal such as landing a job at a high-powered corporation, which seems to be about earning money, may require you to get some additional education or purchase suitable interview attire.

If you find that your goal requires capital, do your best to quantify the amount. Then determine whether you have enough money to achieve your goal or whether you need more. Ask the following questions:

>> Do you have time to earn the amount needed to fund your endeavor?

>> Can you borrow the money?

>> Can you leverage another of your resources to balance the shortfall?

Expanding your knowledge

Knowledge can dramatically increase the prospects of attaining your goal in the time table you've established. Trial and error is a costly means to reach your destination — especially when it comes to time investment. So if you assess your success-list goals and determine that you need more information to succeed, ask the following:

> » What, exactly, is the knowledge you need to realize your goal?

> » What's the best way to attain that knowledge? Formal study? Online research? Talking with experts?

> » How long will gaining this knowledge take, and does it fit in with your goal's timeframe?

Increasing your skills

For the fulfillment of many goals, additional skills are required. Don't confuse knowledge with skill. Knowledge entails the gathering and processing of information in a way that you gain a deeper understanding of a subject. Skill involves putting that understanding into effective action. You can study the heart and understand how it works — even know how bypass surgery works to prevent heart failure — but you don't want to perform such a procedure without having the skill of an experienced surgeon.

Examine your success list again to evaluate where additional skills may be necessary:

> » What skills are required for each goal?

> » Are these skills that you already claim, or do you need to acquire them?

> » Are these skills that you can learn within the timeframe? If not, then how can you make up for that skill shortage? Can you find someone who has the skills and ask for his or her help?

Bringing in the help of others

Most people have accomplished what they have because someone else helped them along the way, so don't overlook the people component as you tally up your resources. The right contacts can be valuable in helping you attain your goals. Consider that dream of working for the high-powered corporation, for instance. Knowing someone who works for the company — or who has inside connections — is one of the best ways to get your foot in the door.

But people resources can help in achieving other types of goals as well, from buying that cabin in the woods (Uncle Sydney always believed that real estate is the best investment) to learning to play the saxophone. (The waiter at the local coffee shop is only too happy to earn some extra money giving lessons.) Here are some questions to ask yourself as you evaluate your human resources:

>> Do you know anyone who achieved a goal similar to yours, someone who may be willing to advise you?

>> If you need additional schooling but are short on funds, do you know people who may be able to help you acquire the knowledge you need?

>> Do you know someone who has the knowledge, skill, connections, or money that you need to reach your goal?

>> Can you tap into your people resources and use the skills of someone else to compensate for skills you can't attain yourself?

>> Do you know someone who knows someone else who may be able to help you?

Think of ways that the people you plan to approach can benefit if you attain your goal. Can you compensate them monetarily for their help? Can you offer something in trade that has value for them? Even just asking for help and saying thank you in advance is enough for some people. (Though many times, people are more willing to help when there's something in it for them.) If you can't find anyone to help, you're forced to take the personal education route. The good thing, though, is that lots of books, classes, and seminars are available to help you, so take advantage of them.

Chapter **6**

Dealing with Adversity and Setbacks

In order for us to win in life, we must push through the adversity we face. Without facing it, we are poorly prepared for winning. The truth is, most of us don't welcome adversity like a long-lost friend. We don't embrace with passion the pain and setbacks that occur. Without a healthy relationship and desire for adversity to happen, we are not prepared to seize opportunity when it presents itself in the present or future. No one has ever achieved a high level of success without overcoming setbacks, failures, and adversity.

Alfred Russell Wallace was a famous botanist of the late 1800s. One day, Dr. Wallace was observing an Emperor butterfly struggling through the life-and-death adversity of escaping its cocoon. He wondered if he assisted the butterfly in its exit, what effect that would have on the butterfly. With a knife, Dr. Wallace made an incision the length of the cocoon that allowed the butterfly to exit the cocoon with ease. The butterfly emerged, spread its wings, and died. The butterfly did not have to encounter adversity in struggling to exit the cocoon. Through the struggle, the butterfly would have grown in strength. Since it failed to struggle and grow, it did not have the strength necessary to survive.

We often try to make similar incisions in our challenges and take the easy route. But when taking the quick exit, we fail to acquire the strength to compete. We often take the easy route to improve our skills. Many of us never really work to achieve mastery in the key areas of life. These skills are key tools that can be very useful to our career, family relationships, wealth, health and prosperity. Highly successful athletes don't win because of better equipment; they win by facing adversity to gain strength and skill. They win through preparation. It's the mental preparation, winning mindset, strategy, and skill that set them apart.

REMEMBER

Strength comes from struggle, not from taking the path of least resistance. Adversity is not just a lesson for the next time in front of us. Adversity will be the greatest teacher we will ever have in life.

We all have areas where we fall short. We all fail at times. Abraham Lincoln said, "My great concern is not whether you have failed, but whether you are content with your failure." This chapter will help you learn from your failures and turn them into success. You will discover how to remove doubt, fear, and indecision from your life, and you will fire up your perseverance to power your quest for success.

You Will Learn More from Your Failures than Success

We all need to reprogram our minds and understand that failure only happens when we stop striving, trying, or progressing. For me personally, it took me over 30 years of my life to grasp that belief. For a long time, I didn't have a refined enough philosophy of life to accept that making errors, mistakes, and not accomplishing goals within specific timeframes was failure. Instead, it was learning, advancing, discovering, and growing. It was a natural process to self-improvement and success. The challenges we face are merely learning experiences to prepare us for a better future.

I learned that failure is *not* doing; it's *not* taking action. It's staying down after you have been knocked down by life. The greatest achievers are not the people with the fewest errors, or what the world would call failures. The greatest achievers are less affected by failure. They don't fear failure. They embrace it. They even go boldly after it, speeding up the process.

Don't be paralyzed by fear of failure

The vast majority of people in life play defense against failure. We become defensive, trying to avoid "the mistake." You never win consistently or accomplish great objectives in life by playing defensive or being fearful. Fear, when connected with a potential negative outcome, saps the willingness to try in most people. The fear takes over the six inches between our left and right ears. If we focus on it, then it consumes our thoughts. When it consumes our thoughts, it controls our actions. When fear of failure takes hold, it leads to other challenges.

Timidity

Successful people are bold. Being bold does not mean being reckless or foolhardy. Being bold means you have gathered reasonable information about taking an action that is needed. You understand that you are correct in taking your thought-out course of action. You then resolve to implement the evaluated action and do so until you reach a favorable conclusion.

Being timid is being overly cautious. Being timid means that you are unwilling to advocate for yourself, your conclusions, or your recommendations. In a sales career, it's not asking the prospect to take action to use your product or services. I love the title of a classic book on sales by Judge Ziglar, the younger brother of Zig Ziglar, *Timid Salespeople Have Skinny Kids.* Being timid is not a virtue in sales or in life.

Indecision

A close cousin of timidity is indecision and the need for ever-expanding amounts of data and information. Some people want to secure 100-percent certainty before they act. They do this to avoid errors. I am not advocating being reckless, but if you reach 80-percent certainty in a decision, you have enough probability for the outcome to be favorable, and successful, a large amount of the time.

Think about it: The amount of time and resources to secure the extra 20 percent to reach 100 percent, which can be stated as guaranteed success, is likely more than what you expended to secure the first 80 percent. In that quest for the remaining 20 percent, you're going to miss out on the opportunity that you've been evaluating. Indecision is a thief that steals your chance for success.

Doubt

Being successful requires self-confidence. At times, you have to act and push your doubt aside. The most harmful doubt is self-doubt. We need to be constantly replaying the victories we have created, both large and small. As Yogi Berra is famous for saying, "It's not over until it's over." If we have self-doubt, we have declared it over before it's over, or worse yet, before we even begin. You must believe in yourself. Robert Schuller, the famous preacher, said, "If it's to be, it's up to me." Requiring a mandatory belief in yourself leads to success.

I have never allowed my kids, Wesley and Annabelle, to use the word "can't." If they say they can't do something, I quickly correct them and express that isn't a word we use in the Zeller family. I don't want "can't" to enter their minds, or more importantly their subconscious minds. That's because your subconscious mind believes everything you place in it. It doesn't evaluate for truth the statements, thoughts, or ideas entering it. Your self-consciousness believes all of it as truthful. It then works even while you sleep to figure out how to go about accomplishing what it believes to be true. Who wouldn't want to hit the on switch to such a wonderful success tool?

ANECDOTE

For more than 34 years, I have replayed a successful life experience that almost everyone watching it unfold highly doubted would go my way. I was 22 years old playing in the semifinal match of the Seattle Open, a professional racquetball tournament. My opponent, a young, up-and-coming player from the area, was giving me a tough match. We had split the first two games. I was down 10-0 in the tie-breaking game to 11, which means I was one point away from being eliminated. If you asked anyone of the hundreds of people watching the match, I had no shot at winning. If there was betting, no bookmaker could have enticed anyone to bet with any favorable odds.

I took a timeout to clear my head, create some space, and to make my opponent wait for his chance to close me out at 11-0. I can honestly say I didn't have doubt; I was confident that I would win. I knew I was not going to get all the points back or pull even in one big, final swoop. I also realized that I had to focus on each point. I knew that if I could get to 8 points, the pressure would be completely shifted from me to my opponent. If I could get to 9-10, he would likely crack under the pressure of blowing such a large lead. I remember making the decision to act as if I had nothing to lose . . . because I didn't. Sometimes that is the best mindset when faced with a difficult task with long odds of success. When your back is against the wall, acting as if you have nothing to lose frees you up to just go for it.

As we played along, I got to 10-3 in one service side. Then I managed to get to 10-6 and then 10-8. At that point, my confidence was sky high and his was slipping. We then were knotted at 10-10, having numerous side outs back and forth. Finely, after five side outs, I hit the game-winning shot. The feeling of accomplishment was the most overwhelming I had ever experienced in my life. Even as I write this 34 years later, I can still vividly feel the emotions of overcoming long odds of success, the exhilaration of proving the gawkers and bystanders wrong. Beating the hometown Seattle wonder-kid 34 years later is still sweet.

I have used that event in my life to drive out doubt countless times. It's one of my go-to success stories that I replay in tough situations. I have had many successes since then, even recent ones. But this one continues to serve me well.

TIP

We all need stories of our success that we can draw on to drive out doubt. What are yours? We all have them, both large and small. They need to be used and recalled to drive performance higher.

Worry

The enemy of joy, happiness, and even success is worry. Most of us worry about things that are highly unlikely to happen. The act of worrying wastes energy and emotion. It robs you of passion and enthusiasm for positive pursuits and results. We can't let worry run free and unfiltered. It needs to be controlled and pushed into a corner to take up as little space as possible.

There are legitimate things to worry about. Your child is out late at night and was supposed to be home hours ago. That is a legitimate concern. My response to worry is prayer. Prayer acknowledges in that situation my lack of control and acknowledges God's ability to protect my child from situations. Prayer acknowledges my smallness and God's largeness to create outcomes as to His choosing. It lowers my ego to its rightful position.

Get your ego out of the way

Most successful people have a healthy ego. There is a fine line between an over-developed ego and self-confidence. You have to be confident in yourself and be a cheerleader for yourself. To be successful, we also need to remain balanced in our evaluation of our strengths, weaknesses, errors, and mistakes. But if we take it too far, when our ego is outsized, we try to find fault in others, in our work, and in our personal life. For example, we look to place the blame of a failed relationship on our spouse or significant other if our ego is unable to be objective. And everyone knows that in all failed relationships, there is more than one person responsible. The out-of-touch ego wants to protect itself from the real truth.

Because I have been in sales for more than 30 years, I see salespeople with high egos blame "the leads" or prospects for low sales numbers. It's a personal defense mechanism to not have to look at the more common problems that are staring back at us in the mirror. These problems include lack of sales calls and contacts as well as poor quality of presentation. In short, what matters is what salespeople say when talking to a prospect and how many calls or conversations they have consistently. Having an inflated ego removes one of the most powerful motivators for change and protection from future repeated failure: disgust.

You might be thinking that disgust is a negative emotion, and that is true, but it can be used well to create behavioral change. Negative emotions like disgust can drive us to make changes that will allow for greater success.

You might feel disgust when you look in the mirror and see an extra 20 pounds of fat that you know shouldn't be there if not for your poor diet and fitness habits. You can turn that disgust into "I am going to do whatever it takes to change this body, and I'm starting right now."

Saying "I've had it" is a powerful moment that guides you to success. When you have that moment of disgust, it moves your ego out of the way. You can have this experience in any area of life: health, wealth, career, relationships. It breaks through the fake reality we might be fooling ourselves with. It can be a life-changing moment when we say, "Enough is enough!"

Think of failure as merely an event

Failure is really a moment in time. It's a snapshot of what happened at one time. It's not a marker of what will happen in the future. Because we experienced failure, it's not fatal or final. Countless people have lost it all financially and rebuilt from zero to astounding wealth. We all make errors and mistakes. What happens in life happens to all of us. We have to treat our setbacks as such.

Victor Frankel, Nazi concentration camp survivor and author of the landmark book, *Man's Search for Meaning,* said, "It's not what happens to me that matters, but what happens in me." He experienced firsthand one of the most horrifying events in modern history. But he understood that his inner thoughts could not be controlled by the Nazis. His exterior circumstances were an event of the present rather than his future. He could not control the events in his life, but he would control his reaction. He could control his mind and his thoughts. Don't let failure or a negative event in your life control your mind. Don't let it control how you think about yourself, your opportunities.

The Power of Persistence

Part of being successful in any area of your life can be boiled down to simply holding on a little longer. The ability persevere frequently creates a winning outcome. For the parent whose child has lost his or her way, the continuation of loving support, prayer, and patience can be rewarded with that child coming back home. The truth is, when we're tackling tough situations, we never know when we are going to have a breakthrough. It might feel like we are miles away from achieving our goal. But in many cases, if we had known how close we were, we could have persevered a little longer.

Let me share this story with you. Florence Chadwick wanted to be the first woman to swim the English Channel. For years she trained herself to keep going long after her body needed rest. When the big day arrived to challenge the channel, things went well until she neared the coast of England, where heavy fog, cold, and rough waters impeded her progress. Not realizing she was within a few hundred yards of the shore, she became completely exhausted and quit swimming. Think about it: She quit a few hundred yards from her goal after swimming miles! She was heart-broken when she found out how close she was. She was quoted by reporters as saying, "I'm not offering excuses, but I think I would have made it if I would have been able to see my goal."

She tried again after she developed a mental image of England and the coastline. She memorized every feature of the distant landscape and held it firmly and clearly in her mind. When she made another attempt, she was again hindered by fog, frigid water, and turbulent seas, but this time she accomplished her objective. And the reason she reached her goal was because she never lost sight of it. It was in her mind's eye the whole way across.

Amazing things can and do happen when we keep our objective in sight. Don't lose sight of yours.

REMEMBER

Facing discouragement in life

We are faced with a lot of opposite extremes in life. We all understand the opposites of light and darkness, success and failure, joy and sorrow. We wouldn't know how good joy feels without the opposite emotion of sorrow. There wouldn't be winning if there also wasn't losing. We will all encounter discouraging situations in our careers, our relationships, our parenting, and our finances. But these are obstacles we must all overcome.

We also could not feel the encouragement that comes from being persistent without experiencing discouragement at times. We often feel discouraged when we miss an opportunity. We look back and say, "If only," and that feeling is part of any life. "If only I had paid more attention to my kids when they were younger," we state. "If only we had bought investment real estate between 2009 and 2012." If we are honest with ourselves, we can all look back and feel discouraged at the decisions we should have made.

The key is to use discouragement to motivate change. Take responsibility for the missed opportunity and resolve to not miss it the next time it comes around. It's the next opportunity that now matters, not the one you just missed.

TIP

Connecting patience with success

We want it all yesterday. I can include myself in that group as well. If patience is a virtue, I am not very virtuous. I am certainly more patient as I have aged, but not by much. Success is progressing to your stated objectives, not just arriving at the finish line of those objectives. We need to give ourselves time for the achievement part of success to grow and blossom. Ultimately, there are no unrealistic goals but merely unrealistic timelines that need patience to come to fruition.

We are all dealing with multiple learning curves in our lives and in the pursuit of success. You can see what I mean by a learning curve in Figure 6-1. In observation and evaluation, we have to ask ourselves this question: "Where am I on the learning curve now?" Sometimes pinpointing an exact location is tricky for most of us. If we knew exactly where we are, then it becomes easier to be patient and persevere the upward climb. I know that evaluating where I am on the learning curve has developed more patience in me.

Learning curve

Effort

FIGURE 6-1:
On the learning curve, things get harder before they eventually get easier.

Return

We need to guard against having too many learning curves going at once. That can lead to overcommitting and overexposure to the steepest part of the curve in multiple pursuits, and then you'll be faced with frustration, discouragement, and a lack of patience. It's easier to have patience when you are confident of the outcome. That's why patience connects to self-confidence and self-esteem.

REMEMBER

The primary rule of the learning curve is "Everything is hard before it becomes easy."

ANECDOTE

The amount of effort we must put forth to climb the learning curve is substantial. When my daughter, Annabelle, was 13 months old, she was trying to walk, and the effort she was putting out was impressive. Her return had been limited to bonks on the head, plops on her rear end, and a few shuffles with her feet by hanging onto anything she could get her hands on to maintain her balance. That's when she was at the steepest part of the learning curve, and I could see the frustration in her face. The lack of success in walking like her 4-year-old brother, Wesley, affected her attitude once in a while. She was committed to overcoming this challenge of life. In a few short months, she was over the steepest part of the curve where the effort dropped and the return was constant and had improved. It just took her time, like for all of us.

When we are not patient in our approach to success, when we lose sight of where we are in the learning curve, we can leap prematurely to another strategy that we feel holds better promise. We don't work through the learning curve long enough to fully understand and test our progress and results. We leap to someone's better mousetrap or the latest and greatest strategy for success, wealth, happiness, and prosperity. Because of the advent of social media, our Facebook, Twitter, and Instagram accounts are inundated with new, latest, greatest ways to lose weight and get rich quick. It's easy to get sucked in because we are climbing to success straight up the face of the learning curve. It feels like no progress is being made, but it is.

I personally filter the pursuit of success through traditional, historic strategies and principles. Whether that's my age, era, or because I have seen too many late-night infomercials, the success principles that have stood the test of time for thousands of years of recorded history appeal to me. King Solomon is arguably the wisest and wealthiest man to ever walk the earth. According to *MarketWatch*, King Solomon's wealth would be more than 2.2 trillion in today's dollars. Solomon wrote in Ecclesiastes 1:9-10, "What has been will be again, what has been done will be done again; there is nothing new under the sun. Is there anything of which one can say, 'Look! This is something new'? It was here already, long ago; it was here before our time."

Solomon knew that success principles can't be created or exclaimed as new. The right strategies and principles will be standard bearers throughout history. I am creating a different combination of words, phrases, and thoughts to convey them to you in this book. I hope I have done it well so that success is more understandable and readily implementable. My desire is that your results fulfill the goals you have set for your life. That's the greatest reward of life. The foundations of what I write about have not changed from Biblical times. They will work for you today, as they did for Solomon, even in today's technology enabled world.

Knowing the ratios to any successful endeavor

We need to expect setbacks and changes to come in life. When we attempt the grand adventures of developing new skills and new strategies, the only thing that is constant in life is change (and the love of a dog), and that's true whether you decide on the change cogently through research and reflection, or a change is thrust upon you suddenly by outside forces. In either case, preparation and resil-iency are required. And you also need to know how to quickly evaluate the success ratios.

ANECDOTE

Let me give you an illustration. My father, at 65 years of age, knew something was not right with him. He was reasonably healthy, playing golf and tennis a few times a week. He just didn't feel right. After months of prodding from my mother, he had tests for his heart. They found he had four heavily blocked coronary arteries. He was faced with a big decision about the odds or ratios of success. He could do angioplasty procedures on the four arteries and avoid the open-heart surgery that was a far more difficult and invasive procedure with a long recovery time. The angioplasty could work well, but he might need further procedures to keep the arteries fully open. It would require monitoring and review.

The open-heart bypass surgery would be riskier and longer, and it would require a more painful recovery. Done well, in a few months, he could resume his normal activities. And with diet change and cholesterol-lowering medicine, he would be better than before. Each had ratios of success and failure. Each had an influence on present and future lifestyle. Because he is a "do it once so you don't have to do it again or worry about it in the future" type of guy, he chose to have the open-heart bypass procedure. The recovery was challenging and painstaking, as he expected. More than 20 years later, he is still going strong at age 87. He has lived 20-plus years with the benefits of making the right decision. He also stuck to a healthy diet and increased exercise to drive his odds of health success even higher.

Being able to evaluate the ratios to create success is an ability one needs to acquire. You might ask yourself a few key questions:

>> What are the odds, on a scale of 1–10, of this goal or objective being achieved?

>> What can I do specifically to increase the odds?

The leverage points to know the ratios of success are knowledge, skill, attitude, activities, people to help, capital, and increased time.

When you want to increase the success ratios, the changes required to increase the odds will come from the first four about 90 percent of the time. It will come from acquiring new knowledge that you are lacking, learning new specific skills, chang-ing your attitude to be more positive, or increasing your volume or consistency of activities.

In my experience as an observer in my life and having a front-row seat in coach-ing tens of thousands of people over 20 years, changing and improving consis-tency in our activities is the leading way to alter the ratios of success in our favor.

If you want to lose weight, it's the activity of eating less and moving your body more. In creating wealth, it's the activity of putting a portion of your earnings aside. If it's relationships, it's the activity of spending more time doing what the other people want to do that speaks love to them.

In your business, it's still activities in making more sales calls or increasing the frequency of your marketing and lead generation. This is especially true in economic or marketplace changes. Because a slower economy creates its own new success ratios, lowering the odds, it requires more activity inputs to create even the same output of sales and revenue as before.

Protecting Your Attitude

According to Zig Ziglar, "Your attitude in life will determine your altitude in life." There is little doubt that Zig was correct in this statement. When adversity strikes, we must prevent our attitude from moving to the negative. Even the age-old thought of "Why me?" is basically a step toward the negative side. Using a negative emotion like disgust, which I mention earlier, to fire you up is not the same as having a negative attitude. A negative attitude lingers and hangs over you, reducing your expectation of being successful. Using a negative emotion lights the fire of resolve to change and achieve.

A positive attitude is a *decision* that needs to be protected. Our positive attitude is connected to our gratitude — how grateful we are for our lives, the people in our lives, our faith, and success. Maintaining a sense of gratitude is the best strategy to keeping a positive attitude.

The second best strategy is through action or activities. The vast majority of people say, "If my attitude were better, I would do _____." They have the belief that attitude controls action. For most people, that would be correct, but not for high achievers. The very successful are actually the opposite: Doing the activities or changes, which are needed or which lead to success, fuels their attitude to be positive. This small shift in your mind to take action, even when you don't feel like it, leads to greater self-discipline, self-confidence, and self-worth.

The following table illustrates the relationship between attitude and action:

Attitude Influences Activity	Activities Influence Attitude
If I only felt better, I would . . .	I'm going to the gym even though I don't feel like it.
If I felt more motivated, I would . . .	I'm going to save this money even though I would rather spend it.

The thoughts of "if only" versus "I'm going to anyway" create very different results in your attitude and success.

Maintaining your optimism

Being positive and optimistic at its core is a decision, and it's one that you make each day when you wake up. The difference in your success that day, as well as for your whole life, will be dramatically different due to that one decision each day. If you have a specific aim or series of goals you are trying to achieve, it becomes easier to hold onto an optimistic view. You have likely been able to check off a few of those goals as accomplished. The checking off of your goal, or creating a dramatic completion moment, engrains it into your mind, setting it apart and creating memorability and easy recall when needed.

I remember being in financial difficulty in my early 20s. I hadn't found a good career, so I was working low-paying jobs. I borrowed money from a local household finance company at an exorbitant interest rate. It was a few thousand dollars, but after a while, I realized the interest rate, at almost 25 percent, was killing me. I resolved to pay that thing off in the next 8 months. I still remember the exact amount I owed: $1,367.34. When I finally had the money to pay off the loan, I brought it to them in one-dollar bills. I could have done it in pennies, but counting it out would have taken forever. I thought about it for a moment: I wanted the drama that counting out $1,367 and 34 cents in single dollars would create. I wanted this event etched in my mind forever for a couple reasons. First, I never wanted to be back in that position. Second, I wanted evidence that I can do anything that I set my mind to. That achievement fueled my optimism that I can tackle anything life throws at me.

Using positive affirmations

There is so much negative in the world. All you have to do is open up social media, watch cable news, or read the newspaper. The world has an abundance of negative events. Our brains are bombarded with negative. We all consciously need to counteract the negative stimuli we receive.

Using positive affirmations help in that waging battle. Affirmations are positive statements vocalized about positive present and future events. To be most effective, they need to be vocalized out load so that your ears pick them up and transfer them to your brain. By saying the affirmations aloud, they become more than just thoughts that can be easily dismissed. Your auditory receptors transfer them into your subconscious mind as truth. Your subconscious mind, because it believes them as truth, goes to work on creating the solutions and circumstances that are consistent with what you have said to it.

Here are some examples of affirmations:

>> I'm a great problem solver.

>> I am intelligent, and I learn more each day.

>> My value to my company is large, and my pay soon will be.

Some affirmations are said to support your current level of success, skills, and attitude. Some affirmations are future-based to promote your goals:

>> I'm worth one million dollars.

>> I will weigh 125 pounds in six months.

>> I will receive a raise in less than three months.

>> I will earn an A this semester in Algebra.

TIP

Craft some affirmations centered around your goals and desires in life. Say them aloud as you are preparing yourself for work this week. Look at yourself in the mirror as you say them. Be authoritative, powerful, and confident in your body language when you say them. Your subconscious mind will help you to create in your life what you affirmed with your voice.

Holding onto your faith

Faith is an important part of moving through setbacks and adversity. A spiritual faith keeps you grounded personally and also gives you a sense of connection to a higher power or God. If you are in an organized community of faith, you are surrounded by people who share your burdens and experience. That community of faith can be an integral part of navigating life challenges.

I receive great comfort knowing that God is walking with me through adversity. I know that I am not alone, and this fact reduces my anxiety during adversity. I can seek His wisdom through prayer and reading the Bible, and that has provided solutions to my challenges in life. It still amazes me that I discover new meaning in chapters and verses of the Bible that I have previously read numerous times. These discoveries are revealed to me in the right moment when I need them most. I have faith because this has happened thousands of times in my lifetime of Christian faith.

Being in a community of faith enables you to connect with people who have experienced similar challenges. You gain practical insight from these people who have walked down the road further than yourself and have experienced similar family, business, health, and financial challenges. Because of the common connection of faith, you see what God is doing in their lives as well.

The intercessionary prayer of the community of faith is powerful and comforting when you are experiencing adversity. God makes a clear promise of that power in the Bible: "For where two or three are gathered together in my name, there am I in the midst of them." (Matthew 18:20)

I am comforted by that verse knowing that God is among those who pray together. I believe that God will answer our prayers when we gather to pray together, and that deepens my faith. That deepened faith reduces any apprehension I might have when dealing with negative circumstances and setbacks.

3

Achieving Optimum Health

Examine the habits you need to stay physically healthy.

Work on improving your positivity and your overall self-esteem.

Evaluate your spiritual beliefs and convictions to live consistently with them.

Chapter **7**

Here's to Your Physical Health

Physical health is frequently ignored as we pursue success. But poor health can affect our concentration, energy level, and stamina, which leads to lower performance in all other areas of our life. When we neglect our physical bodies, we are fatigued more easily. We contract more illnesses, so we miss work and miss opportunities. We have trouble sleeping, and that can affect all aspects of life negatively, including our overall attitude and mental well-being.

In the Untied States, we face a litany of health problems, most of which are self-inflicted through poor diet and lack of exercise. Physical health and well-being, like every other area of life, is fueled by our habits. Eating well, sleeping enough, and being physically active all result from developing good habits.

We invest billions of dollars in weight loss programs, fad diets, and supplements. According to the Centers for Disease Control, or CDC, more than 70 percent of people are overweight or obese, but only 36 percent of the population thinks they are overweight. That's a staggering amount of ignorance and denial. I must admit that I presently have more weight on my body than I should. To get my weight in healthy proportion to my height, I am going to have to grow exponentially taller or, more likely, continue to work at reducing the extra pounds on my body.

My public admission, as I write this chapter, is a clear indication of the gap that exists between knowing and doing. The foundational principles and strategies for health have not altered that dramatically in the last 20 or 30 years. Sure, we get new information all the time about foods and exercise strategies. And experts can also change their minds about what is ultimately good or bad for us. Bottom line: What is the primary cause of cancer, heart disease, and many other diseases and conditions that reduce our quality of life? It's poor diet and lack of exercise.

The objective isn't to have the latest, cutting edge, or experimental strategy for optimal health. There are no magic pills that will make you fit. The goal is to implement foundational habits that result in a long-term sustainable lifestyle change and bridge the gap between knowledge and action. When we are in the action zone, we have the opportunity to form new habits of health, and the habits are critical to success in our physical lives.

We Only Get One to Live In

We have seen significant advancements in medicine in the last half century. The diagnosis of cancer, years ago, was a diagnosis of premature death. In the ensuing years, cancer treatments have extended lives far beyond what was once imaginable. The odds of being cured from common forms of cancer, like breast cancer in women or prostate cancer in men, have climbed exponentially.

Your body is a temple

As a teen growing up in the 1970s, one of my favorite shows was *The Six Million Dollar Man* with actor Lee Majors playing the role of Steve Austin. Steve Austin was the bionic man who had been put back together after crashing a test flight plane. He was, to paraphrase from the show, "better, stronger, and faster" than before. That futuristic depiction, while in the 1970s, seemed farfetched. But fast-forward to present day and there are a whole host of replacement parts that orthopedic surgeons now routinely implant in our bodies. Hip, knee, and shoulder replacements are done in almost every hospital in the United States each day. And then there are cardiovascular advancements. Heart valves can be replaced and blocked arteries can be opened, increasing the longevity of our most important organ, the heart.

All of these advancements, while miraculous, do not change the one undeniable fact: We are only given one body in which to live in on this earth. The most important principle is to take care of the one we are given at birth. While we might replace some body parts, we can't swap the whole body for a new one.

It's common in life to take for granted something we receive for free. Our body falls into that category. We've all heard the old proverb that our body is a temple. In ancient times, a temple was the most valuable and used piece of real estate in the city or town. It was a place of honor and reverence. If we are to treat our body as a temple, we need to sustain it with high quality food and nutrients, exercise it, and always take care of it. Unfortunately, many of us treat our bodies like a trash can.

Everything in moderation

We all enjoy foods that aren't good for us. They might be high in sugar or high in fat (or both), but we consume them anyway knowing that we aren't helping our health. I don't feel, however, that complete abstinence from these foods is sustainable. For example, I have a weakness for ice cream. It's one of those desserts that can get me into trouble. You bring a half gallon of ice cream into the house and I am likely to sit down and eat the whole thing. Should I cut out ice cream completely from my life? We know that plan is destined for failure, right? That's why I force moderation on myself. I only buy ice cream in pints so that I have no choice but to enjoy a much smaller amount.

TIP

A good habit to establish is forced moderation. I firmly believe we can have a few things we truly enjoy eating as long as we enjoy them in small amount.

If we eat a few unhealthy foods in moderation, our bodies are equipped to process the toxins out. If I enjoy a soft drink every once in a while, it's likely to have minimal damage. But if I drink four diet sodas per day, which are loaded with chemicals and artificial ingredients, over time, my body will feel the effects of me treating it like a trash can.

REMEMBER

The unhealthy foods we occasionally indulge in are supposed to be *treats*, not daily staples. Have a small soda or a small bowl of ice cream once per week, not every day, as a reward for your good work.

The only exceptions I would make to the rule of moderation are smoking and taking drugs. Those two habits have addictive qualities that cause psychological and physical dependence as well long-term health problems. Why take the risk?

Creating Your Health Team

We all need to surround ourselves with experts who help in keeping us healthy. The doctors, nurses, nutritional experts, personal trainers, meal preparers, and friends play a large role in our family's quest to stay healthy.

Get yourself a primary care doctor

Your primary doctor is the foundation of your health team. A doctor who stays well read in the medical journals, medical advancements, as well as new drugs and treatment options is essential. You and your physician form a team that works together to improve your overall health. A doctor also requires us to do our part by communicating clearly what is ailing us. The doctor prescribes a treatment plan. We must do our part to follow it exactly through the whole process. Having confidence in your doctor through personal experience or from referral and reputation aides in the healing process.

Good doctors also assemble a team of specialists they have confidence in. Every doctor should have a dream team of specialists in cardiology, orthopedics, gastrology, surgery, urology, and gynecology. As you age, these specialists play an ever-increasing role in your health and quality of life. Sometimes unexpected disease strikes, like it has for me. You might also do research on your own to give yourself peace of mind and perhaps seek a second opinion.

ANECDOTE

I was diagnosed about eight years ago with Meniere's disease. It's a chronic disease that causes fluid buildup in my left ear. I have severe hearing loss in that ear. The most significant challenges associated with Meniere's for me are bouts of vertigo that can cause nausea, dizziness, and in some cases, a visual spinning of the world around me. When that strikes, all I can do is to lie down in a dark, quiet location to try to settle the vertigo down. To think that in my college years, getting the bed spins was a badge of honor after an evening of drinking. I get that same feeling at times without touching a drop of alcohol.

Once diagnosed with Meniere's, I was on a quest to find a specialist of significant experience and skill in treating patients like me with this disease. I fortunately found one at Oregon Health and Science University in Portland, Oregon. Truly, I would travel to the ends of the earth to find a specialist to help manage my treatment of a disease that I will have for the rest of my life.

Be cognizant of your genetics

Our family history and genetics plays an important role in our overall health. It's crucial to record and keep track of your family history of disease. There are genetic influences in most health categories, and that's especially true with regard to heart disease and cancer. If your father, mother, or other close relative has elevated cholesterol levels, as my father does, or has had heart disease, again like my father, it's a marker of risk that you can't ignore. I can assure you that I have received many benefits from being Norm Zeller's son. The only thing he has passed down to me that I don't want is the genetic predisposition to high cholesterol. Even with a proper diet, I am at the high end of the acceptable scale for my cholesterol levels.

It's critical to know your genetic markers for high blood pressure as well. My wife Joan is on blood pressure medication because hers is high due to genetics. Many people in her family are also on high blood pressure medication. Most people are unaware that they have high blood pressure. Get yours checked regularly.

Bring on the specialists

We all need specialists at times on our team. As we cross the threshold of 50 years old, our visits to specialists become more frequent. We need our eyes checked more frequently by our ophthalmologist. Men need to see the urologist because our plumbing flows less freely (or too freely). And don't forget the gastroenterologist, who will take care of your first colonoscopy screening. I didn't have my first colonoscopy until I was 53 years old. The truth is, the reason I got it then was because my younger brother was diagnosed with colon cancer. Fortunately, they caught it at an early stage, and after surgery and radiation treatments, he has been cancer free for a few years. I am thrilled with his early diagnosis and return to health. I am less than thrilled due to shared genetics. I must get a colonoscopy every five years rather than every ten years from my gastroenterologist.

Taking Care of Your Mental Health

The foundation for good health is being positive and optimistic. We need to expect that we will be healthy and successful in life, but that involves crafting a plan for good health through proper eating, exercising, and abstinence from vices that will reduce our quality of life and shorten our length of life. When you decide each day to feel good and expect to accomplish what you desire, your health and well-being is significantly enhanced.

The power of positive thinking

The influence of optimism, positive thinking, and positive expectations are all linked to better mental health. Each morning when you wake up, remember that you have been granted a new day ahead of you, that you are actually alive, with

86,400 seconds to invest as you choose. That realization can set the tone for mental health and success.

We need to start each day with gratitude and appreciation for what we do have and not lament what we don't. With a grateful attitude, it's infinitely easier to accomplish your goals and objectives. Get in the habit of listening to positive music, like worship and praise songs, during your morning routine. Music that is upbeat and soul filling will elevate your mood.

Another option is to listen to motivational talks from Zig Ziglar, Earl Nightingale, Tony Robbins, Jim Rohn, or anyone else who you feel has a positive and valuable message. Dr. Norman Vincent Peale, who wrote the book *The Power of Positive Thinking* in 1952, is a dynamic communicator in print and as a speaker. You might want to listen to him first thing in the morning.

TIP

So many good, positive voices of success are available in free or low-cost downloadable podcasts. I cut my teeth in an era when you bought cassette tapes to play in your car. I would wear them out I playing them so much, and I'd have to buy a new set. Today, it's easy to download positive messages and voices into your phone to improve your attitude and skill. There are no excuses that are reasonable to avoid this habit. As Jim Rohn used to say, "What is easy to do is also easy not to do."

Affirm, but don't live in delusion

It's important to set your mindset to positive. Try doing verbal affirmation statements. Affirmations said aloud can focus, sharpen, and set strong expectations of success for the future. Here are a few examples:

>> "I earn $100,000 a year."

>> "I will lose and release 30 pounds from my body in the next 6 months."

>> "I save money so I can have a vibrant, fulfilling retirement."

WARNING

But I would caution you about one thing: Don't affirm the ridiculous.

Affirmations, to be effective, need to be aspirationally real and relevant. For example, don't affirm in front of the mirror that my body is lean, toned, and at my ideal weight when in reality, I am 50 pounds overweight and in horrible condition. The audio of my voice does not remotely match the video of what I can see. You can state affirmations in future tense using "I will" or "I will in 6 months." The "I am" that is a country mile from the truth is easily rejected by your logical mind that sees the image staring back at you in the mirror.

Health and motivation are connected

As with so many things in life, the better you do, the better you feel. The motivation you create through doing well and feeling well helps you to continue the progress. When it comes to health and fitness, once you get the ball rolling with new habits and begin to see the slightest bit of progress, you'll have increased energy and motivation to keep up the good work. The positive results will begin to snowball, and we feel even better about ourselves.

If you want the science behind this greater feeling of well-being, here it is:

1. Our brain is flooded with dopamine and norepinephrine: These two neurotransmitters energize and stimulate our brain.

2. We also have increased endorphin levels. This is an endurance neurotransmitter.

3. Our serotonin levels increase. This is a make-me-feel-good neurotransmitter.

All these changes in our brain lead to a natural increase in our motivation level. We can even trigger these neurotransmitters through music, a motivational message, or a workout partner. When we are more motivated, we are more likely to follow through on the commitments that we have set for ourselves. We have a higher confidence level that we will achieve what we desire.

TIP

Most people have a drop in their motivation level or energy level in the afternoon. Plan for that drop in energy by putting your most important tasks earlier in the day when your energy levels are higher. Then have the right kind of snacks on hand to give yourself a nutritional boost. Avoid high-sugar junk food as your fuel source. The sugar rush you get won't last. Instead, have something natural and healthy, like fruit, nuts, raw veggies, low-fat cheese, or cottage cheese. We need high-quality fuel in the afternoon to keep our focus and motivation high.

Dealing with Health Events

We all have health events in our lives or the lives of loved ones that can derail or change our plans for success. Whether it's a disease that we contract unexpectedly or a mental health challenge like depression or drug dependency, there is almost no one that hasn't directly or indirectly dealt with health issues as they climb the mountain of success.

I guarantee that health events *will* happen to us all. There's no avoiding them. They will differ in their intensity and duration. The how or what to do will vary.

Additionally, I want to state that I have been dealing with health events that influence strategies, systems, and timelines of success for more than 50 years. What I can declare with the upmost confidence is that your goals don't have to change. You may simply have to change how you go about achieving them.

I learned this truth in observing my mother, who battled multiple sclerosis and all its physical effects for more than 40 years. The disease *never* changed the power of her mind or altered what she planned or wanted to do. In fact, the MS steeled her to a level of determination that was probably not previously there. She was determined to not be defined by the disease and instead was defined by what she accomplished.

Resetting expectations

When a health event strikes, whether it's a short-term illness or chronic condition like my Meniere's disease, you want to first address its influence on your life both long term and day to day. You might not be able to gauge things with 100-percent accuracy, but ask yourself these questions:

>> Is this going to affect the number of hours I can work?

>> Is this going to affect the number of days I can work?

>> Will there likely be a difference in my financial picture?

>> What financial costs will there be?

>> How will this affect my family?

>> How will this affect friendships and relationships at work?

>> What goals or objectives in the short run do I need to adjust or increase the timeline on?

Once you have collected the information from your physician, explored treatment options, seen a specialist if you needed to, and asked yourself these questions, you can then make adjustments to your timelines for goals and objectives.

The biggest change for me in my Meniere's disease has been my reduced travel schedule for speaking events. My old travel schedule of speaking in a new city and venue each day that I am the road is off the table. I can no longer take the stress of giving a talk in the morning, being on a flight in the afternoon or evening to another city, and then repeating the cycle the next day and throughout the week.

Ask yourself these questions each week to better focus and create powerful habits:

>> What can get accomplished in a week?

>> What is the new normal?

>> What's really important in my job that I do?

>> What are the most important goals?

>> What is most important to the well-being of my relationships?

When you are dealing with health events, it helps you to focus quickly on what is really important. It's amazing how much we can cut out that is peripheral in our lives, which allows us to reestablish reasonable margins. I call that finding the "white space" in our lives. If you notice on either side of this page, there is white space where you can make notes and draw arrows to key parts of the text. Life has a way, especially during health events, of removing the white space from our lives.

TIP

If you are dealing with a chronic condition, journal how you feel each day. Read how you feel in the morning, midday, and at the end of your workday. Also, journal what you eat and how that affects your energy and focus levels. Is your feeling of well-being cycle based on the day of the week or the day of the month?

I know this sounds a little out there, but journaling is very effective. Through the process of journaling and observation, I found that of all days, my severest vertigo episodes were on Mondays. They happened late in the afternoon between 4:00 p.m. and 6:00 p.m. I can't explain it, and neither can my doctors and specialists, except for stress. Once I understood the pattern, I began the habit of ending my Mondays at 2:30 p.m., which has eliminated the issue.

Creating new steps and measures to success

Frequently, we need to recalibrate our definition of success and what is truly important to our business, career, financial life, and family. Adversity and change are wonderful teachers that most of us would rather avoid. If we are to arrive at our desired goals, we need to ask ourselves these questions that relate to our better use of resources:

>> What amount of time am I wasting each day or week?

>> What activities am I doing to waste that time?

>> What amount of money am I spending unwisely?

>> What routine life maintenance items need to be removed?

These types of questions help you refine your daily and weekly resources you use to achieve success. As you evaluate, you might discover, for example, that you watch too many hours of TV. A few hours a week is entertainment; a few hours a night is wasted time.

We all have things that we waste money on. When I was diagnosed with Meniere's, I reviewed our family budget and found thousands of dollars we wasted monthly. By cutting out the waste, I increased savings, which helped us decrease our time needed to achieve complete financial independence.

I also removed some of the life maintenance tasks that I did too much of as a younger man. I removed hours a week out of my schedule mowing, weeding, and maintaining our yard. With our corrected family budget, I had plenty of money to spare to hire a yard guy. We can easily delegate house cleaning, yard work, grocery shopping, meal preparation, and laundry to someone who would be happy for a job. Doing so frees us up time to both accomplish more and rest more.

Stay focused toward success

As I've said earlier in the book, the act of intense focus always proceeds success. When balancing the health challenges with the achievement of success, it's easy to treat success as an event, or worse, as a destination. If I could only _____ . You fill in the blank: earn more money, feel better, take more time off, save more money, buy that bigger house. When we have the rug pulled out from under us, we become hyper-focused on the destination aspect of success.

Earl Nightingale has the best definition of success I have heard in my life: "Success is the progressive realization of a worthy goal or worthy ideal." The key element in this quote is the word *progressive*, which refers to the movement toward, not the arrival at, success. When dealing with a health event for you or a family member, you need to focus on answering these questions:

>> Are we moving and taking steps toward resolution or control of the health issue?

>> Are we still moving or taking steps toward the goals we have set that define our success?

Eat for Success

Diet or exercise? Which is more important for health and weight loss? Diet wins every time. Multiple times in this book, I refer to the 80/20 rule, and it applies when comparing diet and exercise options when you need to lose weight. The

80 percent is your diet, and the 20 percent is exercise. Rather than exclusively taking my word for it, let's do the math. As the saying goes, the path is in the math.

If you want to shed a single pound of fat, you need to achieve a 3,500-calorie deficit. That's the number most dieticians use. Let's shoot for losing a pound per week, so that's 3,500 calories divided by 7 days, so you need to have a calorie deficit of 500 calories per day. If you just exercised to burn 500 calories every day, you would be spending a lot of time working up a sweat. For example, a 150-pound person would have to run at a 10-minute-mile pace for around 45 minutes to burn 500 calories. And lower-intensity exercises require even more time to burn that many calories.

There's an easier way. You're better off eating less than exercising more. If you're eating 2,500 calories per day, cut back to 2,000 per day, which is still a lot, and you'll achieve a 3,500-calorie deficit each week. That's so much more doable (and much less painful) than running 45 minutes every day. Or cut your food intake by 400 calories and throw in some exercise to burn 100 calories. That's 80-percent diet and 20-percent exercise.

Let's look at a few fundamentals of eating:

>> **Track how much you eat.** It's no fun to count calories, but there are plenty of free smartphone apps available to log your meals, and tracking calorie intake requires just a few minutes per day. Get in the habit of using such an app for a minute or two after each meal. It's really easier than you think.

>> **Eat at regular intervals.** It's better for your body to get into a regular rhythm when eating meals. If you are inconsistent in eating, you can get too hungry. That extreme hunger causes you to eat more. Your blood sugar can also drop, so your cravings for a quick fix or sugar can intensify.

>> **Decide how much you will eat before mealtime.** The key is making a decision on what you are going to eat beforehand. Be sure it's aligned with your predetermined plan and strategy.

>> **Eat healthy snacks between your meals.** If you get the hunger pains or sense a drop in energy and cognition in the afternoon, then grab a small, healthy snack of nuts, fruit, hard-boiled egg, or even low-fat cheese.

>> **Drink water before every meal.** Our bodies need far more water than the typical person drinks. Drinking water will increase the sensation of being full. You will be more fully hydrated, so your body can more easily remove any toxins you ingest.

>> **Have your last meal or snack no later than 8:00 p.m.** This is the hard one for me. I frequently get hungry in the evening. I have to discipline myself to not eat after 8:00 p.m., especially when I get up in the middle of the night to write or read.

Avoiding the poisons

The excuse of not knowing that cigarettes and other tobacco products are unhealthy went out in the 1950s. Everyone knows the negative effects today. We have ten states where it's legal to smoke marijuana. Whether you believe the drug is a poison or not, the smoking of it leads to lung problems for certain. There are differing opinions on alcohol and especially red wine. Many heart experts suggest that a glass of red wine per day can be good for your heart. But drinking more than that offers no health benefits and leads to liver issues along with other physical problems, including obesity, as many alcoholic drinks are loaded with calories.

The most common poison we ingest is processed sugar and high fructose corn syrup. The explosion of processed sugar in our foods has added significant weight to our society and increased the rate of diabetes exponentially. It's literally a problem of epidemic proportions. Whether it's processed sugar or processed foods, we eat too many processed poisons in the United States.

Choosing the right foods

Our diet in the United States is *over-carbohydronated*. Now that's not a real word, but it should be. The bottom line is that we are consuming too many carbohydrates in our diet. Many experts agree that our diets are too high in carbs and don't have enough protein, fruits, and vegetables.

There are a number of excellent resources in the *Dummies* line of books about eating right. Here are just a few: *Nutrition For Dummies*, *Weight Loss Kit For Dummies*, and *Controlling Cholesterol For Dummies*. Any of these titles will get you on the path of healthy eating.

We all need to eat more clean, rich protein. Some excellent protein sources are fish, especially salmon, which is high in the right kind of omega-3 fatty acids. Poultry is another excellent choice for rich protein with low fat. There are excellent sources of lean protein from game meat such as venison, elk, and bison. Steer beef is higher in fat than other types of red meat, but it's still is a valid source of protein in moderation. Using nuts to supplement your protein needs is also a good option.

Eating ample helpings of fruits and vegetables is key to your personal daily diet. There is no such thing as eating too many green vegetables. For most of us, it's a matter of finding some items we like and deciding on a low-fat and flavorful way to prepare them. Green vegetables are the gold standard, so try to eat lettuce, spinach, celery, cucumbers, peppers, kale, collard greens, green beans, peas, or broccoli. There are enough options, so if you are like President George Bush, you can swear off broccoli for the rest of your life and be just fine.

Fueling your most important muscle

Our heart works overtime every day to pump oxygen and nutrients to the cells in our body. It never takes a break. That level of sustained effort demands our full attention to fuel it well. Besides the aforementioned green vegetables, what are some of the foods that are heart healthy?

>> **Whole grains and especially oatmeal:** The higher the quality and the lower the processing of whole grains the better. Oatmeal has been proven, when eaten regularly, to lower your LDL cholesterol (the "bad" cholesterol) and reduce heart disease.

>> **Berries, and especially blueberries:** All berries are rich in antioxidants, which reduce inflammation of the heart and prevent the development of heart disease. And Dr. Oz swears by them. What more could you want?

>> **Almonds, walnuts, and seeds:** There are better things to do with chia seeds than put them on your chia pet. They are rich in fiber and omega-3 fatty acids. Adding nuts and seeds can increase protein in your diet, and they make a great snack.

>> **Olive oil, rather than other oils:** Olive oil is rich in monosaturated fatty acids. It's packed with antioxidants.

>> **Dark chocolate:** Studies have indicated a connection between eating dark chocolate and lower rates of heart disease. Plus, who doesn't love chocolate?

Enjoying your food

Food is made to fuel our bodies, but it should also be enjoyed. We were designed to taste food and enjoy the texture of it. The combining of flavors, coupled with wine or beer, can create a memorable evening of enjoyment. We can use meals to create a sense of well-being, deepen our relationships, and strengthen family connections. Gathering for a great meal lowers our stress levels. All these pathways converge in success. The key is moderation in everything we put in our bodies for fuel and enjoyment of life.

Let's Get Physical

We all require some amount of movement to maintain our level of health, stamina, and cognition. The population in the United States has become too sedentary. There are incredible benefits to being physical. Let's check out a few:

>> Regular exercise will improve your sleep and mental alertness.

>> Physical activity can reduce stress and increase your energy levels.

>> Exercise reduces the typical aches and pains of the back, shoulders, and neck.

>> Being physical reduces weight and increases stamina.

>> Regular exercise increases our feelings of achievement and improves productivity.

>> Participating in exercise regimens allows us to set concrete goals: run faster, bike farther, lift more weight, or hike a new trail. Working to achieve those goals causes us to develop successful habits.

Exercise does not have to be drudgery

I have to admit, getting on the treadmill is not really my cup of tea. Walking on a belt going nowhere is, in my book, boring. If that was my only option, it would be drudgery. In order to be consistent in exercise, you have to find people, equipment, and types of exercise that you look forward to.

There are so many options that are available in the gym or fitness facility or just in the plain outdoors. Even playing golf is a reasonable level of exercise if you walk rather than ride a golf cart. The typical golf course is 6,500 yards. That's just short of 4 miles for 18 holes if you only walked in straight lines from tee to green. Even the best of golfers hit the ball left or right of center. Tiger Woods might be walking closer to 4 miles, but the average golfer like me is going to walk more than 5 miles (and lose a few balls along the way).

You have to decide what exercise type would be enjoyable and even fun. I am best when I mix in some competitive games in my exercise routine. I played the professional racquetball tour for about four years. I cut my teeth on one-on-one competition. I don't play racquetball anymore because I would certainly not be as good as I once was, so I play squash instead. It's a better workout aerobically. My heart rate is more sustained because the rallies are longer than in racquetball. My competitive juices still flow, and my heart gets strengthened all at once.

When it comes to exercise, there is no right or wrong, only right or wrong for you. Know what motivates thyself.

Using common sense

Before your motivation gets way ahead of your current physical condition, check with a few experts. Start by going to get a complete physical from your physician. Then discuss what an appropriate exercise program might be for you given your present physical condition and goals.

At least see a personal trainer to have them design an exercise program that encompasses both cardio and resistance training. If you feel the need for an extra push, hire them for a handful of sessions to get your started. They can teach you the right techniques for lifting weights so that you can avoid injury and work your muscles more effectively. You might even enjoy the experience of having a coach and continue working with them.

Common sense in an exercise routine comes from two primary things: We must find a good balance and then listen to our bodies. We need to balance our time so that we can accomplish fitness as well as our other goals in life. We have to find the balance between good, sensible exercise levels and not overdoing things to the point where we injure ourselves, especially when instituting a new routine. Our body tells us when we overextend by being too sore and taking longer than normal to recover. When that happens, give yourself time to rest.

Creating a sustainable program

The key to good health through exercise is not accomplished in a day, a week, or a month. It's the consistency of activity for a series of months. Once you get that far down the road, you have established new habits and a new lifestyle. Here are a few final tips on exercise:

>> **It has to be enjoyable or fun.** You won't always feel like grinding it out. There will be days you don't feel like doing it. Create an environment of fun and variety in your exercise routine.

>> **Exercise enough times per week.** Most people need to see results in their exercise regimen. To achieve progress and results, we have to exercise four times per week. Five is better. Think about it this way: If you went out this afternoon and ran 10 miles, but then you wait another week and run another 10, would you see significant health benefits? Not really. If you took those same 10 miles but ran 2 miles per day for 5 days and then repeated that

routine next week, would the health benefits be more? It's the same 10 miles per week. I think we all know the answer.

>> **Develop specific exercise habits.** You need to create a routine, like doing the activity of your choosing every morning before work. Or you can skip lunches at work and go for a walk or run. Or make appointments with your buddies to meet regularly at the gym. Physical activity has to be a part of your schedule, just like picking up the kids from school or attending your weekly status meeting at work.

Rest Is Required

I have come to realize that rest has an important role in our lives. We all need rest to help us recharge our emotional and physical batteries. You can't always run your car's engine at really high rpms before you have a major failure. The same is true with humans. The action of just resting is sometimes the most productive thing you can do. Ask yourself these questions:

>> What amount of rest do you need each day?

>> How long can you work in a day before you hit the wall?

>> How many days off do you need per week?

>> What activities allow you to rest and recharge well?

Find your rhythm

I discovered my rhythm a number of years ago through monitoring my energy levels and stamina. I hit a wall at about 13 weeks without taking an extended break. I could maintain a high productivity pace for 13 weeks with weekends off. When I hit 13 weeks, my energy, effectiveness, and intensity drop like a rock, and fast. If I was out for 15 or 16 weeks from my last vacation or break, I was a shell of my former productive self. I might be at the office in body, but my mind, energy, and especially intensity were all lacking.

In this discovery, I tracked how many days off I needed to recharge fully. I found out it wasn't a full week but 5 days. That was enough time off for me to come back rested, recharged, and raring to go.

We all have a rhythm to our energy levels and ideal work patterns. I know you might not be able to take off that amount of time from your job, but you do need to know your personal rhythm of life. You might be able to go at higher intensity for longer and need less downtime than I do. My 13 weeks shouldn't be your benchmark. The most important thing is for you to discover your unique pattern.

Sleep is all it's cracked up to be

We all require a certain amount of sleep. Our bodies are actually hard at work when we are sleeping. The brain is creating essential chemicals; muscles repair themselves after the stress of exercise. We all have responsibilities and deadlines that sometimes require us to burn the candle at both ends. For example, as I write this chapter, it's 11:38 p.m., about two hours past my normal bedtime.

We all have different levels of sleep required for our health and well-being. If we deprive ourselves of our proper amount of sleep for a few nights, or even a few weeks, we open ourselves up to sickness. We are more fatigued and prone to mistakes and errors. Our energy level is reduced, and our irritability is increased.

REMEMBER

Certainly, you should have a consistent daily rhythm of going to bed and waking up at the same time. The avenue to success and success habits is through consistency of routine.

I am certainly looking forward to tomorrow when I will be back to my normal routine. Goodnight!

Chapter **8**

Developing the Right Mental Attitude

There is no doubt that positive thinking and a positive mental attitude can carry you a long way in life. The right attitude can speed up the process to success in your endeavors. Your attitude can make the obstacles and challenges you encounter more manageable and even turn them into blessings. Being able to turn the lemons of life into lemonade can only happen through a positive attitude.

But having a positive attitude isn't everything when it comes to achieving success. To transform your life, you need to apply a positive attitude to proper habits like working hard, controlling spending, increasing your knowledge and value, and focusing on relationship building. In my experience, more people lose their job due to a poor attitude than lack of skills, errors, or poor work ethic.

Our attitude affects many people around us. At work, it can affect your company and coworkers and influence your clients and customers to appreciate your service and want to do more business with you. Your family and key relationships in life also benefit from your positive attitude. People who have less than a positive attitude in life tend to have a small a circle of friends or none at all. We've all met those people. They also have more problems with their health and mental well-being. So developing a positive mental attitude has countless benefits.

Determining to Be Positive

My belief is that attitude is certainly a decision that one makes. In fact, it's a decision of habit that can be made in spite of circumstances, hardship, and present challenges facing us.

There are at least two points of view for every day and every encounter we have in life. The easiest way to observe life is through the lens of being pessimistic versus being optimistic. Pessimists, when facing situations, look for the difficulty. When an opportunity or change confronts them, they focus on the challenges they are facing. Optimists encounter those same difficulties and they see opportunity. They are encouraged to try to make something good happen in their life or in their business.

REMEMBER

A problem is merely the exterior wrapping to an opportunity. Do we want to focus on the wrapping or what lies inside the wrapping?

Setting your personal thermostat to positive each morning

You start each day with a clean slate, and you get to decide what's written on it. When you wake up in the morning, your first action should be deciding to have a positive attitude. You don't need to make the commitment to have the positive attitude all day. What you have to do is create the habit each day that your attitude will start out positive.

REMEMBER

Creating a positive attitude is both a decision you make and a process you create.

Let me share a process or series of habits I use to set my thermostat to positive.

Step 1: Make a plan

Each night before I go to bed, I organize the goals, objectives, and projects that I need to accomplish the following day. I make sure to prioritize based on importance and value. I then ask myself, "How deep into my list can I realistically get?" Setting reasonable levels of accomplishment for a single day feeds our well-being, feelings of accomplishment, and self-esteem.

By setting my goals, I also engage my subconscious mind to work on my list while I sleep. While I am resting, my subconscious mind is hard at work figuring out solutions to tomorrow's problems and challenges. There are times when I wake up in the morning and the solution to one of my problems slaps me on the head. Other times, my sleep is interrupted by a solution in the middle of the night. I then get up immediately to write it down so that I don't forget it and can implement it in the morning.

Step 2: Start your day with gratitude

Establish the habit of being grateful for what you do have in life. We all are more fortunate than countless others in life. You may be struggling to make ends meet and keep a roof over your family's head. It may seem like you have nothing to be grateful for at the present moment. If you can create a habit of writing two or three things down you are grateful for each day, it can turn the mental tide from negative to positive in short order.

Step 3: Create and review positive affirmations

The words that we speak to others and speak to ourselves matter. When we use positive words of affirmation out loud, we can raise our attitude, enthusiasm, and belief in positive outcomes to our day, week, and life. How we feel can rule what we do, so start each day programming how you feel to the positive side.

You can't change your mindset from negative to positive without changing your negative talk to positive self-talk. Here are some examples of affirmations:

>> "I have vibrant, valuable, and meaningful relationships in my life."

>> "I discipline myself to take actions that I need to do when I need to do them."

>> "I have 86,400 seconds to use today. I will use them well to accomplish great things."

>> "I will earn $_____ this week."

Here's an affirmation I got from Zig Ziglar years ago that's fantastic: "I clearly understand that if I develop yearning power and apply learning power, I will increase my earning power."

Create your own affirmations based on your goals, objectives, and desires for your life. Focus them on habits, attributes, and actions you desire to take today and every day. If you want to really ramp up their power, stand in front of a mirror and say them aloud. You are combining the audio of hearing them with the visual confirmation of seeing yourself say them.

Step 4: Use focused meditation or prayer

Being able to draw from a source more powerful than yourself in the early morning pulls you to positive. I know personally, when I pray, there is a calmness that comes over me. Anxiety and apprehension are reduced. The feeling of calmness turns into confidence knowing that God is on my side; that God is larger than the problems and challenges I may encounter. And then I realize that I don't have anything to be anxious about.

Personal happiness is a decision

Being personally happy is a decision that we make for ourselves. The habit of choosing to be happy in circumstances and situations is powerful. Most of us base our happiness on having what we want, so not having what we desire causes unhappiness. That approach allows emotions to control too large a portion of our lives. Not everything is going to go your way, and you're never going to have everything you want, so does that mean you're going to allow yourself to be unhappy? The vast majority of people equate happiness with a level of financial achievement: the larger home, more exclusive address, luxury car, fancy trip to Europe, and so forth. I must admit that I have fallen into that trap as well.

The balance of contentment and complacency

I personally feel that happiness is achieved in the proper balance between contentment and complacency. We are created to strive, seize, learn, advance, and grow. That's why you are reading this book. You desire to grow your life and self beyond where you are presently, whether that increased success is personal, relational, professional, financial, or all of the above. We were created for growth and improvement. When we stop growing, and we have that choice, we wither away.

How tall does a tree try to grow? That's an interesting question. A tree tries to grow as tall as it can. It tries to shoot down its roots as deep as it can. It tries to absorb as much water and sunlight as it can. A tree innately has only one choice: to be all it can be given the sun, rain, and soil it encounters. As humans, we have the choice. A tree does not. We can choose to be less than we were created to be. We can become complacent; trees don't have that option.

But you can find a balance between complacency and contentment. The need to strive to be more, improve, and grow as large as we can in life is innately wired into us. And we also must achieve contentment, or happiness, in the present place that we are rooted. We want to find the joy we can experience in life right now, today, based on where we are with the knowledge of being still short of our more successful self in the future.

ANECDOTE

At this point in my life, I am personally working on being content while raising two teenagers. And it's the first time as a parent when I really needed to search for happiness and contentment. It was easy when they toddlers. The world was opening up to them. They had a desire to learn from Mom and Dad. In fact, we were likely the smartest people they knew at that time, and they treated us that way as well. Now, if you asked them, we are likely the dumbest people they know. Did we gain more ignorance and lose brain cells in the last decade? Finding joy and happiness in this phase of the teenage years is one of my daily prayers and desires.

Do something daily for your happiness

Doing something for others creates wonderful feelings of happiness. Giving to someone else is one of the purest forms of happiness you can enjoy. The saying, "It's better to give than receive," is very true for personal happiness. Creating the habit of doing selfless acts for others moves us all toward personal happiness.

TIP

Taking small actions of happiness for ourselves can help us recharge so that we can do more for others. Even though you might have a deadline that you've been grinding toward, when the sun comes out, take a 15-minute break to go enjoy the sun's warmth on your face. Treat yourself to your favorite coffee beverage. Schedule a manicure or pedicure later this week as a celebration of completing your task and hitting the deadline.

Rewarding yourself with a few minutes of rest, a walk outside, listening to your favorite music, or eating a type of food you thoroughly enjoy connects you to the feelings of happiness and pleasure. Most of us are so busy working to help and serve others that we forget to take care of ourselves.

Cultivating Your Self-Esteem

Your self-esteem and self-image will determine how you handle the opportunities and challenges of life. The belief in yourself, your achievement, and your success is what kicks in when times are tough. We all will encounter turbulent waters as we sail for our different success ports of call. We create our self-image through our personal evaluation and experiences. Self-esteem comes from past experiences: success, failures, triumphs, and defeats. Our self-image is formed throughout our life but especially through early childhood experiences. These experiences create a picture of ourselves that we believe to be true. What we believe could even be false, but we create actions and habits as if what is false were true.

How clear goals increase your self-esteem

Being clear about your desires in life increased the likelihood that you will achieve them. The process of clarifying your desires into smaller goals or steps creates the ability to measure, shrink, and reward our small actions and habits that lead to greater success. For most of us, the more positive things we accomplish, no matter how small, increase our self-esteem.

Think of a child who's been given the small task to make her bed in the morning. With the bed made, the completed task gives her a sense of accomplishment and room orderliness. As she goes about the rest of her day playing, that made bed is there as a constant reminder of a completed goal. In that small way, she achieved success.

As adults, we frequently fail to break our goals and objectives into small steps that can fuel our feelings of self-esteem and self-image. For more on the power of goal setting and a system for goal setting, turn to Chapter 5.

Setting clear standards and values

To increase your self-image, you have to determine what is most important, and you have to know how to measure its value. That's a critical habit of success.

Ask yourself, what attributes do I value? And what values are most important to achieve success? Is it integrity, creativity, perseverance, ingenuity, discipline, or even courage?

What do you stand for in your life? For example, maybe a standard or value you hold dear is being courageous, which is certainly a priceless commodity. Aristotle said, "A truly courageous person is not someone who never feels fear, but who fears the right thing, at the right time, in the right way." Being courageous, no matter the circumstances you encounter, means knowing that you are never out of options and choices. You know that you can control the outcome of whatever situation you are in. You recognize and accept personal responsibility for your future success.

If you value creativity, then what areas do you wish to develop? Is creativity more in the beauty and harmony of your surroundings? Do you want to create aesthetically pleasing homes and work spaces? Are you more creative in the kitchen creating meals for your family? Do you wish to produce works of art on canvas? Or do you channel your creativity into inventing items that solve problems.

ANECDOTE

I had a neighbor, Bob, who was an inventor. He was amazingly creative man who invented thousands of products. He invented the mood ring in the 1970s, and that invention morphed into the test strip that's included in packages of alkaline batteries. He licensed that technology to a guy in Australia who used it in underwear, calling them mood panties.

If you are a company owner or entrepreneur, what is it that your company stands for? What is important for you and your staff to deliver to your customers? What values or standards would you hold onto even if it became a competitive disadvantage to do so? That's a wonderful question to ponder as you uncover your true values in business. What principles are you willing to hold fast to even if doing so might put you at a disadvantage?

Create and replay success experiences

Our ability to replay our experiences of the last day, week, month, or six months leads to increased success and mid-course corrections. Ask yourself questions like these:

>> What have I achieved today?

>> Did I do as much as I expected?

>> What's important for me to achieve before the week ends?

>> How did I do this week on a scale of 1–10?

>> Why did I give myself that score?

>> What changes do I need to make to guarantee an 8 next week?

You might be thinking, why an 8? Why not a 10? That's a valid question because we all want the highest score. My personal belief regarding success is that if you can link 8s together week after week, if you can mix in a 9 or a 10 every once in a while, you will have a grand and successful life.

The average batting average in major league baseball is .248. That means that in two and a half times out of 10 at bats, the hitter is successful at getting on base with a hit. The average salary is in excess of 4 million dollars per year for being unsuccessful three times out of four. Achieving an 8 out of 10 puts you in a rarified success group. It's also realistic to set that standard so that you don't lose momentum and motivation by setting your standards too high.

We also need to ask ourselves, "What could I have achieved that I didn't?" Asking an honest personal inventory question leads to improvement. Would greater preparation have made a difference? Would more discipline have made a difference? What can I do to achieve my goals that I am not doing? What things do I need to work on that I am not presently working on?

We all have victories in life that we can hold on to and reuse to fuel our desire, resolve, and persistency. Those experiences, whether they are in childhood or adulthood, can be powerful tools that increase our confidence and self-image. What experiences have you had that created an indelible impact on you? Did you have a comeback in life against long odds to claim victory? Has someone shared with you how meaningful and important a role you played in their success in life? Did you ever agonize over a decision to finally take a leap of faith in yourself and it turned out better than you imagined?

We all need these signature stories of success to feed our self-esteem, confidence, and courage in moments when we are discouraged, down, or apprehensive. When you hit the search button in your mind, you don't want to get the wheel of death as your mind grinds to a halt. You want your mind to immediately pull up memories of your successes.

Comparison for Encouragement

All human beings compare from a very young age. I remember the arguments when I was little between my brothers when we would compare who received the bigger slice of cake. My mother solved that problem this way: One kid got to cut the cake while the other two compared the sizes of the slices and selected. The guy who cut selected last. In our home, eventually no one wanted to cut because of the pressure to do so evenly was immense, or so we thought at the time.

When it comes to comparisons, I have failed countless times. My failure was in not using it as a source of encouragement of what is possible, but to focus on the gap — the gap between what someone else possessed and what I had. Too frequently, I used it as a club against myself, bludgeoning my psyche with questions like "Why wasn't I earning more?" or "Why don't I have more in life?" That is completely the wrong approach when comparing yourself to others, and I will freely admit my folly.

Stay positive in comparison

When people other than yourself accomplish anything in life, your attitude has to be this: They proved that it can be done. Further, it proves that it can be done by almost anyone.

Most successful people aren't exceptional or extraordinary. I wouldn't say that I am exceptional or extraordinary. Most successful people are ordinary people executing ordinary success habits and principles extraordinarily well. The *execution* is what must be extraordinary in achieving success.

You don't have to invent Facebook or design a Tesla to be successful. You can be a teacher and be extremely successful because you have always wanted to be a teacher. People who are successful are people who are living out their lives in the manner that they have decided in advance to live them out.

Observe others for inspiration, for clues on the pathway to success. Be a keen observer of both success and failure because they are both good teachers.

We will all be used in comparison by others. Comparison is an inevitable happening of life. We will all be in either the example column or in the warning column. Being in the example column means "Do what this person has done to achieve success." The warning column, of course, means "Don't do what this person's done because it leads to failure and brokenness."

Compare based on your goals

We want to use comparison for encouragement and to stretch ourselves and our goals to think bigger. We all can accomplish more than we typically believe. The true questions in thinking bigger are these: Why do you want it? How important is it to you? What are you willing to trade to acquire it? What price are you willing to pay?

The black hole that's easy to fall into is not being clear about what you want. Our society rewards the beautiful people who have the outward appearance of beauty and wealth. According to the American Society of Plastic Surgeons, there are 7,430 board-certified plastic surgeons in the United States. They did 17.5 million cosmetic procedures last year. That's a whole lot of beauty enhancement. Enhancing your visual image may be one of your goals. If it makes you feel better and it's truly one of your goals (not an attempt to keep up with others), then that is a worthy goal for you.

I have to admit that I have fallen into the comparison trap of houses, wealth, lifestyle, and cars many times and changed my goals to keep up with the Joneses. It's easy to do in our consumer-oriented, more-is-better society. My best advice is to create your plan and work your plan. Use comparison to encourage you to what is possible, and don't use it as a scorecard of where you are in competition with others.

Someone will always have more

It's absolutely true that someone will always have more than you. The current wealthiest person in the world is Jeff Bezos, who founded Amazon. But that will most likely not be the case in a few years. The wealthiest person changes every few years. Whatever your scorecard of success is — money, cars, houses, children, friends — there will always be someone who has acquired more than you have in this game.

Your journey to success is uniquely you. You get to define it by deciding what actions you need to take and what habits you need to develop (and be consistent with) to achieve it. How do you want to be remembered when you're gone? That is all ultimately your decision and your pursuit.

WARNING

It's very easy to slip out of a positive attitude when you are pursing someone else's dreams and goals. When you compare yourself and are further behind someone else in the game of success, it can turn your attitude negative, and that can increase the gap between that person and yourself. Don't go there.

Developing the Habit of Personal Reward

Being able to connect your attitude and protect your attitude can be accomplished through incentives and rewards. Anyone who is working to achieve greater success will have setbacks, frustrations, and moments where their attitude slips. We all can feel like we are swimming in a large bowl of oatmeal with little hope of reaching the other side. As we swim through the muck, we need to recognize and be rewarded in the progress and completion of our accomplishments.

Giving yourself daily, weekly, and even monthly rewards can create a powerful draw to your success habits and the execution of those habits. The annual, or even quarterly, reward is too far out and out of touch with the challenging day where you feel like an attitude adjustment is required. It's hard to connect the daily habits of success (which can be difficult to maintain at times) with the annual goals or lifetime goals we have set.

When setting more short-term rewards like, for example, daily rewards, the key is to both balance the excitement for the reward with the budget you can afford. Establishing inexpensive or no-cost rewards are advisable: an hour of free time, a 30-minute walk outside in the sun, a favorite beverage or meal. Those are all reasonable rewards that are unlikely to break the budget if you end up rewarding yourself a few days a week.

The weekly reward can be a little costlier but doesn't have to be. You can reward yourself with an afternoon at the beach or permission to binge-watch a few of your favorite TV shows. Another weekly reward could be pampering yourself with a massage or evening out at one of your favorite restaurants. The more connected the reward is, the sooner it is enjoyed, and the more it influences our attitude, perseverance, and passions.

A monthly reward for positive attitude and results can be more substantial yet. Allow yourself an additional day off for pleasure and enjoyment. A weekend away with your spouse or significant other can do wonders for your attitude. While it's unlikely you can reward yourself this way each and every month, it is possible to achieve a standard of success every other month or even once a quarter.

The best part of this process of reward is that you are in control. You can make up and use whatever incentives feel right to you. Your goal is to keep your attitude in high gear so that you focus on conquering your problems, creating wonderful opportunities to experience greater success.

Chapter 9

Tapping into Your Spiritual Side

We all would agree that life is comprised of at least three areas: the physical part, the mental part, and the spiritual part. But many of us ignore the spirituality that is inside of us, and unfortunately, we tread through life without developing and refining our spiritual gifts.

The development of our spirituality is one of the great journeys of life. It can bring great joy as well as sorrow. We can be comforted by it and frustrated by it depending on the day. It can enhance our relationships and add meaning, or it can drive a wedge between people who are close. You might be asking, why then would it make sense for me to tap into spirituality when it can cause such diverging outcomes?

I think that's a valid question. I might answer it by saying that we don't want to ignore a major part of our true self. In the achievement of success, you have to risk putting yourself out there. To receive the yang in life, or the good, you have to take the risk that the yin could show up as well. For us to experience joy, we have to risk sorrow.

We Are All Spiritual Beings

Wherever you are on your spiritual journey is okay with me. There is absolutely zero judgement, preaching, or condemnation in my heart, mind, or spirit as I write this. There is no moral high ground I am attempting to stake out in your mind. I hope that you evaluate my thoughts and ideas as they are meant to be, which is guiding, thought provoking, and respectful. I am merely a fellow traveler in this journey of life and legacy, someone who desires to fully develop himself spiritually and find truth for my life.

I believe we are each on our own individual journey to spiritual fulfillment and spiritual purpose. You may have been exposed to your spiritual side early in life and didn't understand it. Perhaps it was confusing or didn't line up with the beliefs about yourself and the world. People can close off their spiritual side because the world isn't as black and white as it might seem. There are certainly plenty of religions in our world that passionately feel that their beliefs are right, true, and the only pathway to spiritual fulfillment. Many have competing doctrine and dogma. The question isn't who is right or who is wrong. The question you need to answer is this: What is right or wrong for me?

There is an element in my spiritual pursuit that requires faith. We can see the beauty all around us in our world. We can see and experience the sun, the mountains, the grassy fields, the wildflowers, and the mammoth trees. We can see the power of the oceans, rivers, and lakes. We can have faith that this beauty around us is a random act of nature that exploded into being in one concise moment. Others can believe through faith that a Creator orchestrated this beauty as part of a master plan. Each of those beliefs requires a level of faith no matter your conclusion.

The development of your personal faith and spiritual beliefs is one of the incredible journeys of life. The twist and turns are better than any John Grisham novel. While there are many different belief systems in our world, I respect all beliefs and people's right to choose and exercise their own beliefs in a way that enhances their life.

I was raised in the Christian faith. As a practicing Christian, who is not perfect by any means, I will speak as broadly or inclusively as possible. I fully disclose my faith to you upfront to establish a clear understanding of where my values and principles are founded. There will be times when I express things in language based on my own faith and use the Bible as a source in this chapter. But I refer to the Bible not to proselytize but merely to use examples to support my conviction that developing your spirituality will increase your success in life. Please feel free to substitute specific terminology that you find more comfortable.

What do you believe in?

Our world is full of belief systems, spirituality groups, and religions with different histories, dogma, and doctrine. The separating question is, what do you believe? How does that belief connect with other people of spiritual faith? Do you believe there is a higher power? Do you believe in a Creator of the universe? Is that higher power benevolent, caring, and loving?

What are the rules and principles that guide your life? What were you taught at a young age that you still believe? Do you believe in the Golden Rule (which I cover later in this chapter in the section "Use the Golden Rule as a spiritual base")? Do you have a belief in karma, the principle that what goes around comes around? Do you have a foundational belief in right and wrong? Do you feel there is a need for atonement or forgiveness?

Some of us are still just seeking, and we don't know what to believe. There is nothing wrong with being a seeker. In fact, having a curious or seeking personality is a clear advantage in becoming successful. A principle of success most of us have heard is "Seek and ye will find." To find and know what you believe in, you must first be a seeker and questioner before you become a finder. In my studies of ancient text, God is not offended by a seeker. In fact, he welcomes the seeker. I realize that might be contrary to how some people perceive God, but it's true. I know many people in my lifetime who have honest questions and doubts about the existence of God. To even ask for God to reveal his presence and existence is a valid thought or question for a seeker.

Consider this basic prayer:

> God (or if that word doesn't connect with you, say "whoever you are"), I don't know if you really exist, but my prayer is, if you do, that you would reveal yourself to me clearly and definitely that I might personally know you.

Alcoholics Anonymous teaches its members to find "a God of their understanding" so that they can pray to whomever or whatever. The simplicity of this approach should not be lost. The objective of this prayer isn't deep spirituality, certainty, commitment, belief, or even faith that you will receive an answer. What you are doing through this prayer is opening yourself up to the possibility of a God or higher power revealing itself to you. It may be a dynamic encounter you have had before, or not. This is the ultimate act of seeking so that you can find spiritual truth.

Developing and expressing your faith

To be able to live out faith, we have to define faith. The dictionary offers numerous definitions:

1. A devotion to duty or a person

2. A belief and trust in and loyalty to God

3. Belief in the doctrines of religion

4. Firm belief even in the absence of proof

I think all of these definitions are interesting to consider as you make your journey to success and spiritual growth.

We can certainly be devoted to and faithful to a cause or person. When I married Joan, my wife, 29 years ago, I had faith based on my devotion to her and the commitment that I made to "forsake all others." I believe it was my duty that day and each day "until death do us part." I also stated that same commitment in the presence of God, as well as all others that attended our wedding.

Your faith also can be rooted in the trust and loyalty you have in God as expressed in the second definition. This is clearly faith for many who exercise their spirituality. Some take that faith to a narrower gate of belief in their specific religion (the third definition), such as being Shiite or Sunni Muslims, Orthodox or Reformed Jews, or Catholic, Methodist, or Baptist Christians, to name a few.

My perspective is that the fourth definition is the most inclusive definition of faith for all of us to embrace: Faith is the firm belief even in the absence of proof. I cannot tangibly prove that God exists, just as someone who is an atheist cannot tangibly prove that God does not exist. Both of us are acting on the faith we have of existence or non-existence in our lives. Faith is something we live out every day of our lives. If I didn't have faith that I wouldn't be in an automobile accident upon leaving my house, I would be a recluse at home. When you buy a United States–issued bond, it clearly states that it is backed by the full faith and credit of the United States. Why U.S. bonds are revered the world over as low-risk investments is because of the faith and credit of the United States government. You wouldn't feel the same way about a bond that was backed by the full faith and credit of Greece or Venezuela.

REMEMBER

In developing your faith, you are developing or improving your relationship with your beliefs, or higher power, or God. And a successful life is about relationships.

In my case, my faith has allowed me to develop my relationship with Jesus Christ. I believe in relationship, not a specific religion. My relationship with Jesus Christ is what matters, not a church building, denomination, church membership, ritual, dogma, doctrine, or even my works (works as defined by good deeds). Christianity isn't a set of rules, or dos and don'ts, to follow and check off. It is not a percentage of time that I need to be good, right, and just to be admitted to heaven. It is the development of a more personal relationship with my Creator, who actually wants to have that deeper relationship with me. How amazing is that?

Improving Your Success by Developing Your Spirituality

You have likely heard the term *spiritual wealth.* Many experts have expressed that spiritual wealth is more valuable than financial wealth. Sir John Templeton, the famous banker, fund manager, and philanthropist, describes spiritual wealth this way: "If we have not developed a reservoir of spiritual wealth, no amount of money is likely to make us happy. Spiritual wealth provides faith. It gives us love. It brings and expands wisdom. Spiritual wealth leads to happiness because it guides us into useful or loving relationships. With spiritual wealth as the foundation and security for our lives, we gain a deep and abiding peace that can't be obtained with material wealth alone."

Money Magazine calls Sir John Templeton "arguably the greatest global stock picker of the century." He obviously had more financial wealth than all of us writing or reading this book. He found spiritual wealth a worthy life pursuit. I believe that Sir John Templeton is correct in his view, regardless of your religious beliefs.

Learn to forgive

People who develop their spiritual side have to develop more faith as well. It's true that people who lack faith frequently carry more resentment, anger, hurt, and fear. We all have been wronged by other people in life. Some of these hurtful experiences come from people who clearly love us, and other negative experiences come from our enemies. If we carry these feelings around and store them for easy recall, reliving the burden and weight of those feelings of resentment and hurt can be overwhelming. Over time, we can turn ourselves into very unhappy people who lack peace of mind and joy in our lives.

The development of your spiritual side through forgiveness is a significant part of your spiritual growth. The mindset, focus, and act of forgiveness are not religious, although most religions have very profound teachings on forgiveness. When we fail to forgive, we are choosing to hold onto and retain that anger, frustration, and bitterness inside of us. It's doing a lot more damage to your peace of mind, soul, and physical body than the person that wronged you. The act of forgiveness enables you to release those feelings and frustrations. It enables you to move past them to focus on more meaningful pursuits in your life.

Find comfort in faith

For me, my faith gives me comfort knowing that God is in control. There is a security I feel in my heart and soul that no matter what I am experiencing, God wants the best for me. I know that my God is bigger and more powerful than any problem or challenge that I am experiencing or will ever experience, and that the ultimate solution doesn't rest 100 percent on my shoulders.

But I'm not saying that I feel that "fate" holds all the cards. There are decisions and actions I take that influence outcomes, both positive and negative. The philosophy of "whatever happens, happens" is a little too fatalistic for my tastes. Our journey through life includes an element of personal choices and personal responsibility.

I am confident in my relationship with my Creator that when my strength and faith is running on empty, He is just getting started with a full tank. I believe that His vast storehouses of knowledge and resources far exceed mine in the present and future. My success in my spiritual life can be attributed in part to this truth: All things work together for the good. Now that doesn't mean that each and every thing that will happen to you will be good. If you've lived a day, you know this isn't true. There will always be bad things that happen to good people. There will be unexplainable happenings or unfair and unjust outcomes. What I am expressing is that if we have faith, a spiritual grounding, we can recognize that all events of our lives will be combined in a grand combination of good, and that also requires faith.

The Apostle Paul, who wrote 13 books included in the modern-day Bible, was temporarily blinded, imprisoned multiple times, shipwrecked three times, bitten by a poisonous snake, beaten, stoned, and ultimately executed. All those events are likely to pale in comparison to any bad things that have happened, or will happen, to us. Paul says in Romans 8:28, "And we know that in all things, God works for the good of those who love him, who have been called according to his purpose." What an amazing spiritual perspective of faith and comfort.

I know what I believe in, and I know where my faith resides. What can you draw on in times of crises that bring you comfort? Is it being in nature? Is it the sound of the ocean or the tranquility of the mountains? Do you have a favorite spot that brings you peace and comfort? Is it surrounding yourself with family and friends? Is it just being alone in solitude?

FAITH AND OUR JOURNEY TO BECOME PARENTS

Joan and I had desperately wanted to be parents. For years, we did what we thought was right in praying for, preparing for, and trying to conceive a child. The "trying" part I will admit was fun at times. The rest was anguish most of the time. We miraculously conceived but only to experience the heartbreak of miscarriage. It was difficult to hold onto the understanding that all things work together for good.

When the miracle of adopting Wesley in fewer than 24 hours happened (and we weren't even in the adoption process), we had renewed faith. Now all those years of "being barren" without child made some sense. It didn't erase the hardship, but it did provide comfort, perspective, and praise. We had a deeper sense of gratitude, humility, and faith.

When we decided a few years later to adopt a girl to complete our family, we encountered the emotional wringer of two failed adoptions. In one case, the birth mother was taking living expenses from not only us but also two other families. She intended to keep the baby all along. In the second case, we were at the hospital for the birth, named the little girl, and expected to walk out of the hospital the next day with her. But at the last minute, the birth father, who had a questionable history of drugs and incarceration, stepped in and asserted his rights. Again, our hearts were crushed, but our faith remained. We knew the promise that was fulfilled graciously before in Wesley by God.

Finally, our daughter Annabelle was born, bringing joy and completing our family. We would not have had the strength for this roller coaster ride of disappointments and heartbreak without our faith in God, knowing that He works in all things for the good of those who love Him.

Increase your feelings of belonging and security

We all want to be connected in community with others. The feelings of isolation and loneliness lead to depression, lack of vitality, poor physical health, and even death. Men are three times more likely to die after being widowed than their normal risk of mortality. We all have seen instances where in long-married couples, one spouse dies, and in a short timeframe, the other spouse passes away as well.

Being invested in a spiritual community truly can be a life-giving and life-changing experience. We feel a sense of safety, security, and belonging when engaged with a community of like-minded people with higher aspirations than just self-fulfillment. Many of these faith-based communities do outreach to their local community and in some cases to the global community at large. Being in service to others is a wonderful way to achieve gratitude, humility, and purpose in life.

Connect your faith with love

All the religions of the world have one common theme or basis: the explosive, exponential, life-giving power of love. The experiencing and acting out of love enables us to live life to the fullest. In fact, the act of love alone qualifies you as successful. If we do nothing other than think and demonstrate love to all other people and other living things on earth, we have been successful. Love is the greatest power in the universe.

By faith we can extend forgiveness, which is an extension of love. To guide others to feel love and to demonstrate love to others both rewards them and you. It's easy to act in love when we feel love to others. The true habit of success is to act in love, even when we don't feel like it. Love is sometimes a *decision* that we make. We decide that no matter what happens, we will love. When life deals us negativity, hard feelings, and frustration, make the decision to return the fire of love rather than retaliate with pain and anger.

REMEMBER

Whatever your beliefs, religion, or faith, the decision to love one and all will change you and also change the world.

Use the Golden Rule as a spiritual base

The Golden Rule is a wonderful basis for your spiritual beliefs. It comes from Jesus' famous Sermon on the Mount in the Book of Matthew in the Bible. Here it is in all its simplicity: "Do unto others as you would have them do unto you."

The Golden Rule knows no geographic or spiritual limitations. It is the same the world over in concept, and I feel that it's a universal constant for spiritual health. No matter where you live or how you were raised, the Golden Rule's power should resonate within you. Living your life on the basis of the Golden Rule will enhance your spirituality no matter your underlying personal or religious beliefs.

Some might say that the Golden Rule is a Christian principle, but I would not agree to Christianity's exclusive ownership. I feel that the Golden Rule is aligned with the values and beliefs of all religions. Compare these proclamations from several religions:

>> **Buddhism:** "Hurt not others in ways that you yourself would find hurtful."

>> **Christianity:** "Do unto others as you would have others do unto you."

>> **Confucianism:** "Do not unto others what you would not have them do unto you."

>> **Hinduism:** "The true role of life is to guard and do by the things of others as they do on their own."

- » **Islam:** "No one of you is a believer until he desires for his brother that which he desires for himself."
- » **Judaism:** "Whatever is hurtful to yourself do not to your fellow man. That is the whole of the law, the rest is merely a commentary."
- » **Taoism:** "Regard your neighbor's gain as your own gain and your neighbor's loss as your own loss."

It's clear to see that the Golden Rule connects with all people, and it's a basic aspirational principle in all major religions of the world.

Growing Spiritually

To grow in your spiritual faith, you must invest time and resources in it. Your spiritual growth is like growth in any other area of your life. It needs focus, effort, study, and application. It's naive to think that you will grow and discover all that your spiritual side has to offer without putting in a solid effort.

Your spiritual growth is both an internal pursuit of self and the pursuit of knowledge linked to emotion and wisdom of a higher power or the world around us. It can be closely linked with the awareness of how small we are compared to the world and universe. Understanding our level of humanity in the world leads to greater spiritual awareness. Unfortunately, in countries like the United States, where we have so much prosperity, it's easy to lack awareness of others in our society.

Find a spiritual community

I believe that finding a community to connect with and feel part of is one of the significant benefits of spiritual growth. It's uplifting to be practice your beliefs with others who are like-minded. We all desire to be part of a community, to feel a sense of belonging, to in essence be part of our tribe. There are clear physiological and social benefits to connecting with people who share your faith, and those benefits come from, say, attending a daily Catholic mass service, an evening prayer at the mosque, or taking a walk in nature with your animism community to observe the spirit in the trees, animals, and plants.

The act of fellowship in a spiritual community is one of the best-kept secrets of being of part of spiritual community. As we connect and interact with people in our spiritual community, our faith is deepened. We expose ourselves to people who share their life experiences and wisdom with us. We are able to tap into vast storehouses of knowledge they have through years of study and application of a common faith. In time, we can provide that same mentoring, support, and guidance role to others. Good and wise leaders are important to our continual growth and development in any area of life, and especially the spiritual area.

Community and fellowship make us better people. Engaging in your spirituality in a community of believers has specific and personal benefits. We become more loving and compassionate husbands, wives, and parents. We enhance our skills as friends. We sharpen each other.

Building relationships

Fellowship builds relationships. Being present and together in a faith community creates relationships. The regular attendance at spiritual gatherings each week or month creates connections with others. Our lives become more meaningful because of these connections we develop. We were built and created to be in relationship with others, and I'm talking about friends, family, and even God. It's one of the more meaningful parts of life.

The spiritual part of us desires to be in relationships with others in the world around us and with a higher power, be that God, Allah, or Jesus Christ. Being successful spiritually means developing a personal relationship with the deity who is the foundation of your spiritual being. King David acknowledges this relationship in Psalms 139:13: "For you created my inmost being; you knit me together in my mother's womb."

Building friendships

Our personal being desires to be in relationships and friendship with others. Think about your closest friends. It's probable that among all the people you know, they are the ones most like you when it comes to how you think, act, and communicate. Because they're like you, you're attracted to each other. The "like" factor of the law of attraction is as powerful as the law of gravity.

We need deep, abiding friendships with others. We need them to fulfill our lives and be successful in life. We also need them for encouragement and security. Ancient scripture tells us "a person standing alone can be attacked and defeated, but two can stand back to back and conquer." It further states, "for a triple-braided cord is not easily broken." I doubt that many of us fear the return of Genghis Khan to attack our world with swords, where we need to stand back to back with a friend for shear physical survival. I do believe that we all need friendships in faith, friends who would have their proverbial swords drawn and will stand back to back with us to protect our families in the battles of modern life. These are the friends I count on to stand with me when financial problems arise, or when a parent dies, or when my kids get in trouble, or when I just lost my job. I am extremely blessed to have friends who, with me, form a triple-braided cord in our collective lives.

Building unity

Unity is beyond relationship and friendship. Unity is a focused resolve by a collection of like-minded people to achieve a specific purpose. The collective buy-in has occurred, and the pursuit of specific objectives can proceed. The founding fathers of the United States of America were in unity in their quest for life, liberty, and the pursuit of happiness. Now it took them awhile to reach unity among themselves, but when they did, something extraordinary was set in motion through the signing of the Declaration of Independence. For all of us who live in the United States, we receive the passed down unity of their fellowship.

The Christian religion was established through unity of thought that Jesus Christ is the Son of God; that he sacrificed himself on the cross for the atonement of our sin; that he rose again and conquered sin for all eternity. It has spread worldwide due to the unity of faith of the 12 disciples, and now 2.28 billion people recognize themselves as Christians today. Talk about the compound effect!

REMEMBER

Nothing that is significant, history making, or lasting has ever been accomplished without first having unity. Unity is a critical building block in creating success in a community and our lives.

Invest time with spiritual study

Whatever our spiritual beliefs, we all must exercise our learning muscles on them. The pathway to growth in any area of our lives is to immerse ourselves in study and learning. Most of us, when we found out we were blessed to have a child, went straight to Amazon or a local bookstore to grab a book to start our learning journey. You might have grabbed *Pregnancy For Dummies,* or as your trimesters passed by, you grabbed *Your Baby's First Year For Dummies.* Making the commitment to life-long learning is a habit that successful people instill. The study of spiritual texts that align with your belief is life enriching.

If your faith is based in Islam, then reading and studying the Koran should be a daily pursuit. You might be of the Jewish faith, so studying the Torah beyond just preparation for your bar mitzvah or bat mitzvah increases your spiritual growth. If you are Christian, the study of the Bible, especially the New Testament section of the Bible, is necessary for spiritual development.

For your spiritual development to continue, it must be viewed as a seed. That belief you have in your own personal spiritual philosophy is like a seed planted in your mind, heart, and soul. For that seed to fully germinate, develop, and grow, it requires good soil, water, sunlight, and weed pulling so that the water and nutrients are used by your seed of faith. You don't want your seed to be robbed by the weeds that grow in the most fertile soil of our heart, mind, and soul.

For spiritual study to be effective, you need to establish habits. You should invest time daily in reading and studying the wisdom contained in ancient texts. If you are Hindu, then studying the Vedas or Bhagavad Gita brings enlightenment. This study is like watering the seed of faith planted in the soil of our heart. Without water, the seed won't germinate, put down roots, and sprout.

Daily prayer is sunlight to our soul. It's where that wisdom is transferred into our minds. Napoleon Hill, in his landmark book, *Think and Grow Rich,* calls the higher power "Infinite Intelligence." Whether you pray to God, Buddha, Allah, or Jesus Christ, the act of prayer provides sunlight for our spiritual seed to grow. The memorizing of spiritual text and scripture is a powerful tool to pull weeds that grow in our garden and threaten our seed of faith. Knowing the words by heart gives you the ability to recall wisdom developed and tested over the history of humankind. When life has you flustered and your thinking becomes off base, you can rely on the texts you know to recenter your mind, and you can pull and discard the weeds that may be crowding out your faith.

Harness the power of prayer

In our spiritual life, prayer creates clarity of self. Through the act of prayer, changes that we need to make are revealed to us. People who need our help and comfort are brought to consciousness. How we might live more fully and abundantly is frequently revealed. The ability to help, support, and intercede for others is one of the ultimate acts of love. It is also one of the most powerful tools in our toolkit.

ANECDOTE

I affectionately called my mother a prayer warrior. She went into battle every day against the evil forces that try to influence our physical world and spiritual world. She was well armed with intercessory prayer for others. She was not able bodied for many years of her life. As I've mentioned earlier in this book, she was diagnosed with multiple sclerosis when I was 3 years old. By the time I was completing second grade, she had taken her last upright step. She couldn't physically do what many other mothers could, but what she could do, even lying in bed, was pray. I know that she prayed for her sons' safety every time we walked out the door. She prayed for our protection against the rampant drug use that gripped our community in our teen years. She prayed for her physical health, not to be miraculously be cured, but for her strength and wisdom to carry out the plans she had for many years. She was a warrior of prayer because of her deep faith and her infirmity. She prayed her way through life.

She even prayed for things unseen and to come. She prayed for her unborn grandchildren, and especially a granddaughter because, having three boys, she never got to experience the joy of a daughter. She passed away before Annabelle was born. Oh, how that granddaughter would have filled her with joy! I know she is delighting in heaven watching over us. I remember her saying to a young mother one day who was holding a new infant, "Being a parent is a wonderful blessing. I have three boys. Do you know why I have three boys?" To which the young mother said, "No, I don't." My mother replied, "I have three boys because I didn't want four." My mother probably prayed mightily to keep her sense of humor.

I have discovered that, rather than starting with my laundry list of personal needs in prayer, if I start in humility and gratitude, the sunlight of prayer is more meaningful. When I begin with gratitude, it repositions my heart to understand how blessed, fortunate, and favored I am by God. I then move to interceding for others: my family, wife, children, parents, and other relatives. I then pray for friends in need, relationships, my employees, and my clients. I then move to the problems and challenges, praying for wisdom and resolution. I also pray for any desires I have that I hope to be fulfilled and answered.

REMEMBER

Whatever your spiritual beliefs, prayer or meditation has benefits for our mental well-being. Too many of us have been led to believe that prayer is formal, or we have to use flowery words and phrases. Prayer is merely a conversation that you are having in your spiritual life with someone or something that has more power than yourself. It's the appeal and recognition that we all need help from the universe or the Creator of the universe in our daily lives. We're hoping for a little more of that "Infinite Intelligence," as Napoleon Hills called it, in our lives.

There is an ancient principle of truth in play when you take part in the act of praying: "Ask and you will receive." "Knock and the door will open." There is no receiving without asking. Do your kids fully pick up after themselves and clean their bedrooms without you asking? Does it usually take multiple asks or prompts for them to complete the task? The same is true in the act of prayer. We often have to ask more than once for what we desire for ourselves and others.

But that doesn't mean that prayer is the big cosmic vending machine in the universe, where all I have to do is drop a coin of prayer into the slot, pull the lever, and out pops my selection. Sometimes prayer is answered, but not in our expected timeline. Sometimes it's answered in an unexpected way or through different life circumstances. There are situations when we pray for a particular door to open, and what opens instead is a window. The fresh air feels the same blowing through the open window as the open door.

REMEMBER

It is an absolute guarantee that there is no receiving without asking. It's assured that the door, window, or slider will not open unless we knock.

Memorize spiritual passages

The practice of memorizing spiritual passages is a powerful way to grow in your spiritual depth. There are useful, valuable, and life-breathing words contained in, for example, the Bible, Koran, Torah, and the writings of Confucius. Being able to memorize them for recall in times of need and times when others need comfort is an invaluable tool.

TIP

Establish the habit of weekly memorizing spiritual passages. Doing so will increase your cognition, fill your soul, and expand your intellect.

When you are faced with difficult challenges, you will be able to recall and use the ancient wisdom to help you overcome your present circumstances. Spiritual passages can bring you comfort and clarity, lighting a pathway of escape whenever you face danger. Memorizing spiritual passages helps us pull the weeds in our garden of life. By weeds, I'm talking about our errors in judgement, unfortunate circumstances, and even evil forces in our world and beyond.

As I stated earlier in the chapter, all spiritual faiths recognize the existence of good and evil. Evil is the opposite of good, and you see opposites at play in all aspects of life. You can't have success without failure. It would impossible to have joy without sorrow. So logically, there must be both evil and good. Memorizing spiritual passages is a way to pull the weeds or even weaponize ourselves against the forces of evil, if that's how you choose to think about things. Here's an apt quote from the Bible in Ephesians 6:13:

> Therefore, put on every piece of God's armor so you will be able to resist the enemy in the time of evil. Then after the battle you will still be standing firm. Stand your ground, putting on the belt of truth and the body armor of God's righteousness. For shoes, put on the peace that comes from the Good News so that you will be fully prepared. In addition to all of these, hold up the shield of faith to stop the fiery arrows of the devil. Put on salvation as your helmet, and take the sword of the Spirit, which is the word of God.

St. Paul, who wrote this spiritual text, knew that we as human beings are in battle daily. We need protection from the fiery arrows of evil. I can attest to using memorized scripture as a weapon against self-doubt, discouragement, frustration, and self-pity. It has provided protection in time of need.

Knowing spiritual texts by heart gives us protection against so many personal follies: lust, gluttony, greed, sloth, wrath, envy, and pride. Memorizing scripture is "the sword of the spirit" that you can use effectively to vanquish the enemies that are determined to create casualties in their wake.

REMEMBER

A spiritually developed life is an abundant life. Our spirituality was placed inside of us before birth. It was hardwired into our being. To ignore or disclaim its existence inside of us is to reject our true self. I am encouraging you to develop your spirituality as passionately as you develop other areas of your being.

4

Success Through Relationships

Chapter **10**

Developing Valuable Friendships

Your success in life is a direct result of the relationships that you cultivate. The journey of life is meant to be experienced with others. Our relationships add to the complexity of the tapestry that we are weaving all the days of our life. The friendships we develop add beautiful thread to the tapestry, and the stronger the threads, the more durable the fabric.

Developing lasting, loving, and meaningful friendships is not difficult, and it doesn't require some secret formula that few have ever been able to uncover. The development of life-enhancing friendships has been written about, talked about, and demonstrated for thousand of years of recorded history. A great recent example is Dale Carnegie's landmark book, *How to Win Friends and Influence People*, which was first published in 1936. According to *The New York Times*, this classic has sold more than 30 million copies. It's a book that I highly recommend.

My hope, in this chapter, is to expand your perspective on the value of friendly relationships and give you some practical how-tos and habits to deepen your current relationships while expanding your database of friends. I want you to deepen your influence beyond merely gathering likes, emojis, and followers in our electronically interconnected world of many acquaintances but few deep, enduring friendships.

What We Learned in Kindergarten Still Applies

As we transitioned from our childhood to adulthood, something happened. All the simple truths and simple principles that we learned and followed somehow became complex. Because we are now adults, we feel that life, success, relationships, and friendship all have to be more complicated. But the simple truths and simple rules that we had to follow in kindergarten still apply in the adult world.

Remember the friendship rules we all learned early on? Share with others, be nice, don't hit, don't take things that aren't yours, say you're sorry when you hurt someone, admit when you are wrong. All of these rules apply as aptly in the adult world as in the preschool set.

One key principle of both worlds is that playing together is more fun than playing by yourself. We were designed for community, relationships, and friendships. We weren't meant to live our lives alone. You may feel at times more comfortable by yourself, which is fine. But the most rewarding experiences in life are vibrant, interactive relationships — the ones you have with your spouse, parents, children, extended family, and friends.

ANECDOTE

I must admit that my skills in kindergarten were lacking. I was in the afternoon class at St. Matthew Lutheran Church. Those were the days when you kindergarten classes were only a half day. I was in the afternoon because the morning was full, but I can assure you, my mother wanted me out of her hair first thing in the morning as I was always bouncing off the walls when I woke up. My teacher was Mrs. Locke, who had likely been there since the dinosaurs walked the earth, or at least it seemed like it to me at the time. She was a rare combination of Mother Theresa and Attila the Hun all rolled into one. When we failed to follow the friendship principles of sharing, being nice, don't hit, don't take things that don't belong to you, and so on, you had the pleasure of occupying the "sinner's bench." Let's just say, I was on a first-name basis with Mr. Bench, and I am not talking Johnny. If it wouldn't have scarred me for life, Mrs. Locke should have renamed the bench to be the "Dirk Zeller's Sinner's Bench." Nevertheless, in that kindergarten class, the fundamental principles of friendship success were ingrained in me and gave me a wonderful foundation. And thanks to the sinner's bench, I learned about consequences. I just wasn't a quick study, but better late than never.

Applying the Golden Rule

The most effective way to created and deepen friendships is to follow the Golden Rule, which I talked about in Chapter 9. "Do unto others as you would have them do unto you." Or simply treat others the way you want to be treated.

The Golden Rule has a close brother in the basic principles for living, which follow. This list I share with you applies to your most valuable friendships that live with you in day-to-day life (like your family, friends, or roommates who live under the same roof with you). The author of these rules is unknown, but Zig Ziglar used them in *Success For Dummies* as well.

>> If you open it, close it.

>> If you turn it on, turn it off.

>> If you unlock it, lock it up.

>> If you can't fix it, call in someone who can.

>> If you borrow it, return it.

>> If you value it, take care of it.

>> If you make a mess, clean it up.

>> If you move it, put it back.

>> If it belongs to someone else, get permission to use it.

>> If you don't how to operate it, leave it alone.

>> If it's none of your business, don't ask questions.

True friends are there for you in both joy and sorrow. They understand the unparalleled joy that we can experience and are ready to party the night away celebrating your victories. They immerse themselves in the joy with you. The joyous friend situation is likely the easiest to attend.

The friends who really count are the ones who are with you in sorrow. The sorrowful situations in life truly reveal who your friends are. I have a friend, Steve, whose 20-year-old son was killed in a single-car accident. Another friend of mine, Ken, was first to reach Steve after the news of his son's death was conveyed to him by the police. Rather than talk and recite the "Seven Ways to Overcome Indiscernible Grief," Ken merely just sat by Steve and said nothing. He was there for Steve to cry with and cry on for hours. In times of sorrow and grief, let's be honest, no one knows what to say that will mean anything; being there is what matters. In friendship, your presence in times of sorrow speaks loud enough. The value of friendships, if just limited to moments of grief and moments of joy, would be a priceless treasure.

Taking the Golden Rule to another level

I have another rule for you, and it's also named after a precious metal: the Platinum Rule. I learned the Platinum Rule from Dr. Tony Alessandra, who is credited with its creation. Whereas the Golden Rule assumes that people want to be treated as I do, the implication is that we end up treating everyone the same, or that we all want the same thing.

REMEMBER

The Platinum Rule teaches me to "treat others the way *they* want to be treated." The Platinum Rule requires us to be in relationships because in order for me to know how you want to be treated, I first have to *know* you.

Steven Covey, author of *Seven Habits of Highly Effective People,* says, "First seek to understand, then to be understood." In the realm of friendships, this means I must first seek to understand others before I can hope to apply correctly how to treat them. The mandate of the Platinum Rule is to accommodate the feelings and true desires of your relationships.

The Platinum Rule doesn't mean you have to become a pushover, acquiesce, or submit to others. Our desire must be to understand what others' needs are, what drives them, and factor that into our relationship and interactions. Do you know what your friends really like? Do you know what their goals are for life, business, and family? Do you understand their struggles? What is truly important to them? What are their fears? What is their favorite brand of Scotch?

TIP

One of the most meaningful ways to apply the Platinum Rule is to understand clearly your friends' behavioral styles, which covered extensively in Chapter 4. The awareness and understanding of human DISC behavioral styles can be applied to great effect in interacting with existing friends and also turning acquaintances into meaningful friendships. Treating others in alignment with their behavioral style is the ultimate success habit when it comes to applying the Platinum Rule.

Creating Friends through Personal Connection

We all desire to be connected and in community. We want a sense of belonging to a like-minded group of people, which adds purpose to our life and creates the opportunity to serve others. That's why religious, fraternal, business, and social-cause organizations exist. Whether you belong to a mosque, synagogue, or church, friendships are easier and more meaningful to develop within an aligned belief system. That also rings true with membership in Rotary, Kiwanis, and Lions clubs in your community. If you desire to help the disadvantaged and needy in your community, a service group is an excellent way to give back and build connection as well. If you are a business owner, it's also a wonderful way to expand your network of potential clients and customers.

I often speak to business owners, executives, and sales teams, and I address a disturbing trend that I've noticed, which is the loss of personal connection between the service provider and customer or client in today's social-media-based society. The wonderful technological world we live in has led to a loss in true social connectivity. Now the social media companies like Facebook, Instagram, and Twitter would likely disagree with my assessment. I'm sure they have exhaustive research to support how their platform increased personal connection. For example, the average number of Facebook friends per user is 338. I would venture to say that out of that 388, you've seen less than 20 percent of them in the last few months. The personal connection has been through electronic likes, emojis, and tweets.

A social media platform can bridge the gap between personal face-to-face interactions. It can continue the relationship or dialogue between personal connection opportunities. It can keep you connected with an old friend from high school that you had a previous face-to-face relationship. But in the realm of establishing and growing a new relationship, there are limitations to social media's ability to personally connect and create friendships.

Developing habits and characteristics that are welcoming

The best way to be welcoming is to smile. A warm friendly smile can thaw out even the chilliest conditions.

Be genuinely curious about people, their interests, and life experiences. The hardest thing in conversation for some people is to stay curious about whomever they are talking with. Most of the time, they are thinking about what to say, or they're waiting for a pause in the conversation to express their views. Be a good listener. Don't just listen for the break in conversation. Earnestly listen to the speaker at the moment. If you catch yourself thinking about your response, then your ears might be listening but your brain is not hearing.

One of the keys to effective listening is to encourage others to talk. The best way to accomplish that is to ask questions. Most people believe that whoever is speaking is controlling the conversation. The opposite is actually true. Whoever asks the questions is actually the guider or controller of the conversation.

Most people believe that the smooth-talking, fast-talking salesperson will have the highest sales. That's actually false. The salesperson who asks the best questions and has the best order to those questions is able to uncover problems and challenges to provide the right solutions. In most companies, that is the person with the highest sales.

But, you might be saying, what if I'm not a salesperson? Well, it doesn't matter how you earn your living. The truth is, whether you are a doctor, dentist, administrative staff member, manager, student, or parent, you actually are in sales. Earl Nightingale, the "Dean" of the motivational speaking industry said, "You will be successful in life based on your ability to sell." He didn't say salespeople will be successful in life based on their ability to sell, which certainly is logical. He said *you*, as in all of us. I believe Earl is brilliantly spot on.

REMEMBER

No matter your vocation or relationships in life, the ability to sell your ideas to others is imperative.

I have been in sales successfully for 30 years. My toughest pitches involve selling to my children the principles of behavior along with cleaning their room, making their bed, and picking up after themselves. And then I have to sell them on doing their homework, handing it in on time, and respecting their parents and siblings. The essence of a successful life with successful habits is effective sales skills. We are all trying to sell something to someone. If you prefer, you can substitute the word *persuasion* if you are challenged by the word *sales*.

ANECDOTE

The most skilled and high earning professionals are effective in persuading people to their recommendations and points of view. I watched my father do this countless times as a dentist. In his era of dentistry, the gold standard of a permanent dental procedure was a gold crown instead of an amalgam filling. The amalgam filling was about 10 percent the cost of the gold crown. The out-of-pocket cost, because only a portion of the gold crown was covered on most insurance plans, was even higher. My dad could "sell" you on his philosophy of exceptional dentistry. He believed in doing it once and doing it right. He was so persuasive that you were happy to pay the additional cost for the permanent solution to a painful and uncomfortable problem. I personally have a gold crown or two that he installed in my late 20s. Because of the quality of the workmanship, they are still going strong after 30 years. They will likely outlast me. You will be successful in life based on your ability to sell!

Making a great first impression

Leading with a smile, as I have mentioned a number of times, is a wonderful habit to establish. In addition, leading conversations by addressing someone by name lowers potential barriers. The sweetest sound to any person is their own name. It is truly the most important sound in any language.

ANECDOTE

There is only one exception to this rule that must be noted. I can personally attest to the anxiety and angst I felt when my first name was followed by my middle name when my mother spoke to me. The worst was Dirk David Zeller, the full enchilada. I knew instantly I was going to be in deep trouble. Mothers and the use of your full name are the only exception to this name rule.

Being well dressed and well groomed plays a big role in making a great first impression. The old adage, *dress for success,* is still an important habit for anyone who wants to be upwardly mobile or who wants to establish some level of credibility and authority. Now we can think that people should be not judged by their appearance but for their character and deeds. While that might be true in a utopian world (or if you are a contestant in the blind auditions of *The Voice*), but that's not how things work in the real world.

As the son of an English teacher, who was a combination of Ms. Manners, Mother Teresa, and Sister Mary Punctuation, the way you speak and use proper language can lead to a lasting first impression both positively and negatively. Abe Lincoln had a unique way to express this thought, "Better to remain silent and be thought a fool than to speak and remove all doubt."

The place of proper grammar in verbal communication is missing today. My mother always said, "You can gain a clear indication of intellect, education, and upbringing by proper use of grammar." Even to this day, it pains me to watch interviews with athletes after the game. My amateur analysis is that 80 percent talk about how "good" they played, hit, performed, or whatever. My mother's voice is ringing in my head: "You can't do things 'good'; you can only do them well." Thanks Mom!

WARNING

If you really want to avoid a poor impression, then cut out the flowery metaphors. And what I mean is cursing and course language. Over the last few decades, the discourse in our society has devolved to be more crass and uncouth. The use of swearing is commonplace, but it's wrong.

We have politicians, business leaders, news commentators, and my personal least favorite, professional speakers and authors, publicly dropping F-bombs. I think some do it because they think it's hip or cool, or it makes their point more dramatic. I personally couldn't disagree more.

When you use course and crude language, you have instantly lost a percentage of the people you are trying to connect with and influence. There are hundreds of thousands of other words that can be selected in the English language to get your points across and make a quality first impression. There is little need for such crude and boorish language and behavior.

TIP

If a word isn't appropriate in a PG-rated movie, don't use it when you're trying to make a good impression.

Engaging in good conversation

The essence of good conversation is to talk about things that are interesting to the other people you are conversing with. When we talk in turns about the other people's interests, we draw them into the conversation. After a while, they start to think that you are a wonderful conversationalist.

TIP

Using a simple system like the *FORD* system still works very well. FORD stands for Family, Occupation, Recreation, and Dreams. When I ask questions about family, kids, spouses, and parents, it creates a connection, and I learn more about someone that I've just met. It enables me to see if there are common life experiences we are going through together. Most of us spend at least 40 percent of our waking hours at work, so the FORD system is a great way to get to know your coworkers. If you get more in-depth and talk about recreational activities and dreams, you're moving the relationship to a higher level. Someone you "see at work" is now an acquaintance. If good conversations continue, you have an opportunity to establish a new friendship.

Finally, to engage in high quality conversations, make the other person feel important. Use active listening skills:

>> **Engage in direct eye contact:** This shows people that they are important, that you care about what they are saying.

>> **Avoid distractions:** Avoid the temptation to look at your phone, your watch, or other people in the room. These actions can make the speaker feel less important and destroy the conversation.

>> **Open body positioning:** Your body can signal boredom or a stand-offish position. Avoid crossing your arms, and use open-handed arm gestures.

>> **Engage in feedback:** Ask questions or use confirming comments like "I hear you" or "Tell me more."

>> **Demonstrate you are listening:** Smile in reaction to the other person. Nodding your head in agreement is also an effective tool.

Being well-read is another way to engage in good conversation. Be a student of what's happening in the world today. I like the feel of the newspaper in my hands, so I still read a few physical newspapers each day. I am able to easily inject ideas or current events from multiple sources into any conversation.

TIP

If you are going to watch television news and opinion commentary shows, be sure to watch both sides of the spectrum. You have to watch both Fox News and MSNBC or CNN. It doesn't matter whether you are conservative or progressive. To be well informed, you have to watch both sides. Think of it as doing a recon mission to know what the enemy is doing and saying.

Developing Your Likeability

We all desire to be liked by others. It's a human and basic need in all of us. What if there was a system or habit that we could establish in our lives to create likeability in relationships and encounters with others? Would that be worth knowing, learning, and implementing? I believe that system would be extremely valuable, not only to our success in our career, but more significantly, for our health, peace of mind, and well-being.

I have a dog named Lily. She's a very likeable dog. She is very cute West Highland White Terrier, which certainly doesn't hurt her likeability. She has one great attribute: She is genuinely excited and interested in everyone she meets. She focuses so much on the experience of meeting someone new that she will piddle on the floor; she can't contain herself. Now I am not suggesting that the secret to likeability is to do as she does, making a small oops on the floor. What I'm suggesting is that you have such a genuine interest in others that you lose your self-focus.

REMEMBER

People are not interested in me or you; they are interested in themselves. Ponder this: We can create more friends in two months through becoming genuinely interested in people than we can in two years by attempting to get other people interested in us. When we attempt to impress people or focus attention on ourselves or maneuver people to be interested in ourselves, we will fail to make real connections and will consequently lack true friendships.

Making others feel good about themselves

Whether you are conversing with a friend via face-to-face interaction, text, e-mail, or social media, interact with a smile. You might be wondering, "Well, what if they can't see me to know that I'm smiling?" But you can see and feel yourself. By placing a friendly smile on your face, your attitude turns more positive. Your thoughts and voice become more positive and optimistic as well. Optimists spread positivity and good cheer wherever they go and to whomever they interact with. Your optimism will make them feel better about themselves. It's a simple way to guarantee that you develop new friendships and deepen existing ones.

TIP

Another key habit is to speak in an upbeat tone. If I can connect on an upbeat level with people as if they were my best friend, it will only increase their feelings of self-worth and self-esteem. When you can increase others' self-esteem, you have made their day better, and they will connect that feeling of well-being to you.

Being empathetic to others

Everyone has tough times and tough days. One of the most powerful connectors is grace. What I mean is the grace to feel for others as they deal with their struggles and challenges. When we live in close relationship quarters with our best friends, grace is invaluable. After all, our closest friends have a better vantage point to observe our true nature, and they are friends with us anyway.

We have to better recognize the tough times and game faces of our friends to enable our responses to display well-timed empathy. We all go through different seasons in life. In spring-like times, everything is blooming, growing, and expanding. In summer, the world is warm, revealing, and even relaxing. In fall, there is so much to be done that we risk becoming overwhelmed because we know that winter is coming. And we go through winters that are so cold, barren, and seemingly endless.

Our friends experience all these seasons, just as we do. These seasons are not aligned with the calendar but on the rhythm of our life. Our friends' winter can be a whole lot longer than a few months. They could experience a winter season for years due to kids on drugs, estrangement from parents, tough financial times, divorce, and so on. Our empathy speaks volumes to them when they need it most.

Engaging in complimentary behavior

We all prefer to be around people who are friendly and make the effort to express kind and complimentary things. The base nature of most humans is that we see faults clearly and quickly in others (and often more readily than we see them in ourselves). Ask yourself, what qualities does Steve have that make him a great friend? What about Susie in her work makes her effective at getting things done? What about Kirk and Marcia as a couple? Do you admire how they interact and treat each other? When you ask yourself these types of questions about your friends and acquaintances, the answers you come up with will enable you to say far more meaningful complimentary things about them than "I like the broach you're wearing today."

Obeying the law of reciprocity

The law of reciprocity states that we pay back what we have received from others. In fact, in most friend relationships, we pay back, or attempt to pay back, more than we have received from others. A quality, strong relationship with a friend has reciprocity. As friends, we feel the need to reciprocate when one of our friends does something for us. This isn't a matter of keeping score, but it's a constant effort to return a favor, to compliment, or to pick up the tab next time. Even the sharing of a good idea, book, or article with a friend or business associate can have lasting and relationship-building benefits.

In the process of passing along, we receive the benefits of reciprocity again and again. As a speaker and author for 20 years, I invest my time, energy, heart, soul, and mind in impacting other people's lives for their good. It has been, and continues to be, one of the true joys of my life to occupy, as I call it, "the front row seat to watch someone else's success show." Nothing is better than to hear people say that they used my thoughts and ideas to create wealth, security, prosperity, and meaning in their life. I receive far more than I give out in this experience.

In friendship, we need to recognize that sharing and giving are the objective. Now you may have some friends who are lucky enough to never need anything, and some friends may need more from you. That's life. I am always trying to catch up in the reciprocity game with my friend, Chuck. It's been that way for more than 15 years, and I can say that he is truly one of my closest, most treasured friends. I have to admit that I am frequently trying to think of ways to rebalance the scoreboard because he is so generous to me as a friend. When you have friends who challenge you to keep up with their generosity, you are blessed beyond measure, as I am with Chuck.

Asking for a turn

When you have generous friends, which makes life rich, vibrant, and meaningful, sometimes you need to be creative in taking turns in generosity. When planning a special evening or activity with a valued friend, announce in the invitation that this is on you. This announcement is usually met with a "You didn't have to do that" or a "No, let's split it." My advice is to hold your ground and insist that it's your invite; it was your idea so it's your treat. If you are on a budget, that's fine. You don't have to select an activity that breaks the bank. Just going out for a walk along the river and quick cup of coffee afterward as your treat can guarantee a wonderful experience with a good friend.

REMEMBER

As we learned as children, it is better to give than to receive. My counsel is to deliberately plan to be the giver in advance so that there is more enjoyment, connection, and reciprocity in the relationship. (This advice also helps to prevent those awkward situations when the bill comes and everyone is looking at each other with alligator arms.)

When Disagreements Arise

Any friendship or relationship will have disagreements and even challenging periods. That is true for newer friendships and even ones formed in childhood. Not seeing eye-to-eye or not being simpatico doesn't have to be unpleasant and shouldn't drive a deep wedge between friends. In fact, moments of disagreement can be healthy for a relationship. They can expand our thinking, allow us to demonstrate grace, and align our values and priorities with greater clarity.

Being at odds with a friend in your relationship can refocus you on what's most important. The typical disagreements between friends that truly care for and love each other become trivial compared to the value of the friendship. Disagreements allow us to hone our conflict resolution skills, strengthen our moral character, and prioritize what's most important in life. These are all worthwhile pursuits in developing ourselves to be more successful.

Take the high road

Taking the high road when disagreements arise means appealing to our higher self with care, concern, dignity, and integrity. Before tempers flare or your tone gets testy, pause and ask yourself these questions:

» How can I get my point across without offending my friend?

» What tone do I need to take so as not to elevate our disagreement?

» What medium would be best to communicate through?

Because the options of communication are so broad in our world today, the selection of the right delivery vehicle of the message is almost as important as how the message is crafted. We can select e-mail, text, social media, private Facebook message, phone call, or face-to-face meeting. I have found a disagreement of any significance is poorly resolved through electronic communication. If I'm not careful, when working through a disagreement via e-mail, text, or private message, my tone could be interpreted as corrective or disagreeable, and the reader could respond negatively, regardless of my intent. The bottom line is that unless you're a skilled writer, it can be difficult to convey a nuanced tone in written communication, especially if the medium, such as texts or social media messages, forces you to be brief.

If I am communicating via phone or face-to-face, other people can hear the sincerity in my voice to resolve the issue. They will also hear how I value our friendship, and that's hard to convey in a text. A large part of communication is carried through body language and tone of voice. The actual words we select carry the least amount of influence in total communication. In taking the high road, always evaluate which road that might be. The text road? The face-to-face road? Just because a communication medium is more time efficient doesn't mean it's the most effective.

Give a little grace

We all make mistakes in our relationships. When faced with disagreement, frustration, and impasse in your relationships with friends, extend grace. If you are trying to figure out the motives behind why your friend acted inappropriately toward you, there are usually two conclusions you can come to: They deliberately and intentionally tried to harm you, causing strife and disagreement, or they made a mistake. When faced with those two options, allow grace to extend the benefit of the doubt.

I have unfortunately said or did the wrong thing countless times in my life. My intent was not to injure someone, but that is what I did. I would hope that my friends, rather than assume the worst about me and my character, would extend grace and understand that I am a human who is prone to error. I would like to think that they would assume that I made a mistake without malice intent.

There is a historic text that supports this position of grace: "First remove the beam out of your own eye, and then you will see more clearly to remove the speck out of your brother's eye." This ancient wisdom of self-admission of our own faults and unseen errors allows us to see more clearly and extend grace to others.

If you are wrong, own it

There is no possibility of being error free in life or in our relationships. By owning your errors, rather than hoping that others don't notice them, the whole confrontation can be defused. How can anyone argue with you when you make these statements:

>> "I am sorry. I made an error."

>> "I made a mistake."

>> "You are right to feel angry. It was my fault."

SOCRATIC THINKING AND CONFLICT RESOLUTION

Socrates was reported to be one of the wisest men of his era, or any era. He advocated a methodology of asking questions to guide people through to a logical or predetermined solution. There is much wisdom in Socrates' thinking when disagreements arise.

When we are asking friends questions, we develop a deeper understanding of what makes them tick. It enhances their level of importance because we are gaining more information from them. Most people would rather talk about themselves than listen to what you have to say, especially if it's a criticism of them, their actions, or their thinking. Use Socratic questions like these:

- Can you share with me why that's important to you?

- How did you feel when you made that decision?

- What are you hoping this will do for our relationship?

- What would you like me to do?

- If you were in my shoes, how would you feel?

One of the keys to resolving conflict is mediation and finding a middle ground. Another key is to make the other people happy about doing the thing you suggest. By asking questions, you can guide them to the conclusion or action that you want them to do. By not mandating it, but guiding it, there will be less resistance because you didn't just tell them through edict but through logic and persuasion by asking questions. They came up with your solution, but they feel like they arrived there themselves.

When you fully own your error, you remove some of the hurt and emotion. If you own it so completely without trying to qualify, hedge, or backtrack, you remove the ammunition from the injured party's gun. The chance of escalation from a small battle to all-out war is reduced.

WARNING

You know you haven't accepted or owned your error when you use the word "but." The word "but" in language negates whatever you said in front of the "but." I could say, "Bob, I am really sorry for our argument, and I was wrong to say _____, but I was under so much pressure." What I really wanted to say came after the "but." My true message actually was "I was under so much pressure." And what I'm doing is really trying to justify my behavior rather than apologize freely, openly, and completely for what I did to cause the disagreement. And don't make the mistake of replacing "but" with "however." What you're doing is putting a bowtie on the word "but," and you pretty much mean the same thing. So own your mistakes without using either word.

Cheer for everyone

To be a friend is to be a cheerleader. Always assume the role of encourager in the lives of your friends. If your friends are resolved in a decision or course of action, your reaction should be nothing but encouraging. I do, however, have a caveat to this general rule: Don't be a cheerleader for any decision that might adversely affect their relationship with their family, spouse, or significant other.

If your friends are starting a new business venture, tackling a new health regimen, seeking spirituality, or dealing with the challenges of life, our mandate as friends is to encourage, pray for, and support their efforts. And then go the extra mile to provide a safe harbor when they need to rest and recharge.

Embrace the greatest gift: Love

The glue that holds all relationships together is love. We must clearly demonstrate love even when our friends are unlovable at the moment. When we are in disagreement with friends, it's hard to feel, or especially act, in love. It requires discipline to do the right thing anyway, even when we don't *feel* like it. To love someone is not only a feeling but also a *decision* that we make and act on, especially in times of conflict.

Ancient wisdom says, "Love your enemies, bless those who curse you. Do good to those who hate you and pray for those who persecute you." While your friend is not your enemy, in times of disagreement, they can be your frenemy. Rather than returning fire for fire, take the more positive position that leads to healing and restoration, and that means choosing love.

Display loyalty (a close second to love)

There are few things more valuable in our lives than the loyalty of friends when we're faced with challenges and conflict. The old saying goes, "You will know who your true friends are." When we are at loggerheads with others, if our friend is coming to us in love and standing by our side in spite of our disagreement, you are wealthy because you have a true friend.

We can also experience disagreements between more than two people. You may have to deal with three-sided disagreements in your circle of friends at times. That is clearly a time to demonstrate your loyalty to your friends. Even in spite of the battle lines, put down your arms to visit both fronts with the message that your loyalty to each is unwavering.

Transform foes to friends

Some of my closest friends did not start that way. Some competed for business. Others had differences in thinking or conflicting political beliefs that created a clear chasm between us. But I kept my mind open and began to think about their beliefs, viewing their character in their actions. I began to gain respect for them. As my respect grew, I started to see the commonality rather than the division.

ANECDOTE

Ben Franklin has a famous story about how he turned a foe into a friend. When young Ben was in the General Assembly in Philadelphia, there was a particular wealthy man who disliked him. His dislike was so severe that he denounced Franklin in a public discourse. Franklin resolved to make the man like him. One day, he asked the man to do him a favor. This favor gave the man recognition and expressed, be it subtlety, Franklin's admiration for this man's knowledge and success. Ben wrote to him to borrow a rare book for a few days so that he might read it and learn from it. The man quickly sent the book to Ben, who then sent the book back the next week with a kind note expressing his appreciation and indebtedness to the man. When they met in the assembly a few weeks later, the man spoke to Ben, which he had never done before, with great civility. He helped Ben on many occasions after that.

What's the lesson here? You can turn foes into friends by placing yourself in debt to your foes.

Chapter **11**

Developing Your Most Important Friendship

A good marriage or long-term relationship is easy to recognize when you see it. A happy couple demonstrates many outward signs of a vibrant relationship. You will see them smiling, laughing, holding hands, hugging, and gently touching. A connected couple doesn't become that way by accident. They become that way through work, trials, struggles, commitment, and effort. A quality marriage of lasting love does not occur by accident but by design and commitment.

Joan, my wife, and I have been married for 29 years. The number of years and the quality of our marriage is a testament to our endurance and philosophy of commitment to each other — along with a little secret I learned before we were even married. In fact, I learned this secret on our first date.

ANECDOTE

When I first met Joan at Cherry Creek Presbyterian Church in a young singles group, I knew she was special and someone I wanted to get to know better. In fact, I asked her out right away. I wanted to go out on Friday night. She replied and said she was going to a conference, and if I wanted to go, I was welcome to join her. I found out that she was going to a conference by Gary Smalley called *Love Is a Decision*. Gary is a relationship and marriage expert. I have to admit I tried to convince her not to go so we could go out on a more normal date. She was having none of that, so I had to decision to make. Be with her at the conference on Friday evening and all day Saturday, or not. I decided that going and being with her was better than not. Who goes on their first date to a marriage conference?

We got to the conference Friday night. Gary came out and did his warm-up of the audience by having a contest. Who came the farthest? Who has the most children? Who has the most grandchildren? As he ticked off the numbers, more and more people would sit down. As the numbers got higher, there were fewer and fewer people standing in each of these categories. Then finally there would be only one couple standing for each of these questions. The applause would come, and the people would be recognized.

This was his final question of the game: Who had been married the longest? As the couples sat down after he called out 10 years, 20 years, 25 years, 40 years, 50 years. The field was narrowing fast, and finally, at 63 years, there was one couple left standing. Again, the room filled with applause. Then Gary asked them, what was their secret of success? The woman looked at the man and the man looked at her. You could tell this was a hard-working couple their whole lives. He was in overalls that looked worn and broken in. He took his hat off, scratched his head, a head with almost no hair on it. He looked at his wife then at the crowd and back at the speaker. He then said, "Yes, dear" and promptly sat down.

That moment and its wisdom have never left my consciousness. In fact, for you men reading this, you can probably stop right here. If you apply that one statement to every circumstance, you will have a successful marriage. Success is contained in doing simple things well. If you want to dig beyond "Yes, dear," I'm happy to oblige.

Committed Personal Relationships Are Not Automatic

Whether you are in a long-term relationship, civil union, or legal marriage, the glue that holds any relationship together is the commitment level you have to each other. And if these long-term relationships end, the split or divorce is a devastating outcome for each person. It shatters their world and the world of their children. Staying committed to the long haul should be the goal of any marriage or similar relationship. Increasing the love and romance in your relationship is one of the main ways to achieve that goal.

A committed relationship is supposed to be edifying, stretching, life giving, and fun. I have more fun with Joan than anybody else, and I would rather be with her than anyone else. I would honestly love to play golf with her more than any other golfing buddy I have. Unfortunately, she doesn't want to play as frequently as I do, which is fine. When we have fun together as a couple, we're investing in positive memories, good feelings, and laughter. The chances of divorce are limited if you're having fun together.

Making the decision to love

As I mentioned in the chapter opening, on our first date, Joan and I attended a marriage conference called *Love Is a Decision*, and like the title of that conference, I'm convinced that you *decide* to love. You make the conscious, intentional, mature choice and resolve to love. And no matter what happens, you decide to lead with love.

The best statement of what love is comes from the Bible, 1 Corinthians 13:4–8. It's a beautiful piece of wisdom that aptly describes love:

> Love is patient, love is kind. It does not envy, it does not boast, it is not proud. It doesn't dishonor others, it's not self-serving, it is not easily angered, it keeps no record of wrongs. Love does not delight in evil but rejoices in truth. It always protects, always trusts, always hopes, always perseveres. Love never fails.

What an amazing and brilliant description of love. Allow me to emphasize a few sections of this passage.

>> **When we are in love and want to express love, we must do it in patient and kind ways.** Telling your wife to hurry up at the top of your lungs or honking in the driveway would not qualify as patient or kind.

>> **Love does not dishonor.** What can I do today to honor Joan? That is a question I frequently ask myself. Would bringing her a bouquet of flowers honor her? Would writing out a card to express my appreciation, or telling her I will handle the kids tonight so she can soak in the tub and relax show her my gratitude?

One small way I try to honor Joan is by opening her car door, and I realize it's pretty old-fashioned. She is certainly capable of doing it herself, but I've been doing it for 29 years and honestly don't plan to stop anytime soon. It's also a public statement to anybody who sees the gesture that my wife is incredibly valuable to me, and I'm willing to serve her in both small and large ways.

>> **Love keeps no record of wrongs.** This is a powerful illustration of love. Some of us have every offense our spouses have committed organized, categorized, and recorded on a mental spreadsheet for easy recall. And what's worse,

many of us take it a step further and share that spreadsheet with others. I'm all for community and friends to help you navigate tough times, but the sharing every negative detail of a relationship will not achieve a positive result unless you positively want to divorce. When relationship conflict comes up, if you're dredging up your transgression spreadsheet to use as a weapon against your loved one, I guarantee you will do more damage than good in your relationship.

Some of you might be thinking, "Well, you don't know how much or how often my spouse has hurt me." And you're right, I don't. But I know there can be a lot of hurt and wrong actions by spouses in marriages. I've inflicted pain on Joan. I've been unkind. I've not been patient. I've dishonored her and have gotten angry quickly. I've made mistakes and needed to ask for her grace and forgiveness when I didn't deserve that grace or forgiveness. That is the measure and expectation of true love.

>> **We must protect our relationships and our love from the evil influences that want to destroy our relationship.** Through hope for a better future together and the willingness to persevere through trials, love will always prevail.

Achieving harmony through compromise

In a relationship, you should have the attitude and resolve to achieve harmony. To achieve harmony in marriage means having to compromise in service of each other. Joan and I don't agree on everything. We are very different. We make compromises, both big and small, every day, and that creates happiness and oneness in the relationship. Wherever your marriage is at the present moment, there are actions you can take to improve your harmony. Here are just a few:

>> **Complement your spouse today.** Express that they prepared a great meal. Or remind them that they are a wonderful provider for the family. Say that you're thinking about them. Thank them for helping out. Compliment them on how they keep the home warm and inviting. Or mention how good they look today. Thank them for picking up the dry cleaning or grabbing your prescriptions at the store. The list is really endless. Most of us receive more complaints and correction in a day than compliments.

Make it a habit to give five compliments for every one corrective statement. That's the right and loving balance.

TIP

>> **Do something special today.** Pick up a card and write a heartfelt note. Stop and pick up dinner so it doesn't have to be prepared. Knock off an item on the honey-do list without being asked. Wash the car. Put in a load of laundry. Go out to dinner together just because. Buy tickets to a great show.

>> **Take something off their plate.** Step in and do the dishes, the laundry, the floors, the lawn, or the gutter cleaning. Whatever the division of labor is in your house, do something that you normally don't do. That one act you don't normally do speaks volumes.

>> **Plan a memorable evening or weekend away.** When we can connect with each other as a couple outside our familiar surroundings, it's special to be able to get away from the ongoing pressures of working, paying the bills, raising the kids. When Joan and I get away, it rekindles how life was when we were younger, when we had more fun, fewer responsibilities, and fewer pressures.

The Value of the Institution of Marriage

I will admit that I am an advocate of the institution of marriage. We have clearly adjusted in society to people being committed to each other without the "piece of paper." But I personally think marriage is incredibly valuable, and its value goes far beyond the marriage license and the ceremony.

The institution of marriage is a clear and public declaration of your union and commitment. You do it before your friends, family, and God. You make the statement that you'll forsake all others and ascribe to the vows that you ultimately recite. It's a reflection of your personalities and relationship with each other. I attended a wedding recently where the bride and groom used the "unity cocktail," which was combined from two separate martini shakers. Now if you knew well the bride and groom as I did, it was extremely appropriate for their personalities.

The true meaningfulness of marriage goes far beyond the wedding day. If you're entering marriage, even with the right mindset, there will be rough seas ahead. In the heat of the acrimony that happens in all relationships, the marital bond is more difficult, emotionally and legally, to be broken. Because of that increased commitment and difficulty of undoing a marriage, when we experience a rough patch, it can allow us to reconsider, gather ourselves, and weigh out if it is really all that bad. Often, we compromise and work through the tough times.

Marriage provides security, and in any relationship, there is likely one of the two partners for whom security is a big issue. That person will feel more security and comfort, as the relationship develops, if marriage is a topic of conversation and is the ultimate goal. More than 40 percent of the world's population is a Steady behavioral style, which is the highest percentage of behavioral styles (discussed in Chapter 4). The number-one need and number-one motivator for a Steady is the achievement of security. Later in the chapter, I provide some guidance on communicating with your partner's behavioral style.

There are countless legal benefits to marriage as well, including the ability to make health decisions for your spouse in case they are incapacitated. In addition, there are survivor benefits and disability benefits afforded spouses through Social Security. I recognize that no one enters into marriage expecting a catastrophic event to happen in life. The truth is, catastrophic events do happen, and far too frequently, and being married provides spouses with the rights to protect each other.

Before you say "I do"

We all intend to be married once and forever. I have never met anyone who planned to get divorced on the way to the altar. Because of this, I believe that some level of premarital counseling is a big benefit. You can hire a professional counselor who's trained in premarital counseling, or, if you and your betrothed are spiritually inclined, you can arrange to meet a few times with your pastor, imam, or rabbi. With a professional guiding the conversation, you can talk about conflict resolution, values, beliefs, children and child rearing philosophy, money and spending, and even domestic division of duties. All are worthwhile topics that should be discussed *before* marriage.

TIP

If you can't find or can't afford premarital counseling, consider attending some classes for premarriage or even marriage classes. There are many that are held each weekend around the country by different marriage and relationship experts.

When marital success goes off the rails

Whether you are married or not, any relationship can get off track. Disagreements and conflicts are part of any relationship, but the biggest relationship killers are disrespect and dishonor. Examples include small mistakes, like speaking in a harsh or condescending tone, and much more serious transgressions, like adultery. Both of those instances and everything in between stem from disrespect and dishonor.

I must admit that there have been times when I did not address Joan with the respect and honor she deserves. Early in our marriage, I tried to be funny at her expense. I was clearly being stupid, immature, and disrespectful. She informed me of such, and she was absolutely right. It took me a short while to get rid of this bad habit forever. I'm grateful that she was committed enough, patient enough, and filled with grace to enable me to put it behind me.

WARNING

There are a lot of traps in this world to snare us and take us off the pathway of oneness, honor, and intimacy in marriage and into the realm of disrespect and dishonor. For men, I believe there's no bigger trap than pornography. The accessibility of porn and the "normalizing" of viewing porn damage both ourselves and the relationships we are in. In watching porn, we demean our partners. It causes them to feel that they can't measure up. Our expectations of sex are distorted by the made-up, silly, and often degrading tropes of the world of porn. The intimate, loving extension of physical connection can devolve to unrealistic demands and discouragement. We have a generation of young men who, because of porn, do not have a healthy view of sexual intimacy in a committed relationship.

Commitment Is the Key Ingredient

I've been married to Joan for 29 years, and in my opinion, commitment trumps everything. The other aspects of your relationship — attraction, good looks, and feelings — can ebb and flow with the changing seasons we experience in life. For example, I'm not the young hunk in amazing physical condition that I was at 27 when Joan and I first met. So I can admit to being more physically attractive at 27 than 57, but that hasn't shaken Joan's commitment to our marriage.

ANECDOTE

My father has been my greatest mentor in my life. As I've mentioned throughout this book, he taught me numerous lessons about life and business. But I feel that his most significant accomplishment in life was the almost 50 years of marriage to my mother. You might think that lots of people celebrate 50 years of marriage, and that's true, but it's uncommon to cross that milestone with a spouse who for 40 years was engaged in hand-to-hand combat with a devastating disease like multiple sclerosis.

My father stayed committed in his marriage when he knew that my mother would lose all her motor functions at some point. That's special. That takes a great person, one of character, integrity, and commitment. He knew the disease would be a big drain on financial resources, and he knew at some point, he would occupy the role of her primary caregiver. And keep in mind that she was only 32 when she was first diagnosed. My father was faced with the challenge of needing to earn a substantial income to afford to pay for her care.

Let's be honest. As I have been reviewing my father's options at 34 years old and a wife with an MS diagnosis, it would've been easier to bail, to exit out the back door, to divorce my mother rather than walk side-by-side with her. According to Focus On the Family, the divorce rate in marriages where one partner has a chronic disease is more than 75 percent. A married woman diagnosed with a serious disease is six times more likely to be divorced than a man with a similar diagnosis. That sums up how rare my father is as a man.

He stuck it out, played all-out, and has earned not only the respect and admiration of his sons but also from every person who watched his commitment, honor, and integrity lived out each day during my mother's 40-year battle with MS. His commitment stemmed from the simple, heartfelt resolve contained in the statement he made when they got married: "I do." I'm blessed beyond measure to have witnessed firsthand the power of personal commitment to others.

Observe before you dive in

If you're thinking about tying the knot or are in the early stages of a serious relationship, be observant of the level of commitment demonstrated by your loved one. Do they commit and follow through on even the little things in life? Do they do what they say they will do? If they don't, do they give all-out effort to the best of their ability? Do you feel they will be truly committed to you when the times are tough? If you were in the heat of battle, and they were in the foxhole with you, would they fight with you side-by-side to the very end, until death? There are times in marriage you're in the foxhole of life with battle raging around. You're low on ammo and all you have is each other and the will to survive together.

Observe and evaluate their past, as well as any familial examples they've had in their lives. Does their family have a history of long marriages and keeping commitments? Are their grandparents, if still alive, still married? Are their parents still married? I recognize that you can have a successful long-term marriage even if your parents didn't, but numerous empirical studies have found that those that experience parental divorce are significantly more likely to divorce themselves. They even have a term for it, which is *intergenerational transmission of divorce.*

TIP

If you or the person you are dating has a tumultuous past, you might pause and increase your courtship timeframe to really get to know in depth your significant other. It would be wise to go to counseling together to uncover some of the hurt feelings and potential damage from the past.

Joan has expressed to me numerous times that one of the things that comforted her was that my parents were still together after 34 years of marriage when we were dating. Joan unfortunately experienced the pain of divorce when she was a teen. It was a tough time for her to watch her parents go through a divorce. She lost a lot of respect for her father that took years to rebuild.

Draw a line in the sand together

The line in the sand is the commitment that we are going to stay married. We are going to work through the minor and major problems of life together. The line in the sand is that we aren't going to threaten divorce or even use the word in our conversation.

Dropping the D–bomb is not relationship building, respectful, or honoring to your spouse. But many married couples use it as a weapon against their mate. The spouse that uses the D–bomb to correct behavior or attempt to correct behavior is wrong. The behavior might need to be corrected in their spouse, but wielding a weapon like the D–bomb is like shaking a container of nitroglycerin. It might go off unexpectedly and with horrible consequences.

Remember that you both are on the same team

Marriage is a joint venture. To be successful long–term, both people have a part to play. I am not talking about stereotypical gender roles, which really don't come into play for two people that are committed to success together. The objective is to figure out what individual strengths and weaknesses you bring to the table. What are your gifts, as well as your spouses?

For example, Joan and I started with her organizing and handling our money and paying the bills. Certainly, we didn't have a lot at the beginning, but it's how my parents handle the household, so I felt that's the way it should work. I was only copying my parents' example. We found out that being the family accountant was not one of Joan's many gifts, nor did she particularly enjoy doing it. At that point, I was tasked with the yard, which I did not enjoy, nor was I particularly good at it either. The truth is, Joan is wonderfully creative and has the imagination and skill to design and care for a yard as well as our home. It's one of her gifts. So we ended up swapping responsibilities and working together. And the Zeller team is much better for switching.

You're both two individuals with a unique combination of needs, skills, and desires. There is no one "right" way to divide the labor in a marriage. Your parents had a certain way that they did things, and you've probably seen how other couples split up responsibilities. But it's up to only you and your partner to evaluate your talents and figure out what works best for the both of you.

Communicating Creates Oneness

Happy marriages are created through the habit of consistent and regular communication. When we regularly share our feelings with our loved one, in both words and actions, we increase the honor, respect, and personal connection we feel for each other. We must embrace the spirit of open communication. We must have a genuine desire to understand our spouse and the patience and commitment to really hear them. To really hear, we need to understand the emotions and feelings that form the basis of their communication. To be connected in communication, we need to listen to the needs behind the actual words. Affection, appreciation, respect, empathy, assurance, and acceptance are some of the needs we all have in our relationships.

REMEMBER

When we can encourage our mate to express their needs clearly, we are better able to meet and even exceed those needs.

Deciphering how to communicate best for your mate

We all have different natural ways to communicate with our spouse. We all use verbal and nonverbal cues to communicate. Silence can even be a form of communication between marital partners: You come to know each other so well that you don't have to express yourself verbally to fill up the gaps of silence in life. I'm not talking about the silent treatment, which is the immature, retaliatory silence of I'm getting even, teaching you a lesson, or making you squirm for what you've done to me. I'm talking about the comforting silence that you can have with someone that you know well, when you can just not say anything and instead just enjoy being in each other's presence.

One of the best books on communication in marriage is Gary Chapman's *The 5 Love Languages*. It's a wonderfully written book that describes how to express love in the language of your mate. The book has sold over 11 million copies since it was first published. Talk about a bestseller! In it, Gary goes through the five love languages in detail:

>> **Words of affirmation:** For some spouses, the encouraging word or affirming statements of value are soothing music to their ears. We all like to hear we did a good job. The spouses who have words of affirmation spoken to them are edified by these verbal words of praise.

>> **Quality time:** Our willingness to give undivided attention to this spouse communicates value, love, and importance.

>> **Receiving gifts:** In communicating well to somebody who connects love to receiving gifts, as their spouse, you have to find things both small and large to present to them.

>> **Acts of service:** For some spouses, the love language is doing the dishes, cleaning, and completing the honey-do list without being asked.

>> **Physical touch:** For some spouses, a physical connection is desired (and not exclusively in the sexual realm). It's reaching out your hand to theirs. It's communicating love through rubbing their feet, giving back rubs, or snuggling up next to them while they're watching TV.

REMEMBER

A couple with a happy relationship is in constant communication with each other using texts, photos, playful GIFs, voice messages, phone calls, and face-to-face discussions. Any form of communication that is meaningful and significant to your partner builds the relationship.

Communicating in your mate's behavioral style

We're all different in our behavioral style. I cover this topic in detail in Chapter 4. It's common for married people to have different behavioral styles and even polar opposite behavioral styles. Joan and I are very different in our behavioral styles, which also means we're very different in how we ideally like to be communicated with. We have each had to learn to adjust our natural communication tendencies to meet the needs of the other.

My belief is that person who is speaking at the moment is tasked with altering the delivery of their words. They need to adjust pace and tonality to match the pattern for better alignment with the listener's behavioral style. Why go to the trouble? Because the speaker is responsible for the hearer's ability to understand and process the communication. So if I want to be heard, then it's my responsibility to talk in a pattern, manner, pace, tonality, and words that connect best with Joan's pattern of listening. If she is listening, that's hard enough work on her part, or any spouse's part.

Communicating with a High Dominant

A Dominant is someone who sees the world through results and outcomes. In marriage, they want to create efficient and effective ways to communicate and achieve a successful marriage. They are more logical in their thinking. That does not make them unemotional. In fact, the emotion they feel when frustrated or road-blocked to success is anger.

Dominants, while their outward appearance is in command and in control, inside of a marriage relationship, they need to be complimented and encouraged. They have the outward appearance of having it all together, yet toward their spouse they need that encouragement and that recognition that they're doing a great job. The positive comments, appreciation, and pride of a spouse demonstrated to a Dominant goes a long way in the pursuit of them being better, meeting their spouse's needs, and changing less appealing behavior. Dominants like to win, which they associate with a long, fulfilling, vibrant marriage. They make decisions with fewer details and are decisive in doing so. They want facts, but not ten truckloads of them. Short, concise, and focused conversations are the way to reach a Dominant in communication. They will become bored in long, protracted, highly detailed conversations.

Communicating with a High Influencer

The Influencer is very focused on connection, approval, and appearances. They are extremely relational. Their beliefs are that if they could just talk it out and hug it out, everything would be okay. They're extremely optimistic people, so a spouse needs to remain positive. They can interpret even a small cautionary concern as being negative. They want feedback that they "look good" because appearance matters to them. They have a need for change and innovation.

In communicating feelings, use phrases that connect with them. Asking them how they feel about something is a powerful conversation tool. Being open about how you feel also leads to oneness with the Influencer. They want to know your feelings, and they want to share their feelings. Always support their right to feel a certain way, even though you may not agree with their conclusions. Use excited words and emotions to communicate and feed off their energy.

Communicating with a High Steady

Because over 40 percent of the population is Steady, it's likely that one of the two in a relationship is the Steady. The keys to communication with a Steady are patience and sincerity. If we try to rush communication or shorten communication, it leads to disconnection. A Steady wants all the details, the description, the backstory, the exact steps, and feelings. They want reasons and personal assurances. They want to know that you are making the decisions of life together. They're very supportive people and want to get behind a good cause. You will infrequently need to question the loyalty or endurance of the Steady. They are in it for the long haul. The key to communication is a warm, patient, and nonconfrontational discussion. Even if you're having a disagreement, it's important to communicate in a warm and patient manner.

The communication should be easy going, cooperative, and team-based in words and phrases. They view a marriage as a team pursuit, which it clearly is in life. Compliment them on their process because they have one for everything they do in life. Provide them sincere appreciation and feedback. Lower the level of emotion if you're talking about a tough subject or if a disagreement arises. If the emotions get too heated, they will only focus on the emotion and shut down. They are unlikely to hear what you say if it becomes too emotionally charged.

Communicating with a High Compliant

Compliants are like Joe Friday on the old TV show, *Dragnet*: "Just the facts ma'am." They want data, evidence, analysis, and proof of your assertions, opinions, and conclusions. If you don't come prepared, don't expect them to be persuaded in the least. When you're conversing, tell them both the "why" and the "how" in the conversation. They want to know how and why you came to a decision or to a conclusion. They want to know the process you used to reach it. The Compliant is very process oriented, so a discussion does not necessarily lead to a decision right away by them. In fact, they're likely going to want to fact-check you even if they have been married to you for a long time. The fact-checking is how they work through to a decision.

The more pressure we apply to Compliants, the more they will dig their heels in. Be grateful if you're married to a Compliant and express that to them. It's likely that they've helped you avoid a lot of mistakes during your marriage. For a Compliant, a 95-percent certainty of success still encompasses a high ratio of risk at that 5 percent. They are extremely risk-adverse, which causes problems with under-appreciating their procedure, their process, and assessment. They have a high need to be right. If you point out that they are wrong, it certainly can be counterproductive. When they discover their error, they will be their own worst critic.

Compromise for Harmony

Based on the political climate in most nations currently, compromise seems to be a dirty word. In all relationships, compromise is needed to accomplish success. If you're more concerned about being right or persuading your mate to your point of view, the process of meeting in the middle, or any form of compromise, is almost impossible. We must start with the admission and understanding that both people have valid points that are likely both right and both wrong. Being open-minded is critically important to compromise.

If harmony is truly the goal in your relationships, then constructive compromise is the pathway to agreement and absence of fighting. All you have to do is look at the history of war. The fighting between countries usually ends with a "negotiated peace." The same is true in marital fights and disagreements. If you approach compromise with an open, honest spirit of cooperation, the solution will frequently be mutual rather than an edict forced by one party on the other.

TIP

Our mindset in compromise situations with our mate should be to go more than halfway. If you are holding out for 50–50 equality in all situations, your compromise strategy is likely to fail. If I am unwilling to give my spouse more than 50 percent, to 60 or even 70 percent, that's where conflict subsides, acceptance begins, and appreciation expands into love and respect. Her mind says, "He must really love me because he was willing to go more than halfway." That creates oneness and harmony.

Know when to hold your tongue

There are some things that are better left unsaid. When we are angry, sometimes we let fly with a retaliatory arrow. Here is some sage wisdom of the ages. "Everyone should be quick to listen, slow to speak, and slow to become angry." Avoid the offhanded comment, the get-even dig, or the careless, inconsiderate statement. That type of communication is best left unsaid.

Consider this ancient proverb: "The words of the reckless pierce like swords, but the tongue of the wise brings healing." Nothing could be more unwise than piercing your mate with a verbal sword. You risk damaging their self-esteem, self-confidence, and their feelings of love and acceptance in the relationship.

REMEMBER

The things we are careful *not* to say can save heartbreak in our marriage. The things you say in love, honor, and respect can energize your marriage. If you are not consciously choosing to hold your tongue on a few comments a day, you are likely struggling in your marriage.

Sometimes it's enough to show empathy

I admit it: I like to fix things. Sometimes that's a good trait, and other times, it just gets in the way. There are many occasions in my marriage when I didn't recognize that Joan didn't want me to fix something, nor did she really want my opinion on how to fix something. In fact, in many cases, the Mr. Fix-It was the last thing she really wanted. Being able to understand those times in your mate is critical to marriage. I can say I've gotten better over the years, but there are times I need to banish Mr. Fix-It back to the tool bench in the garage.

What she really wants is Mr. Empathy to show up and listen to her needs and concerns. She wants to verbally express her thoughts, ideas, and solutions out loud without me expressing anything. She wants me to just listen and feel whatever she's feeling. Then she wants me to say, "Great job, honey." "Hey, I got your back whatever you decide." "I'm sorry that this is happening to you." "Can I ask how that made you feel?" The willingness to be silent, listen, understand, and be empathetic has powerfully positive effects on marriages.

Seek to understand rather than persuade

Communication with our spouse is supposed to bring understanding and connection so that a sense of teamwork develops in the relationship. Some spouses confuse communication with persuasion. They feel because they can't change their spouse's mind that they have a communication issue.

A fellow might say, "My wife doesn't listen to me." The truth is, your wife might be listening to you very intently; she's just doesn't agree with you. Persuasion isn't a direct result of listening. Sound reasoning and eloquent delivery are often required for any sort of persuasion.

Keep emotions in check

In marriage, we are in a small boat together on water that can be sometimes rough and sometimes calm. If I start rocking the boat, then Joan will need to be the one who steadies it. If the seas become rough, then I can't let my emotions get away from me and upset the boat even more. That puts too much on Joan's shoulders to stabilize the boat. Over time, that's a big drain on my wife, and it's unfair to treat her that way.

Cling to Commitment

I realize I have written quite a bit about the power of commitment in the building and expanding of your marriages. Commitment is the life raft in the turbulent seas that insure your survival in open water. The only way to survive the storms of life is to cling to each other and the life raft of commitment.

Recognize the positives

When we are being tossed about by our emotions in the season of turmoil, when we feel less "like" for our spouse and even less love, it's time to focus on the positive rather than the negative. Ask yourself these questions:

>> What do they really want from me?

>> What are the gifts they have that I really appreciate?

>> What am I grateful for about them?

>> Do I believe they have my best interests at heart?

>> Do I want what's truly best for them?

When you get through this list of questions, earnestly think and write down responses, you will have crafted a list that you can use again and again to support your marriage and your spouse. It's easy for our mind to focus on the negatives and what our spouse isn't doing. It's finding the positives that takes more work, planning, and more review.

Remember the beginning or good times

What attracted you your spouse years ago? Where and how did you meet? What caused you to recognize them? I will never forget the first sighting of Joan. I was attending for the first time a young singles group at Cherry Creek Presbyterian Church. She got my attention and empathy because I saw her across the room visibly upset. She headed out of the room crying followed by a few of her friends. I didn't know why she was crying at the time. I didn't know what had upset her. What I did know is that I wanted to meet this young lady. She caught my attention by her beauty but also her tenderness. It was the next week before we officially met, but I will never forget seeing her that first time.

>> What events were memorable early in your relationship?

>> What am I grateful that we are experienced together?

>> What is the most fun we've had when we were together?

>> Why do you feel that was a fun experience?

>> We get along best when we _____.

TIP

The simple act of recalling and writing out your experiences, how you met, and how you got started in your relationship can lead to building a bridge of appreciation between the feelings and the frustrations you currently are experiencing. If we can remember good times and positive memorable experiences that we have shared, it can help us weather a storm. When we come together as a couple, we can restore and enhance our relationship through these memory recollections.

Rekindle the flame

When the flame is flickering or going out in your marriage, the best advice I can give you is to restart your courtship process. Do the things for your spouse that you did before you got into the routine, or into complacency, or in the sameness of marriage. The familiarity of a long-term marriage can cause laziness and low expectations of serving each other. Reach out to your spouse and touch them for encouragement. Give your spouse a hug just because you love being around them and being married to them. It's not a hug with strings attached, hoping it sparks activity in the bedroom later. It's a hug that says you are valuable to me and I appreciate you being my mate.

Focus on specific actions for courtship of your spouse, the courtship you did before marriage was planned. You planned things to give, do, and express to your mate. I know I wrote long notes to Joan before we were married and early in our marriage. I would pick her up gifts, flowers, and chocolates just because I was thinking of her. I would make her a surprise dinner when she came back from a multi-day trip as a flight attendant. I still do those things. I have to admit it's not as often, but I still do them.

Courtship is not one mate's responsibility exclusively. It should be a shared responsibility for both. Now there might not be equality in courtship. There isn't a scoreboard of who did what, when, and how. It's the awareness that without emphasis your spouse is special and needs to be treated that way, like when you first met, were first dating, just engaged, or newly married.

TIP

Create more opportunities to have fun and laugh together. The ability to laugh together is a wonderful extension of the closeness of marriage in all relationships. Your most valuable friendships are the people you have the most fun with and laugh with. If you want to rekindle the flame, create opportunities to laugh together.

TAKE A 40-DAY CHALLENGE

Joan and I were going through a particularly tough time in the last recession around 2008 to 2009. It was a season when business was down, income was down, and kid challenges were up. We were dealing with a lot of curve balls being thrown at us. And I was likely the cause of a lot of issues we were having in our relationship. In fact, I was probably the root cause of many of the problems. This was at a time when the book, *The Love Dare,* had recently come out. It's a book based on the movie *Fireproof.* The book is a 40-day challenge of short reading and actions you do for your spouse. Here are some examples of daily actions from the book:

- Say nothing negative about your spouse today and do at least one unexpected gesture as an act of kindness.

- Buy your spouse something that says, "I was thinking of your today."

- Think of a positive attribute of your spouse and praise your spouse for having this characteristic.

- Consider what need your spouse has that you could meet today? Choose a gesture that says, "I cherish you," and do it with a smile.

I decided that the challenge was worth trying and worth doing. My attitude was it couldn't make what was going on in our lives any worse. Things didn't change overnight or even in the first week when I started following the advice of the book. But by the second week, I had more hope than I did in week one. By the end of week two, I was receiving positive feedback, appreciation, and reinforcement from Joan. I kept going with it. In fact, when I got to day 40, I started back over from day one to go through the process another time. By midway through the second round, we had come out of the winter season and were in the glorious spring in our relationship.

Making your spouse the butt of a joke is *not* laughing together. That actually damages the relationship further by making your spouse feel degraded or diminished in value.

I must admit I love making Joan laugh. I purposely try to do it a couple times a day. It might be recalling funny situations we experienced together that relate to present day. Or sometimes I poke fun at our present challenges in raising children to cut the tension we both are feeling with two teenagers in the house. Or maybe I'll mention current events so that we can laugh about the crazy stuff going on in politics today. Laughter is wonderful medicine when we're hurting, and it's needed even in healthy relationships like ours.

Humble thyself

I have come to the conclusion that Robert Schuller, the famous preacher, was right when he said, "If it's to be, it's up to me." When I take personal responsibility that the relationship challenges we are experiencing are likely caused by me, things improve when I approach the situation with humility and desire for change to better meet my spouse's needs. Our marriage, connection, and relationship improve. That doesn't mean that I'm not on my knees praying for God's help, healing, and wisdom. It does mean I accept my role in creating the problem and act accordingly in humility.

A failed marriage isn't exclusively one person's fault. Clearly, it takes two to tango, but I can only control my own part. If I will commit to change, odds are, everything will change for us. And if I am changing, Joan will also make changes. Those changes will boost our marriage.

To paraphrase ancient scripture, "First remove the beam out of your own eye, and then you can see more clearly to remove the speck out of your spouse's." I think that's a brilliant philosophy for your most important relationship in life.

» **Building character in your children**

» **Protecting your family from the dangers of the world**

» **Keeping your parents in your life**

Chapter **12**

Having a Successful Family

L ike most people, I learned how to build a successful family mostly through observation. We observe from a young age what our parents do, both right and wrong, to raise children, deal with in-laws, and honor their mother and father. Children are also keen observers of how our parents treat each other. Whatever the makeup of your family unit, you and your family can be successful. You can raise happy, healthy, productive, and joyful children who will grow up to be contributing members of society. Relationships, and especially family relationships, are challenging, so crafting a strategy to ensure your family's success is important.

I personally am a proponent of the nuclear family. What I mean is two parents living in the same home. The modern-day family has evolved since the days of *Leave It to Beaver.* There are homes with two moms or two dads. Single-parent families are common. I understand there are life circumstances and reasons why a family may have just one parent in the home. I am not making a value judgement toward any single parents. In fact, I have the utmost respect for a single parent raising children to be productive adults. You are truly a hero by going it alone with the resolve to love, nurture, and teach your children in spite of being overworked and not having help.

I was raised in a two-parent home with my older brother, Kurt, and younger brother, Clark, and clearly, we were blessed. Sure, like any family, we faced challenges, but our family was closer to a Norman Rockwell painting or the *My Three Sons* television show. My father, who was a dentist, provided a lifestyle where we had a comfortable home and never wanted for anything. One major challenge for us was that my mother was diagnosed with multiple sclerosis when I was 3 years old. Her mobility was significantly affected by the time I was 5 years old. I remember she would have my older brother and me on either side of her because we were of similar height. We would walk slowly while she would place her hand on each of our heads. Our role was to be her mobile canes for stability. That lasted a few years until we grew too tall, and her waning strength forced her to get her first wheelchair. Why is this important?

It's because successful families overcome obstacles together. They use tools and each other to create solutions so that they can still achieve success. When an enemy presents itself, they go to war as a united fighting force to vanquish the foe. We as a family waged war with multiple sclerosis for 40 years. The most valiant warriors were my parents, but this affected us kids as well. I was profoundly influenced by this battle.

A family, to be successful, has to have loyalty and love for each member. My father demonstrated very clearly the love and loyalty to my mother. It spoke so loudly he had to say nothing. To walk step-by-step with my mother through that 40-year journey of MS is rare and special. When serious long-term illness strikes a spouse, it's common for the other spouse to leave. My father's legacy will always be love, loyalty, honor, and commitment.

My mother taught us through her hardship and faith that she could still accomplish what she desired. The physical infirmary didn't change what she wanted to accomplish for her family and community. It only changed how she was going to accomplish it.

A successful family starts with parents who are resolved to teach and demand that their children acquire fundamental skills of success. They are teaching and demonstrating perseverance, love, self-discipline, friendship, fiscal responsibility, the Golden Rule, respect, punctuality, delayed gratification, the compound effect, goal setting, and a positive attitude. That's quite a list, but no one ever said that parenting is easy.

Being a Successful Parent

There are tens of thousands of books on parenting. There are parenting classes, systems, and strategies. The greatest influence on your parenting style, however, is how your parents parented. You had parents who either were an example to follow or a warning on how not to do things. While I sympathize with the many who grew up in "warning" households, you are the one who can use that first-hand knowledge of what not to do. You are the one who can break what is likely a cycle of negative. It's common for the negative cycle to carry forward for generations. I want to encourage you and implore you to decide here and now to break the cycle!

Most of us go through life without a plan. That is especially true with regards to parenting. Frequently, we have dreams for our children. We have hopes that they do well in school so that they can go to college and become a doctor, attorney, or some other profession. We want them to do something in life that they enjoy but will also provide a better lifestyle than we have achieved.

Our plan for a successful family and being a successful parent goes well beyond the hope and wish category. It starts with determining what are the important values, attributes, and skills for a successful life.

>> What is the most important characteristic you want your children to adopt and learn?

>> What would be in the top five?

>> What skills do you want them to learn?

>> What values do you want them to stand for?

>> Above all else, what do you want them to know and feel from you?

>> What do you want to protect them from?

The last question will likely create a laundry list in your mind of negative happenings in society. Sometimes it's better to clearly define the negative so that you can create a plan of protection for your child. We can't put our kids in bubble wrap, but we can shelter them enough in their formative years so that later they can protect themselves. Deciding when to remove some of the protections is always the hard part of parenting.

ANECDOTE

We want to protect our daughter Annabelle from the negative and esteem-damaging effects of cyberbullying, predatory behavior, and photo sharing. While most of her friends have cellphones with the open freedom to use their phone as they wish, Annabelle does not have her own phone yet. She is 13 years old and has been asking for a phone for a number of years. She is not ready for the dangers that lurk in cyberspace. Most young teens in 7th grade, as she is, are not ready either. She will receive a phone someday, but her self-esteem, character, and innocence are more important than mobile access to Facebook and Snapchat.

Defining success for each child

There are principles of success that apply to any child, including honesty, service for others, self-discipline, kindness, and generosity. Each child is unique with individual gifts, talents, and goals. One of the wonderful journeys of life is to help your children through the self-discovery process of their talents. We don't all have the same talents and gifts. The quest to discover and develop those unique talents inside us is a lifetime pursuit. As parents, we are required to help our children discover and develop those gifts even in adulthood.

We all have many talents and gifts, but I believe to my core that within each of us, we have a few world-class talents that were placed there for the specific purpose of significant service. As we learn what those few talents are and develop them throughout our lives, our personal joy and self-esteem are increased. Our mission is to uncover those gifts in ourselves. If we can aid our children in their self-discovery process, we give them a leg up on success and joy in their life.

As a parent, of course you want to lead that discovery journey for your child. It's your primary role. The Book of Proverbs in the Bible offers this excellent advice for family success: "Direct your children onto the right path, and when they are older, they will not leave it." On one level, this proverb means that if you teach your children right from wrong, they will use that knowledge their whole life. But I think there's another layer to this proverb that we need to explore. As parents, we must direct our children to discern and develop their unique talents and gifts. If we help them discover those gifts early in life, they won't depart from using them their whole life. The world will be a better place when we all use our talents to benefit our world.

This focus on guiding our children to recognize their unique talents frames defining of success individually for each of our children. When our children are younger, we must take ownership of the definition of success. As they age, our role becomes more of an advisor of success. It was clear at a very early age that I defined success in terms of money and status. I don't believe my parents ever feared for my ability to earn a good income because I was motivated to earn my way and had a strong work ethic. They had instilled that characteristic in me. At the same time, they were also deliberate in working to broaden my perspective through this philosophy, which comes from the Book of Luke in the Bible: "To whom much is given, much is required." They were clear in their stance that being blessed with talents and wealth required sharing, charity, and helpfulness.

ANECDOTE My older brother, Kurt, while not a captain of industry, is a captain of teaching in the music arts. Kurt has had an extremely successful career and a tremendous impact on others through being a university professor teaching vocal performance. He also performs in music and opera throughout the United States. My parents helped him define success for himself in the arts, and his exceptional gifts were apparent at a young age. He enjoyed being in the church and school choirs, playing the piano, giving voice lessons, acting in plays (especially musicals), and playing English handbells. My parents encouraged his passions and talents even though his were dramatically different from the sport-related pursuits of "normal" kids his age. Kurt and I could not be more different than any two human beings. But I could not be more proud of him because he has used his gifts and talents at an extraordinary level to entertain and teach people the love and performance of the arts. We both owe an immense debt to our parents, who brilliantly helped us define success individually and encouraged us to walk our own paths.

Recognizing their differences

Our children are very different from each other. If you are a parent, you clearly understand that. Most of us set family rules, procedures, core values, and characteristics that we want to train our children on, and they should apply to all of the kids. That being said, we must recognize and determine the differences in our children. Asking yourself these questions can help:

>> What make each child tick?

>> What's important to them?

>> What specific gifts or skills are evident?

>> What is my child passionate about?

>> What interests does my child want to pursue?

Communication strategies and mediums can also be different for each child. Ask yourself these questions:

>> What is the best method of communication with this child?

>> How should I communicate corrective behavior needs?

>> What is the best way to assign tasks?

>> What length is their attention span?

>> When talking one on one, is it best to sit, stand, take a walk, or drive in the car?

Both my children are very different in the way they communicate and in their communication needs. Wesley has the gift of verbal communication and needs little prodding to open up and talk. He has been that way his whole life. He is easy to communicate with. The challenge is keeping him focused on the topic at hand. I have to keep that in my mind when I am attempting to communicate effectively with him.

Annabelle, my daughter, is much more difficult to draw out. When she is frustrated or things are not going her way, she turns inward and closes up, which is the exact opposite of her brother. Getting her outside on a walk is one of my key strategies to get her to open up and become more open-minded. Out on a walk, I can then communicate, encourage, and help her become more successful.

As parents, we desire our children to feel safe, loved, and appreciated. We are all working to build their self-esteem so that the world at large doesn't steal their feelings of value and well-being. Being successful requires general and specific tools all labeled by name in our parenting toolbox. As a parent, using a hammer when the proper tool is a crescent wrench can be disastrous. I am always asking myself this question: What's the right tool for this child at this moment?

Celebrating and encouraging their gifts and skills

As a parent, we have all felt overwhelmed. We have all felt inferior and maybe even like a failure in raising our kids. My deepest regrets with my two is not celebrating enough or encouraging enough. First, let me state, having been at this journey of parenting for 17 years, I don't think that any parent can overdo encouragement and the celebration of accomplishments and victories of their children. In reviewing myself, observing other parents, and recalling my childhood, I have come to the conclusion that there is no such thing as praising your kid too much.

Avoid negative comments

In a study conducted by the *Harvard Business Review* about positive versus negative comments in the workplace, the ideal ratio proportion was 5.6 positive to 1 negative. When I read that, I was stunned. I was convinced that I certainly was not even close to that standard at home. Given the value of my children and wife to me, how much I love them, and how much their self-esteem and well-being are important to me, I think that 5.6 to 1 is on the low side. The standard in my mind is to double that ratio and attempt a 10 to 1 range. That's the level of encouragement I want to give to my family.

Negative comments get lodged in their brain far deeper, and they are easier recall, which can shape thinking and self-esteem for a much longer and more accessible period of time. Human nature is that we hear the criticism more clearly; praise gets brushed aside and forgotten.

REMEMBER

Praise connects directly with your children's self-esteem, while negative comments erodes it away like acid.

Recognize achievements and milestones

Create significant celebrations for milestone events in life. When your children do well in school, a hearty "well done" is not enough. It requires a memorable event, like going out to dinner as a family to the restaurant of their choice. Or maybe you can go to the movies, or go bowling, or attend a sporting event. If your budget doesn't allow you to spend much, select a less expensive option like going sledding, having a day at the beach, or hiking at a spectacular location. Getting outdoors with your kids is an amazingly inexpensive way to create a marker.

ANECDOTE

The celebration of even age milestones can have lasting impact for generations. One of my friends who has four boys does a right-of-passage celebration when each of them turns 13. They hike the South Sister mountain in the Bend, Oregon area. The summit of South Sister is 10,358 feet, and the climb is challenging but not technical. All his boys that are older than 13 tag along as a group. He then conducts a knighting ceremony where he awards the new 13-year-old with a sword symbolizing the son's journey to manhood. His sons are now warriors for truth and righteousness. In talking with his sons, it's clearly a benchmark moment of their lives that they can describe even years later.

Preparing and planning gifts and recognition moments and markers can't start too early in your child's life. Joan and I attended a charity auction about six months after Annabelle was born. It was a wonderful event with a silent auction that had some interesting items. As the time ticked away, I saw a pearl necklace and pearl earrings that no one was bidding on. I knew the charity needed the money, and the minimum bid was extremely low compared to the value. So I bid on them with the intent to give them to Annabelle as a memorable rite-of-passage gift later in life. As of this date, I still have that jewelry for her in my closet waiting for her 16th, 18th, or 21st birthday. When she receives it will depend on her maturity to be able to care for and appreciate something I purchased for her when she was a baby.

I understand I am blessed to be able to give her a gift like this, but it's not the cost of the gift that is significant. It's the fact that I did something for her at six months of age and held it all these years, waiting for the right time to present it to her. We can all find ways, in any budget, to create these unmistakable moments and celebrations of our children and our love.

Little Habits to Create Big Success

With any pursuit of success, it's the little things repeated over time that yield the most significant results. The same is true in our family, especially with our children. Raising kids is a lifelong endeavor. You never stop being a parent who is concerned for your children, prays for your children, and encourages your children. That is true even when they are in their 50s and 60s and the relationship has reversed to some degree.

Setting up each day for success

I start each day praying for Annabelle and Wesley. I pray for security, protection, and wisdom for them. Because they are both out and about as teens, with Wesley actually driving, there is a level of comfort I feel knowing they are covered in prayer. I additionally pray for myself and Joan in dealing with these challenging teen years. Mostly I pray for patience and endurance as we deal with new and old challenges that have not yet been resolved. I recently asked a friend how he was doing because his teen son is particularly challenging. His response was, "He keeps me in prayer."

The four probabilities of success are knowledge, skill, attitude, and activities. If you improve any one of these four, you dramatically increase the odds of your success. For both my kids, I focus on primarily on two: attitude and activities.

We talk a lot about our mental attitude in our home. One of our children has always been naturally positive, excited, and expectant of the positive to happen to him. The other has always been less so, to the point of anger, frustration, and venting, especially in the mornings. The lessons of choosing your attitude, controlling one's attitude, and shifting or changing one's attitude are discussed frequently. Many children don't understand the importance of attitude in their daily lives and their overall success.

We then must focus on activities. The right activities can change our attitude and create success. I ask my kids frequently if they are going to have their activities control their attitude today. They know the answer is yes. To be successful, our activities must control our attitude more than our attitude controls our activities. Stated differently, does how I feel control what I do, or does what I do control how I feel?

REMEMBER

The true mark of success is that action controls attitude.

We also talk about their primary goal today at school. What is the one thing that they need to accomplish? I also ask about that once they get home from school. What is the most important thing they need to accomplish after school and before dinner? Even just a day is too long a period of time to be allowed to be frittered away because of poor planning and strategy. As parents, we must seize each day because we don't know how many we really have with our kids.

Looking for encouragement opportunities

It's easy to find fault or error in others. It doesn't take any particular skill to spot when someone messed up. It takes effort and reprogramming in ourselves to catch others doing something well. When it comes to our kids, we don't have to be concerned that giving them too much positive reinforcement might swell their heads. Most kids are their biggest critics. They know when they mess up because they hide it or try to cover it up. Those are the actions people take when they fall short.

TIP

Focus on even the smallest tasks to give encouragement to raise their self-esteem and increase their adherence to your rules and principles.

The nagging of children by parents only leads to dependent adults who continue to need prompting, but their boss won't prompt forever. Did they unload the dishwasher well? Did they make their bed nicely? Is everything off the floor in their room? Did they offer to help you out? Did they get their homework done on time? Did they receive a good grade on a recent assignment or test? Did they play their instrument beautifully? Did you enjoy watching them compete, win or lose?

REMEMBER

As a parent, you need to make the effort to shift your mindset so that you passionately look for what they do right, which you can praise, rather than look for things they do wrong, which you are inclined to correct.

Demonstrating love to your child

The whole world is energized through the demonstration of love. Love is the most powerful thing in the world. We must be vigilant for moments to demonstrate value and love. My favorite actions are "just because" moments of love. It's something that I do for children just because I love them. In fact, earlier today, I sensed one of those moments and opportunities for Wesley. Wesley was going with a few friends to a movie and lunch this afternoon. He had made plans and asked for permission to take the car. He had done his responsibilities, which were a condition of him being able to go. Before he left, I did a "just because." I gave him a ticket to the movies, which I always have on hand because you can buy them in bulk at Costco for a reduced rate. I handed him one along with seven dollars for his lunch. And I made the point to tell him that I was giving him my last seven dollars in cash, because I was. I told him I wanted him to enjoy the movie courtesy of his mother and me, and this cash was his as well. I made it clear that we love him and are proud of him, and he is turning into a fine young man. We were giving him these small gifts "just because" he is our son.

It's also important to know your child's love language. Does it come from spending time with you in recreational pursuits? Is it having a tea party with your little girl? Dads, it speaks volumes when you would do something that isn't considered particularly "manly" with your daughter. That goes for cooking or baking as well. I am not terribly interested in photography, but Wesley is, and he is very good at it. What I am interested in is that my son and daughter know clearly the depth and breath of my devotion to them and love for them.

TIP

There is nothing more powerful than a love note, which you can pen to your significant other or your children. The verbal expression of love is fleeting and can be drowned out by the noise and business of the world we live in. The note of love acts as an anchor of truth. These small notes can stop their ship from running aground into the rocks of depression, drugs, and negative behavior like bullying. I want to provide as many anchors of safety as I can to build my kids' confidence and self-esteem.

I'd like to add another note for fathers. Steve Farrar, author of the book, *Point Man: How a Man Can Lead His Family*, draws a military analogy: As fathers, we are placed in the point man role. We are on patrol in a battle zone with our family occupying the platoon behind us. There is a war being carried on all around us by the world, both seen and unseen. The enemy knows that if he can take out the point man, he can take out the rest of the platoon. This graphic depiction had a profound impact on my thinking because I know it to be true. I don't mean to diminish my wife's value nor her critical role in our family. In fact, you may be reading this book as a single parent. As either the mom or the dad, understand that you are the point person of your platoon without the hope of backup. Our greatest weapon against the enemy is love.

Making time for family meals

In the era of shows like *Father Knows Best*, *Leave it to Beaver*, *My Three Sons*, and even *The Brady Bunch*, families almost always sat down to share a meal each day. By the time we hit *The Simpsons* or *Modern Family*, family meal time was a thing of the past. I will admit that in spite of choir practice, swim team, piano practice, and later, racquetball practice, there was something stable and grounding in family dinner.

The connection over a meal, even a few designated times per week, can build your family. It will help you head off any trouble in a lot of cases because you are engaging eyeball to eyeball for maybe 30 to 60 minutes. It's a way to encourage dialogue in a broad array of topics, including school, friendships, current events, politics, success, society, and philosophy. It's an enriching time for both parent, child, and siblings. While likely viewed as "old fashioned," family meal time has a treasure trove of benefits to families.

Establishing traditions

The traditions of families are many of the most treasured and remembered moments, and this is true for both the parents and the children. The traditions can be anything as long as it's something meaningful and it's done with enough regularity to establish a clear repeat pattern. I would like to share with you a few of my family favorites.

Family Fridays

We have been doing Family Fun night every Friday since our kids were very small. It's something, even now, that they look forward to as teens. Family Fridays can be as simple or as complex as we make it. It can be as easy as getting a pizza and watching a movie as a family at home. It can be as complicated as dressing up to go out to dinner, a play, or performance. We take turns deciding what we do that evening. As Wesley now wants to go hang out with friends in high school, we've had to get more creative and flexible. We've had Family Fridays at the high school football or basketball games, where he is required to sit with the family for one quarter of the game and have a meal with the family before the game. Because, like most teenage boys, his appetite is a bottomless pit, he gladly takes part in the family meal.

Family game night

We have one night per week when we as a family play board games or cards. Once in awhile, we expand the activities to include electronic games, but it's infrequent. Most kids, in my opinion, are too glued to their PlayStations or Xboxes. The interaction and teamwork that comes from classic board games or playing cards still can't be beat in the electronic world. We play some games where it's every man for himself, like Monopoly, Sorry, and Life. And we also play in teams for games like Trivial Pursuit or Beat the Parents. Both Wesley and Annabelle love nothing better than to beat the pants off their mom and dad in a game.

As a child and young adult, my family played card games constantly. We played strategy games like Hearts, Spades, Canasta, and Pinochle. It taught us critical thinking skills, strategy, planning, and teamwork. I want my children to acquire those skills as well. Joan and I believe that family game night is fun and educational, and it promotes family bonding.

Family Sunday dinner

In the television show *Blue Bloods,* the Reagan family gathers each week for family dinner after Sunday Mass. Four generations gather around the table. What a wonderful example of tradition, importance of family, and consistency. They rotate main course responsibility and the menu, but not the venue. Joan and I have operated similarly for 29 years since we were first married. When we were early in our marriage and DINKs (double income no kids), we had family dinner each Sunday after church, usually inviting friends to share a meal with us. When Wesley blessed us with his arrival, we carried on the tradition of the after-Sunday-worship meal in the early afternoon. It is one of the most meaningful traditions we have in our family. I truly hope to have more than two generations at my family table in the future.

BBO: Boys breakfast out

Ever since Wesley was born, we have had BBO, or boys breakfast out. Wesley is an early morning riser and loves to eat, so the combination created BBO. We used to do this once a week, and usually on Fridays. Nowadays, because of my work and the demands of a teenager's life, we still do BBO, but it's about once a month. It's a staple for our relationship.

Annabelle is less excited about the mornings, so going to lunch or afternoon tea is more her speed.

TIP

Find something special that you can do with each one of your children that is uniquely theirs. Then figure out a way to do it with consistency.

The memorable getaways

When you talk to most families, the experiences of camping are some of the fondest and most memorable times of their lives, and that's probably because a camping trip, however well played, usually has twists and unexpected turns in the storyline. The tent collapses, the canoe capsizes, the bears eats the food, someone gets injured with a corresponding trip to the emergency room, or so that's what I hear. We never camped as a family when I was growing up due to my mother's MS. I believe that camping is an acquired taste, and I was never interested because of lack of exposure. My idea of roughing it is having to stay at a Holiday Inn.

I do have rich memories of a lake house that my father built with his own hands and sweat in the 60s and 70s. He worked weekends on it in the late spring through the early fall for a number of years. The memories of swimming in the lake, waterskiing, sailing, fishing, and playing with my brothers are rich and treasured memories. I also have treasured memories of doing all those things with Wesley and Annabelle. As I've mentioned elsewhere in the book, in the last few years, we began a remodel and restoration of the place. Joan and I have done much of the construction work ourselves in an effort to demonstrate the skills to our children and also pay homage to my father and mother for the family legacy that they established in 1964.

Building Your Child's Character

My father always described me as a character. I am sure he was not talking about my values or integrity. He was expressing my level of uniqueness and memorability. We all know what it means to have high moral character: to think *and* act in ways that are noble and worthy, to live a life of integrity, loyalty, and honesty. For our children, instilling in them a sense of high moral character is the foundation on which their whole lives rest. It's important to teach them that we can have high moral character in our thoughts and emotions, but what's most revealing about our character, from my perspective, is action and behavior.

Establishing values in your children

The first steps to establishing values in your children is to define what values are important for the well-being of your child and what values you stand for in your life. If you could state what the top values or characteristics you feel that make one successful in life, what would they be?

A short while after Wesley was born, I asked myself the question, "What values, characteristics, or skills do I want to make sure that Wesley is taught or acquires in life?" For the next 15 minutes, I just brainstormed that question and wrote whatever popped into my head. I wrote a lot of what you probably would write if you asked yourself that same question: honesty, integrity, self-reliance, confidence, moral conviction, compassion, perseverance. My list continued for almost two pages. I then asked myself to categorize them based on a 1 to 5 score, with 5 being the top end of the scale, meaning, the attribute or skill was absolutely essential to success. In fact, my standard was that if this attribute were completely absent, his success was unlikely or severely hampered.

When I had completed my rudimentary ranking system, I asked myself one last question: If I was unable to instill and instruct all top-ranked attributes, was there one that was most important? This was extremely difficult, but after about 15 minutes of intense thinking, I settled on one, which is based on my belief system: the attribute of self-discipline. Now I'm not contending that this choice is right for every child or every parent. The reason why I selected self-discipline is because, in my view, it's a foundational attribute of the successful.

REMEMBER If you acquire self-discipline, whatever skills or attributes you are missing are within arm's reach because you know how to apply yourself.

Self-discipline is a tool that can be used effectively in both work and home life. It takes self-discipline to be successful in business, in relationships, and in conquering our failings in thought and action. In fact, self-discipline prevents us from falling into the traps we tend to encounter on the pathways of life. Ask the people who overspent and lived beyond their means if self-discipline would have made a difference. Ask the people whose lives are torn apart by betrayal because their spouse lacked self-discipline to honor the fidelity commitment in their marriage.

Teaching the power of actions over words

Our children learn the lessons of life much more quickly from video than audio, and they are closely watching the video of our lives as parents. They hear the audio, but what they observe is whether the video and audio are in sync. In other words, they notice when words don't match actions. For example, you can say that you act in an honest manner in your family, but when you go to a restaurant and claim that your 13-year-old is 12 in order to eat more cheaply from the kid's menu, what your video makes clear is that you are not honest as long as you don't get caught or it saves you money. Is that the lesson you want your kids to learn?

Teaching the fundamentals of a pleasing personality

Teaching kids the foundation of respect for others is vitally important. They need to understand some basic fundamentals:

>> Shaking someone's hand properly when you meet

>> Looking someone in the eye when you are communicating directly with them

>> Giving someone your undivided attention when they are speaking to you

>> Resisting the urge check your phone when other people expect your attention

Smiling, making eye contract, and giving a proper handshake will go a long way in establishing a pleasing personality, especially when meeting someone new. Being kind, courteous, cheerful, and nice will enable you to go anywhere and be accepted. The ability to be friendly and inviting in your personality to everyone you encounter will open up doors of opportunity in life. All children want to be accepted by their peers, and a positive attitude makes anyone more pleasing to the people around them.

Teaching responsibility and discipline

Our society has a huge need for people who are able to apply responsibility and discipline.

Being responsible for one's self and one's stuff needs to be taught at an early age. It starts with our children learning and understanding that there is a place for everything, and everything has its rightful place. Being responsible means having a system or process that you repeat so that don't misplace things and you get your chores done. What gets opened gets closed. What we are done using gets put back exactly how we found it. It's basic stuff, but we all know kids and even adults who can't manage these simple routines in life.

WARNING

The error we make as parents is that we don't take the stance that our children need to own the consequences of lack of responsibility.

ANECDOTE

When Wesley calls panicked because he left his homework at home for science class next period, he is out of luck if he thinks we are dropping everything to bring it to him. He usually elevates the consequences, hoping that he will gain the upper hand, by stating, "I will fail science if I don't hand this assignment in on time." The correct answer is, "It's unfortunate that you will be failing. It is your responsibility to complete and hand in on time all homework." As a parent, allowing your kids to suffer the consequences of their actions is your mandate.

Wesley has been in this situation numerous times. I wish I can say we handled it every time like I just described. Joan and I take responsibility for not doing it right often enough in his life. His level of personal responsibility and ownership is too low and not fully developed in the manner it should be. That has been our error.

Setting goals and benchmarks with your kids

Our kids need to understand the importance of goals at the earliest age possible. We can give them simple household chores, set up as goals, to help them develop the habit of successfully achieving goals. As they advance in age, the goals of completed chores can have deadlines or schedules as well, so they have to not only complete the task but also do it on time.

Kids who have goals, plans, and key objectives, especially in their tween and teen years, are far less likely to fall into a destructive pattern of behavior. They are more likely to hang around a positive group of friends. Because of they achieve goals and have self-discipline, they are less likely to be involved with drugs, sex, alcohol, shoplifting, and other rebellious behaviors. When you have goals, a primary aim, and high expectations for yourself, you are less likely to feel pressured by peers to participate in negative behavior.

It's never too early to encourage the habit of goal setting and goal achievement. Soon after kids start going to school, they begin to imagine the careers they'll want as adults — usually exciting professions life firefighter, astronaut, singer, dancer, and so forth. While it would be rare for your child to have in adulthood the career they desired as a first grader, there are exceptions.

In my case, I wasn't thinking about or pursuing a career as an author from a young age. I had a desire to be an athlete and play racquetball professionally. I managed to accomplish that goal. I was not a big name in the sport but won a number of significant professional tournaments. I earned enough prize money to keep me on tour for a few years. If your children are dreaming big at a young age, you might want to show them Chapters 4 and 5 on motivation and goals. They might be ready.

Helping your kids avoid life's dangers

The world is full of countless dangers lurking to snatch away life, innocence, dreams, minds, and relationships from our kids. They are faced with the dangers are drugs, alcohol, tobacco, sex, pornography, teen pregnancy, and sex trafficking. Experts agree that children who have open and regular communication with their parents, attend worship services regularly, and engage in extracurricular activities (drama, music, dance, art, sports) have a lower chance of being involved with drugs.

Idleness

I believe that the old saying, "An idle mind is the devil's workshop," is true. If our kids are bored and have nothing better to do than play *Fortnite*, that's not enough of a meaningful pursuit to keep them busy. I'm not a big fan of video games. The ones like *Call of Duty* and *Fortnite*, which feature nonstop violence and killing, desensitize us to human death. They glamorize war in a mythical fantasy environment. I think we can all agree that there are better ways to spend one's time, even when we just want to have fun.

TIP

Keep your kids active in something that requires physical exertion so that they are stimulated and wear themselves out.

My mother always said, "A tired kid is a good kid." I'm sure that's why she had us in swim classes and competitive swim teams through middle school. She was protecting us by wearing us out so that we didn't get into trouble.

Pornography

To protect your kids from the effects of pornography, install parental controls on every device that can connect to the web in your household. If you're not particularly tech savvy, get help from another parent who is. The main way to protect your children is to block pornographic sites. These sites are predatory to even children. They use URLs (web addresses) that are close or identical to legitimate sites for your children. Their desire is to capture young people at an early age. Watching pornography releases dopamine in minds, especially young minds. They get hooked on the images and the rush of dopamine release.

The images in pornography trivialize women as mere sexual play toys. It's degrading, demeaning, and not an accurate depiction of a healthy relationship between two loving partners. A young man who watches pornography is not a young man I want my daughter to date. He is certainly not a young man I want my daughter to marry. When a husband expects his wife to behave like a porn performer, she's going to feel like she's not enough for him. The resulting hurt and loss of self-esteem is extremely damaging to a marital relationship.

What's worse, there is a connection between the pornographic industry and the sex-traffic industry that preys on girls. They are looking for girls with low self-esteem who are seeking friendship or belonging. What seems like friends at first are only people who want your child as a sex slave to earn them money. Frequently, sex trafficking leads to drug use to cope with the shame and pain of being tricked out. This creates an even deeper hole your loved one must climb out of.

THE BLESSING OF ADOPTION

As an adoptive parent, I have a unique perspective on teen pregnancy. I wouldn't be a father today without two brave and strong teen mothers who chose the love of their child more than the love of self. I am not saying that all teen moms should place their children up for adoption. That decision involves deeply personal and agonizing self-evaluation. What I am suggesting is that abortion shouldn't be a swift or hasty decision. Adoption is a viable option that allows you to bless beyond measure a childless couple who has been praying for a miracle for years.

True, there will be a hole in your heart because your birth child is being raised by someone else. You will think, "I hope my child doesn't hate me for giving them up." You may be fortunate enough to achieve an open adoption, where you are a part of your child's life. Annabelle has a relationship with her birth mother, Amy, who lives locally. They see each other at church frequently and go out to lunch along with her birth grandparents, Nana and Papa. They come to all of her plays, school performances, and ballet performances. Annabelle does sleepovers at Nana and Papa's every few months. While our adoption story is almost too good to be true, it is a story of what can happen and what is possible.

Drugs

The drug problem in the United States is more severe than ever. With marijuana legal in ten states and decriminalized in 13 others, it's only a matter of time before it achieves legal status nationwide. The opioid epidemic is still running wild with a wide distribution of pills, heroin, and fentanyl. Fentanyl is so powerful that a trace amount, which can be absorbed through skin contact, can kill. Never in our history have drugs been deadlier.

As parents, we are at war to ensure our children never try these powerful drugs because it only takes one time for addiction to take root or death to result.

REMEMBER

Involvement and observation are key. Are there changes in your children? Are they getting more secretive with their life? Are grades or attitude changing at school? Do you know their circle of friends? What are those friends' interests and activities? Are your kids busy with sports, clubs, music, or hobbies? A kid who has scheduled activities and goals has a lower chance of experimenting with drugs.

Honoring Your Father and Mother

Our parents played such an important role in our success achievement, so don't forget that they deserve our time, attention, and respect for the physical and emotional energy they invested in us, not to mention the financial resources. Because our life expectancy has dramatically increased in the last 40 years (from 73.80 to 78.69), we have gained five years of extended life. And some, like my father, live far beyond that timeframe and are in good health doing it.

In the Bible, the Ten Commandments were handed down to Moses from God as rules for right living. Commandment number four is "Honor your father and mother." It's pretty high up on the list, so I think we should assume that how we treat our parents is important. Be advised that your children are watching you and will likely model whatever behavior you demonstrate. So if you don't feel obligated to honor your father and mother in meaningful ways for them, then do it selfishly for yourself so that your children give you honor, help, and service later in life when you might need it.

Discovering what's important to them

Many older people slow down in their day-to-day lives. They invest a lot of time in reminiscing about the past. They relive their family and friends in different stages of their lives. They remember when they were more healthy, vibrant, strong, and beautiful, when they could physically do things their body no longer allows. Growing older isn't for the weak-minded or wimps.

Engage your parents in conversation. What are their values? What experiences in life were most meaningful? What did they do when faced with disappointment and challenge? How did they overcome the lows? How did they celebrate their highs?

REMEMBER

Slowing down to gather their wisdom and life experiences will insure that their life wisdom will be captured for future generations.

Getting to know their formative years

Our parents tend to reveal stories periodically from the past. At just the right moment, they will break out the old yarn that they had to walk to school in two feet of snow and that it was uphill both ways. I have had a difficult time dressing up my "get to school" story since my bus stop was at the edge of our property, and school was less than a ten-minute ride away.

Sitting down with parents to talk with them about their childhood honors them. You will gain a clear perspective of how much the world has changed, and you'll learn what shaped or motivated your parents.

ANECDOTE

When I sat down recently with my father, he related some stories that I hadn't heard before. I had no idea of the harsh and squalid living conditions he endured in his early years living in a coal miners' camp in North Dakota. He, his parents, and three sisters barely had a roof over their heads and no floor, other than dirt. They certainly didn't have running water or toilets. Learning of my father's past increased my respect for him because he climbed out of these early life conditions to become highly educated and successful. He was a dentist, land developer, property renovator, and investor. Now in his late 80s, he's a gentleman farmer.

Being there when they need you

It's an honor to serve your parents in their time of need. It's a way to work to rebalance the debt we all have to them. I'm not talking about financial debt but the debt of love, service, and devotion. We owe our parents for raising us. When our parents are in need, it's our obligation as children to support and uplift them.

ANECDOTE

When my mother died after her long battle with MS, Joan and I spent large amounts of our time with my father, and Joan stepped up as a daughter. She and my father have a special relationship; she has never been a daughter-in-law, just a daughter, and she treated my parents as her parents. It's truly a testament that I married up in life. My father was capable of taking care of himself, but I know he did appreciate the extra attention and companionship that was provided by Joan and myself. He was as anyone would be after 50 years of marriage missing his wife. I think what brought him and me comfort was knowing my mom was in heaven and that she was in a new body. That her broken down, poorly functioning earth-suit was replaced with a more glorious heavenly suit for eternity. Her pain and suffering in that earth-suit were over. That didn't remove the emotions of missing her, but it did help.

When Joan's stepmother passed away a few years ago, she knew her father needed her. He was unable to take care of himself due to extensive health issues that her stepmom had handled. In the weeks after her death, Joan was staying with him a few nights and days per week even though he lived more than five hours from our home in Bend, Oregon. She found him a clean, friendly, and well-kept assisted living facility. Then she proceeded to set up his room with a new bed, chairs, and family photos so that he felt welcome. She visited him at least once week until he passed away over a year after her stepmother's death. She demonstrated to our children how to follow the commandment, honor your father and mother.

Putting praise in writing

Any parent knows they have made countless mistakes with their children: the times you made the wrong decision, or you were too hard on them, or you didn't give them enough encouragement, or you assumed they did something bad but they actually didn't. One of the best ways to value and edify your parents is to do so in writing, and that can take the form of a journal you give them, just simple note cards, or a letter or a postcard from a trip you took. You can certainly send an e-mail with your feelings and appreciation expressed in it.

A phone call is good, but it's not as permanent as a letter or note. You can't tack a phone call on the bulletin board or put it on the mantel. It's hard to show it to friends or even review it later. I remember helping my mother one time clean out a closet in my late 20s. She had numerous athletic shoe boxes stacked in the closet. She had kept every letter that her children had ever written her. I must admit that my brother Kurt had the lion's share of those shoe boxes, but I had one or two. That moment was a great illustration of the value of a note or letter that comes in the mail to a parent or loved one.

Crafting a tribute

One of the most powerful experiences I have had personally has been crafting a tribute to my father. I was just introduced to this concept in reading the book by Dennis Rainey called *The Tribute: What Every Parent Longs to Hear*. In his book, Dennis describes the inner longing of parents to know that their children feel they did okay or even well as a parent, that they didn't screw up their kids too much. Parents need validation that their lifetime of hopes, dreams, and worries were all worth it.

I wrote a tribute to my father about six months before I started this book. It was a difficult and wonderful journey as I thought about events of my life, lessons he taught me, ceremonies, and milestones. After a few weeks of crafting and editing, I was weeping with humility and gratitude. As I am writing about it now, the emotions of gratitude for his investment in my life are swelling within me.

The crafting of a tribute to my father was one of the most rewarding experiences of my life. I titled the document "The Sentinel" because of his always watchful eye of protection and security for our family. It is being printed on fine paper and framed so that I can present it to him the next time I see him. I am sure it will be an emotionally meaningful experience for us both that we will never forget.

Chapter **13**

Building High-Quality Business Relationships

Work, business, and commerce take up a significant part of our lives. The vast majority of people have experienced a number of business relationships and business interactions before their formal education is complete. You might have had a paper delivery route, sold cookies for the Girl Scouts, raised money for your basketball team, sold ads in the high school paper, babysat younger kids, lifeguarded, or worked at a fast-food restaurant.

Even at a young age, we start to learn and develop business relationships and skills that allow us to establish success habits that we can use for life. We have both employee and entrepreneurial business relationships. Whichever position you occupy presently, in order to have quality business relationships, you must be well versed on the needs and expectations of each. To have success in business, you need a healthy relationship between employee and employer, regardless of whether the employer is a large company or a small business entrepreneur.

The most important business relationship is between the people in the business and their customers and prospects. The second most important relationship is between the employees in the business so that they can fulfill what has been promised to the customer. Your true objective is to provide more for the customer than is expected.

Providing More Service Than You Are Paid For

ANECDOTE

The key to sustainability in business is delivery of value. Let me give you an example. I don't drink coffee. I just never have acquired a taste for it. But I do enjoy tea and usually have a few cups throughout the day. Tea is something I reward myself with, so I buy higher quality teas rather than grocery-store tea bags. I've tried numerous brands and flavors, and my favorite is Harney & Sons, which is a high-quality product. Their online shopping experience is easy, fast, and responsive. And what I really like is that they always add a few extra individual tea bags of different flavors or varieties as a bonus in my order at no additional cost. This plussing strategy has created brand loyalty and increased sales. They know by that giving away a few extra tea bags of different flavors, customers can enjoy trying other types of tea without having to buy a box of 20 tea bags. This bonus removes the risk of trying out a new tea that I might not enjoy.

What's your plussing strategy? What can you provide to your customers and clients beyond what they are paying for? But keep in mind that your plussing strategy will not make up for a poor customer service experience. Your core service needs to be of high quality and an excellent value or the plussing strategy won't be effective.

As an employee, providing more service to your boss and company leads to loyalty, increased income, and advancement. As you are climbing the ladder of job success, you must ask yourself these questions:

> » What is my plussing strategy toward my boss and company?
> » What can I do to add more value and service to them?
> » What responsibilities can I take on that would free up my boss?
> » How can I increase service and efficiency to our customers?
> » What can I read or learn that will help my value to the company?
> » How can client communication be increased or enhanced?

If you are in a service-based business, a plussing strategy is essential. The typical customer service experience in most businesses is transactional. We as customers are provided a product or service by a business. The communication frequency and quality diminish when we have received the product or service. If we are unlikely to need the specific service again soon, the frequency plummets.

One of the big keys to providing more service than paid for is communication. A lack of communication in many professions is the biggest complaint by most customers. For example, for more than 30 years, the number-one complaint about real estate agents has been lack of communication and responsiveness. In that time range, the methods of communication have broadened and expanded. Thirty years ago, we had snail mail and telephone communication on landline phones. Some people had answering machines. Now we have mobile phones capable of voice, text, e-mail, Facebook, Twitter, and other social media platforms. Yet the lack of communication is still the number-one complaint about a real estate agent. The problem hasn't been solved with the advancement of communication methods.

REMEMBER

In business, you have to constantly work to solve problems, build customer and employee relationships, and provide more service than you are compensated for.

Increasing your value

Increasing your personal and business value in the marketplace isn't an event; it's a process. The value you have to your customers and company as an employee is based on the service you render. It's based on the skills you possess and have proven up until this moment. We attract our success by the person we have become at this point in our life journey. That doesn't mean that we will be at the same level of value our whole lives. We all have the option to learn, improve, come in early, and stay late to increase our value. We all have the opportunity to achieve greater responsibility for our outcomes in life.

Your value in life and business is attached to your willingness to take on more responsibility. The declaration of "I'm responsible" is one of the most powerful you can make in life. It means accepting responsibility for whatever outcomes leads to success in thought, deed, and actions. It embodies the willingness to be accountable to yourself, to put yourself on the line, and to evaluate and objectively compare progress. That is a key characteristic of success and value.

Few people truly want to accept responsibility, even in their 30s, 40s, and 50s. The people who shrink away from responsibility provide more opportunities for those around them. If your company has employees who lack the willingness to take on responsibility, that void creates an opportunity for you to lead. You lead by taking responsibility. When you embrace responsibility, you will be more valuable and will deserve to lead. Winston Churchill said, "Responsibility is the price of greatness."

TIP

To increase your value takes one commitment: to work harder on improving yourself than you do at your job. To be more valuable and successful, you have to develop skills that are valuable. Here are just a few:

>> Problem solving

>> Efficiency analysis

>> Sales force productivity

>> Positive mental attitude

>> Exceptional customer service

>> Marketing, social media marketing, and communication

These value-enhancing marketable skills don't all need to be acquired. You only need a handful of these skills to increase your value.

Looking for and seizing opportunity

When you meet with people who have achieved success and ask them where they feel opportunities in your community are in the future, you are harnessing the brainpower of more than yourself. You are gaining a valuable and fresh perspective on economics, business problems in the community, and even potential solutions.

REMEMBER

To be a successful entrepreneur means to take action. Everyone comes up with good ideas, and one good idea implemented well can change your life and bank account. In most people who desire to be entrepreneurial, the true difference between success and failure is simply in the decision to take action or not. Do you have the willingness to act?

If your desire is to have an entrepreneurial business someday, here are a few ways to find and seize opportunities:

>> **Actively look around for opportunities in other markets:** What business opportunities work well in other markets and locations from your home area? What geographic areas are in front of your market by 24 to 36 months? What business opportunities are doing well that have not hit your market yet? What trends are they selling that will likely come into your marketplace in the near future?

>> **Actively look for problems to solve:** In evaluating opportunities, ask yourself what is not being done? What problems are my friends and family experiencing that no solution has yet been created? The best opportunities are to solve problems that are common to just about everyone.

>> **Actively look for economic trends:** By studying economic trends, we can see patterns from the past that will likely repeat themselves in the future. The housing market crash in 2008 created opportunities for people and companies to help consumers. Burgeoning industries were born in helping people short-sell their home. Advisors sprung up to teach people to avoid or stall the foreclosure process. After these opportunities were winding down, helping people clear up and reestablish credit became a trend.

>> **Actively look for opportunities that run counter to the herd:** The biggest opportunities frequently run counter to the herd, or the masses. They run counter to an established trend. Many times, when a trend, especially an economic trend, is losing momentum or has run its course, that is when opportunity is highest. The highest opportunity is likely being a contrarian to the trend.

The most famous contrarian is Warren Buffett. Mr. Buffett has attracted his most significant wealth and best opportunities by moving contrary to people and the marketplace. When everyone in 2008 and 2009 was selling stocks and bailing out of the stock market, he was buying positions in high quality companies. When the banks were on the financial ropes in 2008 and 2009, they had bad assets and bad debt on their balance sheets, so investors fled investment in banks. He, in contrast, was loaning money to Goldman Sachs and Bank of America. In the Goldman Sachs deal, he loaned out 5 billion dollars. In less than two and a half years, when Goldman Sachs bought him back out, he made a profit of 3.1 billion dollars, which was 62-percent profit in less than 30 months. That is the power of the right contrarian opportunity in combination with the willingness to act.

REMEMBER

Few of us have the asset base of Warren Buffett to work from, but we can observe economic trends. We can prepare for opportunity by living below our means to save cash and assets. Then when the right opportunity presents itself, we can act, decisively, contrary to the trends and the masses. Conventional wisdom and following the herd are usually result in average achievement or worse.

What Makes a Great Employee

Every business owner has their own definition of what a great employee is. Whether you are running a large international company or a local mom-and-pop convenience store, you are looking for people who will be good employees. Employees and employers both have to work together to create a wonderful company, with products and services that benefit the customers and the communities they serve.

Showing that you care

Beyond the nuts and bolts of skills and experience, I think the most important quality of employees is that they care. An employee who really, truly cares about others is an important person in the success journey of a company. The best employees care about the customer. They care about the customer's experience in engaging with your company. They care about how the customer is served.

I have been in countless businesses encountering employees who treat my presence there like an intrusion on their day. These types of employees are just passing the time until the end of their shift. They have failed to grasp that their number-one job is serving the customer and that their paycheck is aligned with the service of people who come to the business, whether that's a physical location, website, or call center. Great employees listen to a customer's problems fully before they speak. They care enough to hear customers out and work diligently to solve their problems.

The characteristic of caring extends beyond the customer. It extends to other employees in the company: leadership, executives, and ownership. It extends to the vendors for your company whom the employers must treat with courtesy and care even when they might drop the ball. These people and companies are working to extend service to the company and its clients and customers.

Choosing the right work situation

Small companies have the greatest need for exceptional employees. I have a particular belief that I have shared with every employee I have ever hired in the last 20 years: Employees in small companies are required to work harder than in large companies. This is a fact and it's very much unfair to the employees who accept a job working for a small company. As a multiple small-business owner for more than 30 years, I acknowledge the imbalance between the expectation and workload on small-business employees versus large-business employees. The acknowledgement doesn't change the need for employees in smaller businesses to work harder. I fully acknowledge that a small-business employee is required to be more and do more. Here are the reasons why:

>> **Fewer workers to pull the weight:** There are basic functions in any business, small or large that must be done. Just because your company is small doesn't mean sales, marketing, accounting, and customer service are lessor priorities. In all likelihood, most of these are a higher priority to success. As a small-business owner, you have less margin for mistakes. Your access to capital to cover those mistakes through borrowing is lower. There are fewer people to perform all those functions.

>> **Each customer is more critical to the business:** In a small business, because of fewer customers and customer opportunities, each interaction, customer, client, sales opportunity, and service opportunity carries more importance to the health and prosperity to the business. One less person going through the doors at MGM Grand in Las Vegas has less influence on the bottom line than one less person through your neighborhood dry cleaner.

>> **Employees can hide in larger companies:** Because small businesses have fewer employees, a poorly producing employee more heavily affects the customers, company, and other employees. The other employees have to pick up the slack, but there are fewer of them to do so. If an employee wants a job to just punch the clock, get paid for showing up, and do minimal work, then a small business is a poor fit (not that a large company would want that type of an employee either). That attitude will not lead to success, but a termination will happen in most cases much faster in a small company than it would in a large one.

There are benefits in both large companies and small companies for employees. Being a wonderful employee means selecting the right setting that allows you to grow, thrive, and achieve success. No company offers a one-size-fits-all experience to its employees.

Expressing appreciation and loyalty

As a small business owner, loyalty is a quality I am looking for in employees. Applicants for a job opening can express reasonable frustrations with their previous job or current job. But when they reveal too much detail, or breach the trust of their previous employer, or divulge what is likely internal or proprietary information, and then they're crossing the line of loyalty. That is an employee that nobody wants.

A good employee is loyal to the company and boss. Being loyal encompasses a broad base of actions. It's showing up on time and taking only the break and lunch times allotted. It's working a full day with as much passion, focus, and productivity as you can. It's being courteous, helpful, and kind to all other employees and customers. Loyal employees also don't bail when challenges or problems arises. They're ready to stay late or come in on weekends to help the team.

Quality companies put the employees ahead of management and ownership. In my case, there have been times in the last 30 years of economic ups and downs that I was the last to get paid, and sometimes I didn't get paid. I have gone without compensation so that my employees and vendors were paid on time. I have borrowed money from banks to meet those obligations when economic times were lean. That is the code and responsibility of an employer. I did my best to keep the workforce employed, but I also terminated people who were not performing with dignity.

It's not easy running an entrepreneurial business. There are a lot of sleepless nights if you stay in business for any length of time. Good employees are cognizant of those sacrifices and pressures and express appreciation to their boss or owner. Business owners are also human, and appreciation from the people they work with lifts their spirits and gives them energy. They need that more from their staff in times of challenge.

Looking for opportunities to serve

The best employees are constantly looking for ways to serve customers, other employees, and bosses. It can be as simple as leading an effort to celebrate and recognize other workers around you, which can increase company moral. Other examples include sending notes of thank you to your coworkers, bringing in special snacks and treats, and celebrating victories and life milestones with others. A employee whose attitude and actions spread positivity is valuable to any organization.

One of the most important actions for any company is sales. The vast majority of companies fail due to lack of sales. There is a big opportunity to remove administrative and servicing activities from sales staff so that they can invest a greater amount of time in the core sales actions of prospecting, lead follow-up, and sales presentations. As an employee, when you look for opportunities to better serve your sales force, you increase your value as well, and you will have a direct influence on the company's bottom line due to increased sales.

Serve by solving problems in whatever department you are in. If you are someone in the trenches working with the systems, processes, and procedures of the business, you have a unique vantage point that your boss or business owner does not possess. Get in the habit of finding problems, but you should also find solutions to bring forth.

REMEMBER

Valuable employees come to their boss with a solution or two for any problems they have identified. Don't just drop the problems at your boss's feet. There are countless problem spotters in companies but few problem solvers. By bringing solutions, you show that you care about the company. It's easy to identify what's going wrong or what needs to be improved. It's harder to create solutions. If you can bring both to the table, you will be a success.

What Makes a Great Employer

The vast majority of us have had both good and poor employees. We've had employers and managers who encouraged, valued, and praised our work. They built our self-esteem and self-worth as employees as well as human beings.

We've also had employers who cared little about us. They did little to train, support, or reward our efforts.

An employer that takes a genuine interest in their employees is one who will create a successful and caring culture. The genuine interest needs to extend beyond the workplace environment. It extends to their family and the challenges they are experiencing outside of the workplace. As an employer, I have always strived to be flexible when employees need time off to deal with health issues for themselves or their immediate family. That caring and flexibility in almost all cases has paid business dividends. Unfortunately, a few employees have taken advantage of my generosity for a period of time. My hope is to screen out that person in the interview process.

Providing a sense of security to employees is critical. When employees feel insecure, they start to look for other opportunities outside the company. When the paycheck is delayed or bounces, they start to feel concerned about their family's well-being. There are untold stories of companies failing to pay employees as agreed. As an employer, it's your obligation to have sufficient credit reserves to pay employees on time, even when your business has a bad month or bad quarter. If the financial challenges continue, it's your obligation to make the right decisions in cutting unnecessary expenses or even making staff reductions so that you can meet the long-term obligations to the remaining employees who are your best performers.

Communicating clearly vision and goals

Any company or employer has a business vision and business goals. The business vision is a foundation for creating success and sustainability for a company, large or small.

Being able to establish a business vision for your company separates you from the other businesses in the marketplace. When building your business, you must pause and work to define your business vision. Enduring, successful people and successful companies establish their core values and core purpose. They then remain fixed on those core values and purpose throughout their business life. The changing elements are their business strategy and tactics due to the marketplace changes and the influence of competition.

The core ideology of a business defines the timeless character of any company. It has two parts: core values and core purpose. Jim Collins, best selling business author of *Good to Great*, describes core values and core purpose this way:

» **Core values** are the handful of guiding principles by which a company navigates.

» **Core purpose** is an organization's most fundamental reason for being.

As a company, knowing who you are and what you stand for is actually more important than where you are going. The innovation part of "where you are going" is in constant flux. Ralph Larsen, former CEO of Johnson & Johnson, sums up core values eloquently. He said, "The core values embodied in our credo might be a competitive advantage, but that's not why we have them. We have them because they define for us what we stand for, and we would hold them even if they became a competitive disadvantage in certain situations."

REMEMBER

Your principles in how you run your business will be influenced by your core values and core purpose. If your core values and purpose don't match, you will have incongruence in your business. The first people who will see it are the employees of the company. You will lose credibility, trust, faith, passion, and commitment to you and your cause. Your employees will believe that cutting corners in your business is acceptable because you do it.

If you continue to stray from your core values and core purpose, your customers will soon become aware. This is especially true if you publicly state your core purpose and core values in your marketing pieces. Even if they don't read it or hear it publicly, they will observe it. It is impossible to get away from the observable elements.

My belief is you can't just tell people to adhere to and believe in your core values. You can't just hand them a piece of paper with your core values and core purpose on it and consider it done for good. You need to offer constant education about the meaning of your core values and core purpose. Through training, education, and coaching of your core values and core purpose, you want your employees to internalize those principles and apply them to their decision making. If a staff member doesn't share your view, you can't change it; you can only improve it.

TIP

And if you can't change people, you have to change people. You might have to read that line a time or two for it to sink in. It's always a better statement from the platform than on paper. What I am trying to express is that if someone on your team won't improve or change, you will have to find someone else for the position. You will have to change to someone else.

As a business, if your core vision and core purpose define the service and experience for your clients at this level, you'd better make the commitment to have enough staff to pull that off. You will need to guarantee that your systems are customer oriented; that they are easy to understand for your staff and clients. The clients you select can't be focused on a service model that Joe Cheap Discount service provider uses.

Business goals are more granular, usually numbers-focused in sales, customer service scores, revenue, net profit, and development of new products and services. A good company will have managers, senior leadership, and executives who communicate clearly the vision and goals that are most important for the company's success. The best will organize them into a few key objectives and measures. Success and especially success habits are simple and few in number. A well run company doesn't try and make too many changes at once. The leadership has figured out what is most important to the growth and sustainability of the company. You have to walk a fine line when changing initiatives or risk overwhelming staff.

REMEMBER

Employees need continual communication from leadership. In a small company, that could be a weekly personal update on progress toward goals and key initiatives of change. In a large company or division, it could be a video e-mail weekly or monthly from divisional heads to inform the rank and file of progress on goals. This communication could also be used to highlight how an employee lived out the business vision of the company with a customer or client.

Setting clear and compelling standards

Accountability is a big buzzword that entrepreneurs, executives, and managers use all the time. "We want to hold our people accountable." For your staff members, the word might conjure up images of a drill sergeant in Marine Corps boot camp. The word is overused and misunderstood by most managers and employees for the process of setting clear standards and measuring them. Quality employers and quality companies want performance improvement. They desire to serve their customers better, earn a higher profit margin, and increase pay for their key people.

Charles Coonradt, in his landmark book, *The Game of Work,* shares how to make work and workers more effective and enjoyable. His primary tenant in the book is this: "When performance is measured, performance improves." The act of measuring the performance of a company, department, or of a human being creates an internal trigger or internal pressure on a quality employee to do better, faster, sell more, serve more.

He further states, "When performance is measured and reported, performance improves faster." The reporting and sharing of measured performance can speed the process of improvement to another level. When employees know they are being watched, monitored, or compared, it tends to increase the performance improvement process. For example, sharing sales data and performance across a sales team creates healthy competition for recognition. Sales is an inherently competitive business. If you are in sales in a company, you have both competitors from other companies that provide similar products and service that your company does. You also have other sales people inside your company. You might not be competing with the other salespeople on specific accounts, but everyone wants to be the lead dog in the pack. If you aren't the lead dog, your view is always the same.

Here are a few tips for setting standards:

>> **Be clear on what is expected from each employee.** Do your employees know and fully understand the expectation? What are the timeframes of completion? What must they get accomplished daily? What quality standards are expected? How should they prioritize projects and deadlines? You can't expect employees to hit a standard that hasn't been communicated or that they clearly don't understand.

>> **Set a clear standard for each employee.** Employees need to be able to gauge how they are doing. When we fail to set standards or require adherence to standards, what happens is that we create new habits of substandard performance. We create feelings in employees that "it doesn't matter" or that the management is based on talk, not action.

In sales, setting a standard means sales quotas. That means top-line sales revenue standards per week, month, quarter, or annually. It could also include the quotas for action or effort as in specific number of presentations, lead follow-up conversations, or prospecting conversations. A standard or quota could be set for talk time, which would be how many minutes on the phone each day or week a salesperson achieves.

>> **Remember that failure is an event, not a person.** When we have taught employees to perform a specific task, set a specific standard of quality and performance, inform them of measuring and reporting timelines, and they fall short, then it's time to recognize the gap or failure. The failure was not the person but the performance. In our correction strategy, we need to both correct and encourage the belief that they can do it to standard and beyond. We need, in essence, to praise the person and criticize the performance.

Praising performance creates winners

People are motivated to perform better when you catch them doing something well. What we reward and praise tends to be repeated. Most people are more motivated by other rewards at work than money. But you can't pay a substandard wage and retain good people just on verbal praise. People do not live on verbal praise alone.

Most people are motivated by positive attention they receive from owners, managers, or colleagues in the business. Public praise and recognition are powerful ways to create a team of high performers. Praising your people is a habit to be developed. If the only time they hear you express a hearty "well done" is when ordering a steak, you will likely lose your best people over time.

Expanding your employees' opportunities

We should all want our employees to expand as people, both inside and outside our company environment. There are a number of ways that we can help and support the growth of our staff. The main one that comes to mind is advancement inside the company to higher positions of value and earnings. The development of new skills can enable an employee to feel more valuable and integral to the success of the business.

Investing in your employees through training indicates a willingness to increase their performance for today's job and also prepare them to handle additional responsibilities in the future. The cross-training of employees is an integral step in any business or department. It's just good business practice, so when employees are absent through vacation or sickness, productivity doesn't crawl to a halt.

I truly believe that expanding opportunities reaches far beyond the walls of your office or factory. I want my employees to be able to fund their life presently as well as in the future. That's why, as a small-business owner, I have always offered a retirement plan to my employees with a company matching feature. It does cost my company profit to match their contributions, pay for the plan's administration, and organize the records and documents. But the value to my staff who participate is significant. I have a few employees who don't participate, and every enrollment period, I personally talk with them to encourage them to sign up and at least start small in their savings, but the key is to start (as I discuss in detail in Chapter 16).

Building Customer and Client Relationships

Businesses operate in a competitive environment, and that's true whether you are a professional, operate a restaurant, have a sales-based distribution business, manage a local dry cleaner, or own a large conglomerate. You have key competitors that are attempting to take your customers and clients away from you. To think, "Oh, that will never happen" is to be naive.

The quality of service you deliver and the depth of the relationship that you have with your customers will determine your success, profitability, and longevity in business.

REMEMBER

There are plenty of competitors that do an outstanding job in the moment that service is delivered to the customer. The key habit is to come up with *after* services — and by that I mean what you do after service is rendered. What do you do after customers have picked up their dry cleaning for the month? After they've bought hedge clippers at the hardware store? After they've bought a home from you and won't buy for another one for five to ten more years?

The after service, value, and communication is where you truly build the customer relationship. Up until that service is fully rendered, a customer assumes that you are providing the service because you want to gain compensation. All the calls, texts, e-mails result in your service being delivered in exchange for funds. But after the exchange of service for funds, all service and value you deliver from that point onward shows that you care about your customers. That's a powerful difference.

Solving problems and creating value

The value of any product or service can be summed up in this equation:

Value = Benefits – Cost

We as consumers feel like we received value from a service provider or business if the value exceeded the benefits we received, subtracted from the costs we paid.

For example, let's say you are having a wonderful meal at a restaurant. The food was delicious and ample in quantity. The waiter was prompt and attentive to your needs. The ambience was comfortable and enjoyable. Who you spent the evening with can also influence your perception of value. The received benefits of enjoyment, fun, well-being, satisfaction, wonderful tastes, and pleasant experiences are all there. If all those benefits you felt about the restaurant exceeded what you spent, you will likely be back and even tell your friends about what a good time and wonderful meal you had there. That's the power of Value = Benefits – Cost.

In business, we deliver value to customers, but we also solve problems. The best products and services are designed to solve problems for people and other companies. Why do you go to the doctor? It's to respond to a present health problem you are experiencing or to head off, through preventative medicine, a problem in the future. We might also learn how to enhance the quality and longevity of our life. Doctors ask a lot of questions because they want to solve problems for their patients. That's a good model in business as well.

As a business owner or employee, you should be asking your best customers these questions:

- » What are the key challenges you are experiencing right now?

- » How might we be of service to help you solve them?

- » If we could improve our products or services for you, how could we do that?

- » What are you not getting from us you wish you could?

- » What other companies like ours are you receiving service from?

- » What are you receiving from them?

- » Why did you select them to receive _____?

These types of questions give you insight into your customers and will help you improve service and solve more of their problems. This strategy of solving problems increases your value with each person, client, and company you do business with.

Under-promise and over-deliver

We have all heard this advice: "Do what you say you will do." In the business world of today, I think that is expected at the bare minimum. And that bare minimum standard will not prevent your clients and customers from going to your competitors in the future.

REMEMBER

In business, we all need a way to "plus" our clients. A *plussing strategy* is a unique way that we can add value, which means under-promise and over-deliver.

Doubletree Hotels has a unique plussing strategy. When you check into a one of their hotels anywhere in the world, you receive a warm, freshly baked chocolate chip cookie. They have a warming drawer built into the front desk in every hotel. It's their way to add value, make you feel welcome, and place you in a delightful chocolate-chip-sugar coma all at the same time. What's your plussing strategy in your business?

Connecting in business integrity

Business is about, first and foremost, trust — the trust between company and customer. Customers need to be able to trust that the company will perform as promised. Employees of the company must believe that the company will fulfill promises made by the company to the customer. What I'm talking about is essentially integrity among all parties in this relationship. People in leadership breed a culture and environment of trust. That foundation of trust creates a thriving business that benefits both customers and employees.

Employees have a key responsibility to their employer's of integrity. For example, significant productivity is often lost through employees being on their phone at work. Checking Facebook and Instagram accounts and answering texts outside of break time show a lack of integrity on the part of the employee. The arriving late, leaving early, or extending your lunch break is stealing from your employer. These habits are pervasive in the office environment of today.

TIP

We need to put our phones down, leave them in our purse, desk drawer, or car. The businesses we work for will be significantly enhanced by this simple practice.

Establishing long-term service relationships

The true value of a customer doesn't come from a one-time transactional sale. You want your business to become an indispensable part of their life so that you gain the honored and hallowed position of serving them for years, decades, or generations. I have some clients that I have been serving for close to 20 years. I consider it an honor to have established our relationship and helped them grow their business for almost two decades. Let me share a few tips to help:

>> **Communicate frequently with value.** Set up a video blog, e-mail newsletter, Facebook group, or some method to communicate regularly with your customers and clients. The communication should be valuable to them. If you are a doctor, focus on health, new medical discoveries, reminders of new immunizations available, eating and exercise tips, and so on.

>> **Communicate personally by sending texts, making calls, or writing personal notes to key customers or clients.** The mass communication of value through e-mail, social media, or blogs is wonderful, but if you want to deepen personal relationships, it must be personal. All relationships are deepened through one-on-one connection. Most of us get busy and fail to make time. The habit of personal communication creates success, and it takes less time than you think. Set a reasonable standard so that you can establish the habit. Start with making one personal call per day, each workday, to a key client. Resolve to not leave for home until that's completed. In a year, you will have 240 conversations with key clients. Can you think of a better way to establish long-term relationships with them?

>> **Recognize milestone moments.** Milestone moments can recognize how long you've worked with a client or customer. Or you could commemorate personal events like weddings, anniversaries, births, promotions, or birthdays. When you recognize milestone moments, you deepen the customer relationship. Select one or two types of milestone moments that you will recognize in your best customers.

5
Success with Wealth and Money

IN THIS PART . . .

Define what wealth means to you and why you want to achieve it.

Approach wealth like a game you can win.

Craft a plan from your earnings, savings, and investments to achieve financial independence and wealth.

Chapter **14**

Achieving Financial Success

E veryone has their own ideas of what financial success would be for them. It might involve income, lifestyle, possessions, and retirement security. The truth is, whatever your definition or objectives of financial success, it must be defined and planned for to achieve it. Most people spend more time planning a one-week vacation than they do their financial success. Long after the beach cocktails are gone and a distant memory, most of us wish we had a better plan to achieve wealth.

My objective is to help you build a solid financial strategy so that you can achieve financial success and wealth. My thoughts, observations, ideas, and strategies come from the self-inflicted wounds and road abrasions I have experienced in defining and executing a wealth plan and strategy for more than 30 years. I have personally read hundreds of books on wealth, investing, real estate investing, retirement planning, and wealth planning. Additionally, I have coached thousands of entrepreneurs, many of whom make a lot of money but have achieved limited true financial wealth. Wealth and financial freedom is not based solely on how much you earn. There are countless stories of people from modest means who made million-dollar donations to charity later in life or upon death through their estate.

REMEMBER

Achieving wealth is first at its core a state of mind. It is a decision to be made. As Napoleon Hill said, "What the mind can conceive and believe, the mind can achieve." To become wealthy or financially independent, at its core, is a decision you resolve to acquire. Because wealth is a long-term pursuit, rather than a short-term pursuit, like I want to lose 10 pounds, the mind has to remain in the state of resolve for a longer period of time. The decision is the first step and requires establishment beyond the "I wish" stage.

The Search for Financial Freedom

My observation is that financial security and financial freedom are desired by the vast majority of people. The definition of financial freedom is personal for each of us. The lifestyle and level of freedom desired varies. Some want to live comfortably; others want a higher level of opulence in their golden years. The exploration of self and personal definition of financial freedom is crafted through your life experiences and reflecting on the desire you have for your life and family.

My definition of financial freedom and wealth was shaped initially by observing my parents. My father had established a productive dental practice. His and my mother's philosophy was to live below their means, which meant to enjoy life but save substantially for the rainy day that may come. They further demonstrated that the freedom of choice to work, or not, was something to aspire to. Being able to achieve a level of wealth that allows you to stop working at an earlier age creates freedom. It provides options, choices, and enjoyment because your time is now your own. You are not required to trade your time to earn an income to fund your lifestyle and living expenses. You have amassed enough assets or wealth that you can live your chosen lifestyle for the remainder of your life, removed from the pressures of work to create income. That place of freedom creates abundant peace of mind and lower stress.

My personal definitions of wealth are more rooted in security and freedom rather than the cars, homes, and lifestyle markers of being affluent. I again state that I am not exclaiming that my way or thought process is correct for everyone. Security for my family and freedom for me with regard to my time are most important. Those desires have pulled me to wealth. The clarity of my drive and the emotions connected to that drive have made the journey motivating and filled with satisfaction.

What drives you?

The key to achieving financial wealth is understanding what it is you really want. Then understand why that's important to you. You create the target and then go after it in a consistent way. What is it that you want in your life with regard to wealth?

>> What type of home do you desire?

>> What type of an annual income do you need?

>> Is that the income you need to replace in retirement?

>> What's the timeline to achieve it?

>> Why is financial freedom important?

>> Why do you want it?

>> What will financial freedom do for you?

>> What emotions will you feel having achieved it?

The why you want something is the big driver of success. The why, if it's deeply rooted, provides an avenue of moving beyond the adversity you face. You will encounter challenging roads in the quest to achieving financial freedom. Any objective you desire will likely involve roadblocks you will have to overcome. The why is the fuel to increase your determination during those trials. It's the passion that causes you to stick to the path when conditions get tough. It's the focus that needs to be present for 10, 20, or even 30 years to achieve wealth.

Few people achieve financial wealth in a few years. There are certainly examples of people who did. The vast majority of financial independent people have achieved it over 10, 20, or 30 years. You must be prepared to endure economic downturns, lost jobs, bad investments, and emotionally draining life events and still continue on to financial wealth. The Internet is full of too-good-to-be-true opportunities that claim to create wealth in the blink of an eye. The vast majority of them offer the same glowing opportunity that Bernie Madoff did for his investors.

What emotions are connected?

You are reading this part of the book to learn better how to attract the money and wealth you desire. But in truth, money is not what we are after. The money is not the causality of success. It's not even the result, although you will have more of it. What we desire are the feelings and emotions of being empowered: freedom, security, pride, and acceptance. We want to have choices, give our children a better lifestyle, and give to charity. These are what drive most humans to acquire, save, invest, and work hard to achieve wealth. So the question is, what are your drivers? It might be none of what I have listed, and it's something else for you. Your ability to define and acknowledge the driver in you is step one.

ANECDOTE

Most of us are driven by our feelings. What feelings will wealth create for you? In the fall of 1994, Joan and I were celebrating our fourth year of marriage. I had just completed my third year in real estate sales. I was 32 years old and wanted to make a statement of "I have arrived" and that I was a success. That year we bought a building lot in a golf course community in Bend, Oregon. Our intent was to build a second home that next summer in 1995. Because my parents had a second home, the emotions of accomplishment, success, and wealth for me were attached to having a second home. It was a realization of a dream from my childhood. We started construction in June of 1995 and moved in mid-February 1996. A sense of self-worth welled up in me as each stage of construction was completed.

Looking back, it's safe to say that my ego was out of balance. I was over my skis and likely to have a yard sale crash on the mountain. For those non-skiers, a yard sale is a big wipeout where your gear is scattered all over the ski run. Frequently, our most basic drivers and motivators come from childhood experiences and expectations. The good ones we want to re-create; the bad ones we want to never have happen in adulthood. It's the desire to have what my parents achieved (or even achieve more than they did). For some, it could be that moment in childhood when there wasn't enough food on the table, and you never want to experience that again.

The financial independence driver for me at its core is all about freedom and choice. Those are my drivers for me personally. I have always wanted the options and freedom that financial independence brings. I choose how to spend my time and answer to no one. The bills of life are being paid through what I already have in financial wealth, and I have passive income sufficient enough that I can choose to do what I wish at all times.

When I started my real estate career, it was in the same year my father was retiring after 30 years as a dentist. I saw firsthand the freedom of choice he had in his life. He had worked hard, but now he had achieved that choice to retire. He was ending his career while I still had the vast majority of mine ahead of me. The timing was curious and not lost on me at the time. If I had been further in my career, or even younger, it might not have had the impact that it did. Some of success is being there at the right time. The timing, in looking back, was fortuitous.

TIP

You have to tap into that driver for you. What are you seeking? What is the emotional need or feeling that is going to drive you to wealth? What is your definition of wealth? The best thing you can do is pause here for moment and review these questions to create your clarity. The second best step is resolving to achieve your why and your wealth objectives. In essence, to make the decision to start crafting a plan and sticking to the plan no matter how small.

The secret of getting ahead is getting started. —Mark Twain

It doesn't matter where you are right now. Some of you are on solid footing. Some of you are deep in debt. You might be hanging on by a thread financially with large debt on credit cards or student loans. Wherever you are . . . it's okay. You can finish where you desire. Some of you have a lot of years left. Some of you, only a few. What matters is right now, right here. What is in the past is there. Don't bring it forward in a big chorus of "if only."

When you resolve to get started, your mind can often say, "It's so small that it doesn't matter." This change is so small; this savings amount is so small; my income is so small. The truth is that it does matter because it's movement in the right direction. When you start an exercise program, you don't expect to run five miles on the first day. Even walking around the block is progress toward the new, healthier you.

REMEMBER

The best time to plant an oak tree was 20 years ago. The second-best time is right now. Get out of the past and into the now. Leave the whole "what if" or "if only" behind. Those thoughts really will not serve you at all. They're a waste of energy and feed a negative mindset.

Wealthy People Are Different

77 percent of Americans have financial worries.

40 percent of Americans have a savings or investment plan.

1 in 3 baby boomers have less than $1,000 saved.

When I read these stats, I was shocked. How could the wealthiest nation in the world be creating such poor results? It's because we lack emotional clarity of why. We lack a specific plan of execution. We lack the discipline to carry the plan out. We get distracted by the need for speed in achievement.

Creating wealth, being wealthy, and having wealth is, first, a state of mind. You have to have the right state of mind to create and attract wealth in your life. You have to resolve to accomplish it in your state of mind. If you are not doing as well financially as you would like, all that means is there is something you don't know. The not knowing creates the barrier to what you don't have. Most of us lack knowledge in wealth. It's not a class we take in high school or college. In fact, most high schools have taken personal finance courses out of their curriculum.

Most people would contend that wealthy people are different because they possess wealth. I would contend that they were different before they acquired their wealth. They focus on positive opportunities and expect to achieve financial success. They don't dwell on the unfair or imbalance of life. That wealth is a result of different thinking and different actions than the masses.

Following the herd will create what the herd possesses in life. There is a reason that the crocodiles of life wait patiently for the herd of wildebeests to cross the river. They know that once a few of them come into the water, there will be several more that will just follow the herd. Their meal of wildebeest is coming soon. When you recognize a trend in which everyone is going in the same direction, that's when you need to pause and potentially head in the opposite direction. Be careful whom you listen to, even if you believe their motives and desires for your success are good.

REMEMBER

Successful and wealthy people ignore their critics. They don't let the naysayers back off their resolve in key areas of their life in executing their plan. They don't take rejection or "no" as personal. The fact that someone didn't agree with you, your plan, or your objectives isn't personal. It's also not fatal or final in nature.

ANECDOTE

In 2010, when the real estate market was in turmoil and the United States had gone through the worst economic recession since the Great Depression, I was convinced that the catastrophic drop in real estate values was over, the real estate market was stabilizing, and the "bottom" had been reached or was close at hand. I shared that view with a number of close friends, colleagues, and family members. There was no one in my circle saying, "Dirk, you are so right!" Their response was more like, "Are you nuts?" Their reaction just fed my resolve that I was correct.

I had to ignore the critics and negativity and plow ahead with my plan in putting all my eggs in the rental real estate basket. I was so convinced that I was correct that I risked it all. Not in a gambling sort of way. It wasn't like going to Vegas and putting everything I owned on black or red. I was not gambling. I was clearly moving contrary to the herd who were handing back properties to the banks through short sales and foreclosures left and right. It's easy to look back years later and have proof that not following the herd, making the investments into real estate that I did at that time, was the correct decision.

If you don't follow the herd, if you will patiently bide your time, the reward financially will be exponentially better than you expect. You will make mistakes as well. When you recognize them, admit them, and take your lumps. In the end, it will work out well for you.

The difference in their thinking and their attitude

Wealthy people expect positive outcomes. That's the biggest difference in the way they think. They expect to achieve their goals and objectives. Wealthy people, when they launch a new business venture, expect it to be a success. That doesn't mean they all are successes. If they are in sales, as I have been most of my adult life, they expect to make sales and do it in sufficient numbers to acquire the new car they desire, the large home, college savings, or anything else they set their mind to.

Their attitude and expectation are set to positive. A positive attitude means that each day they decide to focus on the positive progress they are making toward their goals and dreams. Being and having a positive state of mind is a choice that we all make every morning when we wake up and approach a new day. We have the new opportunity each morning with a clean slate to make that decision. We can be grateful for what we do have in life.

Creating the difference daily

Your results are the effect of a series of causes you engage in over time. The record of your wealth is merely a scoreboard with numbers on it that are influenced by your daily thinking and actions. A financial scoreboard is all about the numbers. It's like a golf scorecard: The story of how I parred a hole doesn't go in the square, which is only large enough to write in a number. It doesn't matter that I hit my drive poorly, landed my second shot in the bunker, chipped out of the bunker, and sunk a 50-foot impossible putt. There is only room to write in a 4 in the box. In the next few sections, let me share with you a few things to do daily to increase your wealth and status.

Step 1: Get up early

Not all of us are morning people, but most early risers tend to compact more work and productivity in their day. If you get up one hour earlier than you're doing presently, if you use it to make more sales calls or complete more reports, if you use that hour to work on self-improvement through reading and studying, then that one hour each work day equates to 30 extra full workdays in a year. It's like having 13 months in a year to achieve your goals. You won't miss the hour of sleep.

Step 2: Invest at least an hour a day learning

Warren Buffett spends over 80 percent of his day reading. He reads five newspapers per day, each day. You don't have to read newspapers or books; you can listen to podcasts or attend classes or take online courses. And with audio books, you can even use your drive time in the car to educate yourself. Whatever knowledge has brought you to the level of success you are enjoying, it will not be enough knowledge to ever keep you there. As my friend Jim Rohn used to say, "Your formal education will help you make a living. Your personal education will help you make a fortune."

Step 3: Move your body each day

Don't neglect the temple in which you live. There is a direct connection between physical health, mental health, and wealth. Becoming successful takes energy and stamina. It's hard to take charge, go against the herd, "stand your ground," and delay gratification of now when you're tired and not physically ready. In the competitive world we live in, it takes physical stamina and energy to build your business or brand to attract customers and client.

Step 4: Rest

High achievers are frequently poor at rest. I know from personal experience that it's easy to underestimate the value of rest. Your body and mind requires downtime to operate well. You need fun, recreation, and friendships to be able to achieve a fulfilled life of success. Your body requires enough sleep nightly to be prepared for a new day of challenges and opportunities ahead. Most of us need eight hours of sleep. We can be short of that for a few days if we are facing deadlines. Eventually, too frequently, our mind and body break down. And often, we wear like a badge of honor the number of hours we work, bragging about how little sleep we need. That philosophy of overwork can lead to physical and mental health issues, which can lead to disastrous consequences.

The First Step: Define Your Wealth Number

Knowing your financial wealth number, your net worth goal, or your specific financial target creates the measuring stick you need to become wealthy or financially independent. These goals must be known by all people that desire wealth and financial independence. Being financially wealthy is the outward result of an inner focus and clarity of purpose to draw you toward wealth. The journey starts in your mind and concludes in your bank accounts or asset accounts. Obviously, the journey doesn't stop there, but the realization of arrival, the "I have enough" moment, is there in your number, along with feelings of freedom and well-being.

How do you define financial wealth or financial independence? My definition I adhere to is this: Someone who has accumulated an asset base that allows them to live off that asset base for life.

The definition implies a passive income earning position. It implies that no work, or no additional income, is required to maintain a specific lifestyle. When you strip all the flowery language away, it really boils down to a number. We are going to start with that premise.

The question is, what's your number?

ANECDOTE

A few years ago, I actually asked my dad how he knew when he had enough assets and retirement was an option. In essence, what was his number? I had honestly never asked him that. In fact, I had never asked anyone that. But isn't that the quintessential question to ask yourself or the people you respect about wealth and financial independence? How much is enough? How much was enough for you?

It was a wonderfully memorable and vivid conversation. I received much more than I expected. My expectation was that he was going to give me a number and then move on. What I received was far more than a number. What I heard was his thinking, strategy, and planning. I heard his expression of freedom, relief, passion, and opportunity that achieving that number provided.

In reality, when he got his number, he worked about another year or so, and then he pulled the ripcord and parachuted off into retirement. He had enough and was confident even though, at the time, my mother required a lot of financial resources due to her multiple sclerosis. She needed full-time, around-the-clock care to be able to live in the home. The physical care of my mother, without considering other life expenses, was more than a six-figure commitment annually.

He had factored all that into the number that was needed to be able to fund his retirement and the substantial healthcare needs of my mother. He is 87 now and has been a wise steward of his money. He is closing in on 29 years in retirement with plenty of assets to enjoy life on his terms. I am blessed with a personal road map to observe at close range.

There are a number of strategies you can employ to arrive at your number. Each of these that we explore has merit and value. The true question is, which of these speaks and motivates you?

Earning replacement income

The first method is to focus on the replacement of income. The goal would be to acquire enough income-producing assets to replace all, or a part, of your current earnings. What is the amount of money you need to acquire to replace your present-day income, plus a factor for inflation. The goal is to buy enough bonds, annuities, pension payments, dividend stocks, real estate, and mortgage notes that create a cash flow to cover your expenses. This is certainly a viable way to create a number that you craft a plan too. This plan creates a replaced income without reducing your asset base. It allows you to spend your income freely, knowing you have future safety as well.

Setting a gross asset number

Another way to develop a wealth strategy is to calculate a gross asset number. What overall net worth number do you need where the income plus drawing on the asset will create years of income to fund your lifestyle? It gives you a very specific target, which allows you to plan as well as check your progress too. It becomes a simple math equation of lifestyle and length of life. You then apply a standard 4-percent rule to your net amount.

The 4-percent rule has been around for years as a benchmark for retirees. This rule describes how much a retiree can withdraw each year in retirement while also retaining enough of an asset base in their account to last 30-plus years. So if you have $1,000,000, you can draw out $40,000 per year and likely never run out of money. This rule is just a guide, so if your asset base drops due to a stock market crash, you might have to adjust.

REMEMBER

Beware of being general, arbitrary, or having round ballpark numbers. My belief is that specificity creates attraction. The law of attraction states that you will be attracted to what you are looking for and what you desire. If you are specific, the power of the pull will be greater. As you march along to your specific goal, your intention, energy, and excitement will increase because you can clearly see the progress. The law of attraction is a powerful tool to the achievement of wealth.

Getting help from other sources

I have scoured numerous websites and information sources to help you on this journey of defining your number. A good financial planner can really be invaluable in defining the number and factoring for inflation. If you want to go it alone in your calculation, I have found what I think is an outstanding resource. Kiplinger has an easy-to-use retirement savings calculator. Check it out at www.kiplinger.com/tool/retirement/T047-S001-retirement-savings-calculator-how-much-money-do-i/index.php. It will take you about ten minutes to work through it. It factors in the variables of time, returns, inflation, and years in retirement. You can include Social Security in the calculations or not. I have found this tool to be invaluable for the do-it-yourself planner.

The objective is to give you a target. That target is reasonably accurate in what you need plus what you need to save on a regular basis for how many years you need before retirement. When you use the retirement savings calculator, be sure to adjust the timing, rates of return, and length of retirement. All those factors can influence significantly the nest egg number. What I am saying is that you should play with the numbers. Create some variation so that you understand how different economic conditions might affect your results, or higher savings rates will affect the outcome, and so forth. I suggest taking a screen shot of a few different scenarios or even printing them out for discussion. Discuss all of the factors, variables, and expected outcomes with your significant other. Talk about risk tolerance. Then you might discuss your ideas of investment avenues: stocks, bonds, mutual funds, real estate, and commodities. There are unlimited options that all carry differing levels of risk and management with them.

Deciding what you need

Take a look at Figure 14-1, where I've used the Retirement Savings Calculator. I realize that for some, a 1.5-million dollar nest egg goal seems big. For others, it might seem small. The $159,000 annual income goal in the figure is two and a half times the median income the United States currently. That's not in the 1-percent income level, but it's certainly an upper-middle-class lifestyle in terms of annual income. The real question is, what do you need?

Retirement Savings Calculator

Our online tool helps you figure out how much money you really need to retire.

Here is an estimate of how much you need to save initially each month to match your retirement nest-egg goal. You will need to increase your savings in future years to keep pace with inflation. The results below assume 3% annual inflation and 2% annual home appreciation.

Annual Retirement Income In Future Dollars:	$159,280.00
Annual Social Security and Pension Benefits:	$76,020.00
Nest-Egg Goal:	$1,507,006.00
Projected Future Value of Current Savings:	$609,900.00
How Much You Should Be Saving Each Month:	$1,543.00

This amount includes how much you are already saving plus any employer match

FIGURE 14-1: Kiplinger's online retirement savings calculator is easy to use.

The $76,020 in Social Security income might also seem like a lot, but it's only 47 percent of the overall income. The Social Security Administration quotes that Social Security is designed to replace about 40 percent of a person's income in retirement.

In this example, the savings still needs to be at $1,543 per month toward retirement. According to Vanguard, about 12 percent of 401k plan participants contribute the maximum amount to their 401k plan each year. The present maximum level is $18,500 per year if you are under 50 years of age. If you are over 50, you are allowed another $6,000 for a total of $24,500. Interestingly, the example I share, the $1,543 a month, would be achieved just by maxing out your 401k plan each year.

This first step is looking at the "what is your number" target. Is that a number that makes sense for your nest egg goal? Then review the monthly savings. Is that something you could save and achieve? Will you need to make adjustments in your family budget or increase your income to achieve that target? I find that people are more willing to make a change if they understand clearly the reward and what price they must pay to achieve it.

REMEMBER

Most people want financial wealth or financial independence but have never even taken the 10 minutes I am asking you to invest to define what that number is for you. You can't hit a target that you have not defined or aimed for. Imagine going out to shoot guns but not having specific targets to actually aim at. Your guns would merely be big noisemakers.

The path is in the math

You have to do the math so that you can work effectively to craft your plan and set the strategy. Let's look at a few more basic math calculations to check how you are doing. The goal is to give you a perspective of exactly where you need to be long term, as well as compare it to where you are right now. If you used the Kiplinger tool discussed in the preceding sections, you understand clearly where you need to be.

I realize for some of you, you don't want to look at this or deal with where you really are. I know it's uncomfortable. It's like looking in the mirror when you are overweight. You see where those love handles are, especially if you turn on the lights. No one is comfortable with this kind of self-scrutiny. The truth is, you can't finish well off or wealthy without a wealth number and a willingness to look at where you are now or where you should be. You have to be able to recheck yourself at intervals along the way. Doing so drastically improves your odds of it even happening. You won't get where you want to go by burying your head in the sand. The common occurrence is to think about crafting a wealth and retirement plan in your 40s or 50s. That's too many years of being the ostrich with your head in the sand.

A good financial plan is not really glamorous. It's not exciting. What creates excitement is having the plan and starting the process to achieving it. A good plan works because it is just common sense combined with simple savings disciplines. It has savings targets and savings goals. For example, consider forced savings out of your paycheck. You decide to deduct $200 per paycheck and place the money in a savings account or a 401k.

The complex stuff makes for great conversations at cocktail parties. But the strategies of paying off non-deductible debt, forced savings, solid real estate cash flow investing, and compound interest don't make for great conversation at cocktail parties, but they can eventually pay for great cocktail parties!

What is your current savings goal monthly? How does that relate to your needed goal of monthly savings you calculated? If it's short, how much short is it? What steps in your family budget are you going to take to increase your savings? What extra work, overtime, or side jobs can you do to increase your monthly savings rate? What is a reasonable timeframe to achieve the increase in savings? You might not be able to do it now due to other debt you are paying off. That won't sink your ship if you can eventually improve your position. If I am off by $500 a month now, but through raises and expense cuts, I can get there in two years, I have only missed paying in $12,000. That might be $60,000 to $70,000 total at retirement, which is only 4 percent of my 1.5 million dollar nest egg, so it's not a big calamity.

What is a reasonable timeframe to close any gaps that exist? You don't have to make up the shortage this month, or even this year. If you, through a deliberate plan, close that gap in the next few years by even placing 100 percent of the raises or periodic side job earnings into savings, the fact that it took you a few years to reach your savings goal will likely be a non-event 30 years down the road in retirement.

The power of compound interest

The eighth wonder of the world is compound interest. "He who understands it, earns it. He who doesn't, pays it," stated Albert Einstein. Compound interest is one of your best friends in crafting a wealth plan.

Compound interest is like a snowball that is traveling down a hill. It continues to pick up more snow, growing in size as it travels. That is the principle as well as the outcome of compound interest. Compound interest does all this work of growth automatically. It does it while you sleep. As long as your investment is paying you a return in interest, dividend, or rent, you reinvest those gains. The longer the timeframe, the wealthier you become. Time is actually your ally with compound interest.

If you start to save $5,000 a year at age 20, by age 60, in 40 years, you would have 2.4 million dollars. You would have saved a total of $200,000 in that 40 years. At 80 years old you would have 16.7 million by saving only $300,000 of income over 60 years. Look at the difference between ages 60 and 80. In 20 years, with only $100,000 added through savings, you went from 2.4 million to 16.7 million. It's astounding!

Why am I so excited about compound interest? Because it's simple success reality is lost by so many people. We are focused on the now too much. For most people, compound interest effects and results are like watching paint dry: boring. But it is what the Warren Buffetts of the world have used to acquire huge sums of wealth. According to *Business Insider*, 99 percent of Warren Buffett's wealth has been created after the age of 50. One of the wealthiest men in history has used the eighth wonder of the world to his advantage. That is how powerful compound interest is over the long haul.

Net worth targets

There are a number of factors that influence your wealth and net worth. Net worth is defined by taking your assets and subtracting your liabilities to create a net asset number, or net worth number. If you sold everything you owned, paid off all your debts, and had money left over, that would be your net worth. Your net worth is one measure of how you are doing in your quest for financial independence and wealth.

The net worth number can be influenced by a number of factors. Your income is certainly a factor, as well as your age. As you age, because you have been working more years, your net worth should be increasing. You also have more assets. You have cars, boats, furniture, and real estate. The home you own is likely one of the biggest influences on your net worth, but be careful. A home you own, rather than an apartment you rent, can help you increase net worth through the home's appreciation, as well as paying down the mortgage debt each month.

Thomas Stanley wrote the landmark book, *The Millionaire Next Door*, one of the classic wealth books of our day. He describes a formula for checking your net worth based on your earnings and age. If you earn more, you should theoretically have a higher net worth. This formula gives you a simple way to check the math.

Net worth target wealth formula to success:

Age x Annual household income ÷ 10 = net worth at age

The following table gives you an example of how this formula works:

Age	x	Annual Income	÷	10	=	Net Worth
35	x	$250,000	÷	10	=	$875,000
35	x	$100,000	÷	10	=	$350,000
36	x	$50,000	÷	10	=	$175,000

As you can see in this example, the age is the same but the income is different. Someone who has a higher earning power should have far more in net worth than someone in a more normal earning level. That is often not the case because the higher earner might be *income* wealthy but not *really* wealthy. If you are ahead of this formula, don't get complacent or comfortable. If you are behind, don't panic. You can make simple changes to catch up.

This formula provides a gauge on how you are doing with your personal expenses, savings, and net worth. The largest portion of most people's net worth in their 30s and 40s is likely the home they own. That is to be expected. When you reach your 50s and 60s, if that is still the case, you need to step up your savings, and fast.

You might find that you are behind the benchmark, at it, or ahead of the benchmark number. I think this quick calculation shows you how you are doing in your savings and spending. It's not an in-depth report, but it's a quick, easy way, as my late friend Zig Ziglar used to say, to get "a check up from the neck up."

Home ownership and net worth

I have a personal view about your primary residence that I must express. It's obvious that I am a proponent of homeownership. I believe that a home that you own is a foundational building block to wealth. Unfortunately, too much of our net worth is attached to homeownership. We all saw the affect of the recent recession and housing crisis that hit in 2008. The net worth of so many people was devastated. Most people say that my home was the best investment I ever made. I am sure that is true for most because it's the only investment they have ever made, and that is the problem. I believe you should have a home that you enjoy, that's comfortable and meaningful to you and your family. It's a wonderful asset, but I think we can get too attached to a home, and then we risk becoming house-rich and asset-poor.

If your home presently is a significant portion of your net worth, that is fine for today. When that is not fine is ten-plus years from now. Your goal should be to change the influence of your home from a significant portion of your net worth to a small portion of your net worth. From being 60 to 80 percent of your net worth to over time being less than 20 percent of your net worth. I can hear it now: "But Dirk, my home is worth 400,000 dollars. That means I need a net worth of 2 million dollars" That's right!

Before I lose you completely, hear me out! It all boils down to one simple reason: You can't spend your home. Your home doesn't create income. It's not an asset in classical terms. It doesn't create income or return. Yes, it can appreciate in value and likely will. But you can't spend that increase unless you mortgage it or sell it. You are not creating more assets from your home like you would stocks, bonds, mutual funds, or rental real estate assets. You will likely achieve appreciation in value of your home. The only way you can spend or live off that appreciation is to sell your home and downsize to a smaller home or lower standard of living. The truth is, few people do that in life. They might when their health requires it, but then they have expenses in an assisted-living facility.

Now there are folks who might sell the older home they raised their family in because it's too large for them or the maintenance is too much. What happens most frequently is that they buy a smaller, newer home with more quality and amenities. They say, "I deserve a nicer home with new hardwood floors and custom cabinets. I want to be able to live on a golf course and have a three-car garage where I can park a golf cart." That gap between their larger, older home and the new home is not as significant financially as they first imagined.

REMEMBER

So your home is part of your net worth, but it should not, in my opinion, be a large factor in your asset base or nest egg calculations.

Understanding the Different Types of Wealth

The average person might ask, "What do you mean by different types of wealth?" I believe there are three different types of wealth that people can achieve when comparing or focusing on monetary wealth. There are a whole lot more important factors of success than just straight dollars and cents.

>> In the financial wealth area, you can be **aspirationally wealthy.** This is where we are trying to project the image of wealth.

>> Next, we have **income wealth,** where we have a high income or have high earning power. We use that high income and consume a large percentage of it to fund a wealthy lifestyle.

> **»** Finally, we have **balance-sheet wealth,** where we have assets that create more wealth. We aren't using our income or going into debt to fund a lifestyle.

The roadblock to success for aspirationally wealthy people

There is a difference between being wealthy and acting wealthy. There is a difference between looking rich and being rich. In reality, most people who look wealthy are not. They are generally living at the top or above their means. They have the appearance of wealth and they are aspirationally wealthy, but they aren't really wealthy, nor do they have freedom. They don't have freedom because they are in bondage to the image of wealth. They are in bondage of debt.

ANECDOTE

I was doing very well income-wise by my fourth year in real estate. We had moved into a large home on a golf course in Portland, Oregon a few years previously. Joan and I were building a large luxury second home in Bend, Oregon, also on a golf course. I was 33 years old. I was working hard, earning well, and I wanted the lifestyle of success. I wanted the outward appearance of success. I wanted people to know I was successful. At that point, I had more the appearance of wealth rather than true wealth. I had aspirational wealth but was not really wealthy. I had a big consumption lifestyle because that is what I thought wealthy people did. Don't get me wrong, I was doing very well income-wise for my age. I was house wealthy and lifestyle wealthy. I was aspirationally and income wealthy but not balance-sheet wealthy. I had put 20-percent down payments on both houses, so I was not sliding in with 5-percent-down loans. If you knew me at that time, you would have said, "He is doing very well. He is wealthy." The truth was different from the outward appearance.

The upshot was the vast majority of what I earned went to paying taxes and funding this lifestyle. I had a very small amount left over to save. We can fall in love with keeping up with the Joneses. We can consume more and more, but that keeps us in the aspirational category for life. It's okay to be aspirationally wealthy in your 30s but not in your 50s.

I don't think there is anything wrong with rewarding yourself for your hard work. In fact, I think to stay motivated, you must reward yourself periodically with tangible things you need and want. You can't be only focused on financial independence and wealth creation without having some fun along the way. If I have made mistakes along my path to wealth, it's this: I probably over-focused on the wealth and freedom of the future at the expense of the present. I might have delayed too much in gratification.

The perils and pitfalls of being income wealthy

Income wealth comes from having achieved a high income but also a high spend rate. Income wealth is frequently associated with advanced-learning professions like doctors, dentists, and attorneys. They have high income but frequently also high consumption. In the modern day, many of these advanced-degree individuals have high debt levels due to student debt. When they finally get out into the workforce, their earnings can support higher spending but not higher spending, high savings, and a debt-reduction strategy. The higher spending tends to win out because of the desire to reward oneself after all that toil in school.

REMEMBER

Human nature is to spend up to and even beyond your means. When your income increases, so does your spending. I am speaking from personal experience that I continued far too long. I spent years of my life being income wealthy before I figured it out.

Becoming balance-sheet wealthy for life

Balance-sheet wealthy is the objective. Your goal is to have assets that create income. You want to have assets that are not overleveraged, so you have peace of mind and freedom. The goal, if you desire to achieve financial independence, is to be *balance-sheet affluent.* Balance-sheet affluent is where you have strong assets, meaning equity that automatically creates new wealth for you, with limited effort. What does your balance sheet look like without your home? Remember, you can't spend your home, or in my case, even my second home. In fact, they actually were a negative drain on my monthly budget. For many years, in my 30s into early 40s, the largest portion of what I had saved over the years had gone into my two homes. I had high income with high consumption. I was income-statement affluent but not balance-sheet affluent. I was not saving enough and in danger, if my income dropped, of losing everything.

If you looked at what I was making for listing and selling real estate, you would think, "Wow, he is doing very well financially." If you looked at our cars, homes, clothes, and travel, you would say Joan and I were well off or wealthy. It's what you have besides the houses, cars, and clothes that will make you wealthy, financially speaking.

If your net worth is in the millions and 85 percent of it is tied up in your homes, you really aren't wealthy. And if the value of your homes depreciates by 50 percent, like they did from 2008 to 2011, much of the wealth is gone, so the wealth isn't real. You are at too much risk when an economic downturn happens. All you can focus on will be survival. But for wealthy people, when economic downturns hit, they think thrive! They can thrive because they have the funds to capitalize on the opportunity.

To be balance-sheet wealthy, you want your primary home to be less than 20 percent of your overall net worth asset base. The lower that percentage is, the more balance-sheet wealthy you will be. If your nest egg goal is two million dollars and your home net value (home value minus debt) is, say, $400,000, which would be 20 percent, then you have 80 percent, or 1.6 million dollars, working to create more assets. You are using compound interest on 80 percent of your assets. Now that's balanced! Your age plays a role in this calculation as well, as I stated earlier.

ANECDOTE

Looking back, I made a lot of errors but managed to figure it out early enough that I recovered well. I learned a lot from that period of being income wealthy and aspirationally wealthy. I would not trade the experience of being aspirationally wealthy. Joan and I, through that second home we built in Bend, received something more valuable, rewarding, and amazing than anything. I sold real estate in Portland, Oregon Monday through Thursday, and then we would go to Bend for Friday, Saturday, and Sunday each weekend. Without spending three days a week in Bend, Oregon, we would never had gotten connected to our church in Bend. Westside Church changed our lives, but not in the typical church experience way. Through Westside, we finally became parents. Both my kids, Wesley and Annabelle, were adopted through a series of miracles and God's blessings that were orchestrated because of our church family. If we had never built that home in Bend, I would not have experienced the richness of being a father. That's ultimately true wealth in life.

Chapter **15**

Becoming Master of the Board

The quest for financial success has been written about extensively. There are literally millions of books published on the subject. Jesus talked more about money than he talked about heaven or hell combined. Money is referenced more than 800 times in the modern Bible. Yet most people, even successful ones, lack understanding, a plan, and strategy to attract it, acquire it, save it, and invest it well.

In this chapter, I reveal rules to create more wealth. I also focus on foundational truths relating to debt, including its use and abuse. Debt and its improper use in American society have devastating effects on personal wealth. Most of us have had, or currently have, challenges with debt.

Personal Wealth Is the Board Game of Life

Being wealthy and successful is much like playing a board game. You have pieces you move around the board with skill and strategy to create the opportunity to win the game. In life, like the game of Monopoly, you acquire assets and have chance encounters that you are either prepared for or not. You are thrust into situations that are new, exciting, and opportune, or these situations can create havoc, stress, and frustration. While Monopoly has a real estate focus, the board game of real life is not solely based on real estate. Although many who have mastered the board of wealth have used the Monopoly approach to achieve their financial goals.

My hope is that you have not just read the preceding chapter but also took action by calculating your nest egg goal:

>> You have broken it down into the amount of money you need to save.

>> You have done some thinking about your income and personal budget in relationship to that monthly savings goal.

You might be looking at that number and saying, "Wow, how am I going to do that?" "How am I going to be able to save at that level?" "I have too much month at the end of the money to save much."

I have heard those comments countless times. I will also admit, that is a fair initial reaction. I think the first step is to look at this question: Can you cut expenses to save enough based on the income you are currently at? Can you drive spending down enough to increase savings? The likely answer is "no" unless you want to dramatically alter your lifestyle, which most of us don't want to do. Most of us want to expand our lifestyle, amenities, and experiences as we progress through life. I clearly fall into that camp along with you.

ANECDOTE

A few years ago, I sold the big trophy home that I had owned for more than 20 years. I originally built it as a second home in a golf course community. It was my "I have arrived at success" statement asset. My ego was very attached to that home. That was one of the reasons why I had to let go. In truth, it was more ego than practical, but if I'm being honest, the decision was hard. I didn't want to let go. We gave up what we really were not using in space and downsized. I cut my overhead and gave up what I didn't need. I released something that was controlling my ego and self-worth for too long. (I didn't give up living on the golf course. I'm not nuts.) That decision opened up the door to increased savings rate, less overhead, and greater peace of mind.

Some of our very best financial wealth decisions are tough. They are connected to us letting go of our ego. We have to change our thinking and connection to "stuff" so that we can achieve what we really desire: freedom, peace of mind, lower stress, and a more enjoyable lifestyle. Let me share with you a financial truth, which is . . .

A dollar saved is two dollars earned

Please reread the heading above. If you increased your income earned by $2, by the time you pay overhead and taxes, you would likely have less than a dollar that's left for you to spend. If you are a business owner or have a side job or side hustle, like if you drive for Uber, the money you make from it doesn't go 100 percent in your pocket. You have vehicle maintenance, gas, tolls, insurance, and employer side taxes. But a dollar saved is $2 earned. You need to see what you can do to cut overhead and expenses personally to fund your nest egg number.

REMEMBER

Financial wealth is, in most cases, a consumption equation rather than an earning equation. The greatest short-term influence on your savings and wealth is based on the consumption side of the equation. The definition of short term: from now and outward to the next six months. If you can shift the savings rate in the short term, it can establish a new habit that will enlarge your wealth long term.

A wide variety of people are reading this book. Some of you are paid on a salary; some of you earn an hourly wage plus tips; some earn commission income; others are business owners. A few might even be presently unemployed. Whatever category you fall into presently, your wealth life mantra must be, "A dollar saved is two dollars earned."

As a business owner who has created my own income and personal economy for more than 30 years, I have lived by that philosophy — not because it's catchy and pithy, but because I have done the math. I have done the calculations over time — each month, quarter, semiannually, and annually. They confirm the truth.

All business owners have overhead to run their business. They also have local, state, and federal taxes to pay. They have Social Security taxes to pay for both the employee and employer. If you do the math, you will quickly see what I am expressing.

Let's say the goal, from the calculations in the previous chapter, is $1,000 savings a month or $12,000 a year. I realize that might be more than you calculated or can afford at this point. I want to share a solid example that is both aspirational and reasonable. Here is the true math:

Entrepreneur		Costs
$12,000 saving		20% Federal tax
	+	4–12% State tax
	+	15.3% FICA, Medicare tax
	=	39.3% Total Tax

$12,000 savings × 39.3% = $4,716 Total Tax Paid

$12,000 + $,4716 = $16,716

Salary Employee		Costs
$12,000 saving		20% Federal tax
	+	4–12% State tax
	+	7.65% FICA, Medicare tax
	=	31.65% Total Tax

$12,000 savings × 31.65% = $3,798 Total Tax Paid

$12,000 + $,3,798 = $15,798

The path is in the math (as I discuss in Chapter 14, but it's worth repeating). If you need to increase your income to achieve the savings to achieve wealth, you must recognize that a sizeable portion of that increased income will not flow to savings but actually to taxes. For every dollar you earn, now an ample portion is being taxed presently.

TIP

If you can save more of your present income because it has already been taxed, this creates the need to earn less. It insures that when you increase your income, you will save even more of it.

Most business owners have 50- to 70-percent overhead before they pay themselves. That further cuts down the equation and savings opportunities before they even pay their 39.3% in combined taxes. I am not making an anti-taxes statement here. My objective is to reveal the truth of what is really left over to save and enjoy life.

Wealth does not equal income

ANECDOTE

Wesley, my oldest son, recently started his first job. He works in guest services at a country club. It has been a great experience for him. When he received his first paycheck, he was so proud and excited. He merely wanted to look at the net amount of the check. We spent 5 to 10 minutes going line by line through each deduction and talked about what was drawn out, where it went, and for what purpose. I had him calculate the overall percentage of his check. I wanted him to understand wealth and income.

You might be thinking, "Wow, Dirk. This is a whole new way of thinking." Or, "This is more detailed than I want to get." My response is that this is how wealthy people think, plan, and strategize. They understand the board game of wealth. They set true and accurate benchmarks and objectives. They plan out their expenses, taxes, and earning needs, rather than using the typical strategies of the herd.

Wealth is not the same as income. You can use the surplus of your income to create wealth. You can have wealth and utilize it to create income. There is a design here that must be followed, but income fully spent will not create wealth. Wealth is accumulation, not spending.

REMEMBER

Wealth is a result of planning, hard work, perseverance, a system of savings, self-discipline, and delayed gratification. If you notice, "income" is not listed in this group of skills and attributes. While a higher income can improve your odds of wealth or increase the speed in which you attain wealth, it is not the sole factor nor most important factor to acquisition of wealth. Which of these are you lacking? If you have a high income, for example, but are unable to delay gratification, you are unable to wait to buy stuff. You put stuff on your credit card, paying 17 percent, 21 percent, even 24 percent interest, you will never have wealth no matter how much income you create.

I am not expressing that frugality and miserly behavior is the pathway to wealth either. Being able to provide extras and amenities to your comfort and lifestyle adds enjoyment. It's prudent to evaluate for yourself the value exchange between those amenities or even luxuries compared to debt, savings, and investment for the future. My philosophy: Owning the beach is better than a day at the beach.

Factor in some enjoyment

We all work to "fund" our life. We all have different things that are important to us and give us enjoyment and meaning. We all are traveling through life, and there are vastly different ways to travel in comfort and amenities. Some people have to travel by bus; others fly economy class; and still others can afford first-class flights. (And then there is a whole other level of flying in a private jet.)

I think that we all need to determine how we are going to travel on our journey of life. What type of travel experience can we aspire to and afford now and in the future? Each of these travel experiences I just mentioned is an illustration of a lifestyle one could aspire to or set a goal based on. I have taken all the aforementioned "classes" of travel in my lifetime. This analogy can relate to where you live, what type of home you live in, cars you drive, vacations you take, and restaurants you eat in. You have to develop your plan of lifestyle because it determines your level of fulfillment and feelings of success.

Please understand that I'm not judging how anyone chooses to travel through life. But I can say, after having traveled millions of miles, that I am no longer a fan of economy travel. I've been on the road for years speaking worldwide, and frequently, I get upgraded to first class. In my contract to speak internationally, I require business class. The travel part of speaking domestically or internationally is grinding. A little more space and amenities makes it less so.

You are the one who needs to decide for yourself. Then you will need to evaluate the financial and wealth requirements that will allow you to travel through life in the lifestyle of your choosing. The vast majority of us would not require 50 million dollars in net worth to live the life we desire, but we may require a million or more in net assets.

We trade our energy, time, emotions, knowledge, and skill for the income we create. You do that whether you are a brain surgeon or a fast-food worker. The value per hour is clearly different in these examples. One gets paid $10 an hour and one get paid $10 per second. Each likely has different views of what wealth is. Each person's level of planning, perseverance, saving strategies, self-discipline, and delayed gratification will influence the outcome to his or her definition of wealth success.

At the end of the day, you need to answer these questions:

>> What is the income you need?

>> What lifestyle attributes are important to you?

>> What constitutes financial security for you?

>> Are you working toward your plan or someone else's?

The most important missed rule of the success board game

Each game we play has rules. In board games, the rules are printed out, so players can clearly understand those rules to make the game fair and fun for all. When we start playing a game, the objective is to have fun, but we also want to win. Let me share with you truth: We all want to be master of the board. You want to master the board when you are playing Monopoly by buying as many properties as possible and placing larger rental structures to increase rents and cash flow. You have to have total commitment to acquisition. No fear. No mercy. Buying properties, putting up houses, upgrading to hotels, all in the pursuit of winning the game.

That's a solid lesson for success, but it's not the best lesson that Monopoly or any other board game teaches. You could be the master of the board in Monopoly, but most people miss the best lesson with all the money changing, properties, houses, hotels, bankruptcies, and triumphs.

REMEMBER

The best lesson, no matter who are you, how many hotels and how much money you acquire, whether you ultimately win or lose, at the end of the game, it all goes back in the box.

When the game is over, you can't take it with you

Here's the truth: You aren't going to take your hotels, money, and saved get-out-of-jail-free cards with you. You won't move past Go ever again for this game and collect your $200. It's all going back in the box. This is the same truth with our lives. When the game is over, even if you have mastered the board, it all goes back in the box. If you are number one on the *Forbes* wealthiest list or down to your last nickel, when the game of life comes to a close here on Earth, it all goes back in the box.

A few years ago, I read a book by John Ortberg titled *It All Goes Back In The Box*. Full disclosure: I loved this book. It spoke to me. It is also Biblically based with scripture quoted throughout. If that's not your thing, I understand and respect that. It's why I am saying that up front. What I drew from the book was a renewed and refined philosophy for how to play the game. And I decided that I want the pieces I return to the box to be used to bless others. I want to be able to fully play the game for as long as I am blessed to be on this Earth. My desire is to play the game of life well.

I don't want to have the last dime in my hand when I die. I want assets to go back in the box for my kids to use, and their kids' kids. I want to create a legacy and live well while doing it. I have thought through what I want to put back in the box for Joan, Wesley, and Annabelle. And I know what I want to leave to my church and charities.

We all get to choose the what and how our game pieces go back in the box at the end of the game. What do you choose? What pieces create meaning and a legacy for the blessing of others?

Debt: Your Foe or Friend?

Wealthy people think differently. They prepare differently and live differently than the rest of the population. They also think differently about the role of debt and the use of debt in their lives. There are different types of debt. The discovery I have made is that there is good debt and there is bad debt. There are some experts, like Dave Ramsey, who declare all debt to be bad. I respect Dave. Dave has impacted many lives through his books and teaching. His stance that all debt is bad is not accurate. To say that most people's relationship with debt leads to financial trouble is accurate. That few people use debt in a positive manner is consistent with reality. That most people have periods in their life where they make poor choices about debt is true. I personally made poor choices with debt in my 20s. Fortunately, I learned and did not become an anti-debt zealot.

Success principals about debt

My belief is that *consumer* debt must be avoided if you want to achieve wealth and financial independence. Consumer debt is credit card debt, consumer loan debt, retail store or gas credit cards, revolving accounts, and even car payments. It's any debt you would take on for consumption purposes. Any debt entered into on a non-appreciation asset should be questioned. So what about a car loan? A car is a depreciating asset. The car loses value the minute you drive it off the lot. It depreciates in value over time. But the use of loans to buy cars today is commonplace. In fact, 43 percent of the adult population has a car loan to pay. In the 1960s and 1970s, it was rare for people to have car loans. If you want to join the ranks of the wealthy, avoid bad debt and consumer loan debt.

Now the use of debt on *appreciating assets* is a valid tool to create and increase wealth. An appreciating asset could be the home you live in, an investment property you purchase, or business that you acquire.

ANECDOTE

There are periods of time when what should be appreciating assets don't appreciate. We all watched from 2008 through 2011 our homes dropped significantly in value. I bought a commercial building in July of 2007. I couldn't have timed my purchase any more poorly even if I had tried. The building lost more than 50 percent of its value over the next few years. So you can still make wrong choices, as I did in this case, with leveraging debt with appreciating assets. I was fortunate that the rents covered my expenses, so I just keep waiting, paying the debt, and the value has rebounded nicely over time. There are countless examples of people over-leveraging and getting into trouble.

TIP

By and large, an appreciating asset with reasonable debt amounts will help you create more wealth.

The desired wealth needed to achieve financial independence influences the need to use debt as a tool. If your nest egg goal is one million dollars and you have 30-plus years to achieve it, a solid savings and investment plan will produce the results. You won't need the use of even good debt to achieve your financial goals.

The type of debt that more than 65 percent of all Americans have is consumer debt: bad debt, and much of it is credit card debt. I had trouble with the proper control and care of credit cards in my lifetime. I think most people, no matter their background or knowledge, have at one time or another and can say the same. Successful people don't avoids mistakes; they make the mistake only once and learn from it.

I'm not going to just tell you, "Hey, don't get into credit card debt!" That's not very helpful, especially if you have debt presently. What I am going to say is that there are some strategies to create efficiency and value in using credit cards sparingly and well. And there are ways to get out of credit card debt efficiently and permanently. Read on for my advice.

Reducing credit card debt

If you presently have credit card debt, you need to work out of that situation. This non-deductible debt, in my view, is the worst form of debt. When you combine that with the high interest rate that credit cards usually charge, it really is an explosive problem. Putting the credit card down and not using it is certainly the best strategy.

Maybe you have some ongoing business needs or personal needs that require a credit card. Most business service providers will take an EFT charge direct from your account. If you have a credit card with a balance that you cannot pay off and you need the use of your credit card for some reason, here are a few steps you must take:

Step 1: Resolve to pay all new charges off in full on time

The worst thing about credit cards that most people don't know about is not just the high interest rate. The interest rate is obviously incredibly high. No one ever got wealthy paying 17-percent interest to someone else. I think the worst is the fact if you carry a loan balance on a credit card, when you charge something to that specific card, large or small, from the moment of the charge processing, you will accrue interest charges. The normal 25-day grace period to pay with no interest charged is gone. Because of the balance on the card, you will be paying interest from the moment you bite into that hamburger you just charged. It means that $15 lunch will cost you 17 percent more!

Step 2: Establish a going-forward credit card

What you need to do is pay off one card that will be used as your going-forward credit card for emergencies and necessities. Reread that sentence: The key words are *emergencies* and *necessities,* not discretionary spending.

TIP

You want any balance moved to a very low-interest card or credit line. Frequently, if you have good credit, you will receive offers with a 2- to 5-percent one-time fee on the balance you are transferring. You can then receive 12 months with no interest to pay it off. It's not no interest, because you paid the 2- to 5-percent fee upfront, but it's a lot better than 17 percent interest ongoing month to month.

The key is that you must use a credit card with zero balance as your emergency need card. And you won't ever use that emergency need card unless you have the ability to pay the full balance each month. Your goal is to only spend at all times what you can comfortable pay off each month. And if you have to transfer a balance to a spare credit card and pay the one-time fee of 2 to 5 percent, do it. Then budget out paying off that card in the timeframe of the zero interest year. The worst thing you can do in this strategy is run up debt that you can't pay off monthly. You will be in more debt than before.

Do the math of figuring out how much you need to pay each month to erase your debt in the specified time. Then pay that specific amount, or just a little bit more. That way you are only paying 2- to 5-percent interest on the transferred borrowed amount.

REMEMBER

Again, I caution you, do not charge a thing on this card. The credit card companies apply payments to the lower interest rate balance owed first. The only thing that you will pay for is the annual fee charge if any. That will be charged at your normal interest rate charge. Get yourself out of credit card debt as quickly as possible by paying the lowest rate possible. Then never go back into credit card debt.

Crafting your debt-conquering strategy

Let me take you through a system to help you get out of debt. Now there are a number of systems to help you control and get rid of credit card debt. Dave Ramsey has a good system he calls the "debt snowball." If you have learned Dave's system, that's great. Go ahead and use it. The key is getting out of high-interest, non-deductible consumer debt.

If you are in debt you must create an organized strategy to retire that debt. I have created and included a tool, shown in Figure 15-1, from our Champions of Wealth course for your use. This Debt Management tool looks at your number of credit cards. It helps you organize your debts and set a strategy to become bad-debt free.

The tool provides you a place to simply organize and list all your debts completely. You will want to just brainstorm and fill out the form. List everything on the document rather than organize as you go. Don't evaluate based on an amount or interest rate. The purpose is to just create a complete accounting in one spot of all debts you owe. The debts you have will become easier to organize a plan from once you have identified them and collected them all in one document. List all bad debt first.

Picking your strategy

Now that you have your list of debt, you need to craft a plan to get rid of it. It will be hard to invest and save at the level you need to without getting out of debt. There are two schools of thought in the strategy of paying off debt. One school is the financial strategy for debt reduction and one is more of an emotional strategy to pay debt off. There is not a quantifiable best option here, so choose what's best for you. Each of us is driven by different emotions and feelings. Either the financial or the motivations emotional strategy will connect with you.

How many credit cards do I have (include spouse and dependents): _____

WHAT DO I OWE?				
Name of Creditor	Account Number	Outstanding Balance	Monthly Minimum Payment	Interest Rate
1.				
2.				
3.				
4.				
5.				
6.				
7.				
8.				
	TOTALS:			

FIGURE 15-1: Debt Management tool.

Total amount of credit card debt: $_____

Total monthly minimum payment: $_____

The financial strategy goes back and organizes your credit card debt cost based on interest rate. You list your highest interest rate debts at the top, pay the minimum payment on all other debt, and power excess funds in paying the highest interest rate one first. That strategy makes greater financial sense, but it might not be right for you. In fact, it might not be correct for most people depending on whether you can create momentum and feel good progress about getting out of debt. Maybe your highest interest rate debt is also the largest amount. It takes a greater discipline to pay debt off through this method.

The strategy that has the highest likelihood of success is tackling the credit card or debt based on amounts. You organize your debt based on smallest amounts at the top. This way you start to see progress sooner. The strategy of ranking which to pay off is based on the principle of momentum and positive progression. This way creates emotional excitement and rewards sooner and more consistently. The goal is paying off the card then cancelling the card forever. This is especially true for store credit cards.

Store credit cards carry the highest interest rates. They also have the enticing money-saving offers. We shop at Old Navy for my kids. Every time, they offer a credit card where I can save 15 percent off our total purchase. If we are spending a few hundred dollars, it's $30 to $50 in savings. Let's be honest, a good deal is enticing to any of us, but I always turn it down because my time of having to deal with another credit card is just not worth the one-time savings.

REMEMBER

The goal is to reduce debt, reduce expenses, and hassle. Every card you carry has an expense, usually an annual fee, and the hassle of dealing with more bills and tracking. It's just not worth the one-time offer in savings.

Laying out your GALP (Gone After the Last Payment) plan

What you want to do is base your strategy on the Gone After Last Payment system, or GALP. Pull together your statements and balances and then calculate your GALP number. Take the outstanding balance and divide by the minimum payment to determine how many months it would take to pay off the credit card or debt. The goal is to pay more than the minimum so that you do it faster. You also have to recognize that if you only pay the minimum you won't have it paid off in the GALP number because you are not factoring the interest charged each month you will pay, but you will be close. Take a look at Table 15-1, which shows a sample debt scenario.

TABLE 15-1   A Sample Strategy to Pay Down Debt

Account	Outstanding Balance	Monthly Minimum Payment	GALP Number	GALP Ranking
VISA	$550	$50	11	1
MASTERCARD	$720	$60	12	2
AMEX	$1,400	$40	35	3

At a minimum, to hit your GALP number, you have to pay the minimum payment plus the accrued interest that the bank is charging you. Only then can you pay off and close the account out of your GALP number. Then you add the snowball concept: Once you pay off a card, you then add what that payment would have been to your next debt plus the minimum payment and accrued interest. You then start paying that card down and just continue repeating the process until all debt is gone.

TIP

I am convinced that laying it out on paper (see Figure 15-2) and tracking your progress is a powerful way to create excitement and momentum. It's the way for you to be ready to create the wealth you desire, save the money you need to create the wealth, and fund your present and future lifestyle.

Account	Outstanding Payment	Monthly Minimum Payment	GALP Number (Outstanding Balance ÷ Minimum Monthly Payment)	GALP Ranking (Lowest GALP number is ranked #1)
1.				
2.				
3.				
4.				
5.				
6.				
7.				
8.				
9.				
10.				
11.				
12.				
13.				
14.				
15.				

FIGURE 15-2:
The GALP tool.

IN THIS CHAPTER heading area

Chapter **16**

Crafting Your Wealth Plan

n the previous chapters on success and money, we dove deep into defining how much money you need and what your goals and lifestyle needs require. We have explored the use of debt as a help or hindrance to achieving the wealth you desire. If you have debt, I hope that you went through the planning process of the GALP (Gone After the Last Payment) plan from the end of Chapter 15.

My desire in this chapter is to put a bow on the whole process of wealth and money. I want to encompass everything you've read into a comprehensive wealth plan.

REMEMBER

The fundamentals of wealth and financial independence are quite simple: Control your spending, reduce debt, live below your means, save a portion of what you make, and avoid the get-rich-quick schemes.

If all the wealth in the world were redistributed evenly among the population, there is no doubt in my mind that people like Bill Gates, Jeff Bezos, and Warren Buffett would figure out how to deliver enough value to the marketplace that they would be able to reacquire the wealth that was redistributed to all people. And without change in behavior and strategy, the people who received the redistributed windfall would in short order continue their error-filled ways and lose the gifted funds.

Realizing Your Market Value

Whatever income level your earnings are at is based on your value to the market-place. The income per hour, or salary you earn, is based on the value you deliver to your company, clients, or customers. People who produce more output, have specialized skills, possess a more positive attitude, or provide exceptional customer service are the ones who earn increasing income throughout their work lives.

In a capitalistic society, the intent is to climb the ladder of income. The objective is to develop your skills and giftings to increase your earnings. The bottom of the ladder is minimum wage. We are not intended to stay at that level of income our whole life. Minimum wage is the starting point, not the finishing point.

The *scarcity* of one's skill, or *replaceability* of your position, affects income. For example, there are a lot of people who have enough skill to work at McDonald's in some capacity, whether they are cooks, counter workers, or drive-through clerks. The pool of potential workers is fairly large, ranging from kids getting their first job at 16 to senior citizens who want to supplement their income. The number of people who would qualify for such a job creates an ease of replaceability compared to more highly skilled jobs.

An airline pilot is a less replaceable position, so the income is higher. The highest paying jobs and careers in life have fewer people who qualify for those positions. The people occupying them have invested time or money, or both, to reach proficiency. Commercial airline pilots now must have 1,500 hours flying a plane before an airline can hire them. The flight time requirements have tripled in the last ten years. And the pay for new hire second officer pilots has tripled because of the scarcity of new pilots.

Part of your wealth plan must be the realization of where you presently are on the income ladder. Are you climbing upward or stagnate? If you are plateaued or stuck, what changes are you making in your career to unstick yourself? Are you at a place income-wise that provides you the opportunity for wealth? If you are stuck at the bottom, wealth is not impossible, but it is much harder.

Fighting Against Human Nature: Wants Become Needs

For all human beings, wants become needs. In other words, the things we want become, over time, the things we need. It's typical human nature. Here's a common example: We want that new car because we become bored with the old one.

Over time, our dissatisfaction with the car we've had for four years grows until we decide we deserve or need the new one. The want transitions to need because of perceived status, the need to keep up with the Joneses, boredom, inferior feelings about ourselves, and a host of other reasons. We eventually convince ourselves that we need the new car. And frequently, we still have payments left on the old car. We then roll that old debt into the new car payment, and we have higher payments. Those payments might be taking up too much of our monthly budget, so we feel like we can't save money. When we drive off the lot with the new car, that new car becomes a used car in the blink of an eye. We just lost 15 percent of its value in that moment.

Far too many of us beat ourselves up because we feel we lack the discipline to avoid what is human nature. But if we recognize that it's in our nature to turn wants into needs, the problem becomes easier to deal with. There are people with better reasons than you or me who spend more than they make. There are people with greater willpower than I possess who spend more than they make. So spending within your means has nothing to do with your moral character or your willpower. All you really have to do is understand the math and create simple systems to help you avoid wants turning into needs. You also must set up an automatic plan, strategy, or system to save money.

The path to financial success is in the math.

To create financial wealth, I really believe that you need just two systems in your life:

>> A math-based wealth plan

>> An automatic savings system

The vast majority of wealthy people haven't achieved wealth through staggering earnings. I haven't earned an astronomical amount of money. My income over the last 30 years has been substantial, but it's not so high that the math, strategy, and controlling of spending were irrelevant. I think there are few people who earn at such a high level that their plan, savings strategy, and investment strategy are unimportant to achieving wealth. That group is incredibly small, and it's unlikely that you or I will ever be part of it.

There are countless examples of people who were at the top of their field in skill and earnings. Take athletics, for example. Evander Holyfield, Björn Borg, Scottie Pippen, John Daly, Mike Tyson, Lawrence Taylor, and Sheryl Swoopes all have two things in common: They were among the best of the best, and they also all lost it all or spent it all. These athletes made more than 50 million dollars in their playing careers. Think about that: More than 50 million in earnings passed through their bank accounts. And for most of them, they earned that money in less than 10 years! It's unfortunate but true that 73 percent of all NBA players, within five years of retirement, are broke. And over 60 percent of all former NFL players are broke.

A large income, or even a large windfall of income in a short period of time, does not guarantee that the wealth won't leave you. In fact, studies show a high percentage of lottery winners are broke within seven years of winning the jackpot. And it's not like they all get swindled. They and others within their circle spent all of the money.

ANECDOTE

A SAD EXAMPLE OF POOR WEALTH MANAGEMENT

I've done a couple real estate transactions that have really saddened me. I felt bad for the individuals who were forced to sell due to economic hardship. Much of what I have bought over the last eight years have been distressed properties. These are properties that are either foreclosed on or the banks are willing to entertain a short sale. A short sale means the bank is willing to take less than the amount owned and release the borrower from liability. When you are buying from banks, you know there was someone who was living there previously. And those previous owners lost their homeownership position. You don't know their story, but it is likely unfortunate and emotional. Because I was dealing with Wells Fargo, Chase, and any other number of banks, the transaction became a faceless, nameless experience.

In the summer of 2016, I encountered a property that I wanted to buy. The seller was in early stages of distress. He wanted to sell his property immediately and close within a few weeks. He needed someone who had the ability to cash him out in a few days. He wanted $60,000 for his three-bedroom, two-bath home that was in decent shape. He needed the money to live on because he had no money left. He couldn't even buy groceries to feed himself. It was truly sad.

What happened? He had won the lottery less than five years ago. He had received, after taxes, more than a million dollars in one lump sum. That million dollars was spent and gone. This house was the last asset he had from the lottery winnings. The reason I got the call was that his agent knew I had cash and knew I could close fast. The agent also knew I wouldn't take advantage of the situation. I wasn't going to negotiate the guy down or delay closing to gain the advantage and get it cheaper. I was saddened by the whole experience but came to realize that I was actually helping this guy out of a dire position. When you are prepared financially and honest in your dealings, these types of opportunities will come your way.

What you earn doesn't determine your wealth

The real confusion for so many is that income is viewed as wealth. The media and the government view them as one in the same. The advent of social media and technology has led to greater confusion. Our social media feeds are filled with consumerism, presenting the bling and shiny objects others have bought. According to a Federal Reserve study in 2015, almost half of all Americans could not pay an unexpected $400 expense without borrowing the money or selling something.

So let's break down income and wealth:

>> *Income* is what you bring home today. It's the pay you receive for the output of production you generate. It's attached to you showing up and using your skills and your time in a creative pursuit of commerce.

>> *Wealth* is what you have presently and what you will have also tomorrow and in the future without any effort being added. Wealth will produce more, but it's not reliant on your additional labor. Wealth compounds even when you sleep.

The most unvarnished scoreboard of financial wealth is your *net worth,* which is what would you have left if you sold all your earthly assets. If you sold your home, cars, stocks, bonds, furniture, and so forth, how much actual cash would you have once all the debts are paid off? The remaining amount is your net worth. That is the number you are working to increase through saving, investing, and reducing debt.

The Federal Reserve, in 2017, calculated the median net worth in the United States to be $97,300. When the equity in one's home is removed from the calculation, the median net worth drops to $25,116. When I read those numbers, I was shocked. Those amounts are frighteningly low. The average person has not enough net worth to even last a year without working. What this demonstrates is that earnings are the least of the challenges; it's the expense side of the equation that causes the biggest issues.

Unfortunately, we spend what we make

Even if you are a high earner and you make more, or even much more, than the average income of roughly $59,000 a year in America, I have found that very high earning people are very challenged by the expense and savings side of the wealth equation. If you truly want to build wealth, it takes discipline in restricting consumption.

I truly believe that social media has played a pivotal role in accelerating our society away from wealth and reduced consumption. We have always been challenged with our consumption as people. Social media has made it easier for marketers to reach us with messages that tempt us with the latest goods we must have. It has created an open conduit of images, experiences, purchases, entertainment, and travel. We are inundated with pictures and tweets about what people are driving, doing, and buying through social media channels. All this leads to greater temptation to spend in our attempt to keep up with the Joneses. What's also evident is the Joneses are going into debt and spending more than they make to keep up appearances.

Thomas Stanley wrote the landmark book *The Millionaire Next Door* in 1996. Since that book, he and his daughter, Sarah Stanley Fallaw, have continued their research of millionaires. In 2016, 91 percent of the millionaires they studied rated being disciplined as an important factor of success. And what do I mean by discipline?

>> The discipline to create income and transform that income into wealth.

>> The discipline to create a budget that balances your earnings and spending in such a way that savings numbers are achieved.

>> The discipline to weigh and balance choices of wants and needs. It requires us to accept that we might not receive everything we desire or at least not yet. We must delay gratification of the now for the long-term freedom and security of the future.

Warren Buffett, widely regarded as one of the wealthiest and most successful investors in the world, made this remark about consumption: "The happiest people do not necessarily have the best things," he asserts. "They simply appreciate the things they have." Warren is a classic example of reasonable wants and needs. He continues to live in the same house in the central Dundee neighborhood of Omaha that he bought in 1958 for $31,500. He says that he has everything he needs in that house, which is not walled or fenced in. He preaches that we shouldn't buy more than what we really need. He drives his own car everywhere he goes, having forgone a driver and security people. He could purchase anything on Earth he might desire, yet his spending has limits.

I think we have to figure out what we really need and focus on living below our means so that we can save at the level we need to fund both our present and our future. The athletes I mentioned earlier in this chapter lived at their income or above their income and had nothing left after the high level of earnings stopped. I'm not saying you shouldn't enjoy yourself, and I'm not advocating that we all live in tents and eat boxed macaroni and cheese. But there is a balance and a plan that we all need to control spending and start saving.

Pay the Most Important Person First: You

You are now faced with the most important decision of your life. It will determine the how the rest of your life goes. It's the one decision that will have the biggest influence on, not only your financial life, but your stress level, retirement, and your kids' lives for generations. What do you think it is? That's a big lead up!

REMEMBER

It's the portion of your paycheck or earnings you have the freedom to keep; the portion that you *pay yourself first.*

I had heard that phrase, "pay yourself first," in my early 20s, but I didn't really understand that it was my choice, my freedom, my budgeting strategy. I didn't realize that if I only did that and nothing else but was resolute in executing it, my wealth was assured. I would need to make reasonable investments and not be tempted to touch those funds, and I knew I would be fine. In fact, I would be more than fine. I would achieve wealth. If you select a reasonable percentage of your overall earnings to pay yourself first, invest it prudently, and never touch it, that strategy alone will be enough for you.

What I failed to grasp was the whole "pay first" concept. When I say "first," I mean before rent or mortgage, taxes, car payment, entertainment, dining out, and so forth. I was doing it backwards. I was paying everything else, and when there was money left over, I would put a few dollars away. But there was rarely anything left over. There was, in those early days, more month at the end of the money. While I heard "pay yourself first," I was last in line rather than first in line. I needed to recognize that I was worth being first and that my future demanded I be first. If I didn't change my thinking and value myself and my family more, I was going to live paycheck to paycheck the rest of my life.

I was in the group that was poor when I first heard "pay yourself first." I was poor because I spent everything and saved nothing. You are guaranteed to be not well off both now and in the future with that exact wealth strategy and wealth plan. You tell yourself, as I did, "When I make a little more income or this certain amount of income, I will start then." The truth is, I whisked by that income and still didn't start.

TIP

When the amounts are small, that's when you start your wealth plan or wealth strategy. It doesn't get easier when the amounts are larger. That's the lie we tell ourselves.

How much should you pay yourself?

If you want to achieve middle class now and beyond, you will save 5 to 10 percent of your gross income. That will allow you, over time, to access and stay in the middle class lifestyle and keep that lifestyle through retirement. That might seem unattainable. You might be thinking, "How could I save $100 out of every $1,000 I earn? My budget is so tight and stretched as it is now." I have never expressed in the last few chapters that any of this would be easy. If you received that impression, I want to dispel that notion right now. It won't be easy but it will be worth it.

Take a look at Table 16-1. It outlines how much you need to be saving, or paying yourself first.

TABLE 16-1

Savings and Results

Life Status	Savings Amount
Poor	Spend everything, save nothing
Middle Class	Save 5% to 10% of gross income
Upper Middle Class	Save 10% to 15% of gross income
Wealthy	Save 15% to 20% of gross income
Wealthy Quickly	Save 20% of gross income

We all need to make the choice. We choose how we are going to spend our money. We can choose to go to Starbucks less frequently and not pay for the lattes that costs $5.75. If we remove three lattes per week, that is $69 per month. If I brown-bag my lunch more frequently than going out for lunch, that can add up to $100 per month or more. If I quit smoking one pack of cigarettes a day, that's $170 per month that I have saved. All tallied, we're looking at $339 in savings that I can pay myself first, and the yearly total is $4,068 per year, not including investment earnings. The median income in the United States is $59,000. That $4,068 is 6.9 percent of $59,000. I only need to find another 3.1 percent to guarantee middle-class income for life.

If you desire wealth and financial independence, you can achieve that through saving 15 to 20 percent of your gross income. That is more than most experts profess. The typical expert will tell you that you need to save only 10 to 15 percent to be well off. But I am talking about the wealth that someone, at retirement, has a few million net worth not including his home. That level of wealth puts you into the top 5 to 10 percent. That level of wealth, invested conservatively at 5-percent return, will provide you with an income of $100,000 to $200,000 per year. For most people, that level of income would allow you to not dip into the asset base.

You would be able to live off the income or interest produced, never touching the principle.

How long do you make the payments?

If you want to achieve wealth quickly, then you must be putting 20 percent of your gross income into savings. Let me qualify the term "quickly." Quickly does not mean 5 years, or even 10 years. I think that quickly, when it comes to wealth, is 20 years.

It's possible to do it in less than 20 years if you find a rare and unique opportunity or investment, or if you save even more than 20 percent and perhaps hit 30 percent. Your definition of quickly might be different than mine. That's totally fine. Do whatever is best for the strategy you are implementing.

PAY YOURSELF FIRST EVEN IN TOUGH TIMES

ANECDOTE

When I fully grasped pay yourself first, at least intellectually, we were broke. I was just getting my real estate career going. We were living commission check to commission check, paycheck to paycheck. We were spending the money before we even got it in our hands to cover our bills. So wherever I am finding you, I was there and have been there. I have dug out of a deep hole as well.

True, I have made a very good income for some time, with a few exceptions, in the last 29 years. I have been on the ropes financially a few times as well. In fact, in 1999 during the dot-com stock crash and real estate correction, we had extended ourselves in Joan's building company. She had six spec houses under construction or recently finished. We were writing interest checks coming out of our ears to the tune of $15,000 per month. That was above and beyond our normal household expenses. We had everything for sale, and I mean everything, except each other. (And I'm sure if Joan could have gotten anything for me, she would have sold me, but she would have to come to closing with money to get rid of me.)

We had both our primary home and our second home in Bend for sale. We had two duplexes we owned with very little equity for sale. It seemed like we were cutting checks for interest for an eternity, but we held on, mostly to each other and weathered it until the last of the spec houses were finally sold. We gave a few away where we made zero profit by the time all the interest was paid. During that time, it would have been easy to stop paying ourselves first, but we never did that. We knew that if we stopped that habit, we might never get it started again. Even in tough financial times, you have to continue the habit of paying yourself first.

I first created my income and savings plan at the age of 28 with the goal that it would be completed by 59 and a half. (That's the age when retirement accounts are free from the 10-percent penalty for early withdrawal.) There was a family component as well. My father worked as a dentist for 30 years. He was able to retire before his 60th birthday due to his own 30-year plan.

You have to determine the number of years for your plan. Some of you reading this don't have 30 years or don't want to take 30 years. That means that you will have to go to the top end of the savings scale. If you only have 15 years, then you better execute the "Wealth Quickly" strategy of 20-percent pay yourself first.

The habit is more important than the amount

Many of you are again thinking, "I can't carve 10 to 15 percent, or even 5 percent, out of the money I am making." I completely understand, but that is just an excuse to not do what you know you need to do. I am not saying to do the 10 percent anyway. I am saying that you have to start with something at some level. I didn't start saving 20 percent of my income. In fact, it wasn't even 5 percent. I started with 1 percent.

One percent was it. It's all I could justify. I really didn't feel I could even afford that, but I knew if I delayed starting to do something, I ran the risk of never starting. I recognized that if I didn't start the habit, if I delayed even for one month or one commission check, then I was doomed. "Doomed" is a strong word, but I realized that about myself at the time. As the years have gone by, I recognized I was just like everyone else. You and I are no different. In fact, you might be saying the same things I said to myself: "That small amount won't be worth it. It really won't make a difference. I should put that toward my debts instead. That small amount won't get me to wealth or retirement." But it's not the amount at first that creates the magic.

What percentage or amount works for you? There is no right answer, only your answer. What does your gut tell you?

What's easy to do here is to let that small voice of doubt talk you out of doing what you know is right. Ignore that negative voice saying that the small amount you are thinking about saving doesn't matter. The truth is, it's the start that stops most people. Don't let a small start influence the big finish you will achieve and desire to achieve.

Before you read another word, make the decision . . . right now! It will be the most important decision you ever make in your financial life.

TIP

Making your wealth commitment

There's a truism in life called the law of diminishing intent, which I mention in Chapter 3. We've all experienced it on some level. From the moment you intend to do something, your emotion and resolve are at a high level. But the longer the span of time from thought to action, the lower the odds you will actually ever do what you intended. My goal and desire is to help you beat back the law of diminishing intent. I am asking you to fill out the Wealth Commitment document right now:

Wealth Commitment

"I, _____, hereby promise that I will begin paying myself the first ____ percent of my gross monthly income, or per each gross paycheck, no later than _____ (insert date).

Signed, _____

I expect my gross monthly income to be $_____.

Of this, I will pay myself first the following percentage each month: $_____.

By doing this, my monthly savings will total $_____.

In one year, I will have paid myself first $_____.

The next step is to share this commitment with someone. The act of sharing your commitment solidifies it in your mind. It drives a stake in the ground that says, "This is important. I will do this!" Also, give that person permission to ask you how you are doing with your savings and wealth commitment.

Finally, I want you to open up a separate account to put your wealth commitment funds into. Don't just save them in your other accounts. You need a separate account because you want to see your progress. You don't want to comingle it with other savings or debt accounts. You want to establish the philosophy that you won't touch it or dip into it when times get tough or money gets tight.

The amount you start with won't be the final amount. My suggestion is that you review your wealth commitment. Decide for the year ahead what the amount or percentage should be. Then write up a new commitment contract with yourself. My guarantee for you is that in five years you will be saving vastly more than you can commit to now.

Institute forced saving mechanisms

The use of forced savings that transfers money automatically is one of the secret weapons of the wealthy. Whether you are an employee of a company or owner of your own company, setting up deductions out of your regular earnings to pay yourself first is the pathway to wealth.

Left to our own discipline and commitment, the outcome for many of us will fall short. Most people who achieve wealth have instituted forced savings mechanisms. The secret is to automatically transfer the funds, so you don't see or miss the money. It needs to automatically be transferred at a set time each month. The other option is to have the money taken out of your paycheck. That's why I truly believe in company-sponsored retirement plans like a 401k. These programs help you automatically live on less because it is never missed from your paycheck.

I realize that some people are paid less regularly or have swings in income, which makes an automatic savings plan more challenging but not impossible.

Forced savings as a business owner or entrepreneur

Whether a part or all of your income comes from a business you own, it's easy to not control your earning, income, and savings. You may have a side hustle like Uber, multi-level marketing income, or a side landscape business. I said in an earlier chapter, I have created my own personal economy for more than 30 years, and in that time, I have made numerous mistakes but have also come up with a system of wealth control for business owners.

The first rule is this: Put yourself on a salary. I have been on a set salary for almost 25 years. I take the same salary every month. Joan, my wife, takes a set salary as well for working in our business. The savings contribution to our retirement comes from our paychecks. We are normal, payrolled employees. Our taxes are collected and paid as well. I don't get my hands on that money. I send it away, so I live within my means. And it becomes easy to max out your retirement contributions through forced savings. We have learned to live on the salaries. Then we put the surplus dividends away in savings or buy new investment real estate with the surplus in company profits.

So how do you determine the right amount for your salary? I think there are a few ways to look at that figure. You can come up with a number based on expenses and savings, and even Social Security can play a role in this wealth strategy plan. I am going to start with the most complex one, which is Social Security.

Most people do not understand even basic strategy with Social Security. The truth is, the strategy for Social Security does not start when you are reaching retirement age. The strategy and planning start 20 to 30 years before then, especially if you have an entrepreneurial business. Using Social Security as an evaluator of what salary or income you draw is important, but few people even factor Social Security into their thinking.

There is a Social Security Benefit Formula in monthly earnings. You get credit of 90 percent of the first $856 months earnings. What that means is that you would receive in benefits if you worked for 35 years and made $856 a month. You would receive 90 percent of that number at your full retirement age, which is $770.40 per month until death. You only need about 10 years of working to qualify for Social Security retirement benefits. For every year you work less than 35 years, the Social Security formula will apply a zero income into the average.

You receive 32 percent of credit toward income from $857 to $5,157 in monthly earnings. That means you receive 32 percent of every dollar earned and Social Security tax paid on the next $4,301 of monthly income. If you drew a monthly salary at the top end monthly of $5,157, you will receive an additional $1,376 in Social Security monthly income at full retirement age. Again, provided you earn that amount for all 35 years, your total retirement benefit would be $2,124 per month.

Beyond the $5,057 per month in earnings, you receive a 15 percent Social Security credit based on earning above the $5,057 per month threshold. So the credit decreases as your income increases. The maximum Social Security income for the year is $128,400. That would be $10,700 per month in income. You can earn more than that, but that is the maximum income that will be subject to Social Security tax.

You can also set your base salary level based on savings. Your salary would be filtered through the savings goals and automatic savings mechanisms you put in place. If you commit to saving 20 percent of your income and need $2,000 in savings going to your retirement nest egg (based on the Kiplinger calculator covered in Chapter 14). Then you need to set your salary at $10,000 per month.

You certainly need to factor in your expenses. What do you need in income to pay your obligations, food, shelter, and fun (along with savings) to reach your financial wealth goals? What does it cost you a month for your personal overhead? You want to use that number plus the savings level that is in your wealth commitment. This enables you to live more easily within your means. When your business does better and dividends and extra income are paid out to you, you can save a large portion of the surplus or spend it in a meaningful way.

Guaranteeing Your Retirement Success

The American dream is to retire financially well off when we are still physically able to enjoy the freedom, which means being able to travel, relax, and enjoy our golden years. The age and amount needed to accomplish that goal is a personal decision, but you definitely need a well crafted plan.

The typical length of retirement 30 years ago was less than half the number of years it is today. It's common for people to live into their 80s and 90s, which requires much larger savings and more years in retirement than before. My father practiced dentistry for 30 years. He is 87 years old now and has been retired for 28 years. He is in very good health, so it's likely he will be retired for more years than he worked at his primary career in dentistry. That achievement was unheard of 30 to 40 years ago when our life expectancy was much lower.

Whether you are an employee or business owner, crafting and executing a wealth plan or wealth strategy that incorporates both savings and spending is a must. Selecting the right retirement accounts and amounts can enable you to spend your golden years with peace of mind and freedom.

Simple steps if you are an employee

Whatever your company is offering for retirement savings accounts, take full advantage of them now. Most companies, large and small, offer some type of 401k or retirement vehicle for their staff. The typical pension benefits of the 50s, 60s, and 70s are long gone in most companies. That doesn't mean you can ignore what your company does offer. If your company provides a matching feature in the 401k based on what you contribute, you must fund your 401k to that specific level or beyond. For example, at my company, Real Estate Champions, we offer employees up to a 4-percent match of their salary into a 401k if they at least put in 4 percent themselves.

We have some employees who choose not to participate in the plan, even when they are eligible. I have others who put only 2 percent in. When your employer is providing some type of a 401k match, you are turning down a 100-percent return on your money if you fail to take advantage. This 100-percent return is above whatever investment gain you generate. Where else are you going to generate a guaranteed 100-percent return on your investment with zero risk?

Review your Social Security benefit statement annually

The Social Security you earn through your contributions needs to be monitored. You don't have investment choices to make, but you do need to make sure you are receiving the Social Security income credit you paid in. Social Security is designed to replace about 40 percent of your income in retirement. You will need to save for the remainder in other accounts that you set up and control. The vast majority of people don't plan or check on what could be 40 percent of their retirement income.

Review your statement for income projections and qualification credits. You will need a minimum of 40 credits to be eligible for Social Security benefits. Your

Social Security payments will be based on 35 years of earnings. The lower years of earnings, if you work more than 35 years, will start to drop off in the Social Security calculations. Those years when you were 16 years old working at McDonald's will be replaced by your higher earning years in your late 50s and early 60s, which will dramatically increase your monthly benefit.

Review your benefit amounts for early retirement at 62, full retirement at 67, and delayed benefits at 70 years of age. You will receive an 8 percent increased benefit per year from full retirement age until 70 years of age. This is a large bonus if you can wait until 70 to start receiving benefits. There is no point in waiting longer than 70 to take your benefits. Your benefits will not increase past age 70 even if you are currently working at that age.

A married couple, whether both of them work or only one of them works, can each receive Social Security benefits. The stay-at-home spouse will receive a Social Security benefit that's half of the working spouse's benefit. Few people know this fact and haven't factored it into their wealth and retirement plans.

REMEMBER

It's important to save a portion of your Social Security benefits when you are both receiving benefits. There will be a time in the future when one of you passes away before the other and your benefits will be reduced. It's not that Social Security will reduce your monthly check, but you will only receive one check, rather than two, losing the lower of the two monthly benefit checks through death. To lessen that financial loss, save 10 to 15 percent of your gross Social Security checks each month. This will help the surviving spouse not have to deal with both grief and financial hardship at the same time.

Set aside a percentage of your raises

As you become more valuable to the marketplace and your company, you will likely see an increase in pay. You could be recruited by a competitor for more income. Don't spend all of your increased income and raises on consumption. We all certainly deserve some of the reward of being more valuable to the marketplace. The key is to put some of that increase aside to create wealth.

If you can discipline yourself to put 20 to 30 percent of that increased earnings into savings and investments, you will quickly change your net worth through sacrifices that are unfelt by your current budget. If employees did that one thing over a 30-plus year working life, that one thing would dramatically change their retirement years down the road. It's a painless way to increase your wealth quickly, and you can do it through increasing your contribution to the company 401k. Most employees do not max out their company 401k benefit at $18,500 per year. I would put any raises in a 401k plan to prevent myself from spending them. You can also save outside of the 401k in after-tax options like a Roth IRA or buying an investment property.

Invest in discounted company stock (but be careful)

There are companies that offer employees discounted company stock as a benefit. That stock investment can be inside or outside the company retirement plan. As an employee benefit, it can provide you with a way to buy a good asset at a lower price. Where trouble can come knocking at your door is putting too many eggs in one basket. If a high concentration of your retirement funds is invested in the company stock and the company has a rough patch financially, you could be laid off and your stock could be devalued as well.

Most financial experts suggest that 10 percent is the maximum of your total assets that should be invested in your company stock. That seems a little low, especially if you are working for a company that is currently flying high. If you worked for Google, Amazon, Netflix, or Facebook over the last ten years and had only 10 percent of your retirement funds or after-tax money invested in those stocks, you would have missed out on a fortune.

Because you are participating in employee stock, which I would encourage if the discount is 10 percent or more, it's incumbent on you to keep your ear to the ground at the office. You should know for your ownership and your career if the company is struggling. You should also read all the company communication to stock owners. Compare what you know on the inside to public statements and public comments. Is the communication inside the same as the communication outside? If it's incongruent, it's time to cut back your exposure to protect you and your family from the downside risk.

Simple steps as a business owner or entrepreneur

There are really countless options and strategies as a business owner to guarantee your retirement success. There are numerous retirement account options that you control the decisions on as an owner.

As a business owner, the foundation is a good flow chart of your wealth plan with accounts and amounts clearly identified. Your wealth plan flow chart moves you from hope, theory, or desire, to execution. I have included a few flow charts in this book that I have used personally and taught to countless small-business owners who are now wealthy. You can see them in Figures 16-1 and 16-2. The differences between the models has to do with where you are going to pay taxes and fund retirement savings. Are you going do it at the corporate level or at the personal level? In some instances, your model might encompass doing that at both levels, and that's when wealth can really be exploded.

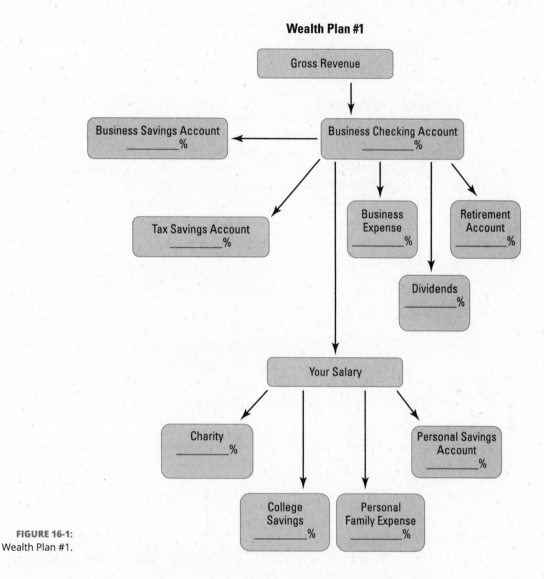

Wealth Plan #1

- Gross Revenue
- Business Checking Account _____%
- Business Savings Account _____%
- Tax Savings Account _____%
- Business Expense _____%
- Retirement Account _____%
- Dividends _____%
- Your Salary
- Charity _____%
- College Savings _____%
- Personal Family Expense _____%
- Personal Savings Account _____%

FIGURE 16-1:
Wealth Plan #1.

As a business owner, it's easy to feel you are doing well because you see the gross revenue of the company. The employees only see their net check. A company owner can easily overspend when gross revenues are climbing. In reviewing these charts, you might feel there are too many accounts to manage. Wealth Plan #2 (Figure 16-2) has at least four accounts at the personal level:

>> Tax savings

>> Personal savings

» College savings

» Retirement savings

I have all those accounts and also a few more for investment savings and all the rental properties. I can attest that managing all those accounts requires work, time, and accounting. I also have discovered, for me, that the more accurate and compartmentalized I operate, the more money I can save through control and budgeting. As a business owner, comingling accounts is a bad strategy that can hide problems with the company or financial challenges personally. It can also conceal a lack of discipline.

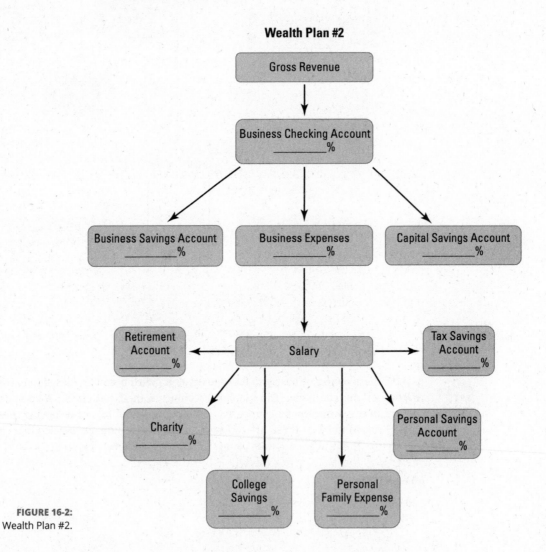

Wealth Plan #2

FIGURE 16-2:
Wealth Plan #2.

280   PART 5 Success with Wealth and Money

The "secret sauce" for small-business owners

As a small-business owner, I have had every type of retirement account known to man. I have had 401ks, Sep IRAs, Keough, Money Purchase Pension Plans, Defined Benefit Plans, and Roth IRAs. There is not one that is the best over all the others. You and your accountant need to figure out — based on your age, income goals, and size of company — what options are best for you. All of the ones I mentioned have pluses and minuses, so a true professional is needed.

But the real "secret sauce" is beyond just the accounts you use. It isn't the type of account; it isn't a type of investment class (stocks, bonds, commodities, or real estate). The secret sauce for a business owner, especially a small-business owner, is setting up your retirement accounts to be *self-directed.* As a business owner for almost 30 years, I spent the first 20 following the standard path. I saved my money each paycheck religiously into my retirement accounts. I selected credible financial planners that invested my money in stocks and other investments. I got slaughtered in 1999 in the dot-com correction. I lost over half of the value of my retirement accounts for Joan and myself. Then in 2008, in the most recent downturn, after my accounts had built up again, I lost another 40 percent. After that loss, I was not philosophical; I was mad. I started to look around for the solution to fix this issue. I had saved consistently and done that well. I had not listened to myself and had trusted the judgment of others more than my own. Big mistake.

I found the solution or "secret sauce" in *self-directed retirement accounts.* A self-directed retirement account allows me more latitude to decide what I invest in. Because I own the company, I can set up all the retirement accounts in my company for the self-directed options. This change in my company's retirement plan has enabled me to invest my retirement assets in a wider range of investment options. It's different than when you have a standard, boilerplate plan that feeds funds to Wells Fargo, Morgan Stanley, Edward Jones, or any of the large financial advisor institutions. They generally don't allow you to self-direct your assets into real estate, businesses, hard money lending, and so on.

WARNING

I am a firm believer that as a business owner, and especially a small-business owner, you must set up your retirement accounts that allow you to self-direct the assets, but I caution you to invest in what you know. Because I have specialized knowledge in the asset class of real estate, that is where I have directed my retirement funds. I proved through losing almost 50 percent of my retirement fund twice in stocks that stock investing was not my cup of tea at least in terms of my knowledge.

My current retirement funds have enabled me to acquire numerous single-family rentals, duplexes, and four-plexes, as well as an apartment building. All the rents and revenue go back into my retirement accounts, and all taxes are deferred until I need them in retirement. I feel very comfortable with my investments. If the real estate market adjusted catastrophically, I honestly can accept that because it's on my shoulders. What I have invested in is strong cash flow properties, so the cash flow is unlikely to go away, even if the values correct.

There are also lenders that will loan you funds to acquire real estate if you don't have enough funds in your retirement accounts to acquire the property. This leverage enables you to control a larger asset while earning income and appreciation without having all the funds presently in your retirement account. Only by establishing a self-directed retirement account do you have access to all these options. It took me 20 years and two financial meltdowns for me to finally get frustrated enough with my situation to learn about self-directed retirement accounts. I moved my company 401k to be self-directed. I combined all my SEP IRAs, Keoughs, and money-purchase pension plans into one IRA to self-direct it all into real estate. If you are a small-business owner, professional doctor, or CPA with your own business, this one move can add millions of dollars of net worth to your retirement and give you stability in your income in retirement. It has been a game changer for me.

6
The Time and Success Connection

Master the key area that will determine your success in life: Time management.

Understand the time and money connection.

Use time-blocking to get things done.

IN THIS CHAPTER

» **Looking at your strengths and goals**

» **Creating a system to manage your time**

» **Minimizing the disruptions from calls and other distractions**

» **Fighting the urge to procrastinate**

» **Becoming adept at making big decisions**

Chapter **17**

Setting Your Habits for Time Management Success

Time is the great equalizer, as everyone has the same amount in a day. No matter who you are, where you live, and what you do, you clock the same 24-hour cycle as the next person. One person may be wealthier than another, but that doesn't earn him a minute more than the poorest people on the planet.

If that simple fact seems a bit discouraging, think of it this way: You may not have the power to get yourself more time, but you *do* have the power to make the most of it. You can take your 365 days a year, seven days a week, and 1,440 minutes in a day and invest them in such a way that you reap a return that fulfills your life and attracts the success you dream of.

That's what this chapter is about: taking control of how you spend your time to make sure you're using it how you really want to. Anyone who does that is a success. You really are in control of your time, even though you don't always feel like it; even if you have a job that demands overtime; even if you have kids who keep you in the carpool loop; even if you have dreams and goals that involve developing new skills or furthering your education.

All in all, discovering how to manage your time well is part mental restructuring and part creating a system. Effective time management requires a little introspection, some good habits and organizational skills, and more than a few logistical and tactical tools. But all are achievable for anyone who desires to be more successful.

Getting to Know Yourself

The better you understand yourself — your strengths, weaknesses, goals, values, and motivations — the easier it is to manage your time effectively. In this section, you look at your strengths and goals, think about how much your time is worth, and observe personal energy and behavior patterns that affect your focus throughout the day.

Assessing your strengths and weaknesses

As a young man, I thought I was good — okay, I admit it, I thought I was *great* — at a much larger group of skills, tasks, and jobs than I do today. In fact, the older I get, the more I realize the list of what I'm *not* good at dwarfs the list of things I *am* good at. Being consciously competent at those few, however, gets me a lot further than being unconsciously incompetent, as I once was. Despite my poor academic record in high school, as a young adult, I was a quick study at what I needed to do to be as successful in life as I wanted to be. At some point, I saw the light and realized I needed to face up to what I had to do to get where I wanted to go.

First, I took stock of my assets: I tallied up my strengths, skills, and even my weaknesses. And I identified things I needed to work on and things I needed to leverage. That's when I realized that although some people were smarter, were more educated, had more money, and knew more influential people than I did, I had the same amount of time as anyone else. And if I wanted to get ahead, it was up to me to harness my time and invest it in such a way to get a greater return. My willingness to invest more time to gain the edge helped equalize the playing field for me and help me achieve the success I enjoy today.

Chances are that by this point in your life, you've discovered some skills that you come to naturally or perhaps have worked hard to acquire. Maybe you're a master negotiator or a whiz with numbers. You may be a good writer, or you may have a silver tongue. Whatever your strengths, developing the handful that brings you the most return on your efforts, propelling you forward to attain your goals, is a more productive course of action than trying to be the best at everything. For most people, these strengths typically number no more than a half-dozen.

In addition to pinpointing your strengths, you need to identify the areas where your skills are lackluster. Then figure out which tasks are essential for meeting the goals you want to accomplish and build those skills. Invest time in honing and maintaining your strengths and improve the weaknesses that you need to overcome to reach your goals.

REMEMBER

To be successful, you need to be selective.

Naming goals to give you direction

You know how it is: When you're working toward something, keeping your focus is much easier. A woman may want to lose weight, for example, but perhaps she struggles to stick to a diet or exercise plan. But if her son's wedding is looming three months away on her calendar, she may be more inspired to stay on track, cutting back on second helpings and getting in workouts.

REMEMBER

Your goals can serve as inspiration in adopting good time-management skills. After all, managing your time isn't really a benefit in and of itself, but managing your time so that you can spend more of it doing what's important to you *is* — whether you're saving for a retirement of travel and adventure or buying the house in the perfect neighborhood.

Using your aspirations to fire up your time management success means you have to identify your goals and keep them in the front of your mind. Pinning down what's most important to you may require some soul searching. Write down your goals — all of them — and follow these guidelines:

>> **Cast a wide net.** Go for the big goals, such as joining the Peace Corps, as well as the not-so-big ones, such as getting an energy-efficient car next year.

>> **Think big.** Don't rein in your dreams because they seem unrealistic.

>> **Be as descriptive as possible.** Instead of "build my dream house," flesh it out: Where is this house? How big? What features does it have? What does it look like? When do you want to move in?

>> **Don't limit goals to a single category.** Think about goals for your career, your personal life, your social situation, your financial status, and any other facet of life that's important to you.

The process of goal-seeking can be a fun and energizing experience, and it's one you can explore at length in Chapter 5. You also see how your current time use can affect the forecast for your future.

Assigning your time a monetary worth to guide your priorities

Most people think about the value of their time as it relates to on-the-job activity. The fast-food worker knows he earns a minimum wage per hour. The freelance artist advertises a per-hour rate. The massage therapist charges for his services in half-hour and hour increments. But to be truly aware of the value of your time, you need to carry this concept into your personal life as well. The value of time in your personal life is at least as valuable as your work lifetime. In some cases, personal time is priceless.

REMEMBER

One of the most important points to remember is that it's okay not to get everything done. What's critical is making sure that the *important* things are getting done. By assigning value to your time and using the skills you acquire from these next two chapters, you can clearly identify what's important and make conscious, wise choices. For example, if you need to save another $200 per month because you want to start an account for your children's college education, you may determine that putting in an extra shift at work may not be worth the loss of time with your family, even at time-and-a-half pay.

Identifying your rhythm to get in the zone

Athletes talk about being *in the zone,* a place where positive results seem to stick like a magnet. Well, I'm here to tell you that the zone isn't some magical place where wishes come true. Anybody can get there, without a lucky token or fairy dust. What it takes is focus, singular focus.

If you know your rhythms — when you're most on, what times of day you're best equipped to undertake certain tasks — you can perform your most important activities when you're in the zone. Everyone works at a unique pace, and recognizing that rhythm is one of the most valuable personal discoveries you can make. Some of the aspects you need to explore include the following:

>> How many hours can you work at a high level each day?

>> What's your most productive time of the day?

>> How many weeks can you work at high intensity without a break?

>> How long of a break do you need so you can come back focused and intense?

Following a System

Effective time management requires more than good intent and self-knowledge. If intent was enough, everyone would be wealthy and healthy. We would all achieve financial independence and have rock-hard abs. To keep your time under careful control, you need a framework. In your arsenal of time-management ammunition, you want to stock organizational skills, technology that helps keep you on track, and planning tools that help you keep the reins on your time, hour by hour, day by day, week by week, and so forth.

Establishing a solid system you can replicate is a key to succeeding in managing your time. Systems, standards, strategies, and rules protect your time and allow you to use it to your best advantage. These skills are applicable whether you're the company CEO, a salesperson, a midlevel manager, an executive, or an administrative assistant. No matter your work or your work environment, time management is of universal value.

Scheduling your time and creating a routine

Sticking to a time-scheduling system can't guarantee the return of your long-lost vacation days, but by regularly tracking your meetings, appointments, and obligations, you reduce your odds of double-booking and scheduling appointments too close. And by planning ahead, you make sure to make time for all the important things first.

For years, I've followed the time-blocking system, which I detail in Chapter 19. The system ensures that you put your priorities first (starting with routines and then moving to individual tasks/activities) before scheduling in commitments and activities of lesser importance.

REMEMBER

Such time-management techniques are just as applicable to the other spheres of your life. There's a reason why I advise you to plug in your personal commitments first when filling in your time-blocking schedule: Your personal time is worthy of protection, and you can further enhance that time by applying time-management principles.

Organizing your surroundings

A good system of time management requires order and organization. Creating order in your world saves time wasted searching for stuff, from important phone numbers to your shoes. But even more, physical order creates mental order and helps you perform more efficiently.

THE SCHEDULE WILL SET YOU FREE

Too many people feel that all this structure is too restrictive. They think the freedom they seek with their schedules and their lives is contained in a more flexible environment. They're afraid establishing a routine will keep them wrapped in the chains of time.

However, most people waste too much time figuring out each individual day on the fly. They react to the day rather than respond. *Reacting* is a reflex action that turns over your agenda to others, and that can't possibly lead to freedom. *Responding* is a disciplined act of planning that determines where and how you'll invest your time.

For example, suppose you have a set place in your schedule to respond to phone calls and problems. You've established the routine of dealing with these issues in predetermined time slots. You can hold off on your response until later — when you're calmer, more focused, and in a problem-solving mentality — instead of reacting because you're dealing with the issue now.

Planning how to spend your time, which at first glance seems opposed to freedom, is the only pathway to the true mastery of time. With the right routine come simplicity, productivity, and freedom. The questions "what am I going to work on today?" and "what's my schedule today?" never enter your mind. And when you get the important work out of the way, you free yourself to do what you really enjoy.

If you're a free spirit and what I'm suggesting just fried your circuits, start with a small amount of routine. Ask yourself, "Can I establish a daily routine to try it out? What can I do without having it send me into withdrawal?" Then implement a new routine every week. You'll add more than 50 new pieces of structure to your schedule in a normal work year and see a significant improvement in your freedom.

Yes, your workspace should be clean and orderly, with papers and folders arranged in some sort of sequence that makes items easy and quick to find. Your desk should be cleared off, providing space to work. Your important tools — phone, computer, tablet — ought to be within reach. And your Google calendar, or day planner, of course, should be at your fingertips. You might say, "Who uses a written day planner anymore?" The truth is, for many, a more technological approach to time management lowers productivity. Don't feel, to organize your time, that you have to use technology.

Using time-saving technology

Organization extends beyond your work area: Not only should your laptop or tablet be nearby, but the files, documents, and contact information on them should be ordered for quick access. If you are in any type of business, you must use a customer relationship management software, or CRM for short. The vast majority of businesses use Outlook or Google Drive or Excel for customer lists. A CRM, like Salesforce, Hubspot, or Goldmine, can be invaluable to organize and correspond to clients efficiently. A CRM stores your address list, tracks your correspondence, and contains your calendar and upcoming appointments.

But that's just the beginning. Today's teleconferencing and videoconferencing equipment means you can hold weekly meetings with your colleagues who live on the other side of the globe without anyone having to turn in a travel expense report. The use of Webex, GoToMeeting, or Zoom can be a game-changer for communicating within a company as well as making video connections with clients and prospects.

Overcoming Time-Management Obstacles

Anyone can conquer time management, but it's not always easy. If your experience is anything like mine, sometimes your days feel like a video game, where you're in constant threat of being gobbled up on your course to the finish line. But instead of cartoon threats, your obstacles are your own shortcomings (poor communication skills, procrastination, and the inability to make wise and quick decisions), time-wasting coworkers and bosses, phone and people interruptions, and unproductive meetings.

Communicating effectively

Communicating effectively is one of the best ways to maximize your time. One of the biggest time-wasters on company time is, no surprise, talking with coworkers. But what may be a surprise is that the abuse *isn't* a function of weekend catch-up discussions that take place at the water cooler or the gossip circle at the copy machine. Rather, it's the banter at the weekly staff status reports, the drawn-out updates of projects that never seem to conclude, and the sales presentations that get off-track. It's all the meetings that could be as brief as ten minutes but somehow take an hour or more. At your disposal, however, is an amazing weapon for taming these misbehaving encounters: your words. With a few deft remarks, you have the power to bring these meetings to a productive close.

The biggest challenge in communicating effectively is selecting the communication channel. We have a much broader band of communication methods at our disposal today. Roll back the clock 30 years. Our methods of communication were mail, phone, and face-to-face. There were only three potential choices, so it was easier to at least select the right delivery vehicle. In our world today, we still have those three, plus we have text, e-mail, instant message, and social media posts (think Facebook, Twitter, Instagram, LinkedIn). We also have video e-mail, video message, Skype video, and FaceTime.

I would first evaluate the purpose of the communication: information, connection, or persuasion. Those three categories can help you select the delivery method. If I am just trying to convey information, I can use any method I choose. Any e-mail, or even snail mail, can create information flow and do it efficiently. I likely would not need a face-to-face meeting to deliver information. The information could also be conveyed electronically via text or instant message. If I am trying to connect with someone, then speed and the ability for a back-and-forth short dialogue could be used. For example, a text or instant message would be better suited. I could even use video e-mail to create connection. While a video e-mail isn't dialogue, the recipient can see me personally, and it shows me to be a very caring person. This is an especially useful tool for communicating someone you haven't met yet.

Being persuasive requires the most effective communication. If I am trying to persuade people to my point of view, I need to be talking with them over Skype or FaceTime, having an online meeting, or be face-to-face with them. Ever try to convince your teenager of something via text? It doesn't work well. If you could see them rolling their eyes when they read your text, you could respond accordingly, but you can't.

Circumventing interruptions

Interruptions creep into your workday in all sorts of insidious manners. Think of the pesky coworker stepping into your office with "Got a sec?" Plus you have interruptions in the form of unproductive meetings, phone calls, hall conversations that drift into your office and distract you, and even the "you've got mail" icon that creeps onto the lower corner of your computer monitor.

Additionally, most poor time managers interrupt themselves by trying to do too much at once. Study after study supports that multitasking isn't the most effective work style. The constant stops and starts disrupt a project, requiring startup time each time you turn back to the task.

Scheduling time offline

Used effectively, the telephone, text, social media, instant message, and e-mail can enhance performance, increase productivity, boost profitability, and expedite career growth. But there's a flipside: Because modern communication allows for easier interruptions, it creates a greater loss of production, performance, profitability, and advancement than ever before. And to a certain extent, e-mail has taken many people hostage. Do you feel compelled to open all e-mail immediately? Do you jump on to the next e-mail even before you've responded to or resolved the previous e-mail? Just as with cellphones, the fact that you *can* be reached easily and at any time seems to dictate that you must be available to anyone — all the time.

REMEMBER

When you stop to open each and every e-mail as soon as it arrives or answer the phone every time it rings, you are, in essence, *multitasking,* trying to perform one or more tasks simultaneously. And as I frequently point out, multitasking is just not time-efficient.

TIP

To keep your focus, set aside time — daily or several times per week — during which you simply do not take calls, check e-mail, review social media, or allow other interruptions. Such prescheduled segments ensure blocks of concentration, a tactic certain to raise productivity and lower frustration. If you're concerned about being unavailable for too long of a time, then limit these periods to one or one and a half hours, with time afterward to return messages.

Letting e-mail wait in your inbox

I am a firm believer in working offline. There's no way I can resist the temptation to check my e-mail every time my computer tells me a message has arrived. During your offline time, turn off your e-mail notice or disconnect from the Internet. Schedule your e-mail time and devote a reasonable time block to take care of it. Then turn your e-mail program off so that you don't see the you've-got-mail icon on your computer until your next scheduled e-mail session.

TIP

The toughest decision you may face is whether to check your e-mail first thing in the morning when you fire up your computer. Wait and knock out a few priorities first? Or open it up and relieve the suspense — and possibly get waylaid by some marauding issue you feel compelled to pursue? It's your choice, so do what works best for you. But by staying offline for the bulk of your workday, you're likely to stay focused on the tasks at hand and get much more accomplished.

Stopping the ringing in your ears

Give yourself times when you turn off your cellphone. The most brilliant innovation with these amazing devices? You can turn them off! This stops the dinging, pinging, and screen popups that distract all of us. Without missing a message, tweet, or post, you can continue with your conversation, errand, or work without distraction and get back to the phone when you're through. Of course, you may already protect yourself against uninvited interruptions by limiting whom you give your cell number to. But unless you're awaiting an urgent call from your kids, your boss, or the state lottery commission, you can likely afford a period of off-time while you attend to important tasks that require your full concentration.

Limiting phone interruptions from loved ones

In some cases, family calls are the primary source of telephone interruptions. Have a frank talk with your family members about when it's appropriate to call you at work.

If you have young children, you know how they want to tell you all the cool things that happened during the course of their day, well before family dinnertime. You likely expect and welcome these calls. Certainly you want to set opportunities for them to reach you, but it's good to establish boundaries at the same time. You may, for example, ask your kids to call you and fill you in on their day at a certain time — say, after they get home from school or in the case of preschoolers, after lunchtime. Same goes for your spouse or partner.

WARNING

Most job environments allow for some personal call time, but few are tolerant of employees who receive calls throughout the day. That type of phone interruption can undermine your productivity, not to mention your career. At work, you really don't need the kinds of emotional distractions that'll dramatically affect your performance and productivity for the next 30 minutes, an hour, or even the rest of the day. Calls from family can move your mind to home even though your body is still at the office.

Secondary Defenses: Minimizing Damage When Calls Get Through

If you set up the defense mechanisms and blocking techniques I cover throughout this chapter, you can avoid more than 90 percent of the interruptions that most people experience each day. But no matter the system or strategy you use to protect yourself, telephone interruptions are certain to penetrate your defenses. When this happens, your best strategy is to accept it and go with the flow. Okay, so an interruption slipped past your perimeter: Instead of expending effort to repel the breach, just deal with it. A negative attitude or reaction is likely to cause more damage and waste more time than simply resolving the matter that made its way to you.

The most effective technique to help you adhere to your time management strategy is to plan for the distractions that'll undoubtedly come. You may use the preemptive strike technique, which allows you to deal with distractions from others on your terms. In this section, you discover a few plans for handling the phone calls that make it through to you.

Delegating the responsibility

When the call penetrates your defenses, attempt to delegate the call to someone who can handle it for you. Inform the caller that you're booked, buried, under a deadline, committed, or heading into a meeting. Then state that you're shifting the responsibility for the call as the fastest way to resolve the problem or challenge. Assure the caller that you're bringing in someone qualified to help.

Shortening or condensing the conversation

When a call does sneak past the fortress guard, your best defense is to bring that call to a close as quickly as possible. Your focus has been broken, and it'll require five minutes from the point you wrap up the call to regain your momentum. You want to keep the conversation short so that you can get back in the groove.

Inform the caller upfront how much time you can offer. You may, for example, explain that you're in the middle of an important project and have only ten minutes available. You can also state that you have an appointment — and if you've implemented the time-block schedule (see Chapter 19), you've blocked out your day, so your claim is true.

Some people feel uncomfortable about cutting calls short in this way, especially with clients or prospective customers. Giving the caller a time limit feels abrupt, but it doesn't have to. Here's one way your speech may go:

> *I know we can resolve your problem, but I have an appointment in ten minutes that I have to keep. If we can't resolve the problem to your satisfaction in the ten minutes, then we can set a time to talk later today to finish up.*

This approach still gets you off the phone in the allotted time but gives you an out. The customer can also feel better that you're offering more time. I've used this technique for years with high-maintenance clients. Rarely do we need the additional conversation, but they appreciate my offer all the same.

Rebooking discussions for a better time

If now's a bad time to handle the call, then reschedule. The caller certainly doesn't know your schedule, and it probably never occurred to the caller that this could be a bad time. Offer a brief explanation — you're in a meeting, on your way to an appointment, or simply tied up at this time. Then without allowing time for a response, offer two options of when you're available:

I'm not able to give your situation the full attention it deserves at this moment. Can we schedule a phone meeting for this afternoon after 3:00 or first thing tomorrow morning?

By offering options, you give back some control to the caller. If you've been caught without your day planner, give a general time, such as Wednesday morning or Thursday afternoon. Then don't forget to transfer the call appointment to your planner.

TIP

Another technique is calling customers back and telling them that they're so important that you squeezed them into your schedule or that you called them first. This technique is extremely effective when you return a call before the appointed time. If you informed them on voice mail that you'll be calling them back at 11:00 a.m. and you manage to get your priorities done early and can start calling the high-interruption clients back at 10:30 a.m., they'll think you walk on water.

Setting expectations

Educating family, friends, and customers about your availability is important. Let everyone know your schedule and the best times to reach you as well as how to leave a message when you can't be reached. As part of this education, you also want to establish how quickly they can expect a response from you after they leave a message: Within 24 hours? The same business day?

What you're trying to avoid is the person who calls you back five times that day because you were in meetings. With every call, that person gets more frustrated that you haven't called her back. Or worse yet, she reaches you on the fifth call before you're walking into your most important meeting of the day, creating the worst interruption of your life because she unloads on you and ruins your focus.

REMEMBER

Creating reasonable expectations is key in good customer relations. Taking 24 hours to return a client's call may be reasonable — but it won't seem that way if the client expects to hear from you within an hour.

You can also reinforce wait times through your voice mail message. By leaving your availability and response details as part of your message, callers are more likely to recall and retain. Here's an example:

You've reached Dirk Zeller. I am out of the office today, Tuesday, September second. Please leave a message and I will return your call by end-of-day Wednesday, September third. If you need immediate assistance, please call so-and-so. Until then, make it a great day!

I've set the scenario: The caller shouldn't expect a return call from me today. And in fact, because I'll be returning to an inbox filled with calls, e-mail, and correspondence, I may not be able to get back until as late as the end of the day. I've offered, however, a back-up plan if the situation is more urgent. This should satisfy virtually anyone who calls.

WARNING

Don't be tempted to include "If it's an emergency, call me on my cellphone" unless you're prepared for lots of interruptions. After all, isn't *interruption* exactly what you're trying to avoid?

Maintaining Your Motivation as You Press Ahead

Everyone has struggled with procrastination, and many still do. I have yet to meet a person who doesn't battle with the temptations of putting off those obligations that seem too big, too hard, or just plain no fun. Recognizing your tendencies is the first step toward recovery. By following the strategies I outline in this chapter, you can make remarkable progress in overcoming the procrastination.

Staying on the right course, however, is a never-ending vigil. The following sections present maintenance tactics that can help.

Keep your expectations realistic

Before you beat yourself up for your woeful procrastinating ways once again, take a look at your schedule and first figure out whether what you're attempting to accomplish is realistic. Have you accepted an assignment you're not qualified to take on, or is too much expected of you? Have you committed to an absurd deadline?

Again, when you begin to feel overwhelmed by your workload, this may be an indicator that you'll slip into postponement mode. So do whatever you can to get over being overwhelmed. It may require some adjustment in expectations of your boss or coworkers.

Handle the big stuff and delegate the rest

When you find that too many obligations and projects are demanding your attention to the point that you're putting off making headway on any of them, it's time to lighten your load.

After you examine your workload and identify what's really important to your job or your career goals, you know what to attend to first. But instead of putting those smaller or less-important tasks on the back burner, see whether someone else can take over for you.

Prevent clutter overload

Another sign that your procrastinating proclivities may soon raise their ugly head — or already have: Your office or home is cluttered with a confusion of papers and files, your e-mail inbox contains more than a week's worth of unread mail, and you've lost control of your schedule.

You can't maintain control of your time or stay on top of your obligations if your life has become so disorganized that you can't keep on top of your work and home. It's no wonder you're procrastinating — if you have a project in all that mess, you don't even know where to start.

You may be overloaded. You may have too many projects at once. At any rate, it's time to clear your head and your desk. Take a day once a month or even just a few hours to purge, file, respond, and clean up.

Focus on maintaining a healthy balance

Both your work life and your personal life are important to your well-being. Keep an eye on the scale to be sure that these different areas are in balance. If you get weighted down at the office, you lose energy and perspective, and procrastination — both at home and at work — creeps in. If family issues take over, you risk your performance at work. When one aspect of your life gets out of whack, do everything you can to regain balance.

Making Decisions: Just Do It

One of the easiest things to put off is making a decision. Even sidestepping the smallest decisions can lead to giant time-consumption. Think about it: You scroll through your e-mail and save one to ponder and respond to later. You revisit a few times and still can't bring yourself to a commitment. So you get more e-mail from the sender. To stave off making a decision, you ask a couple of questions, which requires more time and attention. By the time the issue is resolved and put to bed, you may have invested five times more attention than if you'd handled it at once.

Many factors create the confusion and uncertainty that prevents you from making sound but quick decisions. Often, part of the struggle is having too many options. Most people have a tough enough time choosing between pumpkin and apple pie at the Thanksgiving table. But every day, you're forced to make decisions from choices as abundant as a home-style cafeteria line. Having options is usually a good thing, but too much choice is overwhelming, even paralyzing.

Life is always serving up decisions, and making choices — even wrong ones — is how you grow, mature, and accomplish the things that make life meaningful. Most successful people realize they are going to make wrong decisions frequently. It doesn't stop them from taking action and deciding. The lack of making a decision is actually still making a decision. If you're stymied by small decisions, you never have the time and energy to seek out choices that lead to a more enriching and successful life.

REMEMBER

In other words, decisiveness is more than a useful tool; it's a way of living. Indecision, on the other hand, is a way of drifting, simply surrendering to fate.

It's all too easy to get bogged down weighing and reweighing options in a purgatory of analysis paralysis, but endless second-guessing and falling prey to the tyranny of what-if only bleeds you of energy. Sitting on the fence is inefficient, not to mention uncomfortable. And *not* deciding? Well, that's a decision itself — with its own consequences.

Like many important life skills, effective decision-making isn't taught in school. Most people learn by trial and error and through the experiences of other people. Unfortunately, this approach can leave you floundering in a sea of changing choices. When you begin to feel more confident about making smaller decisions, you find it easier to apply what you've discovered to larger challenges. You see that you can break down what seems confusing, or even overwhelming, into a series of smaller steps. Eventually, you'll be comfortable enough with making decisions that you *invite* them, because being able to quickly and confidently make decisions gives you power and control over your life.

Looking at the source of most decision-related struggles

Why is making a decision so hard? It usually comes down to fear: fear of making the wrong choice or maybe fear of regret. The more afraid you are of tripping up, the more you torture yourself by evaluating, debating, analyzing, and obsessing over every decision.

Before you begin to work on your decision-making skills, you need to see where the problem lies. Take a moment to ask yourself these big-picture questions:

>> What's one area of your life you'd like to change but have avoided taking action?

>> What's really holding you back?

>> What's the worst thing that can happen if you decide to take action?

>> What are the odds that the worst really will happen?

>> Would you be likely to live through — and even learn valuable lessons from — making a mistake?

Armed with the answers to these questions, realize that the fear is probably unfounded — that the worst that can happen is very unlikely. Then decide to take action on your finding today.

Whittling major decisions down to a manageable size

Lucky people make good decisions once in a while. Successful people have a system they consistently use to approach situations that require decisions: a plan of action that works no matter what the circumstances or stress level.

Here's why: Individual decisions rarely exist in a vacuum. Daily decisions, ranging from how and when you discipline your children to whether to stick to a regular savings plan, have consequences that may reveal themselves only years down the road. The key is to make clear-headed choices *today* and build on good results instead of haphazardly cleaning mistakes as you go. Use the following five steps to whittle the formidable task of making a decision down to manageable size.

Step 1: Evaluate the gravity of the decision

The key is to approach situations in every facet of your life with a cool head so that you can accurately assess the size and gravity of the situation you're up against. Following is a list of the larger, more important areas of your life that really deserve some time and effort. Decisions in other areas of your life need not require much time or thought.

>> **Taking care of business:** If you're a business owner, your daily decisions guide the fortunes of your family as well as those of all the employees who rely on you for a regular paycheck and benefits. You have to balance

seemingly small decisions (whether to refund a customer's money) with bigger-picture choices (redirecting the business to take advantage of a potentially lucrative niche market).

TIP

Assessing the size of a business decision isn't always a straightforward process, so look beyond the obvious to possible repercussions. For example, failing to provide a refund to a dissatisfied customer may prompt that person to post a scathing review of your customer service policy on a widely read blog; you may spend months undoing the damage. Redirecting resources to a new niche market, on the other hand, may affect the morale — and productivity — of employees in core business areas.

>> **Furthering your career:** Should you decide to take a higher paying job with a longer commute? Hang up your sales hat and study to become a nurse? If you're changing your job, assess the impact of added travel expenses and less time with your family. A major career change can shake up everything from your budget to your self-image.

>> **Keeping it in the family:** Some of life's major decisions involve your family: whom you choose to marry, when to have children, where to live. Along with these big decisions come plenty of smaller day-to-day decisions. Who takes the kids to school? Should you take a vacation or renovate your kitchen? Even decisions that don't seem significant in the moment, such as giving your kids unsupervised use of the computer, can have unexpected repercussions. To further complicate things, you may have to step in to provide assistance or physically care for your aging parents.

>> **Making sense of your finances:** Money isn't the most important thing in life, yet it's the lifeblood of so many important goals. Unfortunately (but perhaps not surprisingly), most marital conflict is linked to finances. The choices you make about spending, saving, and investing — individually or as a couple — can spark daily arguments and have serious long-range implications.

>> **Staying healthy:** The good news in this area is that the simplest decisions can have the most profound effects. Deciding to eat a healthy, balanced diet, exercise daily, and take regular breaks from the stress of work can prolong and improve the quality of your life. This alone is good preparation for the more serious, sometimes life-or-death decisions you may have to make if you develop a condition such as diabetes, need surgery, or require tests.

>> **Building strong relationships:** Happy relationships are the foundation of a happy life. If you're married, in a committed relationship, or devoted to a circle of close friends, the time and care you invest will pay you back a thousand-fold. If you're still looking for a spouse or life partner, the decisions you make about the qualities you want and need in someone else and the qualities and commitment you're willing to bring to a relationship shape your future for better or worse.

Step 2: Assess the timeframe you have to make the decision

When you're on a time crunch for making a decision, your struggle in making that decision increases. The key: Give yourself a reasonable deadline, allowing a comfortable but finite amount of time to research and consider your options. In decision-making, you may need to slow down your process, timeframe, and expectations in terms of time and results. You have to be willing to take a few breaths to pause and then decide.

TIP

Here are some questions to ask when you're assessing a reasonable timeframe for making a decision. Let your answers to these questions guide your next steps:

» Is there a shelf date on this decision?

» Will something good happen if you make the decision by a certain date? Will something bad happen if you don't?

» What's likely to happen if you make the wrong decision within this timeframe?

» What are the consequences of postponing the decision? Can you (and your family) live with that?

Step 3: Narrow your options down to two

Having too many choices is confusing. The more options you have, the harder it is to commit to just one. Research indicates that you'll be happier with your decision if you choose from a smaller number of options.

The fastest and best decision-makers are people who align their decisions with their personal or business goals, as having this foundation simplifies things by narrowing your focus. Identifying your goals, vision, core values, and core purpose in life is an important first step. (I help you get them on paper in Chapter 5.) Then check to see which of your options doesn't align with your goals and cross them off the list.

TIP

To do a preliminary evaluation of your options, you need to do a limited amount of research. Give yourself a time limit for researching possibilities (perhaps only an hour online, a half-hour making phone calls, or a half day to visit stores). Then, based on your cursory research, decide which two options best align with those goals, priorities, and values. Matching options to priorities can be a bit tricky if each option addresses more than one goal — you have to decide which options meet your most important goals. I often find it helpful to apply the following filters:

>> Impose a price range to narrow down the choices.

>> Establish some basic criteria to whittle down the possibilities (open-toed or sling-back shoes; Asian restaurants on the east side of town; job opportunities in major West Coast cities).

Step 4: Check in with the reliable wisdom of your gut

Your body is a very powerful partner in decision-making, whether or not you act on what it tells you. So before you invest lots of time researching a particular course of action, stop thinking and take note of what you feel deep inside: What does intuition tell you?

Somewhere in the vicinity of their stomachs, many people detect a distinct discomfort about certain decisions they're considering — hence the term *gut feeling*. You don't have to have full-blown indigestion to know you're not feeling good about a decision. And believe me, all the positive data in the world probably won't change your gut feeling about the outcome. The best decisions both make sense logically and feel good in your gut.

Step 5: Determine the most efficient way to get your desired result

Take a close look at what you're trying to achieve, quantifying (where possible) what your decision will cost in terms of time, effort, and resources — both short-term and long-term. Then look at your desired end result to see which path is the best way for you to get there.

Success is subjective. What I may deem important or how I measure the cost of a result is unique to *me*. You have to do what's right for you.

>> How will you know when you've achieved a level of success that satisfies you?

>> How much time will this take? Is the amount of time and money you'll have to invest worth the result?

>> What would a satisfactory outcome be? What would an outstanding result be for you?

>> What are you willing to do to achieve the satisfactory level?

>> Can you tangibly or quantifiably measure the results? How would you accomplish that?

You can certainly use a pros and cons list to help refine the direct route to your desired result. As you make your list, rate your priorities on a scale of 1 to 10 to give each response some weight.

Keeping Motivation High

Like most goals, mastering your time-management skills isn't something that happens overnight.

Throughout the process of working to improve the way you manage your time, you'll occasionally encounter points where you start feeling disappointed, wondering whether your efforts are paying off. Whenever you hit those lows — and you will — remember to give yourself credit for every step you make in the right direction.

TIP

One great way to stay motivated is to link incentive to inducement: In other words, reward yourself. For example, if you complete certain actions that tie to your goals, give yourself Friday afternoon off. Or savor an evening on the couch with a good movie or dinner at a favorite restaurant. Do whatever serves as an enticing reward.

Take motivation to the next level by involving others in the reward. Let your spouse know that an evening out awaits if you fulfill your week's goals before deadline. Tell the kids that if you spend the next couple of evenings at the office, you can all head for the amusement park on Saturday. I guarantee this strategy is a surefire way to supercharge your motivation.

As you work through this difficult but worthy bout of self-improvement, keep your mind on the positive side and remember two simple truths:

>> You're human.

>> Work always expands to fill the time you allow for it.

No matter how productive I am, whether I have just a couple things to accomplish or a sky-high pile on my desk, and whether I leave work on time or stay late, there's always something that doesn't get done. So I don't get hung up on those things I don't accomplish. Instead, I just keep my eyes on the goal, prioritize accordingly, delegate what I can, and protect my boundaries carefully so that I take on only as much as I know I can handle while still remaining satisfied with all parts of my life.

TIP

When you start to get frustrated about the never-ending flow of work that comes your way, remind yourself that you're blessed with more opportunities than time — and that's not a bad place to be.

Chapter **18**

Time Equals Money

uccessful people place a higher premium on their time, both in terms of its monetary value and its psychological value. When you talk about productivity, earnings, goals, family, and health, all of those important factors in overall quality of life are interconnected and influenced by their time utilization.

Success is not measured by any single scale or ruler in life. We all have our own unique way of determining success. Depending on your values, different kinds of numbers may be important to you. To some, it's cholesterol count and blood pressure figures; to others, it's the number of years they've been married. To many, the sum total in their retirement account is the number-one measure, and some people focus on the amount left on their mortgage.

But I contend that your per-hour worth should be among the top-of-mind numbers that are important to you — no matter what your values or priorities are — even if you don't earn your living on a per-hour rate. Knowing the value of your time enables you to make wise decisions about where and how you spend it so that you can make the most of this limited resource according to your circumstances, goals, and interests. This focus will lead to greater success, fulfillment, and wealth.

REMEMBER

Obviously, the higher you raise your per-hour worth, while upholding your priorities, the more you can propel your efforts toward meeting your goals. You will have more resources at your disposal: more money or more time, whichever you need most.

Why Your Hourly Rate Is Important

Your per-hour value translates to your quality of life, both now and in the future. Not only does your income influence how you spend your nonworking hours, but it also determines how much leisure time you have to spend. In traveling the world to speak to success-focused audiences, I have found few people who want to earn less money. There is a direct connection between your income and wealth and your sense of success or achieving success. One measure that has a direct and significant influence on the quality of life is hourly rate.

As you can imagine, your hourly value reaches beyond the basics, as it impacts your health as well. For example, studies show that lower-income earners have more health problems, including heart disease and diabetes, which are often attributed to poor diets and a lack of medical care. Additionally, the challenge of trying to make ends meet can cause great stress, leading not just to physical illness but also to depression and other mental health problems.

And though it's important to live in the present, it's also important to keep an eye toward the future. How well you prepare does have an impact on your quality of life right now. Making enough money to be able to save for retirement and other major life expenses — including a child's education — results in a sense of comfort and safety about your future.

Your personal time has value, too. And by having a grip on the value of your work hours, you gain a better grasp on what your downtime is worth. After all, most people work so they can make the most of their personal time, whether they're devoting it to family, hobbies, volunteer work, travel, or education.

REMEMBER

When you recognize that your free time has a monetary value just as your work time does, you are able to achieve a more successful work/life balance and a more fulfilled mental state. You gain the perspective you need to make choices:

>> Is the extra money you'll gain by working overtime worth giving up your holiday with your family?

>> Could you go part-time and stay at home with your small children?

>> Can you afford to take a leave of absence to do a volunteer stint in Haiti?

>> Should you take on a freelance project that means giving up all your free time for three months to fund your dream trip to Bali?

But what is an hour of your personal time worth? Well, that's not a question you can easily answer. How do you put a price on time with your young children? Or apply a dollar value to travel experiences that bring you in touch with new worlds? Or equate the quiet therapy of a walk in the woods with the stress of a work presentation?

The harsh truth is that you don't get paid for not working. But that doesn't mean your personal time has no monetary value. Just thinking about your time as a commodity with a value helps you sort through and recognize the activities that are most important to you. (For information on valuing your personal time, see the later section "Making Value-Based Time Decisions in Your Personal Life.")

Calculating Your Hourly Income

No matter your occupation, everyone sells time for a price; it's just a lot more transparent in some situations than others. Most obvious are individuals who receive a wage or a fee based on the hours they work, including minimum-wage workers and self-employed individuals such as tutors, house cleaners, and consultants.

Other people advertise their prices based on a per-project basis, but in reality, they base that fee on an estimate of project hours the job takes. Freelance writers, for instance, may charge $1,500 to write a promotional brochure, but that amount is likely a reflection of the writer's value of his or her time at a certain figure — say, $75 per hour.

In today's "gig economy," there are more people in short-term employment, work-for-hire situations, and side job ranks than ever before. Examine the number of people you know who have a side hustle as an Uber or Lyft driver. How many people do you know who take jobs through Fiverr or Upwork to earn extra income? While I'm an author of many books, including several for the *Dummies* brand, writing is not my primary focus. I also speak, coach, and consult.

Some businesses and professions charge customers based on an hourly rate, although workers don't directly receive that per-hour fee. Instead, their salary or compensation is based on the revenue the company can bring in based on those hours. Law firms and plumbers, for example, may charge for their services on an hourly basis and pay their employees a salary or a per-hour rate.

TIP

If you earn a salary, you may not perceive yourself as having an hourly rate. But everyone does. Here's how to calculate your hourly income. This number doesn't affect how you're paid, but it puts you in touch with what an hour of your work time brings you.

1. **Calculate the number of hours you work per week.**

Work hours/day × days/week + overtime = hours/week

To be completely accurate, calculate your hourly rate based on the hours you actually work. If you consistently put in more than 40 hours per week (most salaried folks aren't paid overtime for additional hours worked), add those hours to your total. Here's an example:

8 hours/day × 5 days/week + 2 hours overtime = 42 hours/week

2. **Figure out how many hours you work per year.**

Work hours/week × weeks/year = hours/year

Make sure you subtract time off. For instance, if you take three weeks of vacation each year, subtract that from your total number of weeks worked. If your salary is based on a three-week vacation and an average 42-hour work week, here's how many hours you work per year:

42 hours/week × 49 weeks/year = 2,058 hours/year

3. **Divide your gross salary by the number of hours you work per year.**

Salary × hours/year = hourly income

For example, $80,000 divided by 2,058 hours is $38.87.

Boosting Your Hourly Value through Your Work Efforts

For especially successful people, money isn't the scarcest and most valuable resource; time is. There are plenty of ways to make more money, but there's no way to add more minutes to an hour. You have a limited amount of this precious commodity, so you want to protect it and spend it as if it's your own personal trust fund. For less successful people, they usually feel the lack of money or capital is their biggest issue.

REMEMBER

The truth is, lack of productivity or lack of service value is more stunting than lack of funds.

Most people think that if they work more hours, they'll automatically make more money. That's faulty thinking: You can devote more hours to work, but if you invest the hours in the wrong actions, you gain nothing — and you lose time.

The solution may be to ask for more money for your time. Some workers have a good deal of control over their hourly income and can therefore charge more per hour for their services. The freelance writer can raise her hourly rate from $65 to $70 and bring in an additional $50 on a 10-hour project. A tax accountant can increase the fee for income tax preparation from $450 to $510. If she needs six hours to prepare the average income tax return, the accountant just gave herself an increase from $75 to $85 per hour.

However, the simple fact is that most people don't have the luxury of raising their income at will. So what's the next best step? Change how you use your time so that you get the best return on investment. After all, what you do with your time leads to greater prosperity.

Increasing your productivity

To increase your hourly value, you have to decide whether you'll work toward earning more money or earning more time. Then focus on performing high-value activities to achieve that goal. The process of discovering the really important actions or items you can invest your time in can help you change your hourly rate. The decision of how to increase your hourly value — whether to work toward generating more money in the same amount of time or generating the same amount of money in less time — depends on your circumstances:

>> If you're in a commission or bonus compensation structure, you can increase productivity to earn additional income.

>> If you're in a salary-based position, you can find ways to be more productive within the 40-hour workweek and reduce the additional hours you put in.

Increasing your income

If your job doesn't enable you to increase your hourly value, whether in terms of money or time, then you have bigger decisions to make. Other changes you can make to directly impact your income are to simply do the following:

>> Find a similar job at a company that pays a bigger salary or offers more freedom with your work hours.

>> Improve your performance and earn a raise or a promotion. Know, however, that the success of your efforts toward a raise or promotion is ultimately up to the higher-ups.

Improving your quality of life

When evaluating time-for-money trades, be sure not to limit your definition of return to money: Ask yourself whether the exchange improves the quality of your life. Look at how your life would change outside of work if you were to double or triple your hourly rate. If what you're trading for dollars does any of the following, it's a good trade:

>> Increases your ability and opportunity to earn more money

>> Increases your amount of family time

>> Decreases your work hours

>> Enhances your physical and mental fitness

>> Provides an opportunity for someone who needs it

>> Removes something you don't enjoy or don't do well from your life

REMEMBER

Success is about progression, being better today than you were yesterday. It's about progressing or moving toward your desired outcome or objectives. When you really dig down with the preceding questions to create a plan or strategy to improve time performance and value, you are on your way to success.

Making Value-Based Time Decisions in Your Personal Life

When you consider the way you live your personal life, divide your focus in two: chores/responsibilities and leisure time. Although personal time may seem straightforward, there really is a difference between chores and leisure activities, and the way you approach your time-management decisions hinges on that difference. But however you spend your personal time, you can assign that time a value equal to your work worth — even though no one's paying you — to help you decide how to spend it.

Deciding whether to buy time: Chores and responsibilities

When you have a handle on the value of your time in hourly increments (see the earlier section "Calculating Your Hourly Income"), you have the information you need to make better time choices. The chores have to be done, whether you do them, delegate them, or even pay someone else to do them. The question with chores is whether you want to do them yourself or to exchange dollars for someone else to do them. You have to ask, "Is the cost of the time this task would take me greater than or less than the cost to hire someone to do the work?" Here, you're simply comparing numbers.

Think of the list of household chores and personal errands that can eat up every bit of personal time you have. If you could pay someone to do some of those tasks at a rate equal to or well below your hourly rate, wouldn't that be a good return on investment?

For example, paying $50 to have your grass cut each week may have been a cost barrier you couldn't get over before. But if you've determined that the hourly value of your time is $50 per hour and it takes you 3 hours to mow your lawn, you've just bought yourself $100 worth of time ($150 worth of your time minus $50 to outsource the work). On the other hand, if you have all kinds of free time on the weekend — and you enjoy being out in the yard — paying someone else to cut your grass may be a money-time trade that has no value for you.

If you love to garden but hate cleaning the house, and cleaning the house takes you 4 hours ($200 if your time is worth $50 per hour), why *not* pay a housecleaning service $100, $125, even $150 to buy back the 4 hours it'd take you to do it all? And you buy yourself 4 blissful hours puttering over your zinnias and scarlet runner beans.

TIP

You should reevaluate your trades periodically because your attitudes can change over time.

ANECDOTE

A few years ago, Joan and I acquired a vacation home that my father and mother had built themselves in the 1960s. It needed a lot of work because it was stuck in the 60s. I had grown up doing construction work with my father. I had learned carpentry, painting, finishing carpentry, plumbing, and light electrical. Because I did a lot of maintenance and tenant-improvement work on my father's commercial buildings, to say I was burned out on construction projects is an understatement. I've had numerous properties to renovate and improve that I have bought in the last 15 years. I didn't feel the need, or the desire, to lift a hammer anymore. But at the lake house, where my father physically hammered in every nail by hand, my thinking changed. It has been very rewarding and time consuming to renovate this family property back to life.

Making time-spending decisions: Leisure activities

With leisure activities, your decision simply hinges on whether you want to do them at all. Unlike chores, which you have to deal with in some way, you can get away with forgoing certain pastimes. When you're faced with decisions on whether to accept an invitation or volunteer for a committee or do any other activity, that can affect your leisure time.

Looking at rewards

REMEMBER

A leisure activity has to bring you as much joy or value as your hourly income rate. Some things you do will be priceless, but others are worthless or even less than worthless because they drain you rather than fill you up. So with leisure activities, you aren't comparing numbers. Instead, you simply decide whether a given activity is worth your hourly value. Consider the value of the activity in terms of . . .

>> Your personal enjoyment

>> The service you want to do for someone

>> The support to those who are less fortunate than yourself

>> The desire to pay it forward

>> The legacy you want to leave to others

These are evaluations that successful people make with regard to free time. The desire to retire, for most successful people, is rooted in freedom — the freedom to choose what to do with your time each day or week in a manner you decide.

Factoring in monetary and time costs

Another factor to consider when choosing leisure activities is the cost of your free time. Often, that time isn't so free because you undertake activities that require some recreational funds. When you have to pay to enjoy certain recreational or leisure activities, take the cost of the activity and add it to the monetary time-cost you'd have to pay for the activity. In short, would you pay the cost in your hourly value (plus any costs of the activity itself) to participate in that activity?

Say your income equates to $35 per hour. If an acquaintance you're not all that crazy about invites you to her jewelry party on a weeknight, you'd be looking at, say, a 2-hour cost of $70, plus any money you'd spend while there. Should you go? Probably not, if this acquaintance really isn't someone you prefer to spend your time with.

Or how about this scenario? A local nonprofit asks you to be on a committee that requires an average of 10 hours per month. Total value: $350 worth of your time each month. Is the value earned from your time donation worth the cost to you? How does it factor into your overall goals? Do you enjoy being on the committee and do you feel passionate about the nonprofit's mission? Do you have other more important things you have to tend to first?

The money-to-time-value consideration extends to even the seemingly most mundane of activities — for example, dining out. Going out to a 2-hour dinner with a family of four may cost $100 or more. If you earn $100 in one hour, this may seem like a fair trade, as you're paying $100 for something that would cost you $200 in time. But if your income is $20 per hour, you're essentially paying $100 for something that's worth only $40 in time. That may seem steep for a midweek convenience meal; however, if you're celebrating your child's first straight-A report card, it may feel like a fairer trade.

How about a week of vacation? Travel, hotel, and food on the road can add up fast. If you and your partner total up $5,000 in expenses for a beach resort getaway, at $100 an hour, that's more than a week's worth of work hours — not a bad deal, you may think. The fact of the matter is this: The decision of whether an activity is worth its cost is completely subjective. That idea is certainly empowering and freeing as long as you make conscious choices about where you dole out your hours.

Staying open to experiences and using time wisely

REMEMBER

The process of evaluating your leisure time is meant to help you use your time well, not to limit your experiences. If you're unsure about a certain activity but you had fun and found it worthwhile in the past, you should probably go again. Also consider going if it's part of your current or future goals. If you enjoy the people but not an activity, you can suggest a change of venue and make the outing more worthwhile.

Chapter **19**

Creating the Success Habit of Time-Blocking

What you do with your time is more important than how much time you have. Just as recognizing and understanding your life goals helps you achieve successful time management skills, the effective use of your time goes a long, *long* way to shortening the journey to those goals. By investing your time with care and consideration, your journey toward your dreams is certain to be smoother. In fact, an old time-management adage says that for every minute you invest in planning, you save 10 minutes in execution. Spend an hour planning a trip, for example, and you'll free up *10* hours to achieve better business results, reduce stress, and add quality time at home.

The best way to achieve your goals is to prioritize them and develop an ordered plan to reach them. A universally recognized method for maximizing productivity, called the *80/20 rule,* has proven successful time and again, for more than 100 years. In this chapter, I explain the general concept and show you how to apply it — at work, at home, in your relationships, and beyond.

People who are most productive have another common trait: They treat everything in life as an appointment. These people value their time and the activities to which they commit, whether business or personal. They lend importance to their duties, commitments, and activities by writing them down and giving them a time slot, whether they're one-time occurrences or regular activities. They even make appointments with themselves.

To ensure you act on your priorities in the order that's most important to you, you need to follow a method to your scheduling — and that's what this chapter is all about. Here, I help you match your overall time investment to your goals, prioritize your tasks, and create a schedule to take you safely to your destination.

Focusing Your Energy with the 80/20 Theory of Everything

As I've mentioned earlier in this book, in 1906, Vilfredo Pareto noted that in his home country of Italy, a small contingency of citizens — about 20 percent — held most of the power, influence, and money — about 80 percent, he figured. That, of course, meant that the other 80 percent of the population held only 20 percent of the financial and political power in the country. Pareto found a similar distribution in other nations. In the 1940s, Joseph M. Juran applied the same 80:20 ratio to quality control issues, and since then, the business world has run with idea of the "vital few and trivial many."

The basic principle is that in all things, only a few are vital and many are trivial. This is known as the *80/20 rule* (also referred to as the *Pareto principle*), and you can apply it to almost any situation. I've heard it used in the workplace ("20 percent of my staff makes 80 percent of the revenue") and even by investors ("20 percent of my stocks generate 80 percent of my income"). You can also apply the 80/20 rule to time management.

Matching time investment to return

Generally speaking, only 20 percent of those things that you spend your time doing produce 80 percent of the results that you want to achieve. This principle applies to virtually every situation in which you have to budget your time in order to get things done — whether at work, at home, in your relationships, and so on.

REMEMBER

The goal in using the 80/20 rule to maximize your productivity is to identify the key 20-percent activities that are most effective (producing 80 percent of the results) and make sure you prioritize those activities. Complete those vital tasks above all else and perhaps look for ways to increase the time you spend on them.

The steps that follow show you how to implement the 80/20 rule.

Step 1: Sizing up your current situation

Before you can do any sort of strategizing, you need to take a good, honest look at how you use your time. For people who struggle with time management, the problem, by and large, lies in the crucial steps of assessing and planning. Start your assessment with this process:

1. **Observe how you currently use your time.**

   Through the observation process, you can discover behaviors, habits, and skill sets that both negatively and positively affect your productivity.

   What do you spend most of your day doing? How far down the daily to- do list do you get each day?

2. **Assess your personal productivity trends.**

   During which segments of the day are your energy levels the highest? Which personal habits cause you to adjust your plans for the day?

3. **Take a close look at the interruptions you face on a regular basis.**

   During what segments of the day do you experience the most interruptions? What sort of interruptions do you receive most frequently, and from whom?

Step 2: Identifying the top tasks that support your goals

Some folks tend to follow the squeeze-it-in philosophy: They cram in everything they possibly can — and then some. These people almost always end up miserable because they try to do so much that they don't take care of their basic needs and end up strung out in every possible way. The quality of what they do, as well as the amount of what they do, suffers as a result of their ever-increasing exhaustion.

REMEMBER

To work efficiently, you need to identify your 80 percent — the results you want to achieve. Break out your list of goals. Take a good look at your top 12 goals and identify the tasks you need to do that align with those goals. If your number-one goal is to provide your kids with an Ivy League education, for example, then your priorities are less likely to center around taking twice-yearly vacations to the Caribbean and more likely to revolve around investing wisely and encouraging your offspring to do well in school. (Can you say "full-ride scholarship?")

After you identify what you need to do — your vital few — spend a bit more time in self-reflection to double-check that you've correctly identified your goals and essential tasks. One of the biggest wastes of time for people is changing direction, priorities, objectives, and goals. Successful people and successful time managers take the direct route from point A to point B.

Here's what to ask yourself about these key tasks:

>> How much time do you devote to those activities? Twenty percent? Less? More?

>> What are you doing with the remainder of your time?

>> How much return are you getting for the investment on the remainder?

Step 3: Prioritizing your daily objectives

After you identify the tasks and activities that you need to accomplish to achieve your goals, assign a value to those goals so that you can decide how to order your daily task list.

Take the send-your-kids-to-an-Ivy-League school scenario that I bring up in the preceding section: Even though another of your priorities is to be home for your kids, you — as a nonworking parent who values the type of education you can provide for your 3-going-on-18-year-old more than the short-term joy of being a stay-at-home parent — may decide to return to the workforce as you see tuitions skyrocketing. You can make this decision because you have a clear idea about how you rank your priorities. This clarity may help direct you to a job with hours compatible with your kid's schedule.

To personalize how you prioritize your goals at work, follow these steps:

1. **Look at your long-term career goals.**

   Do you want to advance to a particular career level? Do you want to achieve a particular income? Or is your goal to fine-tune your skill set before figuring out where you want to go next?

2. **Review your company's priorities.**

   Having a solid understanding of the company's priorities, goals, objectives, and strategic thrusts guides your own prioritization so you can get the edge on the company's competition. To get a global perspective, review your company's mission statement, review its published corporate values and goals, and see how they pertain to your position. Ask your direct supervisor for further elaboration on these statements and on his or her priorities so you can make sure you align yours accordingly.

The vital 20 percent: Figuring out where to focus your energy at work

Used effectively, the 80/20 rule can increase your on-the-job performance. From boardroom to lunchroom, executive suite to mailroom, this time-management principle can help you accomplish the most important tasks in less time and help you advance in your career.

The 20-percent investment in the 80 percent of results remains relatively constant. In more than a decade of working with business leaders to improve performance, I've witnessed it firsthand: What's truly important for success changes very little within a given profession. The two global objectives of any successful business are profit and customer retention. What differs among professions is how those global objectives translate to match individual objectives.

For example, here's how the 80/20 rule factors into some major job categories:

>> **Ownership/executive leadership:** As an executive or owner, your most important role is to establish the vision, goals, and benchmarks for the business. What are the core values and core purpose for the business?

What are the goals for the year and then next quarter? What are the most pressing problems that need to be solved? What are the strengths, weaknesses, opportunities, and threats the company or marketplace is experiencing? You then have to convey those answers consistently in clear terms for your lieutenants to follow and hold the lieutenants accountable to the standards.

>> **Sales:** For sales professionals, lead generation leads to 80 percent of your return. Without new leads and new prospects to sell to, your customer and prospect base remains fixed to your current clients. So in sales, your most important tasks are prospecting and following up on leads. You should put a priority on securing and conducting sales appointments and building personal relationships.

Don't forget your existing client base as well. They usually follow the same 80/20 rule, where 20 percent of them contribute 80 percent of the revenue. Spend your time with this group to increase sales and referrals.

>> **Management:** For those in leadership positions, your vital 20 percent is the coaching and development of people. You use coaching strategies to encourage and empower your employees, and you monitor your staff's adherence to the company's strategic plans. In addition, you help your employees acquire the knowledge, skills, attitude, and actions to advance their careers.

>> **Task- or service-based roles:** This group of people varies the most because it's the broadest. To identify your vital tasks, take a look at your company's objectives, your department's objectives, and your own objectives to get a well-rounded picture of how your role fits into the bigger picture. Then decide which of your job responsibilities increase sales or improve customer retention.

After that, consider the value of the product or service you offer, and weigh the importance of quality versus speed or quantity. Your ultimate goal is to serve your customers better so that you retain and grow your relationships with them. (If you're not sure how much weight each element deserves, talk to your supervisor about where you should focus your efforts.)

- If quality takes higher priority, ask yourself how you can deliver a better product or service in the amount of time you're given.

- If delivery speed or quantity is more important, ask yourself how you can deliver that product more efficiently while maintaining quality.

>> **Administration:** If you're in an administrative role, your goal is to enhance the company's performance, whether you're supporting frontline sales staff or assisting the corporate leadership in steering the business toward profit. If you're in sales support, how can you help free up the salespeople to do more selling? Can you fill out reports for the salespeople? Research new market opportunities and get contact information? Can you repeat that help for the sales manager in reports and better tracking of the salespeople's numbers so the manager can do more coaching and shadowing of the salespeople?

>> **Customer service:** If you're working in customer service, is there a recurring customer service problem that needs to be solved? Can you identify it? Can you find at least two solutions to the problem and bring them to your boss for review? You can make yourself an indispensable asset to the company with these actions and save time for yourself and your superiors as well.

Personal essentials: Channeling efforts in your personal life

The 80/20 rule isn't strictly business, so don't lose sight of its influence on your personal life. In fact, the 80/20 rule can have the greatest impact at home. For most, personal and family life is the realm that matters most. But with all the demands of work and the outside world, it often takes the back seat. By categorizing and ordering your personal priorities, you can customize your approach to the people and priorities in your home life and make the most of your time spent with family, hobbies, leisure, and friends.

When factoring in your personal priorities, think of a variety of areas, such as time with loved ones, a worthy cause, your faith, education, and future plans. In this section, I cover the two areas of prioritization that affect most people.

Investing wisely in your personal relationships

One of the great things about the 80/20 rule is that it doesn't apply only to task-oriented items. It's also about the quality of your time and the energy you put into any aspect of your life. If you have a significant other, for example, consider how 20 percent of all the time you spend with him or her shapes 80 percent of your relationship with that person.

Outside of work, personal relationships are number one, so always consider them first, before you even start thinking about chores. Evaluate your connection with each of the important people in your life, both family and friends. In this way, you can customize your approach to the people and priorities in your home life instead of lumping everything into the generalized category of "home" and perhaps not giving any individual or activity its due attention.

When dealing with people, ask yourself these questions to help you identify the 80/20 balance:

>> How can you invest your time with this person to create a better relationship?

>> What's most important to this loved one, and how can you serve and support these needs?

Many other questions can help get you to the root — or the 20 percent — of actions that produce a bumper crop of love, security, appreciation, and experience that build meaningful relationships at home. For example, if you're raising children, you may ask yourself these questions as well:

>> How can you invest your time to nurture this child's developing interests?

>> How can you show that you value this child in a way that he or she understands?

>> What do you need to do each week to teach this child an important life skill?

>> What shared activities allow you to serve as a positive example?

>> What can you do to create a positive family memory?

Balancing crucial household tasks with at-home hobbies

Face it: Your days are filled with tasks that really don't bring much return on investment. Whether it's doing the laundry or filling out paperwork, there are loads of those necessary-but-not-monumental duties that you'll never be able to eliminate. And in your personal life, these activities may include housework, home maintenance, or walking the dog.

SETTING UP FAMILY TRADITIONS

My wife, Joan, and I have a few family traditions that don't take much time but reap huge dividends for our family. The first is weekly Family Friday. We have family activities each Friday with our two kids, Annabelle and Wesley. We go to the movies, have dinner out, ice skate, whatever the family wants. We rotate who gets to select the Family Friday activity.

Sunday night is game night: We turn off the television and play board or card games as a family. It creates an interactive, cooperative, and competitive environment. Frequently, now that the kids are older, it gravitates to "beat the parents."

Your 20-percent time traditions may differ from ours, depending on the age, interests, and unique traits of your loved ones at home. The important thing is to find out what brings the biggest return, greatest connection, and best memories. Of course, I have to confess that applying the 80/20 rule in relationships is much easier to write about than to execute. Although you may understand how the 80/20 rule applies to your home relationships, putting it into practice remains a challenge. Work on it with each passing day.

However, you can apply the 80/20 rule to help balance how you invest your time in chores so that it aligns with your hobbies. Which activities bring you the biggest return? For example, do you spend every summer evening and weekend on your back patio, entertaining or simply admiring your backyard and flower garden? Then for you, trimming, mowing, planting, and weeding may be a wise way to invest that vital 20 percent of your time. If, however, you get more enjoyment from traveling to new places, you may allocate that time to budgeting for and planning exciting vacations.

TIP

Cooking, cleaning, shopping, laundry, yard work, bill paying, and other tasks are essential, but that doesn't mean that *you* have to do them. As I cover in Chapter 18, sometimes the added cost of hiring help is worth the time it frees in your schedule. If you gain no joy or fulfillment whatsoever in cleaning or household maintenance, or feel you simply don't have the time or energy to do all this without sacrificing your most important priorities, hire out those responsibilities.

Sure, there's a cost involved, but you buy back time to spend on the activities that mean the most to you. So send out the laundry if it frees you up to explore new menu ideas in the kitchen, or bring in a personal chef if you'd rather be out in the garden planting tomatoes.

If you can hire someone who makes far less money than you do to do something you don't enjoy, hire out the task immediately. If you can work a few more hours and increase your pay or set yourself up for promotion sooner, then work the extra hours and hire the help. In the end, you'll be doing something you enjoy rather than something you despise.

ANECDOTE

Yard maintenance will never be on my vital 20-percent time investment list. In my adolescent years, I mowed, clipped, trimmed, and hedged a lifetime's worth of yards to earn money. I don't own a lawnmower and never will. And frankly, a prizewinning lawn is not tops on my list of life satisfactions.

However, I do enjoy presenting my family and friends with creative meals, so I put my time into grocery shopping and cooking. It gives me a chance to help lighten the load for Joan, and it offers another 20-percent time tradition with the kids. They love to get creative in the kitchen — especially baking cookies — so we do it together.

The 80/20 rule doesn't stop there. You can also apply it to the quality of those tasks or hobbies and the results they have on your well-being. If you're a gardener, for example, think about the 20 percent of your efforts that bring forth the 80 percent of your pleasure and satisfaction from gardening. For example, maybe you don't need to sculpt a perfectly arranged flower garden to reap the personal benefits, as the very act of digging your hands into the earth may give you the greatest sense of joy. So focus on the act of planting more than on the planning and shopping.

REMEMBER

Don't forget to include those activities that support and improve your physical, mental, and emotional health. Those activities that keep you sane, happy, and fit may seem insignificant when taken one at a time. But if they start getting squeezed out of the schedule, you just may start to see that sanity, happiness, and health start slipping. Be sure to account for all those little pleasures that add texture to your life: reading, study, yoga, your weekly facial, and so on.

Getting Down to Specifics: Daily Prioritization

After you identify the vital few tasks you need to accomplish to meet your top 12 goals, break them down a bit further into daily to-do items. Then prioritize them to make sure you accomplish the most important tasks first, identifying which ones you must do on a given day. In that way, you progressively work through all the minor tasks that lead to the greater steps that, in time, lead you to achieving your goals. The following sections outline the steps you need to take.

Step 1: Start with a master list

Write down everything you need to accomplish today. Don't try ranking the items at this point. You merely want to brain dump all the to-do actions you can think of. You may end up with 20, 30, even 50 items on your list — tasks as mundane as checking e-mail and as critical as presenting a new product marketing plan to the executive board. Or if you want to fill work on your personal to-do list, the items may range from buying cat food to filing taxes before midnight.

WARNING

Remember to account for routine duties that don't have a direct effect on your company's mission or bottom line: turning in business expense reports, typing up and distributing meeting minutes, taking sales calls from prospective printing vendors. Neglecting to schedule the humdrum to-do items creates a destructive domino dynamic that can topple your well-intentioned time-block schedule.

Step 2: Determine the A-list

Focusing on consequences creates an urgency factor so that you can better use your time. Ask yourself, "What, if not done today, will lead to a significant consequence?" Designate these as *A activities*. If you have a scheduled presentation today, then that task definitely hits the A-list.

Same goes for filing your tax return if the date is April 15. Buying cat food probably doesn't make this list — unless you're totally out or have a particularly vindictive cat.

Step 3: Categorize the rest of the tasks

Now move on to B-level tasks, activities that may have a mildly negative consequence if not completed today. C tasks have no penalty if not completed today. Next you have the D tasks, and D is for *delegate.* These are actions that someone else can take on. Finally, E items are tasks that could be eliminated, so don't even bother writing an E next to them. Just mark them out completely.

Step 4: Rank the tasks within each category

Say you've categorized your list into six A items, four B items, three C items, and two D items. Your six A tasks obviously move to the top of the list, but now you have to rank these six items in order: A-1, A-2, A- 3, and so forth.

TIP

If you have trouble ordering several top priorities, start with just two and weigh them against each other: If you could complete only one task today, which of the two is most critical? Which of the two best serves your 80/20 rule? Then take the winner of that contest and compare it to the next A item, and so on. Then do the same for the B and C items.

As for the D actions? Delegate them to someone else! Everyone likes to think they're indispensable, but for most people, the majority of their duties could be handled by someone else. That's where the *85/10/5 rule* — first cousin to the 80/20 rule — comes into play: You tend to invest 85 percent of your time doing tasks that anyone else could do, and 10 percent of your time is devoted to actions that some people could handle. Just 5 percent of your energy goes to work that only you can accomplish. But whether at home or at work, this doesn't mean you can kick back and leave 95 percent of your responsibilities to someone else. This thought process simply helps you hone in on the critical 5 percent, allocate your remaining time to other activities that bring you the greatest satisfaction, and recognize those tasks that are easiest to delegate.

Step 5: Take action based on your rankings

Now you're ready to tackle your to-do list, knowing that the most important tasks will be addressed first. Don't expect to complete as large a number of cross-offs as you may be used to. Because you're now focused on more important items, which likely take more time, you may not get as many tasks completed. In my view, however, the measure of a great day is whether you wrap up all the A-list items. If you follow this system and consistently complete the A items, I can assure you success. Why? Because the B and C items quickly work their way to A items, and you always get the most important things done.

REMEMBER

Don't assume that you just move the Bs and Cs up the next day. You need to complete the whole process each day. Some of the Bs will move up, but others will stay in the B category. Some of the Cs — due to outside pressure, your boss, or changed deadlines — may leapfrog the Bs and become the highest priority As.

ROCKING OUT: PUTTING THE A-LIST TASKS IN PLACE

Steven Covey and A. Roger Merrill illustrated the importance of prioritizing tasks in their book *First Things First* (Simon & Schuster) with a simple metaphor. In short, a guest lecturer was speaking to a group of students when he pulled out a 1-gallon, wide-mouthed Mason jar, set it on a table in front of him, and began filling it with about a dozen fist-sized rocks. When the jar was filled to the top and no more rocks would fit inside, he asked the class whether the jar was full, to which they unanimously replied, "Yes."

He then reached under the table and pulled out a bucket of gravel, dumping some of it into the jar and shaking the jar, causing pieces of gravel to work themselves down into the spaces between the big rocks. He asked the group once more whether the jar was full, to which one suspicious student responded, "Probably not."

Under the table he reached again, this time withdrawing a bucket of sand. He started dumping in the sand, which sank into all the spaces left between the rocks and the gravel. Once more, he asked the question "Is the jar full?" "No!" the class shouted. "Good!" he said, grabbing a pitcher of water and pouring it in until the jar was filled to the brim.

He looked up at the class and asked, "What is the point of this illustration?" One eager beaver raised his hand and said, "The point is no matter how full your schedule is, if you try really hard, you can always fit some more things into it!"

"No," the speaker replied. "The truth this illustration teaches us is if you don't put the big rocks in first, you'll never get them in at all."

Blocking Off Your Time and Plugging in Your To-Do Items

After you identify and order your priorities (as covered in the preceding sections), you place them into time slots on your weekly calendar, broken into 15- or 30-minute segments. This process is commonly called *time-blocking*. You might start with 30 minutes to establish the success habit of time-blocking. A 15-minute schedule, if you are just diving into time-blocking for the first time, will be a challenge. I've discovered no better system for managing time on a daily, weekly, monthly, yearly, and lifelong basis. I've seen miracle-level transformations in the lives of my clients — successes measured in income, health, relationships, personal growth, spiritual transformation, and wisdom.

Like exercise, time-blocking can be tricky because it requires a lot of thought and adjustment, both in the initial stage where you're doing it for the first time and for a while thereafter, when you're developing the skill. Everybody knows what day two after the beginning of a new fitness program feels like: Stiff joints and sore muscles have you moving like the Tin Man after a rainstorm. At first you may feel like you'll never achieve the goals you've set, but sticking to the daily program and creating habits eventually brings the results you want. Figuring out how to best manage your time depends on two things:

REMEMBER

>> **Consistent, diligent practice:** If you want to build those time-blocking muscles, not only do you have to work them regularly, but you also need to increase the weight, stress, and pressure as you progress. Understanding the key to managing your minutes, hours, days, weeks, and so on takes repetition. I was first exposed to time-blocking at a business seminar more than 30 years ago, and for the past 20 years, I've coached hundreds of thousands of people. In all this time, I've yet to meet anyone — including myself — who doesn't need some ongoing reinforcement, repetition, and refresher course of the time-blocking principles I share with you here.

Don't panic when you find yourself a little stressed or sore from all your time-blocking exercises. It's simply a sign that your efforts to build up those skills are working.

>> **A span of time to improve:** Achieving a level of time-blocking mastery does take time — a minimum of 18 months and as much as 24 months. Why so long? Because you're developing a complex skill. A typical day has you switching from refereeing an argument between your kids to making an important presentation to the corporate executives; from putting together your department's annual budget to paying for your groceries in the checkout line. That's a lot to orchestrate, and even Handel didn't write his *Messiah* overnight. If you accept that time-blocking skills require time to develop, you're more likely to remain motivated. As we know, if we lose our motivation, the success we desire seems more challenging to obtain. Your objective is to make measurable progress in reasonable time.

Implementing time-blocking to help organize your schedule takes a bit of time, but you reap huge dividends on that initial investment. The steps in the following section walk you through a general outline of the process I follow.

Step 1: Dividing your day

To start, you need a daily calendar divided into 30-minute increments. Why such small bites of time? Because even 30 minutes can represent a good chunk of productive activity. Losing just two or three of these small blocks each day can diminish your ability to meet your goals, from finishing that project at work to writing your bestselling (you hope) memoir.

I personally feel that designing it on paper, rather than putting your time-block into an online scheduling program or calendar app, is more effective. It connects you to your schedule; it create a more tactile and visual example to follow. You can make changes and annotate easier. As your time-block schedule becomes more solidified in a few weeks or a few months, then move it into your online scheduling system. You can then colorize your blocks of time.

On that blank schedule, begin by dividing your day. Draw a clear line between personal time and work time. When you take this step, you're creating work-life balance from the start. Don't take it for granted that Saturday and Sunday are time off just because you work a Monday-through-Friday workweek.

So block personal time into your schedule, or work activities may creep into your precious downtime. The more you take action on paper, the more concrete the time-block schedule becomes.

TIP

Are you apprehensive about drawing a line between work and personal time because you're wary of having to tell a business associate you can't attend a business function that extends into personal time? Not to worry. You don't have to tell a client that your Tuesday-morning workout is more important than a breakfast meeting with her. Instead, simply say you're already booked at that time. That's all the explanation you owe, and my experience shows that professional colleagues who want to do business with you respect your boundaries.

Step 2: Scheduling your personal activities

Blocking out personal activities first gives weight to these activities and ensures that they won't be overtaken by obligations that have lesser importance in the long run. Personal obligations are almost always the first thing most people trade for work. Because of that, I recommend that you hold fast and tight to the personal area so it doesn't get away from you. Another advantage? You help establish a reasonable end to your workday. If you're scheduled to meet at a friend's for Texas Hold 'Em on Thursday nights, you're more motivated to wrap up your project in enough time to cut the deck.

People who are success-forward and success-minded can have life balance and boundary issues with their personal life. We desire success, wealth, or recognition so much, we flex when we should be more rigid with our time rules.

Scheduling personal activities is twofold:

1. **Schedule routine activities that you participate in.**

Do you have dinner together as a family every night? A weekly date night with your significant other? Do you want to establish family traditions? Don't just assume these activities will happen, so give them the weight they deserve and block out the time for each one. Don't forget to include your extracurricular activities here. All those PTA groups, fundraising committees, nonprofit boards, and other volunteer commitments get plugged in as well.

2. **Schedule personal priorities that aren't routine.**

Put those personal agenda items first before filling in your day with tasks and activities that don't support those priorities.

Step 3: Factoring in your work activities

Begin with the activities that are a regular part of your job and then factor in the priorities that aren't routine. Whether you're a company CEO, a department manager, a sales associate, an administrative assistant, or an entry-level trainee, you're responsible for performing key tasks and activities each day and week. They may include daily or weekly meetings. Or maybe your responsibility is scheduling meetings for others. You likely have to prepare for these appointments. Perhaps you have to write and turn in reports or sales figures on an ongoing basis. You may have to call someone for information routinely. If you report to work daily and always spend the first hour of your day returning phone calls, time-block it into your schedule.

Step 4: Accounting for weekly self-evaluation and planning time

Your goals — whether a one-year business plan or long-range retirement vision — warrant routine checkups. Consider them as rest stops on your journey: Are you still on the right road? Is a detour ahead? Have you discovered a more direct route? I have a weekly appointment time in reviewing my real estate rentals. I review rent rolls, projected cash flow, vacancies, and units in repair stages. Because my rental investments are a business, I need to watch and monitor them.

Use weekly strategic planning sessions — ideally for Friday afternoon or the end of the workweek — to review your progress toward those near-future business projects as well as your larger career aspirations or personal goals. This is an opportunity to review the previous week and jump-start the upcoming week. I recommend spending 15 to 30 minutes daily and then taking a 60-to-90-minute session on self-evaluation and planning at the end of the week.

REMEMBER

This strategic planning time is probably your most valuable time investment each week. It gives you a tremendous wrap-up for the week and a good start to next week, and it reinforces your vision for your long-term success. It also enables you to go home and spend time with your family in the right frame of mind.

Years ago, I booked a weekly appointment with myself to analyze the numbers, sales ratios, and business activities in progress. I found the results of my performance as well as that of my staff improved dramatically. I'd wasted weeks and months as I agonized whether to include this activity into my schedule. My advice: Book an evaluation and planning session first and ask questions later.

Step 5: Building in flex time

Plug segments of time into your schedule every few hours to help you to minimize the fallout from unplanned interruptions or problems. About 30 minutes is enough time to work in at strategic intervals throughout your day. You will likely need three of these segments in your business day. Knowing that you have this free block of time can help you adhere to your schedule rather than get off track.

This strategy makes it easier to delay that "emergency" that really isn't to a more controlled time. Frequently, the emergency will burn itself out or be reduced in the short 60 to 90 minute delay you have created. It ends up taking less of your time and emotion, saving you time and energy that can be better invested elsewhere.

TIP

As you begin to build your time-blocking skills, insert 30-minute flex periods into your schedule for every two hours of time-blocked activity. This may seem like a lot of flex time, but if it allows you to maintain the rest of your time-block schedule and maintain or increase your productivity, it's worth the investment. My experience is that the best time for flex time is after you've put in a couple of hours of your most important work — whether sales calls, report-preparation, or meeting a deadline.

WARNING

Don't schedule flex time right before you go into an important activity time: You're more likely to get distracted and fail to get started with your critical business. Schedule it after the work. Then you can use it, if necessary, to resolve any unforeseen problems.

TIME-BLOCKING: MAKING SMALL INVESTMENTS IN BIG SUCCESS

Time-blocking doesn't require a huge commitment to produce results. A few years ago, one of my clients, a top sales performer in her region, exploded her sales by more than 125 percent in one year! I knew that time-blocking had played an important role in her success. I asked her what percentage of the time she had managed to adhere to her time-blocking schedule. She confessed that she'd stuck to the schedule only 35 percent of the time. The undeniable truth is that *a little goes a long way*. As you continue to use your time-blocking skills, that percentage increases, and your productivity grows accordingly.

Assessing Your Progress and Adjusting Your Plan as Needed

Being successful in your habits, discipline, and consistency in time-blocking is not easy. Each of us will use the principles I have shared thus far to craft a unique plan or strategy with our time. We also must be prepared for making adjustments and revisions. Becoming comfortable with time-blocking takes time and achieving a glitch-free schedule is a likely and reasonable expectation. There is nothing about success that is glitch free. Be ready to work time-blocking for a stretch and make a half-dozen revisions. Even then, routinely evaluate your time-blocking efforts and adjust them periodically to make sure you're getting the desired results. It's not a huge time investment. You can check yourself with a few minutes a day or use 15 to 30 minutes of your weekly time to review your results. Ask yourself the following:

>> What daily habits are not getting done?

>> What took you off track this week?

>> What interruptions really affected your success with your time?

>> What shifts would help your efficiency? In the next section, I discuss this review in detail.

Surveying your results

One way to determine your effectiveness at time-blocking is to check results. In as little as two weeks from when you launch your time-blocking schedule, you can probably see where you need minor adjustments. The best way to keep tabs on results is to track them on an ongoing basis. Getting in the habit of asking yourself the previous questions can really ramp up your success. The ability to self-evaluate, observe, and implement change is a differentiation of success. At a minimum, I suggest a weekly review that focuses on the past week and a periodic review of where you stand in relation to your overall goals.

The weekly review is a time for you to replay the tape of the week, looking at the highs and lows. I guarantee you'll have days where you want to pull your hair out because you face so many problems and distractions. You'll also have days that are smooth as silk. What were the differences in those days besides the outcome? What are the granular differences? What takes you off your schedule?

As for the periodic review, review your job description, key responsibilities, and the ways in which your performance and success are measured. Then ask yourself these questions:

>> Are you moving closer toward achieving your goals?

>> Can you see measurable progress in reasonable time?

>> Are you monitoring your performance well enough to see improvement?

>> What changes do you need to adopt now to increase your speed toward reaching the goal and reduce the overall amount of time you invest?

Your success in meeting your objectives tells you whether the time-blocking is working for you.

Looking at measurable goals

If you can measure your goals in terms of numbers (dollars or sales, for example), then checking your results is a cinch. As a salesperson, for example, you may follow your sales numbers or commissions results over several months in order to get a good understanding of the effectiveness of your time-blocking efforts. Or say you're a magazine editor who's evaluated on consistently meeting weekly publication deadlines; if your goal is to publish three articles per month in national magazines, you can assume that your time-blocking efforts require some tweaking if your review reveals that you're getting only one story in print.

If you are a stay-at-home parent, you have a small window of production between the time kids get on the bus in the morning to the time they get off the bus in the afternoon. Evaluate by your completed to-do list and the stress you feel in getting it done. Did you have some "me" time in the course of the day to relax and recharge?

Evaluating qualitative goals

If your goals aren't easily measured in terms of dollars or sales, you may need to get creative in developing your own tally for results. Family and personal goals are difficult to measure, but you can likely gain a good sense of how your efforts are tracking by just paying attention to your daily life and how you feel about it, rating your day on a 1-to-10 scale. Are your kids comfortable in talking and spending time with you? Do they look forward to being with you? Are you on friendly terms with the people in your community activities? Do you and your spouse laugh together more often than you argue?

You can also turn to other measuring sticks, which are especially useful in the workplace:

» What went well this week? What could you have done better?

» Did you accomplish what you really needed to do? How many high-priority items did you carry over to the next day or week?

» How would you rate your week on a 1-to-10 scale, with 1 being utterly overwhelmed and dissatisfied, and 10 being completely in control of and happy with how you spend your time?

» How do you feel you performed at work? How does your supervisor feel you're performing?

» Did you meet your goals at home?

» Has what you've accomplished this week positioned you better to achieve your long-range goals?

» What are the key improvement areas for you next week?

» What adjustments to your long-range plans do you need to make?

» What's diverting you from your schedule?

» Were you unrealistic in your time estimates for tasks?

» What segment of the day or activity is tipping your schedule off track?

REMEMBER

As you're reviewing your results, be careful to do so with an open, observant mind, not a judgmental one. Give yourself a couple of weeks before you resolve to change your schedule. Doing so helps you get through a long enough period of time to account for anomalies.

Tweaking your system

Looking back at your personal behaviors and skills and the interruptions you routinely face, identify two or three steps you need to take in order to increase your success. Here are a couple of tips to point you in the right direction:

» **If you're not completing the most important tasks or working toward the most important efforts each day:** Weed out some of the trivial tasks to make room for the most important ones.

» **If your most productive times of day are filled with trivial tasks:** Shift the tasks and the time slots you fit them in.

After you figure out what you need to change, you can adjust your schedule accordingly. Unfortunately, I can't give you a one-size-fits-all set of answers to help you figure out what to change. Those decisions depend on your job requirements, your personal strengths and weaknesses, your personal goals and desires, and the amount of control you actually have over those aspects you'd like to improve. I can, however, help steer you in the right direction.

REMEMBER

Even if you aren't religious, you can find some guidance in this prayer: "Grant me the serenity to accept the things I cannot change, courage to change the things I can, and the wisdom to know the difference." You can apply it to the way you manage your time. If you can balance the results you expect to achieve (more productivity, greater efficiency, reduction in time worked, and greater sales) with the results you need to achieve, then you'll be successful.

Following are some examples of quick evaluation questions that can help you make the most effective, results-oriented changes to your schedule:

>> **What's the standard?** Do you have a sales quota that needs to be met? Are you getting your boss's priorities done? Going home, how are you feeling about your progress? Are you completely spent as you walk in the door at home?

>> **How accurate does the time-block schedule need to be?** In time-blocking, a little goes a long way. The real question is how well you did this week with the most important activities — the vital 20 percent of the 80/20 rule.

>> **How much have you improved?** How have you improved since you started working your time block? How large is the improvement? Would you be happy if you improved each week for a year at this level? We vastly overestimate what can be accomplished in a day, but vastly underestimate what we can accomplish in a week, month, or year.

>> **With additional revision, how much additional productivity would you gain?** Before revising a time-block schedule, look at the anticipated return on investment. Is this change going to bring significant benefit in productivity, efficiency, or personal satisfaction?

>> **How good is good enough?** As I have become older and, hopefully, wiser, I understand better how our high expectations in most areas can shape our attitude and success. Some of us expect too much from ourselves and others, especially in the short run in change. What is really the standard of improvement we are striving for? Where is the point where you'll achieve diminishing returns on your effort? At some point, further refining your schedule can lead to reduced results. Where do you think that will happen?

WARNING

Perfectionism is a scourge of people who are trying to achieve more with their time. The obsession with revising, redoing, and readjusting one's time-block schedule every few days — or even hours — leads to frustration. In your time-blocking, clearly define the line of success so that you can achieve your goals without going overboard.

7

The Part of Tens

IN THIS PART . . .

Review the ten characteristics of success.

Discover several measures and models of successful people.

Avoid the biggest roadblocks to creating wealth.

Chapter **20**

Ten Personal Characteristics to Improve Success

My mother always said I was "a character." I'm sure she was not talking about desirable character traits, as I am in the chapter. Being more successful requires us to refine our character to a level few people achieve. You can be successful with fewer than these ten. My estimation is that having a high level of commitment, focus, and proficiency in seven or eight will enable you to achieve the vast majority of your life goals. I can unequivocally state that if you possess all ten at a high level, you will be, as the saying goes, healthy, wealthy, and wise . . . guaranteed!

I present the ten personal characteristics in random order. In the end, it's up to you to evaluate, secure, and maintain these traits, and that will lead to greater success in your life.

Perseverance

Successful people encounter problems and challenges. To think that is not the case because of their status, wealth, or lifestyle is to be naïve. In fact, as you become more successful, you're going to face bigger problems and take on larger responsibilities. The problems and responsibilities I experience today are far greater than when I was unsuccessful and broke. I have a larger company with more staff and more clients, and I have industry recognition to uphold. This all requires a higher level of perseverance. Perseverance is a critical characteristic on the climb upward to success. It is even more necessary when you reach the pinnacle of your profession or career. There will always be competitors attempting to knock you off the mountain. There will be more distractions and naysayers.

As we age into our 40s, 50s, and 60s, we all have to endure the aches, pains, and breakdowns that naturally occur. It requires more perseverance to keep the pounds off, our bodies tuned, and our minds active. Our mind's speed in processing thoughts and solving problems declines with age. Growing older isn't for wimps.

Doing More than You Are Paid For

This characteristic, when started young, yields a lifetime of valuable results. In today's world, to compete as an employee or as an entrepreneur in owning a company, the world wants to know what value you bring to the marketplace. We are all paid based on the value delivered. Recognizing that fact prepares us for our upward climb in income. The attitude of "I will only give a limited effort because my pay is low or limited" does not create the opportunity for advancement.

I've noticed that a lot of teenagers and even adults in their 20s and 30s will take any free moment they have at work to pull out their phone and start playing with it. Let's face it, they're not doing anything important. As far as I'm concerned, unless you are on a designated break or it's an emergency, the time you are wasting staring at your phone on company time is stealing! You might be thinking, "Wow, that's pretty hardcore," and that may be true in today's society. But successful people do more than their hourly rate dictates. It's because every time they do more, they become more valuable, increase their skills, self-confidence, and self-esteem. They also know when they approach their boss for a raise, they are worth what they are asking and so does their boss.

REMEMBER

As a business owner or entrepreneur, our world is based on delivered value and perception of value. If you resolve to innovate, take exemplary care of your customer relationships, and focus on value, you will be able to grow, thrive, and expand in any marketplace and economy.

Lifelong Learning

The passion to learn is the great equalizer in life. Whatever level of skill and knowledge you possess right now will not be enough to keep you at the same level you presently enjoy. The world is always changing, improving, innovating, and learning. It's a race between you and other people, companies, and organizations. Your desire to increase your knowledge can never stop. Successful people always remain curious. They are curious about how to make things better, how things work, and what needs to happen next. They are curious about how they can make more money, how they can have better relationships, and how they can improve their health. They want to learn how to live a successful life, as you are doing by reading this book.

Gratitude

Being grateful for what we currently have in life is a wonderful characteristic that few people embrace. In striving for success, it's easy to focus too much on what we are working to acquire. The pursuit of more can lead us down the road of discontent and unhappiness. You have to latch onto gratitude to achieve more success no matter where my advice finds you today. No matter how small the success, or blessings, you are experiencing right now, you have to hold onto gratitude tightly.

Gratitude positions our heart, spirit, and mind in the correct place to receive more. Without gratitude, we can't make room for more abundance. It's as if our coffee cup is full. We have to pour out some of the coffee to make room for more in the cup. The pouring out is the act of gratitude that makes room for more. The sustainability of your long-term success can't be accomplished without gratitude.

If you really want to improve your attitude and feelings of well-being, personally express gratitude to the people who have impacted your life, helped you, and have guided you. Think of the people whose shoulders you stand on: your parents, teachers, friends, mentors, personal cheerleaders, spouse, significant other, and even your kids. There is an endless list of supporters for any successful person. You will make two people's day through your personal expression of gratitude: you and the person who receives your praise. Do it today, and you start making more room in your cup.

Positive Attitude

Many people believe that a positive mental attitude is the be-all-end-all in achieving success. Through a positive mental attitude, you can avoid all challenges and problems in life. I am convinced that your attitude is highly important and influential in your pursuit of success, but it's probably not the be-all-end-all. People who have the right mental attitude look for and see the opportunity that exists in any problem or circumstance. Someone who has a more negative perspective sees the problem alone. The truth is, problems and opportunities are linked together. You can't have one without the other. It's a matter of perspective to see both.

I have found in my life that attitude is a choice. It's a choice that I control and make each morning when I wake. The choice of a positive attitude empowers each day to success. Whatever circumstances you are facing, how you react to it will always be more important than the problem or challenge staring you in the face. A negative attitude won't allow you to accomplish any more in life than a positive attitude. The likelihood is that you will accomplish less and likely be miserable doing it.

Integrity

Following through on your word and being fair will never go out of style. As a parent, I recognize that my kids are always watching. They are watching what I do more than what I say. They are watching to see if my video (actions) matches my audio (words). If the audio and video align, that is integrity. There are teaching moments and opportunities that come up when you least expect it with kids. The demonstrating of your integrity creates a legacy of success for your children.

ANECDOTE

I remember one occasion when I had an integrity opportunity in a restaurant. Wesley was 7 and Annabelle was 3 at the time. The bill had come, and in reviewing it, the waiter failed to charge for one of our drinks. I remember double-checking the bill, as I always do, because I am frugal and want to make sure I'm not charged for something I didn't order. I called the waiter over and told him he needed to charge me for another drink. He expressed that it was okay, it was his error, so no charge. I knew in my mind that it was not okay. First, we had received the drink, so the restaurant owner deserved the money to help her pay for the costs of her business. She also deserved to turn a profit from our patronage. The waiter's error was an honest mistake. His error was his expression to forget it. In my mind, that demonstrated a lack of loyalty and integrity to his boss, the owner. I am not judging his motives for why he said, "No problem." I knew my motives were to do what was fair and right.

Bottom line: My integrity is invaluable compared to a $2 savings on a beverage. The lesson my kids would learn about integrity was worth a lot more in life than that $2 soda. As the bill came back, Wesley asked why I had asked the waiter to add the drink to our bill. It was a priceless opportunity to educate my son on what is right and how to achieve success in life.

Persuasion

As we make our way through life's journey, we must develop our character and the skill of persuasion. Because we interact with people of all walks in our daily life, we are required to engage in persuasion.

Another word that sums up persuasion is *selling.* The truth is, we are all in sales. To be a successful human, we need the skills and characteristics of a good salesperson. I am not talking about the tactics of the stereotypical hard-closing salesperson with the leisure suit and gold chain; I am talking about being able to cogently reason with people so that they take an action or opportunity to make a change that is beneficial for them.

Do you have children? Are you trying to sell them on a set of standards of actions, conduct, behaviors, and social norms? Are you trying to persuade your spouse or significant other of the needs you have that make you feel accepted, loved, and valued? As a boss, are you selling your employees on the value of producing more so that their income increases and they achieve success for themselves and their families? The skill of persuasion will make all areas of your life better.

Patience

As you've no doubt heard, patience is a virtue. Having patience with ourselves and others is an admirable gift. I use the word *gift* because some of us have it more naturally than others. For some of us, God gave us an extra helping of patience. I was not one of them, as I'm not naturally patient. People who are striving for greater success are demanding of themselves and others. The pursuit of success in relationships, health, business, and finances takes time. We are dealing with imperfect situations and imperfect people. The most flawed and imperfect is likely ourselves.

We create goals to be achieved in specific timeframes. We then take longer to reach our goal before we lose patience with ourselves. When that happens, ask these questions:

>> How far off of my accomplishment am I?

>> Am I progressing, drawing toward my goal, or am I stuck?

>> Am I gaining or losing momentum to my goal?

>> Is this goal as important to me as when I first wrote it down?

The last question is the most important. If you've done the best you can, that's all that you or anyone else could ask for. We are all human, born to make errors. Sometimes we need to lighten up and extend grace and patience to ourselves and to others.

Concentration

The ability to focus in the moment, foregoing all other stimuli and distractions, separates high achievers from the rest. This one characteristic of single-minded focus creates power for achievement. Focus precedes success in all situations.

High achievers' level of concentration sets them apart from others in society. We live in a time where being unfocused is rampant. Our phones and technology are a constant distraction to success, productivity, and relationship building. The dings, beeps, and flashes of our phones create a constant stream of interruptions throughout our daily lives. If you want to learn better strategies in dealing with the interruptions of daily life, check out my book *Successful Time Management For Dummies.* In Chapter 15, "Defending Your Day from Interruptions," I give you secrets and strategies to fight the interruptions.

REMEMBER

The truth is, every interruption that occurs wastes five minutes of time. It will be, at best, five minutes before you can concentrate at the previous depth before you were interrupted. That's a fact, even if the interruption takes less than a minute. It's the break in your concentration that is so damaging to productivity.

Self-Confidence

The world is going to knock you down. Murphy's Law will always take a portion of everything in life. Willingness to stare down and face the storms of life and know you will prevail is self-confidence. Ask anyone who's achieved great victories in life and they'll tell you that belief in yourself is the key.

When you have higher levels of self-esteem, it's easier to be more decisive. Being decisive creates bigger successes, more dominant victories. Being victorious more frequently when faced with life challenges is one avenue to increased success. Another pathway to success is to make your victories larger. Successful people don't win all the time, every time, but they usually win more frequently in life. And when they do win, the wins are more significant in size, so they are embedded with deeper meaning, and they can be drawn on to increase self-confidence, self-reliance, and self-acceptance.

Chapter **21**

Ten Measures and Models of Success

Excellence is an art won by training and habitation. We do not act rightly because we have virtue or excellence, but we rather have those because we have acted rightly. We are what we repeatedly do. Excellence then is not an act, but a habit. — Aristotle

There are countless measures and models in establishing your pathway to success. For anyone who has the desire to be more successful, we have to define what success might be to us. And success is defined differently by each of us for the benefit of all of us. Success in life is really about playing all out at your present level of skill, thought, action, and idea. It's the pursuit of excellence throughout your life journey.

Playing Your Game

Success is a striving for excellence while still playing the game of life within the means and parameters presently in front of you. Here's an example: I am not an exceptional golfer. I carry a handicap that fluctuates between 12 and 15 depending on time of year and how frequently I play and practice. If you ask any of my playing partners, they would describe me as a successful golfer, which means that I enjoy the sport, strive to get better, and play my game.

I have strengths and weaknesses, as most golfers do. The key to being successful in golf is to intimately know what those are in your game. One of my weaknesses is that I'm not a long hitter of the golf ball. So to compensate, my game is keeping the ball in the fairway, having a very good short game, and putting well. I play to my strengths so that I can score well.

Successful people play their game. They know their game, whether it's at home, at work, and in their world. They focus on playing to their strengths. That doesn't mean that they aren't working diligently to improve their game or remove their weaknesses. They aren't complacent or stagnant. They realize that playing to their goals, strengths, and objectives leads to success, satisfaction, and well-being. And playing your game in business and life leads to fulfillment, happiness, and wealth.

Keeping Up with Daily Habits

Success is really achieved in the daily victories of life. It's in the daily habits, routines, and disciplines you execute. If you can win the day, you can create long-term sustainable success. That is true of any measure or category of your life. Here are the questions to ask yourself to check how you did today:

» Did I get up and start my day at the planned on time?

» Did I begin my day with gratitude?

» Was my attitude positive today, especially at the beginning of my day?

» How well did I stick to my morning routine?

» Did I affirm, recognize, and demonstrate love to my kids and spouse before leaving for work?

» Did I arrive early for work?

» How much idle or unproductive time did I allow to creep into my workday?

» Did I achieve my key objectives for the day at work?

» Did I encourage someone at work today?

» Did I move my body vigorously today for health?

» How were my eating habits today?

» Did I spend less than I made today?

» Did I give exclusive attention to the people important to me today?

» Did I listen to or read something for at least 30 minutes to learn?

If you complete the vast majority of these habits daily, you wouldn't even recognize your old life within 30 to 60 days. You would have love, passion, energy, and success filling your whole life.

Staying on Top of Your Physical Health

As I've discussed earlier in the book, when you don't have physical health, you are at a severe disadvantage in creating success. As someone diagnosed eight years ago with Meniere's disease, which can only be managed well rather than cured or eradicated, my views of health have evolved.

My definition of physical health is being free of disease that blocks your pathway to success. It's the ability to control and live well in spite of physical infirmity. And it results in being productive in achieving your goals and dreams.

As we age, we lose strength, flexibility, and stamina. And that means time is of the essence. We all have a limited amount of time to accomplish our goals, but that doesn't mean our goals should change. It means that our focus on physical and mental health needs to be a priority. We need to allow ourselves more time to complete specific tasks and functions, and we do that by striving for good health.

Serving Others

The greatest success I have in life is helping others succeed in life and fulfill their dreams. Success is helping and serving others. Service, whether it's for your family, friends, or complete strangers, is the essence of success. Ask yourself these service success questions:

>> Who could I serve right now?

>> Who needs my help?

>> What organizations in my community could I impact?

>> How could I help them?

REMEMBER

Service to others makes our world better. We all need to look at our own lives and decide how we can devote time to serve others. What can we do to benefit our community?

Maintaining Business Savvy or Entrepreneurial Spirit

The ability to create something out of an idea is success. All large businesses of today started with an idea. Facebook, Google, and Microsoft were all ideas hatched in college dorm rooms across the United States. These companies have grown to become the most powerful technology companies the world has ever known. A wonderful method of achieving more success is starting your own entrepreneurial business. Then invest time in your business and watch it thrive and serve people.

Entrepreneurial businesses are the lifeblood of the United States. Small-business owners provide 49 percent of all jobs, according to the Small Business Administration. Think about it: Just about half of all jobs are in companies with fewer than 100 employees. Having owned numerous small businesses for more than 30 years, I know that I provide a valuable benefit to my community by offering solid, good-paying jobs with benefits to a handful of families.

We all have unique talents beyond what we do for work. These talents can be used to earn more ancillary income. As your side gig begins to grow and flourish, it has the opportunity to expand beyond your current full-time employment situation.

Working toward Security

There is an element of security we all want to achieve that connects with success. This is especially true for the people who have a Steady behavioral style, which is 40 percent of the population. The achievement of security speaks to a large swath of humans. (If you want to know more about your behavioral style and how you are wired, turn to Chapter 4, where I include a link to take an assessment that will help you know your behavioral style.)

Being able to create a model of security for your life requires some introspection through questions:

>> Does money or wealth play a role in you feeling more secure?

>> On a scale of 1 to 10, how big a role does wealth play?

>> How much would you need to feel secure?

>> Would paying off your home enhance your security?

If so, craft the plan in what additional you can put toward the mortgage.

>> Do you have six months of personal expenses in savings? If not, how short are you?

Craft a plan of additional monthly savings to achieve six months of personal expenses savings.

>> What makes you feel more secure?

>> What can your significant other do to help you feel more secure?

>> What actions can you take at work to increase your value and job security?

Building Self-Confidence

The people who achieve more significant success in life have unshakeable self-confidence. Being focused on achieving a growing, thriving confidence in yourself is a measure and indicator of success. As you gain self-confidence, you will take bold action toward success.

All successful people assess risk and take the risk anyway. They take smart risks that have a high probability of a positive outcome. If you are waiting on the sidelines because a lack of self-confidence or an overinflated sense of worry, it will be challenging for you to achieve the success you desire. In order to build self-confidence, ask yourself these questions:

>> What am I really good at?

>> When were some times that I had fear but acted anyway?

>> What small successes have I had that seemed impossible at the time?

>> What large successes have I had that seemed impossible at the time?

>> What actions could I take to help me increase my belief in myself?

>> Who are some of my biggest fans or cheerleaders?

To raise your confidence, spend more time with your fans. Talk with them about your goals and dreams. Those cheerleaders in your life will encourage you, help you, and be rooting for you. If you lack those types of people, go find some because we all need them in our lives. They could be family, friends, or colleagues.

Looking for Self-Improvement

Success is life is the constant pursuit of self-improvement. It's the small incremental improvement in ourselves each day. If you only improve yourself by 1 percent each day, you will achieve a staggering the amount of improvement in a year. Would you care to take a guess as to how much? The normal guesses fall between 365 percent and about 500 percent because some realize there is compounding involved. The truth is, both figures are way off the mark. Give up? The increase within 12 months, based on a 1 percent improvement each day is 3,800 percent. Yes, you read that correctly. It's 3,800 percent! A small improvement in our knowledge, skills, and mindset yields exponential results. That doesn't even factor what it will do to your bank account, health, and relationships.

Staying Mentally Tough

The only guarantee in life is that there will be death, taxes, and adversity. There is no success without failure and adversity. That's why mental toughness is required. You are going to have days where you will want to retreat back to your bedroom, pull the drapes, turn on the electric blanket, and go back to bed. You will have tragedy in your personal life, financial life, and business life. You will have days where you are crying out to God for comfort, where it feels like the whole world is against you in every move you make.

Successful mental toughness is well illustrated in this Mark Twain quote:

> Courage is not the absence of fear, but rather the judgement that something else is more important than fear.

Being mentally tough requires you to want something more, to be willing despite logical and even illogical fear to act in pursuing what you want. It means that you will pursue your goals to the ends of the earth. That you won't quit . . . ever.

Creating a Legacy

The most successful people have created a legacy to have a meaningful impact on the world. Andrew Carnegie is a wonderful example to follow. Carnegie spent the first half of his life becoming the wealthiest man alive. He then decided to give all his money away before he died. We owe most of the libraries that exist today in the United States to Carnegie. A legacy of that magnitude is astonishing and wonderful.

Creating a legacy of success starts with the people you have the greatest influence on. That would be family, friends, church, and community at large. You can create a legacy of love, acceptance, service, and loyalty. You can set up a legacy of the unexpected accomplishment — that you succeeded against the odds and adversity.

You can create a financial legacy through giving to charity, endowing a scholarship at a university, or endowing a needs-based ministry at your church to help the disadvantaged. You can create educational accounts to pay for college for your grandchildren and great grandchildren. You can create whatever legacy you desire to leave behind that demonstrates your love and what you value. A wonderful legacy lives out of your principles and beliefs long after you are gone. You can do as I am doing and write down your principles and beliefs to share. That's why I write books: to help people achieve success with the hope that the positive results live on for generations.

Chapter **22**

The Ten Biggest Wealth Success Mistakes

The truth is, we all make mistakes in when it comes to creating wealth. This chapter presents ten mistakes that are commonly made by many people. Making a few of these mistakes is not catastrophic to your wealth. But if you don't learn from the errors and you repeat these errors, you'll find it difficult to stay on the road to wealth. As you review the sections in this chapter, I want you to ask yourself, "Have I made this mistake? Is this an ongoing problem or challenge? How can I overcome this issue so that it's never a roadblock to my success again?"

Most of these errors are rooted in lack of strategy, lack of action, or lack of consistent action. In essence, what's lacking is the development of key success habits that are repeated over time!

Starting Too Late . . . or Not Early Enough

When you start late, you are up against it. When you say you will begin "someday," it's likely someday will never come. The time to act is now. While I did not start extremely early, I did start before most. I opened my first retirement savings account at 28. It was a humble beginning, meaning I put in very little, but I put something in. At the beginning, it was more of a rounding error in size. But don't go into the mental space of "I'm 40 years old, and I haven't saved anything."

That is wasted mental energy in the "if only zone" of life. You can't change the past. You can only create a new future from this point forward.

ANECDOTE

I literally started by putting 1 percent of my gross commission checks in retirement savings. I was in 100-percent commission sales selling real estate. My average commission check was $3,200. I was putting $32 dollars away into retirement. After a year, I had a whopping $1,300 saved in my retirement account. That $1,300 would have been nothing today without my habit of continuing to save and increase my savings amounts annually. The $1,300 by itself would have turned into $10,000 if I had gotten excellent returns from investing it.

The actual amount was inconsequential. What was consequential is that I did it. What was consequential was establishing the habit that has stuck with me. Then I slowly raised the level of savings. I raised the percentage from 1 percent to 2 percent, then to 5 percent and more. It's the start that stops most of us.

TIP

Even if you just establish an IRA right now and find a small amount from each earnings check, that new habit will create momentum to wealth. It might be less than you need, but it's more than you have done previously. The best time to start is 20 years ago. The second-best time is now.

Lacking Clarity for Your Future

What is it you want? What do you want your future to look like in retirement? What is the lifestyle you desire? When do you want to achieve financial independence? At what age? What type of house, freedom, travel, and philanthropy?

The clearer you are on the *why* and the *what* you want, the *how* you get there becomes easier. You are better able to craft a plan and create projections of how to get there. When you have a plan, you can unleash your subconscious mind to attract and create solutions. Your subconscious mind will turn your plan and process over and over again even while you are sleeping — like a chicken on your rotisserie BBQ until it's cooked perfectly.

Not Having a Written Wealth Strategy Plan

It's not enough to know what you want and why you want it. You must craft and execute a plan. Most people invest more time in planning their next vacation than they do planning their financial lives. I realize that this is uncomfortable, and you might feel ill-prepared to do this. You might be thinking, "I have no idea where to start."

I want you to know that I have felt pretty much the same way. It's perfectly normal to believe you are not prepared and have some fear because of it. What is also normal for most people is to save some for their whole life and hope it turns out okay. If you are in your 30s or 40s now, chances are good that you will be alive 30 or 40 years from now. So there's little question that you will arrive at retirement age. The question is, what will your lifestyle be when you arrive at that age?

You may feel you are vastly behind in where you need to be. I also understand that as well. I am not a financial planner and I don't claim to be. I am a guy who is passionate about helping people achieve wealth and success in their lives. I want to help you craft your success plan to achieve it.

Carrying High-Interest-Rate Consumer Debt

No one should carry high-interest-rate consumer debt, which is credit card debt, consumer loan debt, and IRS debt. That type of debt is always bad. It costs more and lacks deductibility, so the effective interest rate is very high.

A little known fact on credit card debt and fees: If you carry a balance on your credit cards and you charge something on a credit card that has a balance, the interest on that most recent charge starts the moment the charge is applied to your account. The typical grace period or float period is gone. So that tank of gas you just put on your credit card is carrying a 17%, 21%, or 25% interest charge on it from the time you start your car to pull away from the pump. The banks make billions of dollars every year from this cost to you. And you end up paying hundreds if not thousands of dollars per year in additional interest charges.

TIP

If you feel you need the use of a credit card in your financial life, then work to pay one off that you can then use. This strategy will enable you to receive a grace period again of roughly 25 to 28 days before you need to pay the bill. You won't be charged interest on your purchases, and you will be using credit wisely.

Not Using "Good Debt" Wisely

There are only a few types of good debt. The most common good debt is debt on real estate that produces strong cash flow. I am not talking about speculative-only appreciation-return-expecting real estate. I am talking about properties that are leveraged with 25 percent down or more. I'm talking about properties with cash flow hundreds of dollars a month beyond your PITI, mortgage fees, vacancy losses, repairs, and contingency funds. For these properties, the cap rates and rates of return are strong, and you are well covered against the forces of the economy and real estate market. You can absorb a drop in real estate value, higher than expected repair bills, extended vacancy levels, or increased rental competition driving your results down by 10 to 15 percent.

To leverage and use debt under those standards and parameters is not foolish or overly risky but actually wise. To use debt in a long-term, measured way is prudent. The debt must be stable, meaning no teaser or short-term fixed-rate options unless you have a plan for when the balloon comes due for that type of a loan. In this case, the rate of interest and payment creates growth and leverage.

Not Having a Rainy-Day Fund

If you don't have cash reserves or a cash cushion, then you have problems. The adage of having six months of cash reserves minimum that covers 100-percent of your living expenses is sound thinking. If you need a little more to feel secure, that is fine also.

The real key is to define the amount and save the amount you require. Once you have saved that amount, then make sure you use your funds well beyond that. The funds beyond that amount should be invested where your return is much better than a standard savings account or CDs. If your expenses are $10,000 a month, you don't need $100,000. You need at least $60,000. That extra $40,000 can be used to create wealth better than having it in cash, getting a less than 1-percent savings return. The truth is, you are losing 1 percent a year to inflation, which is at 2 percent. You want enough to provide security in liquid assets.

If you lose your job or your income drops, you have savings to weather a short-term bump in the road. I am 56 years old as I write this. There will probably be three more recessions in my lifetime. Many of you will experience four to five or even six more recessions or economic shifts in your lifetime. The rainy-day fund enables you to not act out of desperation, haste, or panic when the next economic curveball of life comes your way. The wealthiest people have the means and courage to seize opportunities when economic shifts happen. Without a rainy-day fund, your mindset becomes just trying to survive rather than to thrive.

Poor Estate Planning

Even if you are young, you need estate planning. At a minimum, you need a health advance directive. It's a document that clearly states your wishes in the event of a health emergency where you have lost the capacity to decide for yourself. You will also name someone you authorize to make those decisions. (Joan, my wife, has that authority, and I'm sure she's going to pull the plug — because I'm worth more dead than alive. LOL, as the kids say.)

Basic estate planning is essential for your loved ones. We recently lost Aretha Franklin, who at death had no will or estate plan. Her children are going through the grieving process of the loss and the nightmare of dealing with her estate without even a basic will.

A revocable living trust creates a trust for your assets and provides clear direction regarding what will happen with your assets and property. If you are married, both you and your spouse need to have one. As an example, Joan and I own several properties either in whole or in part in Oregon, Arizona, California, and Hawaii, and they would all need to go through the probate process in each state if we didn't have the living trust document. It would be extremely expensive and time consuming. We would need to hire probate attorneys in each state and then file all the court documents in each state.

You also need to equally place assets between your spouse's trust and your trust if you have a large number of assets. For example, if Joan and I put all of our property in my trust, the value of my trust could be too large and create an estate tax bill at death to the federal government. There is no avoiding our Oregon estate tax because the threshold is only 1 million dollars per person. We will have to pay that tax at death. The federal threshold is 5.49 million dollars per person, so if we evenly spread out assets between the two of us, we can resolve or eliminate the potential federal tax payment.

If you live in a state with high property values, it's likely you will have an estate tax due at the state level. You must have some type of plan and strategy for yourself and your kids. A good attorney who is knowledgeable in trust estates and estate taxes is worth his or her weight in gold, as is a very good accountant.

Rarely a month goes by where I don't hear about someone who has passed away leaving behind a young family. What is a tremendous tragedy is compounded because the family frequently finds out there was no life insurance policy to pay off the mortgage and other debt, fund college for the kids, or even meet basic family expenses for the next few years. Life insurance is an integral piece of estate planning for your loved ones. For most people, basic term life insurance is inexpensive compared to the benefit and protection it affords. Secure a policy that, upon death, will free your family of debt and financial obligations.

TIP

You should also have life insurance for a stay-at-home parent. If that parent passes away, you will need to cover the cost of the vital role that person played in raising the family and maintaining the household. Even though the stay-at-home parent wasn't earning an income, his or her loss will create a financial as well as an emotional hardship on the family.

Going Alone without a Wealth Team

Most of us, including myself, are amateurs in some areas of wealth, estate planning, tax law, and tax strategy. It isn't our primary job or area of expertise. I understand real estate and the real estate industry extremely well. I have personally been doing it for almost 30 years. I watched my parents initially in their real estate investing for better than 20 years before I bought my first property. I have close to 50 years of real estate experience in active investing or firsthand close observation. So I don't need someone on my wealth team who is versed in real estate investment.

But I will never achieve as much knowledge and practical experience in tax strategy. That's why you have to formulate your dream team. Doing it all yourself will lead to errors, mistakes, stress, and lower levels of wealth. There are four people who make up your primary wealth team: a good tax estate attorney, a good financial planner, a good investment lender, and a good accountant. These are the people who will guide you and advise you about your financial-independence goals. They have been instrumental in my journey to financial independence.

Your accountant

The accountant is really the ongoing foundation of your wealth creation strategy. The other three are important, but the right accountant is the glue that holds it all together. To me, the right person in the accounting seat works to create a strong tax strategy to reduce your taxes to the lowest legal level while also making sure you pay enough income tax so that you are easily financeable by your lender for your home and potentially investment properties.

If you own your own business or have a side hustle, if you offset your income with extremely high deductions to reduce your tax liability and show low or no income, that will save you in taxes, but that strategy will make it unlikely that you will be able to save money. You will also have a harder time securing financing for a home to purchase. If you want to invest in real estate, you are going to need to show enough income on your tax returns for the banks to want to loan you money. If you show large deductions and no income on line 33 on your tax return, banks typically don't like that. They view you as an income risk.

The financial planner

The financial planner's role, in my case, is for short-term investment gains. They hold and invest the funds I am not presently using in real estate investment and the liquid funds I need. I'm personally not a huge fan of having my assets in the market other than the real estate market. That doesn't make it wrong to invest in the stock market. I understand this strategy is not right for everyone. I just personally understand real estate much better than the stock market and am more comfortable with it.

There are many good financial planners who can provide expert wealth guidance. Ask your friends who they use. Find out why they use this person and what their experience has been. Then interview a few about their philosophy of investing, service, and costs. Share with them your goals and expectations so they can craft a plan for you to accomplish your wealth goals.

Your attorney

You need wise counsel for your trusts, LLCs, estate, and estate tax planning. There is a larger amount of work getting everything established initially. The ongoing work after the initial setup is less until you have a lot of assets, stocks, bonds, or properties. Your estate strategies get more complex as wealth increases. Additionally, as you age, your needs, goals, and strategies will change. For example, you might want to leave a larger portion of your estate to a charity rather than to family members. It pays to have a trusted attorney do all the legwork for you.

Your investment lender

If you are going to use real estate as an avenue for wealth, you will likely need to create a lender relationship. The first four properties you buy with mortgages are easy, and almost any lender can do them. It's the fifth through tenth properties with loans that are more challenging to secure. These fall under more stringent Fannie Mae guidelines. Then once you get beyond the ten properties that are single family, duplex, triplex, or 4-plex, that's where you need a portfolio lender: the lender that is willing to hold your loan in its portfolio, rather than sell the loan. That is where the real value of a good lender shows up.

The need for a portfolio lender depends on the number of rentals you need to achieve your financial independence number. Most people who invest in real estate can achieve their desired wealth if they use the right combinations between standard Fannie Mae loans, their retirement accounts, retirement account loans on properties, seller-financed deals, and private financing. Through those sources, you can acquire the rental asset base you need to achieve your financial impendence goals. The time to work through your strategy is now, in the planning process, so you can place the right assets in the correct places and entities to maximize your return and advantages.

REMEMBER

There is more to creating wealth than just saving money, investing it in stocks, or buying a good-producing income property or flip property. You have to decide, for example, where you hold your assets, or whether to place a property in your trust, LLC, partnership, or your self-directed retirement accounts. A good lender can review your financial situation and help you make decisions. You should interview a few and ask about their experience with investors. How many investors do they work with that have more than five loans with them? That will give you a clear picture of their experience. Then meet with your attorney and accountant to learn the ins and outs of the legal entities through which to buy investment properties.

Being Timid When Opportunity Arrives

For most people who have achieved wealth, they have developed the habit of saving consistently toward their desire wealth. That is the single biggest "secret" to their wealth. A close second is bold action when an opportunity presents itself. You won't be able to do the second without the first. You won't have money to use when opportunity arrives. Creating wealth requires boldness. That doesn't mean you are reckless or take undue risk. It also doesn't mean that you follow the herd. Most wealthy people are not herd followers. In most cases, if you follow the herd, you will receive what the herd possesses, which is not much.

The classic contrarian is Warren Buffett. He is arguably the greatest investor of wealth ever. He studies, analyzes, and patiently waits for proper timing. He then boldly makes his move with large positions or large acquisitions. Many of those bold moves have been purchasing distressed assets, or in distressed economic conditions.

"Be fearful when others are greedy. Be greedy when others are fearful." —Warren Buffett

I am certainly not in Warren's league, but I have a few opportunities that I seized and boldly. I saw the real estate market correction coming. I did not predict the depth of the correction that happened from 2008 to 2011. No one could have foreseen a 60-percent correction in value in some real estate markets. What I did see early in 2009 is that this real estate correction was going to be larger than we had ever seen in history and that homes were selling in some markets at half of what it would cost to build them.

At that point, our economy was struggling, so all asset classes were discounted heavily. If you had bought stocks in high quality companies, you would have done very well. Opportunities come infrequently. When it rains gold, put out a bucket, not a thimble. Warren Buffett, being able to see and seize opportunity, creates wealth unlike any other.

I saw the rare moment in time for what it was: opportunity. I went all-in like a guy who was holding four aces in his poker hand. There aren't too many hands better than four aces. The odds of me losing were incredibly low. I pooled all my retirement account funds and available cash, applied for larger credit lines, and established a few more lender relationships. I knew for the next few years there would be great opportunities to buy real estate assets at heavy discounts. This was a big moment: Real estate would never again in my lifetime be discounted and undervalued to this level. I had been preparing my whole financial life for this rare occurrence.

So what was the difference? I get asked that all the time by people seeking wealth. Was I better and smarter than others? Certainly not. The difference is, I acted. I didn't just think about doing something or research every angle. The difference was, once I did my research and knew I was facing a rare moment in time, I acted on what I learned. The same is true for the people who bought Google stock at its IPO in 2004 at $85 a share. It's now trading at $1,575 a share. Had we acted in 2004 buying Google, we would be wealthy as well.

Big opportunity will be presented to you in your lifetime a few times. The question will only be this: Will you act boldly when it comes knocking at your door?

Not Remaining Married to Your First Spouse

When my father was preparing to retire in 1990, I was 29 years old and recently started my new career in real estate sales. Joan, my wife, and I were in our first year of marriage. Norm, my father, and I were out playing golf one day, which we did frequently as I was growing up. Getting four hours of uninterrupted time with my dad was totally worth its weight in gold.

We were talking about financial success and discussed when he knew that he had amassed enough wealth to sell his dental practice and retire. I have been blessed to have those types of conversations over my lifetime with him. They're not the typical conversations between a father and son. He was sharing with me the details of a recent meeting with his longtime accountant, Uncle Bob. They agreed that he was ready financially to retire. In fact, the accountant stated, "Norm, you have done the one thing that made the biggest difference in early retirement and wealth." My father at that moment paused in the story. To this day I don't know whether he was gauging my interest, whether he did it consciously, or it just happened, but there was this moment of silence that seemed like an eternity.

My mind was racing. Was it his choice of real estate he invested in? Was it the fact he wasn't flashy with fancy cars or homes? Was it some stocks he had selected? I was trying to guess what that "one thing" was. The agony of the silence was finally and mercifully broken by my father sharing what Uncle Bob said to him: "You still have your first wife."

Honestly, that was a big letdown. I thought, "Is that it?" But over the last few decades, I've done a lot of thinking about what was revealed that day, and I've come to realize that the longevity of marriage is a significant determining factor of success and wealth in life.

My professional and financial success would not have been achieved in the absence of my wife, Joan. She has been an integral part of that success. Our partnership is the foundation of success. I know that was true for my father and mother as well.

The breakup of a relationship causes untold loss of wealth. There are now assets and liabilities to split up and two households to fund. And don't forget about the emotional toll on all the family members. I am not here to judge or comment on your personal relationships. Relationships do get severed, divorces happen, and some spouses are in abusive relationships. They need to free themselves for their emotional health and physical safety.

I understand how blessed I have been to come from a two-parent home and to have experienced 29 years of marriage with an incredible spouse and partner in Joan. I am blessed to have a thriving business and wonderful staff that make me look better than I am. I have two amazing kids in Wesley and Annabelle. All of these blessings come from the foundation of the relationship I have with Joan.

Index

C

calculating hourly income, 307–308

capital, increasing, 92

career
as a category of success, 12
as goals, 82

caring, as a characteristic of a great employee, 216

Carnegie, Andrew (entrepreneur), 82, 350–351

Carnegie, Dale (author)
How to Win Friends and Influence People, 155

categorizing
goals, 84–85
success, 11–14
tasks in time-blocking system, 324

category tournament, 88–89

cellphones, turning off, 293–294

Chadwick, Florence (swimmer), 101

Champions of Wealth course, 258, 259

Chapman, Gary (author)
The 5 Love Languages, 180

characteristics
of Compliant behavioral style, 66
developing welcoming, 159–160
of Dominant behavioral style, 60–61
of great employees, 215–218
of Influencer behavioral style, 62–63
personal, for improving success, 337–343
of Steady behavioral style, 64

charisma, as a benefit of being motivated, 52

Cheat Sheet (website), 3

cheerleader, being a, 169

children
adoption, 205
building character of, 201–206
defining success for individual, 192–193
demonstrating love to your, 197–198
encouraging gifts and skills, 194–195
establishing values in, 201–202
helping them to avoid life's dangers, 204–206
recognizing differences in, 193–194
setting goals/benchmarks with, 203–204

chocolate, dark, 123

choosing
motivation types, 67–71
work situations, 216–217

chores, buying time for, 311

Christianity, 146

Churchill, Winston (UK Prime Minister), 213

circumstances, mastering your, 41

circumventing interruptions, 292

claiming rewards, 58

clarity, lacking, for your future, 354

Clason, George S. (author)
The Richest Man in Babylon, 29

clinging to commitment, 185–188

clutter overload, preventing, 298

Collins, Jim (author)
Good to Great, 219

comfort, finding in faith, 144

commitment
clinging to, 185–188
creating to goals, 78
as the key ingredient to marriage, 177–179
to marriage, 172–175

communication
in business relationships, 213
as a characteristic of a great employer, 219–221
effective, 291–292
frequency of in business, 226
in marriage, 179–183
personally in business, 226
in your mate's behavioral style, 181–183

comparisons, for encouragement, 136–137

complacency, balanced with contentment, 132

completion, as a motivator, 70–71

Compliant behavioral style
about, 66
characteristics of, 66
communicating with someone who has the, 182–183
downsides of, 67
drivers of, 66
how they operate, 66–67

recognizing
  achievements, 195
  differences in children, 193–194
  milestones, 195, 226
  positives, 185
reducing credit card debt, 257–258
rejection, fear of, as a barrier to goal setting, 75–76
rekindling the flame, 186–188
relationships
  building, 148
  business
    about, 211
    building customer/client relationships, 223–226
    characteristics of great employees, 215–218
    characteristics of great employers, 218–223
    providing more than you're paid for, 212–215
  as a category of success, 12, 13
  investing in personal, 320–321
Remember icon, 3
reminders app, 32
repetition, turning consistency into, 19–20
replacement income, earning, 238
resetting expectations, 118–119
resources, determining needs for, 92–94
responding, 290
responsibility
  buying time for, 311
  delegating, 295, 297–298
  taking, 167–168
  teaching, 202–203
rest, 126–127
Retirement Savings Calculator, 238–239
retirement success, guaranteeing, 275–282
return, matching time investment to, 316–318
revocable living trust, 357
rewards
  claiming, 58
  developing the habit of personal, 138
  discipline as, 36–39
  of leisure activities, 312

rhythm, identifying your, 288
The Richest Man in Babylon (Clason), 29
Rinzler, Carol Ann (author)
  Controlling Cholesterol For Dummies, 122
  Nutrition For Dummies, 122
  Weight Loss Kit For Dummies, 122
Robbins, Tony (motivational speaker), motivational talks by, 116
rocky places, sowing seeds in, 46
Rohn, Jim (personal coach), 11, 25
routines
  creating, 289
  success, 18–19
rules, wealth and, 254

S

salami approach, for tasks, 71
Sales Champion (website), 59
sales professionals, 80/20 rule for, 319
salmon, eating, 122
saving mechanisms, forced, 273–275
savings
  about, 250–252
  rainy-day fund, 356
  starting too late, 353–354
scattering the seed, as a success strategy, 43
scheduling
  personal activities in time-blocking system, 328–329
  planning time in time-blocking system, 329–330
  self-evaluation in time-blocking system, 329–330
  time offline, 292–294
  your time, 289
Schuller, Robert (preacher), 97, 188
security
  increasing your feelings of, 145
  working toward, as a measure/model of success, 348–349
seeds, 123

About the Author

Dirk Zeller started his entrepreneurial career more than 50 years ago with lemonade stands. He has been creating his own economy through numerous businesses since he was 24 years old. For more than 30 years, he has signed both the front and back of each paycheck he earned. He founded Real Estate Champions and Sales Champions in 1998. Both are recognized as leading organizations in sales training and coaching in the business-to-consumer selling fields.

Dirk is one of the most sought-after speakers in success, time management, peak performance, and sales in the world. He has presented worldwide to hundreds of thousands of entrepreneurs, salespeople, and senior executives. Dirk has been awarded the CSP (Certified Speaking Professional) award from the National Speakers Association. Only 11 percent of speakers achieve this lofty award.

Dirk has authored several best-selling books on sales, success, productivity, and time management:

> *Your First Year in Real Estate*
>
> *Success as a Real Estate Agent For Dummies*
>
> *Telephone Sales For Dummies*
>
> *The Champion Real Estate Agent*
>
> *The Champion Real Estate Team*
>
> *Successful Time Management For Dummies*
>
> *Thriving in the Marketplace For Dummies*
>
> *Selling All-in-One For Dummies*
>
> *Effective Time Management For Dummies*
>
> *Running a Great Meeting in a Day For Dummies*
>
> *Success Habits For Dummies*

Dirk considers his most significant achievements to be a successful marriage of 29 years (and counting) to his wife, Joan. He is blessed by his two adopted children: Wesley, 17, and Annabelle, 13. He and his family reside in Bend, Oregon.

You can reach Dirk at

Sales Champions
5 NW Hawthorne Avenue, Suite 200
Bend, OR 97703
541-383-0505
Info@SalesChampions.com
Info@DirkZeller.com

Dedication

No one accomplishes great things in a vacuum or all by themselves. So many people have contributed to my success in life. I must acknowledge a dear friend, Zig Ziglar, who wrote the original *Success For Dummies* book. Zig was instrumental in his guidance and words of wisdom to me entering the professional speaking arena in 1998. He was a wonderful mentor and friend.

My most influential and significant mentor and friend has always been my father, Norman Zeller. I dedicate this book to him as a small token of thanks for the success principles he taught and demonstrated to myself and others through his daily living. I was able to observe first-hand through his words, but most importantly through his actions, many of the principles and strategies in this book. He rose from being raised in a home with dirt floors to becoming a successful dentist, businessman, real estate investor, husband, father, and friend. His loyalty and commitment to my mother through her 40-year battle with multiple sclerosis in nearly 50 years of marriage until her death established a foundation that I have been blessed to build upon. He continues to live out his life principles every day, at 87 years of age, as he tends to his farm and lives life on his terms. Dad, you are truly amazing, and it's my honor to be your son!

Author's Acknowledgments

Any success in life is always a collaborative effort; so is a book. While I receive the unfair lion's share of the credit, countless others are behind the scenes making me look good. There are many who I am blessed to work with in accomplishing a project like *Success Habits For Dummies*.

To the team at Real Estate Champions and Sales Champions, an incredible group of people who change people's lives each day, you are the best. Thank you to our support staff of Julie Porfirio, who has faithfully worked with me for more than 20 years, and Julie Tracy, who has been the wearer of many hats in her tenure and is invaluable. Thanks also to our coaches and salespeople, who really change the lives of everyone they touch.

I also need to thank the team at Wiley: Tracy Boggier, acquisition editor, and Tim Gallan, project editor. You are truly a pleasure to work with on each *Dummies* book I write.

Finally, I must thank my personal clients along with our Real Estate Champions and Sales Champions clients. You constantly challenge us and want passionately to achieve greater success, which drives us to work so hard to stay ahead as we build new programs and intellectual property to enhance your business and lives. You inspire our passion and create our success. It's a blessing and honor to occupy a front-row seat in your success show!

Publisher's Acknowledgments

Acquisitions Editor: Tracy Boggier

Project Editor: Tim Gallan

Technical Reviewer: Anthony Santero

Production Editor: Magesh Elangovan

Cover Image: © gavni/iStock.com